EDWARD VAN HALEN:

A Definitive Biography

EDWARD VAN HALEN:
A Definitive Biography

Kevin Dodds

iUniverse, Inc.
Bloomington

Edward Van Halen: A Definitive Biography

iUniverse books may be ordered through booksellers or by contacting:

iUniverse
1663 Liberty Drive
Bloomington, IN 47403
www.iuniverse.com
1-800-Authors (1-800-288-4677)

ISBN: 978-1-4620-5480-0 (sc)
ISBN: 978-1-4620-5482-4 (hc)
ISBN: 978-1-4620-5481-7 (ebk)

Printed in the United States of America

iUniverse rev. date: 10/07/2011

Cover design by John Luke
Cover photograph © D'Lesa Plunk

CONTENTS

PREFACE

Edward Van Halen is one of the most important and influential musicians that has ever lived. He is up there with just a handful that includes Mozart, Elvis, and Jimi Hendrix. Amongst the things that differentiate Eddie from that group is the fact that he has significantly outlived them all while facing no less tribulation.

I consider myself fortunate to have come of age during his initial rise to fame. I was seven when I got my first Van Halen 45 rpm record, "Dance the Night Away." I was ten when "(Oh) Pretty Woman" came out and swept our entire household, as well as the entire nation. I was twelve when I saw one of the last few shows on the *1984* tour that the original Van Halen would ever play.

My childhood idols, if you will, predominantly consisted of two people in two distinct phases. Roger Staubach was Phase One. I grew up in Houston in a home full of Dallas Cowboys fanatics. Staubach's career as the quarterback of the Cowboys, which included four Super Bowl appearances in the 1970s, faded just about the time Van Halen spilled into our house in early 1982 as my adolescence kicked off with a bang. Edward Van Halen was Phase Two. As far as boyhood heroes go, that was it. Of course, throughout my life, I have come to admire and respect a great number and a wide variety of artists and other incredible people. But my adolescence? I was that kid in high school that played all of Ed's songs—proudly, note-for-note in most cases.

Since playing guitar became such an important part of my life, consequently, so did Edward. I studied him as if I were a presidential scholar. I wore out tape decks hitting start and stop and pause. I transcribed all of his songs that I learned that weren't already published in the guitar magazines.

Ultimately, the *1984* concert would change my life and the life of my best friend Michael. After the concert, we formed our own band and began performing in public that very year at the age of twelve. We went on to establish a popular Austin band in the 1990s, but went into "retirement" after nearly a decade of trying to make it on our own terms. It was for the best. We started having kids. We can still reunite and draw a crowd every now and then. We didn't run it into the ground or let it run us out of our own minds.

As I've aged, I have developed an insatiable craving for rock history. I have read easily a hundred rock history retrospectives, biographies, and autobiographies. I strive to understand the nature of the history of rock music not only because of its direct and major impact on culture, art, and society—but because of the role it plays in defining who I am.

By default, Edward Van Halen plays no small role in that definition. I can play them all: "Eruption," "Cathedral," "Ice Cream Man," "House of Pain," "Little Guitars,"—you name it. Anyone that can do that, someone somewhere is saying, "Man, that guy's pretty into Eddie Van Halen's music."

I am also a huge fan of Elvis and Hendrix. I easily own around thirty books on Elvis alone, and there is no shortage of material on Jimi.

So, I went in search of something that didn't exist: a definitive biography on Edward Van Halen. I had to ask myself why there are dozens of books on lower-tier rock stars and nothing specifically on Eddie Van Halen? He's without question the second most influential guitarist after Hendrix—even though the length of Eddie's reign dwarfs Jimi's. There are collections of interviews with guitar magazines, he's in *Rolling Stone* every once in a while, there are a slim few books on even Van Halen the band. But there is not one single comprehensive, cohesive examination of the life of one of the world's most influential musical artists.

That's where I come in. I decided that if one had to do it, I was going to do it; so I set about putting it all together in one single piece of work.

Although the man was indeed a childhood hero, I have examined every aspect of his life which ultimately includes a horrific battle with alcoholism, adultery, and a host of other unpleasant realities of life for the rich and famous. It turns out I have things in common with Edward that allow me to view him from a few unique perspectives. I have followed him for his entire career. I know his music inside and out. And I am a recovering alcoholic and live with and manage depression. I've been through a divorce with a child.

While I have composed a comprehensive examination of Edward's life, I had absolutely no intention of using sensationalism in any way whatsoever. The man's life story follows an extraordinarily complex path. Ed has had his ups and downs, but who hasn't? There are aspects of his behavior that belie some sort of supposed mental illness. Having conducted an absolutely thorough review, in my opinion, Edward suffers from two of the most common problems in society: depression and addiction/alcoholism.

Both are incredibly complicated diseases, especially when intertwined—and sadly, I know exactly what I'm talking about as I personally endured dual treatment for both diseases. Persons with highly functioning intellectual capacity are especially subject to these diseases, and genetic predisposition plays a hugely important role as well. It is not sensational to review his personal battles—it is simply a matter of fact, and also offers hope to those waging similar battles of their own. And, not to spoil the ending, but Edward—as of 2011—is in a great place. He is sober, happily married, and working with his son, his brother, and his one true creative partner, David Lee Roth.

While this is specifically not a book about the band Van Halen, the fact that Edward has been one of only two consistent members of the band for nearly his entire life, the history of Van Halen is certainly covered extensively throughout. Much the VH lore is debunked. There is also quite a bit of coverage of David Lee Roth, Valerie Bertinelli, and Sammy Hagar—this is solely because of how the relationships with those particular three people affected Edward's own life so significantly. I will state it outright and make no apologies that I believe the most creative and fun Edward gets is when he is working with Dave.

I have never met Edward—although my brother did once—but even my own mother referred to Ed and his ever-present music and posters in our house as being something like a family member.

ACKNOWLEDGMENTS

Edward Van Halen is the reason for so many great things in our culture and in my life. He is the primary reason that I am a guitarist, and being a guitarist is something that plays a huge role in defining who I am as a human being.

I would like to thank the support of my wife Melanie, my sons Evan and Owen, my mother Marjie, my sister Debbie, and specifically my friends Michael, Brando, Nate, Chris, Brendan, Doug, Lyle, Steve, and Larry for helping me out in any way they could—whether it was playing Van Halen's music with me as kids, forwarding me a link to a previously unearthed YouTube video, encouraging me to go for it, or handing over a stack of 1980s *Hit Paraders*. Special thanks to my many back readers including Russell, Matt, Brendan, Wes, Larry, D.J., Dave, Tom, William, and my uncle Lyndon.

I would also like to thank rock guitar journalist Jas Obrecht for his cooperation and assistance by providing access to all of his works. I would also like to give special thanks to author Charles R. Cross for providing encouragement to write my first rock biography. An extra special thanks to Greg Dwyer of the *Dwyer and Michaels* radio show for allowing me to use excerpts of the historic interviews they conducted with Edward.

Special thanks to the staff at iUniverse for their assistance in publication of this work.

Thanks to my brother Brandon for getting me into Van Halen permanently. And thanks to my grandmother "Mama Dodds" for getting me "Dance the Night Away" on 45 rpm for my seventh birthday.

ACKNOWLEDGMENTS

DEDICATION

For my brother Brandon . . .

My brother Brandon made this Frankenstein replica guitar completely by himself in the summer of 1984 at the age of 16. Photograph © Kevin Dodds

INTRODUCTION

It is July of 1984. He is the most popular musician in the world in the most popular band in the world, the band that bears his own surname. The Summit in Houston is sold out not for just one night, but for three nights in a row.

It's the first night of the stand. The rockabilly opening act has come and gone without notice. The house lights have gone down and the lighters have gone up. The crowd roar is simply unbelievable—constant and deafening. Thirty to forty seconds go by with swirling white spotlights streaming up from the stage's edge. And then I hear it. A scream—a scream from a guitar. I know that scream but my brain is laboring in disbelief. "Is this really happening?" And I wasn't sure it was. This was bigger than Christmas, bigger than a thousand Christmases. The guitar dive bombs on the low E and a few choice licks come pouring out of the sound system.

The spotlights continue along with the butanes. I still haven't grasped the reality. I feel like I'm dreaming because it's dark and the lights are trancelike. It continues: the crowd roar, the wailing guitar, pounding drums, the spotlights rotating. The stage announcer steps up, sounding like a WWF wrestler, and delivers the classic Spinal Tapesque "I give you . . . the mighty . . . *VAN HALEN!*" Edward then immediately kicks off the show with "Unchained." I am still in disbelief because I can only hear it and can only barely see it. Ed is backlit, silhouetted in a tight white spot. The introduction of "Unchained" continues and the opening pattern is repeated twice before the drum fill followed by the entire band kicking in. And when it does—the lights explode, and the first thing you see is Dave at the peak of his "splits" jump coming off the drum riser. It was like sleeping and being awakened by being shoved out of an airplane. The wave of applause that followed the opening hit of the lights was simply thunderous and permanently unforgettable.

The microsecond that my mind admits it—*"Okay, you* are *at the Van Halen concert"*—my eyes immediately scan the stage in search of my idol. There he is in a white shirt, patched jeans, a bandana around his neck, and red shoes. And he's playing a red, black, and white striped Kramer guitar.

"It's true," I thought. *"He does exist. He's real. I can see him with my own eyes."* He is a comic book superhero and here he is saving us, 15,000 people at a time. If the roof of the Summit had caved in, I would not have been surprised if Edward were to hold it up with one hand while continuing to play with the other. Honestly, that probably would've just been incidental to the concert.

Permanent After-Effect

Within a week, my best friend Mike and I started a band. The first three songs we learned as a band were "Runnin' with the Devil," "You Really Got Me," and "Ain't Talkin' 'Bout Love." My buddy and I still play together to this day. This all really means something to me. Edward inspired me so greatly, I absolutely had to get to the bottom of what makes him tick. My peers demanded I do it. "You were born to do this" and "If anyone was cut out to do this, it's you" and "You should do it because . . ."

Edward is one of only a handful of legitimate musical geniuses of the past 200 years. Genius is a blessing, but sometimes a curse. And the two are, unfortunately, intertwined.

My own ticket stub from the first night of a three-night stand at the Summit in Houston (only $13.75). Photograph © Kevin Dodds

PROLOGUE

"I think a lot of people enter this business with a lot of problems already. It's just—they're just couched and they won't dish them—certainly won't dish them to you in an interview. They come in with a lot of bitterness and a lot of problems, and then only compound it through drug use, drinking; the stress in terms of hours and responsibilities that are heaped upon them, or that they heap upon themselves through excess, laziness, sloth, egotism . . ."

—David Lee Roth, March 1985

"I've worked with such legendary guitar players as Allan Holdsworth, Ronnie Montrose, Eric Clapton, Lowell George, and Steve Vai, but none of them come close to the having Ed's fantastic combination of chops and musicianship. I rank him along with Charlie Parker and Art Tatum as one of the three greatest musicians of my lifetime. Unfortunately, I don't think Ed puts himself in that class."

—Ted Templeman, September 1991

"Some people tend to take this all too doggone seriously, you know? I wish that we could be articulate enough and poetic enough, and maybe enough like Salvador Dali to paint something of a false reality. The fact is this a rock and roll band, okay? This is . . . not the invasion of Normandy . . ."—Alex Van Halen; "It's rock and roll!"

—Edward Van Halen, October 1996

"I'm very excited, uh, you know, to be makin' music with my son, my brother, my new brother [Dave] . . . It's, it's the shit. That's all I can say."

—Edward Van Halen, August 2007

PROLOGUE

CHAPTER 1
Life in the Netherlands

There is no doubt that when you think of Edward Van Halen, one of the first things that does *not* come to mind is the Dutch East India Company. But if the roots of one human being's somewhat miraculous DNA makeup must be traced to a reasonable starting point, it would be with the world's first megacorporation.

In 1602, the United East Indian Company began colonizing Asia for the benefit of the Kingdom of the Netherlands. The principal territory in which the VOC did business was within a string of islands nestled immediately south of The Philippines and just north of Australia. These islands then became known, fittingly, as the Dutch East Indies (or Netherlands East Indies). This was a world away from their colonial pillager the Netherlands, way up in the northwest corner of continental Europe, immediately west of Germany, north of Belgium, with the North Sea on its west and north coasts.

The VOC endured through a nearly two-century rule until things inevitably unraveled beginning in 1780, brought down by the engine of colonialism itself, corruption. Prior to its eventual disbandment in 1800, it was referred to as Vergaan Onder Corruptie ("perished by corruption"). The responsibilities of the VOC fell to the Netherlands in 1800. Rather than pulling back to appease countries like the United States, who obviously had some issues with colonialism, the Netherlands expanded their operations right up until the mid-twentieth century.

Europeans numbering in excess of a million traveled the thousands of ships on trade missions to perform all manner of potentially unspeakable colonial duties on the beautiful tropical island string. Many of these Europeans decided to stay and settle in the islands, a strange new land a half a world away, presenting new and different opportunities—and a major change in lifestyle. Inevitably, race mixing took place resulting in a people known as Indos or Eurasians, or more bluntly, Dutch Indonesians.

The ratio of race mixing for people under this blanket description runs the gamut and it is impossible to assess that ratio without taking stock of one's physical appearance and making a fair judgment based on what physical traits are most prominent.

Thus was born a Eurasian woman in 1914 with the markedly Dutch name of Eugenia van Beers in the Dutch East Indies. Technically, she was the first "van" in the Van Halen family. Her given name gives no indication of the percentage of European genetics. In fact, on name alone, an assumption would practically be uncalled for. In viewing photographs of Eugenia, it is clear that she retained a significant portion of her native island ancestry. A reasonable assessment would be likely something approaching one-third European descent.

Back in Amsterdam, Jan van Halen was born in 1920 shortly after the end of World War I. Jan's name certainly suited his ancestry without a colonial tint or guesswork; he was a northwest European. Jan was born with the musical gift and was described as a bit of rebel. As a young man, he mastered the saxophone and clarinet so well that he was gigging regularly by eighteen. It's been said "he worked hard to have fun" playing in a retinue of jazz bands, swing bands, and orchestras across Europe. Jan no doubt enjoyed his pick of opportunities as a young man in the late 1930s, from radio events to a circus troupe, and even political rallies.

He only had a few brief years to enjoy both his early gigging and his youth. When perpetual bad neighbor Germany invaded Poland in September of 1939, Jan, like any other Dutch male his age, joined the military. Jan's talents came in handy though, landing him in the Dutch Air Force with the task of playing marches.

In May 1940, the Nazis took over their neighbor's homeland. Starting on May 10, the Germans battled their way all the way to Rotterdam which they bombed into submission in just five days. The majority of Dutch operations were left virtually untouched—they were simply German now.

Hitler's takeover of the Netherlands was less dramatic than Poland. The Nazis considered the Dutch to be essentially 100% Aryan. The Netherlands was simply to become part of Germany following the war. However, Dutch Jews and Jehovah's Witnesses were rounded up and sent to the most notorious concentration camps of World War II. Author Linda M. Woolfe Ph.D. wrote:

> As Nazi oppression slowly took shape, so did Dutch resistance. Hitler underestimated the Dutch people and the Nazis were unprepared to deal with the primarily non militaristic character of Dutch resistance. In many ways, there are some striking similarities between the Dutch resistance and the spiritual resistance on the part of Jehovah's Witnesses. Much of Dutch resistance can be characterized as either passive resistance or non-violent active resistance. For example, immediately following the Nazi occupation, American and British films were banned from theaters replaced by German movies including German newsreels. Dutch patrons took to walking out or booing during the newsreels. Thus, new laws were passed prohibiting such behavior. Subsequently, attendance at films dropped. Radio broadcasts under Nazi control consisted principally of propaganda. Thus, while it was illegal to listen to British radio, many Dutch began to listen to the BBC and radio broadcasts from the Dutch government in exile. In 1943, over one million radio sets were confiscated by the Nazis in response to these acts of resistance.

Author Ian Christie reported that Jan, a member of the Dutch Air Force, was captured by the Nazis during the five-day invasion. When the Germans realized Jan was a talented musician, he was forced to perform propaganda music. This is how Jan van Halen spent his early twenties: playing propaganda music during the Nazi occupation. A gifted musician, who could truly play, forced ostensibly at gunpoint to perform a mandated set of material with no room for individual expression. It was simply a strictly tailored form of hell for him.

The Dutch government operated out of Britain during the period of German occupation, and eventually declared war on Japan, in solidarity with the United States, the day after the bombing of Pearl Harbor. Just a few months later, the Dutch East Indies came under the occupation of the Japanese in March 1942. So went Dutch colonial rule of the islands. Japanese occupation through the end of the war in 1945 cannot be described in terms extreme enough to convey the horror and atrocities that occurred. One's mind need only hear a few—sex slaves, forced labor, random arrests, rampant executions. Worse yet, those of Eurasian descent were specifically targeted and interned.

The end of the war in 1945 had an immediate and profoundly direct impact upon Jan van Halen and Eugenia van Beers. They were each caught directly in the heart of the two locales in the world's most brutal war.

Post-WWII Love Affair

Upon his release from musical captivity, Jan clearly felt a need to leave the scene and find somewhere far away to recover from the madness of the past five-plus years. When a musical opportunity presented itself in the Dutch East Indies, Jan jumped at the chance to test the waters in this strange and different land with clearly little in common with northwest Europe.

Now free and no longer under the command of the Nazis—and trying to erase the memories of the god-awful music he'd been forced to play—Jan was feeling loose and dandy enough to take an interest in Eugenia van Beers. Things moved fast and the two were soon married. Clearly, Eugenia wanted to get out of what would be known by 1949 as Indonesia and start over in a new and different land herself. The newly married couple resettled in the Netherlands. An interracial couple in Dutch territory would have been absolutely unthinkable during Nazi occupation.

Back in Jan's home country, he continued to perform at every opportunity that presented itself. The couple's first son, Alexander Arthur van Halen was born in May of 1953. Edward Lodewijk van Halen followed on January 26, 1955 (his music-obsessed father naming the future prodigy after Ludwig van Beethoven). Jan banked on his boys following in his somewhat bohemian footsteps. Also, like their father, both boys were born in Amsterdam, but the family eventually resettled in Nijmegen. Nijmegen is a city in a province directly on the border with Germany and to this day lays claims as one of the oldest cities in the world at 2,000 years old.

After failed attempts at instruction by Jan himself, where he discovered he did not have the patience to teach his own boys, Alex and Edward began piano lessons at a very young age. "Basically, that's where I got my ear developed, learned my theory, and got my fingers moving." It most certainly did get his fingers moving, and Alex and Edward excelled and soon mastered works by Beethoven, Mozart, and Tchaikovsky.

Whenever Jan's performances were broadcast over the radio, they all gathered around and listened as a family. Jan was always practicing and noodling around the house, often along with records at home. Jan even showed the boys some of the music he performed with pride during his military service: marching songs from the Dutch Air Force prior to the Nazi invasion. As very small toddlers, the kids followed Jan around with pots and pans while he played his proud marches.

As the boys got older, Jan brought them along to his performances around Holland and into Germany. As a result, the boys—neither yet even ten—were exposed to the nuts and bolts, the glamorous and the perverse aspects of the music business and the entertainment industry. Following one of his father's shows, Alex admitted to losing his virginity at the simply unrealistic age of nine.

As the van Halen marriage progressed, for reasons possibly becoming more and more obvious, Eugenia simply turned sour on the idea of the boys becoming professional musicians like their father. Indeed, it was apparent that, personality-wise, Eugenia and Jan were opposites. According to Edward, "My dad is the person who would cut school and smoke cigarettes, and my mom would be the cheerleader. Complete opposites—the conservative and the screw-up. If you sat there and talked to my dad, he'd make you roll over and laugh." (The quote featured no secondary comment about his mother.) Alex recalled that he once as a child told his mother he didn't feel like practicing. Eugenia instructed Alex to place his hands on the table and proceeded to hit them with a wooden spoon.

Jan continued to perform, ultimately developing into a phenomenal clarinet soloist. As noted by Ian Christie in *The Van Halen Saga*, at his peak, Jan's band, the Ton Wijkamp Quintent, was the top act at the Loosdrecht Jazz Festival, a highly respectable musical achievement. Nevertheless, Eugenia was finally ready for the ultimate change. After years of Dutch colonial occupation of Indonesia, followed by Japanese occupation, then resettling in the Netherlands, the base of her native country's subjugation . . . needless to say, she was *more* than ready for a change. Furthermore, she fell under the spell of letters from family members who had emigrated to Los Angeles after the war. These letters were full of stories about the Land of Opportunity and perfect weather, even though they were somewhat fabricated according to Alex.

Coming to America

As winter closed in 1962, Eugenia finally had enough of the Netherlands. Edward said bluntly, "My mom wanted us in the U.S. and out of Holland. She was afraid we'd get into music like my father." Consequently, the four van Halens prepared to embark on that all too familiar journey, the one where the family from a faraway land decides to start over, yet again, in a strange and different new land, willing to take the risk for the potential reward. Alex noted, "Taking a gamble, my parents sold everything they had and moved over here."

Except the family did not quite sell *everything*. It seemed the one family possession they could not part with was their cherished German-made Rippen piano. One can only imagine the reception upon boarding the boat: a married couple, two boys under ten, a few bags, and a piano. A piece of the legend also includes that the family only had "fifty dollars" with them. Of course, the amount of money they spent on freight for the piano would have clearly been a fortune, but obviously that was not an issue of particular importance for the family. The piano was a family member. It was coming, period, no matter the cost.

The nine-day trip on the boat is a pauper's fairytale. Jan played with the ship band to help finance the expedition (and to conceivably help cover the freight cost of the piano). Also, the little boys themselves, likely pushed out as a sympathy act, capably demonstrated their individual piano skills for the passengers. Edward said, "Alex and I actually played on the boat while we were coming to America. We played piano, and we were like the kid freak show on the boat." Alex added, "It was kind of a novelty to have two kids playing the piano." Following their performances, the kids would begin their lifelong routine of working the crowd, getting their start by passing a hat amongst the passengers to collect tips to help raise money for the family during the voyage.

Looking back, it is a rather young age, particularly for seven-year-old Edward, to take on the task of passing a hat for tip money to support the family; it surely left a lasting impression upon this already extraordinarily talented little boy. But Eddie noted poignantly, "Music saved our family." A photo from the journey shows an all-smiles family enjoying dinner on the boat all decked out in paper sailor hats. Clearly, they were a tight-knit group.

The family arrived in New York and promptly had their surname Americanized to Van Halen, because everyone knows Americans would surely just get too confused over van Halen with that funny lowercase "v". The clan, along with the beloved Rippen, next made a cross-country journey via train straight into Los Angeles. One can only imagine the sights they observed out the window along the way—traversing the length of a country a mere 236 times the size of the Netherlands.

CHAPTER 2
Life in America

Eventually, they settled into a two-bedroom bungalow in Pasadena at 1881 Las Lunas Street where they would stay for two decades. One of the first orders of business upon arrival was to find a replacement piano tutor for the boys. One cannot be sure where the pressing need to become fluent in English laid on the priority scale, but it would soon become a major issue.

1818 Las Lunas Street as of 2011. The 900 square-foot home was built in 1922, giving the lush vegetation plenty of time to grow hearty and healthy over ninety years. Edward lived in the home from age of seven until approximately the age of twenty-five. The home was burglarized while Van Halen performed their first headlining show at The Forum in 1979. Photograph © John Adams

Edward and Alex were freshly transplanted Dutch boys in the heart of California in the early 1960s, and not just Dutch boys, but race-mixed kids as well, with Alex bearing more distinguishable Eurasian features than his little brother. At first, of course, they spoke absolutely no English except "yes," and had a habit of smiling and saying "yes" to anything said to them.

Alex said that their mother gave them a book to help them learn English and the very first word in the book, alphabetically, was "accident," which was unfortunately appropriate. The brothers were bearing abuse reserved for weird outsiders. Alex recalled: "One day I was walking in a park and went past a kid carrying a baseball bat. I said, 'baseball,' because it was one of the few English words I knew. He said something to me and I nodded affirmatively, and it turned out he'd asked, 'Do you want me to hit you in the face with this?'" Alex ended up with a broken nose. Welcome to America.

Edward would further add: "I wasn't able to speak English, and used to get my ass kicked because I was a minority [Author's note: part-Indonesian, part-Dutch, 100 percent immigrant]. All my friends were black, and they stuck up for me . . . because I was in the same cage as them, literally. In elementary school, there was a special place for us on the playground. And God, those days . . . Steven and Russell were my first two friends. Sometimes, I think of going back to that school (and) checking the records to find them. They were wonderful human beings . . . Such a trip."

Because of the barrage of abuse, Edward held back, too shy and too scared to make a move on his own. The older and bigger Alex took the admirable route some big brothers take which is to protect their little brother. Rather than be in constant battle like many brothers so close in age tend to be, considering the totality of their circumstances, Edward and Alex formed a tight bond that would prove to be unbreakable throughout their lives. Although, possibly in return for protection, Alex was known to engage in hardcore wrestling with Edward, routinely beating his ass with Ed getting in his own licks as best he could. "We were two outcasts that didn't speak the language and didn't know what was going on," said Eddie. "So we became best friends and learned to stick together."

The brothers continued on, learning more and more the rules of the playground and enjoying the freedom offered to them by their bicycles. In their small backyard, they had their own tree house—a private sanctuary for the two of them to not only commiserate, but also to plot and scheme.

A piano tutor was found that took on the boys with authority. "When we got to the States, my mom and dad did their best to find a really happening concert pianist teacher," Edward later told *Keyboard World* magazine. "They found a Russian teacher named Stass Kalvitis." A well-regarded, however nasty teacher, the septuagenarian instructor was known to have a ruler at the ready to mete out physical discipline upon a young Edward's hand or face were he to commit the sin of hitting a wrong note, or even being late on the right one. Yet operating under the hopes that the boys could possibly become respectable classical pianists some day, the lessons continued.

Hard Work

To support the struggling family, Jan took many different jobs to make ends meet. He went to work as a janitor for the Masonic Temple. He also worked at the Arcadia Methodist Hospital washing dishes (without steady transportation, Jan often walked the ten-mile round trip). He even occasionally took a job answering telephones during a graveyard shift. Eddie recalled learning how to use "one of those big floor waxers" working with Jan on his janitorial shift. Ed said his dad "worked his ass off" and added that "it shows you that you can make something out of nothing if you put your mind to it." Eugenia worked as a maid, though she spoke practically no English at the time.

And of course, Jan picked up gigs, primarily getting his start in the area with wedding and oompah bands. Again, Jan was a great player. Eddie remembered: "I knew what music was really about ever since my earliest memory of hearing my dad downstairs in his music room, holding just one note on his clarinet for as long as he could. I'm serious. He wouldn't just sit there pissing up a rope."

Through every last little bit of hard work through ungodly hours, Jan did everything he could to make their new life in this strange new land as perfect as it could be. But as a respite from the hours and brutal pace, Jan's penchant for alcohol consumption was an out-in-the-open situation. It was no family secret. Ed said, "He was a happy guy. He wasn't an angry drunk." Edward also later revealed the dual nature of his father that he struggled to come to terms with, yet unfortunately would inevitably emulate: "I think my desire to do my own thing came from my dad. He was a real soulful guy. He played sax and clarinet like a motherfucker. Unfortunately, he was also an alcoholic."

Eugenia often oversaw and came down on Jan's activities and behavior just as if he was one of the boys himself. Edward said, "The whole time I was growing up, my mom used to call me a 'nothing nut—just like your father.' When you grow up that way, it's not conducive to self-esteem." How sad for a little boy with such unimaginable potential.

Ironically, it turns out the one that really pushed the boys musically, at least in adhering to the strict, paid-for expectations of their tutors, was Eugenia. According to Edward, "My mom was the one pushing us. You know the father in the movie *Shine*. That's what my mom was like. And my dad, who was a musician, didn't push us at all." It was Eugenia who commanded their electric organ for holiday family jam sessions.

Under the vigilance of his mother, Edward entered and won several talent competitions. He later admitted that he actually was not ever able to read sheet music on sight. All of those years of piano lessons under such strict circumstances, Edward Van Halen, the young child, relied solely upon his ability to memorize passages and rehearse them on the Rippen. "I never learned how to read," he said. "I always fooled the teacher. He'd play the song for me first and I'd watch his fingers and learn the song by ear."

With Mr. Kalvitis as his instructor, Edward said, "He would have us practice all year for this contest they had at Long Beach City College. . . . I actually won first place two years in a row. But I *hated* it." He said, "You sit there and practice one tune for the whole year, and they put you in a category and judge you. . . . [I won] second place the last time, which kind of showed I was losing interest."

Discovering Rock Music and Vices

Ed himself admitted his reason to slipping to second place in the piano recital was his waning interest, mainly as it did not function to advance his burgeoning interest in this rock and roll business. As Ed said, "I wasn't into rock in Holland at all because there really wasn't much of a scene going on there. When we came to the U.S., I heard Jimi Hendrix and Cream, and I said, 'Forget the piano, I don't want to sit down. I want to stand up and be crazy.'" Ed added, more specifically, "We moved to America, and we saw *A Hard Day's Night* the movie—and I stopped playing piano." Ed did in fact cease taking formal piano lessons at age twelve. In 2009, upon further reflection, Edward said, "I stopped playing piano for one reason: I was forced to do it and I wasn't allowed to play what I wanted, so it wasn't fun. So I rebelled and bought myself a drum kit."

Twelve would also bring another change, a seemingly random event that truly changed his life forever. Out with his father, Edward was, incredibly, attacked and bitten by a German shepherd. "Alex, my dad, and I were out in Covina, and a German shepherd jumped through the screen door and bit me. It hurt like a motherfucker." It being 1967, Jan retrieved a flask from his person and dispensed a shot of vodka to his son and followed it up with a Pall Mall cigarette. "Have a shot of vodka, Ed. This will make you feel better," said his father. Jan is absolved from the judgment of twenty-first century child-raising norms, and Jan most definitely lacked any medical understanding of the incredibly complex genetic nightmare that is alcoholism. Nevertheless, this is the fateful moment that Edward begins what will be a long-term problem for him, and ultimately his family, his band, his image, and his fans. It's not often that one can pinpoint the exact moment when *that* ball got started rolling, but this was it.

Almost thirty years after the fact, Edward's recollection was a little different, but no less profound. "I remember when my dad got me into drinking and smoking when I was 12. I was nervous, so he said to me, 'Here. Have a shot of vodka.' Boom—I wasn't nervous anymore. My mom used to buy me cigarettes and it just stuck, it was habit. I don't drink for the taste of it, I drink to get a fucking buzz. I like to get drunk. I really do."

A few years earlier, at the house, like seventy million other television viewers, Edward and Alex watched The Beatles perform on *The Ed Sullivan Show* and were blown away. At the time, Edward was actually more impressed with the Dave Clark Five, the first British band after The Beatles to score a U.S. hit with "Glad All Over"—a song he would come to credit repeatedly over the years for his fairly major shift in musical direction that would follow further exposure to other groundbreaking material and artists.

Before heading full-long into the rock world, they started their first "band," The Broken Combs. They even worked up two original songs while still enrolled in Hamilton Elementary School. The unorthodox lineup featured Edward on piano, Alex on saxophone, with the band rounded out by a drummer, a guitar, and, well, yet another saxophone. While these gigs that took place in the school cafeteria were certainly innocent fun, they had a profound effect on both Alex and Edward in finally reaching the point where they not only belonged, but stood out as unique individuals, extremely talented young men. Edward summarized, "Music was my way of getting around my shyness."

CHAPTER 3
The Stringed Instrument

In what would on the surface appear to be simply yet another attempt by their parents to continue training their children in classical music, the boys were made to learn violin when Edward was near the end of elementary school. However, this move marked the moment that stringed instruments were brought into the house; up to that point, they had been confined to keyboard and wind instruments. By the time the boys were in John Marshall Middle School, they were fully entrenched in violin lessons learning traditional classical music pieces, including Kreutzer's instantly recognizable *Etude No. 2.*

John Marshall Middle School in Pasadena, California. Photograph © Kevin Dodds

Alex progressed impressively and made All City Orchestra, but according to Edward, "I never did. I didn't like the songs they made me play so I just started messing around with it and lost interest." He was easily distracted by the TV, and found himself more focused on plucking out the theme to *Peter Gunn* on his violin rather than study Paganini's caprices. This is the first known instance of Edward's guitarish abilities, revealed when in a form of rebellion against the violin itself; he used it to play along to the theme song to a television show. It's funny how he used the violin in a tongue-in-cheek manner to amuse himself. He would later revisit his violin years while composing what would ultimately become his most important piece of work.

The violin period lasted about three full years before its interest finally bowed. Hoping to capitalize on Alex's talent on a stringed instrument, the parent's next hope was flamenco guitar. Alex was given a nylon-string and an appointment with a flamenco instructor.

Enter the Guitar

Edward's fascination with the Dave Clark Five got a hold of him and he maintained his resolve to buy a set of drums to study their songs "Glad All Over" and "Bits and Pieces." Ed admitted, "I never grew up wanting to play guitar." Although the family was in Eddie's words "very poor," they provided Alex with a flamenco guitar, and Edward was provided with a $125 St. George drum kit for which he had to take a paper route to pay back. Ed cracked, "It was the only honest job I ever had was a paper route."

What follows is the kind of momentous lore that changed the direction of not just the one or two peoples' lives forever, but would also end up affecting millions upon millions of people around the world. Alex and Ed exchanged instruments. One can imagine how protective Eddie was of his new investment, and $125 was not chump change in 1966. Eleven-year old Edward was getting up at the crack of dawn, 5:00am, retrieving his lot of papers, pedaling his bicycle "with a flat tire" for hours to deliver them all, only to return home day after day to find Alex couldn't resist the lure of the St. George. Of course, one can't be sure if it was Alex's mastery of "Wipeout" that really made Ed throw in the towel on the drums.

Having played nothing but piano and violin up to that point, the drums didn't make actual music. He heard melodies and other note structures and combinations in his head, not pitter patter. Alex, on the other hand, must have found the drums a stress-relieving break from the piano, the saxophone, and the violin, and thus took to them with enthusiasm.

Once the flamenco guitar was in his hands, Edward quickly learned The Arrows tune "Blues Theme" but decided that this default acoustic was not at all the type of guitar he needed if he was going to undertake this challenge his way. A trip to Sears brought the first electric guitar ever to grace the Van Halen household or the hands of Edward Van Halen: a $100 Teisco Del Ray. A family photo shows a beaming twelve-year-old Edward strapped with the guitar nearly his own size with his grinning mother leaning down over him.

Surf music being the rage of the day (as illustrated by Alex and "Wipeout"), after Edward mastered the bar chord, he focused on "Walk Don't Run"—the surf masterpiece by The Ventures. In Ed's words: "The very first thing I learned was a bar chord, E, and then I went [demonstrates going up and down the neck holding a bar chord]—hey, anywhere! But this very first thing I learned—I played it for hours—and I didn't have an amp—so I would put my guitar on the table—so it would be louder. So it would resonate on the table. So the first thing I learned was . . . [Ed demonstrated the descending bar-chord sequence, E-D-C-B, for "Walk Don't Run"] I would just play those four chords for hours. I never learned [demonstrated the very distinctive single-note riff part of the song]. I never learned that! Just—[plays E-D-C-B repeatedly again and laughs]."

With their drumming and guitar chops improving at a rapid pace for the boys, it wasn't long before they were sitting in with their father at gigs around the L.A. area. The opportunity first arose when Jan needed a last-minute replacement drummer for the wedding band and Alex kept up with their jazz and salsa repertoire. Eddie started out subbing on bass playing the rather strict up-and-down oompah bass lines. The brothers even performed as a duo during intermissions.

As per usual, Jan sent the boys out with a hat to gather tips in addition to the standard pay for the band. After the first gig as a collective family, upon counting out the money in the hat, the tips totaled $22. After distributing $5 each to the boys, the two were left puzzled. According to legend, Jan revealed an ugly truth to them when he said, "Welcome to the music business, boys." Imagine the tree house conversation that night.

Every gig under the sun was now fair game for Jan and his wunderkinds: weddings, bar mitzvahs, polkas, and oompah music. Edward: "We would play at the La Mirada Country Club. My dad would play at the Continental Club every Sunday night, and we would sit in with him. He'd play at a place called the Alpine Haus off of San Fernando Road in the Valley, and we'd wear the lederhosen. Those polka songs are so weird. They're all I-IV-V, but they're like some odd country song." At an age where most boys were playing baseball—not taking a bat to the face, that is—Edward and his brother were as groomed and as trained and as prepared for a career as musicians as any two young men could possibly have been.

Doing it Wrong

For Edward, his obsession with his Teisco revealed itself to be the ultimate target for punishment by Eugenia. Access to the guitar would be restricted by locking it in a closet for up to a week should Ed be deemed to deserve it after coming home late on a Friday night. Ironically, the worst offense would be forsaking piano lessons, which by that point, must have just been excruciating for him. In Ed's words, his parents expected him to play "something respectful . . . not rock and roll." Eugenia bought him the oft-debated go-to starting point for so many guitar hopefuls and hapless, the *Mel Bay Guitar Book for Beginners.* However, Ed took a look and learned all the chords he felt would benefit him and abandoned it. Guitar would not be to him what piano had been: a chore, work, sitting down, being told "you're doing it wrong," even though that is still what happened.

The first page of the Mel Bay book shows you the "proper" way to hold a guitar pick, but Ed could not hold it as demonstrated—he held it between his middle finger and his thumb. "My mom goes, 'You're doing it wrong,'" he said. "I'm going, ' . . . wait a minute. It's music *theory* not music *fact* . . . so don't tell me I'm doing it wrong." Many years later, Edward said, "When I found the guitar, I refused to take lessons. This was my real emotional release, and I didn't want to be taught how to approach the instrument."

By 1968, at thirteen Ed was smack dead in the heart of the onslaught of the heavy rock guitar music of the day. If you indeed are requiring a point of reference for what music was changing the world at that time, a mini-snapshot would include: *Electric Ladyland* by Jimi Hendrix;

The Beatles by The Beatles (aka the "White Album"*)*; *Beggar's Banquet* by The Rolling Stones; *Wheels of Fire* by Cream; *Vincebus Eruptum* by Blue Cheer. The political upheaval at the time: MLK/RFK assassinations and the Chicago riots, to name a few. Something was in the air. The thirteen-year-old found himself at just the right place at just the right time to soak up the aggressive and inspired music flowing forth from, arguably, one of the most creative and dangerous eras in the history of rock music and the United States.

Unlike other thirteen-year-olds though, Ed was sitting down with these records and learning them note-for-note, songs like "Crossroads" by Cream. The percentage of human beings on planet earth at that time, not just thirteen-year-olds, that could listen to and play back "Crossroads" note-for-note, without the benefit of charted, technical notation or special equipment of any kind, could not have been—using technical terminology—statistically significant. Ed was also a student of The Yardbirds featuring Jimmy Page as well as The Jeff Beck Group. Alex said, "I could tell by how he was imitating and listening to different people and being able to play the same thing that this guy knew what the hell he was doing."

Edward eventually began to experience a slow awakening; a self-realization that perhaps he had a potentially unique ability on the guitar that just might be he just might be able to do some serious damage with. He observed: "Some things were easy, some things were hard. I didn't even think about whether it was easy or hard; it was something I wanted to do. To have fun and feel good about doing (it). Whether it took me a week to learn half a song or one day to learn five songs, I never thought of it that way."

CHAPTER 4
Pasadena High School

The Gladys D. Edwards Auditorium at Pasadena High School. Van Halen performed several legendary shows inside the auditorium. Photograph © Kevin Dodds

In school, Edward said his "friends could get away with murder and I was the only one to ever get caught at doing nothing." However, he did admit to getting busted changing his grades while the teacher was out of the room. About changing his grades in his English class, he simply said, "Right when I'm doing it, the teacher walks in. Got nailed." In general, Edward's scholastic career would never be a real issue, as he and Alex were both destined for immediate admission to Pasadena City College upon graduation from Pasadena High School.

Edward was indeed popular in high school due to his skills. As was the norm, he was a sexually active teenager and his high school girlfriend once became pregnant. The decision was made to have an abortion. Eddie described the ordeal as "very confusing," which included a trip to Planned Parenthood, the works. To their great relief, her parents were supportive and said they would've offered to help. It was a one-eighty from what Edward had expected, saying, "I thought they'd call us scum." It was a rude introduction to the downside of sex.

Edward entered Pasadena High School as a ninth grader in the fall of 1969. Quick points of reference: Apollo 11 moon landing; Woodstock; Manson murders; Altamont. Extraordinary stuff for anything but ordinary times. As a sophomore, on November 21, 1970, Edward saw his first ever rock concert. He and Alex caught Eric Clapton and Derek and the Dominoes at the Pasadena Civic Center. "A friend of mine won two tickets from a local radio station," he recalled, "and, knowing what a Clapton fan I was, gave them to me and Al. The show wasn't sold out when I got there, so I paid a little extra money, upgraded my tickets, and ended up in the sixth row. It was great." Alex later ribbed Eddie about bringing his binoculars to the show. Alex said, "We were sitting in the sixth row, but he had to see everything!"

While Ed was in ninth and tenth grade, he and Al began forming a menagerie of bands with an endless array of floating support musicians and practiced out in the family garage. In 1971, with their teenage sense of humor getting the better of them, the first band name they christened themselves with was The Trojan Rubber Company. Although it was said the name was abandoned when a bass player split, the change to The Space Brothers was a tad more practical, and ultimately, more printable. According to Eddie, "We had to change the name of the band to The Space Brothers, just so we could play these gigs at (a) Catholic school."

1971 was a fateful year for Edward. He had a brainstorm during a Led Zeppelin concert at the Forum on August 21. To *Rolling Stone*: "I was watching Jimmy Page going [sings hammering guitar lick], like that, with one hand, in 'Heartbreaker.' I thought, 'I can play like that, and you wouldn't know if I was using this finger [points to left hand] or this one' [points to right hand]. But you just kind of move it around, and it's like, 'You got one big hand there, buddy. That's a hell of a spread!'"

Edward's Discovery of Finger-tapping

This would be the birth of Edward's signature "double-handed" or "tapping" guitar technique that, when executed correctly, can present a sequence of notes at a theretofore unprecedented rate of speed on an electric guitar. On the surface, it would seem to be an obvious move—after all, you've got two hands. And the truth be told, he is not the inventor or discoverer of the technique. He himself said, "I didn't invent the hammer-on technique. I just put it out there for people to listen to." The origins of the move can be traced all the way back to Paganini in the 17th century, and modern electric guitarists beginning in the 1950s have been well-documented using the technique. Regardless, the technique was not used even on a small scale, and Edward was never, at least not knowingly, exposed to it prior to discovering it himself at the age of 16. Later Eddie said, "As far as the hammer-on thing—I never really saw anybody do it, okay? I'm not saying 'Hey, I'm bitchin', I came up with it,' but I never really saw anybody do it." He began incorporating the move into his playing on a regular basis in 1972.

Ed spent countless evenings alone in high school figuring out everything he could do with his right hand now hitting the fret board in conjunction with his left. "I used to sit on the edge of my bed with a six-pack of Schlitz Malt talls. My brother would go out at 7pm to party and get laid, and when he'd come back at 3am, I would still be sitting in the same place, playing guitar. I did that for years." Although the guitar helped him fit in, he was still shy and couldn't easily relate to kids his age—most likely because other kids his age had not just unlocked the keys to a new musical kingdom.

His devotion to his craft was less like a love affair and more like a mad scientist sublimating a machine to do his bidding. His mother worried about him when hearing some of the sounds coming out of his bedroom. Edward said, "She always used to say, 'Why do you have to make that high, crying noise?'" (Later, Ed would finally retort, "Well, it bought you a house, didn't it?") By high school, he had three steady companions: his six-string, his six-pack, and his cigarette pack (he would later state, "I started playing guitar, drinking, and smoking at the age of 12").

By Eddie's senior year, Alex was well into his studies at Pasadena City College, where surely to his mother's chagrin, he was taking music classes. The Trojan and Space Brother days petered out. When a bass player named Mark Stone entered the picture, it was Ed's ideal combo—a Cream/Experience-based trio, with himself on both lead vocals *and* guitar. However, it was a less balanced act than Cream (where half the attention went to Jack Bruce on vocals and half to Eric Clapton on guitar). It was rather more like the Experience, where Jimi was the focal point on lead vocals and guitar. But Cream was their main thing; even at the band's earliest gigs, they basically were a Cream tribute act with Alex playing the famous "Toad" drum solo and Edward wowing everyone with his stellar recreations—not interpretations—*recreations* of the solos and fills on "Crossroads" and "Spoonful."

With Cream having peaked in the late sixties, Ed had shifted his preoccupation to yet another English band while in high school. At one point, he was intent on naming the band Rat Salad, after the 1970 Black Sabbath song on *Paranoid*. "We played just about every Black Sabbath song. I used to sing lead on every Black Sabbath song we did," said Edward. Genesis was they name the brothers eventually agreed upon and they began their run on the legendary Pasadena backyard party circuit under that name. Of course, it wasn't long before they realized Genesis was already the name of an English group that had been around since 1967 with Peter Gabriel as a founding member. It's not too shocking they had never heard of Genesis, though; kids in the early seventies walked out of the record store with either Black Sabbath *or* Genesis, certainly not both.

College Days

Because the family had so little to get by on, despite Jan working ungodly hours, the boys were forced to get creative to pay for drum heads, drumsticks, guitar strings, guitar picks, and guitar cables—and god forbid a guitar or an amplifier. Without the consent of any particular regulatory authority, Ed and Al took to repainting numbers on street curbs for a fee. Knocking on doors one by one. One holding the stencil, the other holding the spray paint. Short work, quick payoff. Their own resourcefulness funded their growing need to pay for the basic objects of the industry. Basically, Edward had just the two "real" jobs in his life: his "honest" job delivering papers, and the rather fly-by-night house number painting scheme. Both were used to finance music equipment.

Following the Genesis revelation, Mammoth was officially founded in 1972. Mammoth was arguably Edward's first real rock group. With his brother on drums, Mark on bass, and himself on lead vocals *and* guitar, the band's early repertoire included Grand Funk and Cream, as well as Deep Purple and, of course, Sabbath. Very briefly, Mammoth employed a keyboard player, but that tied Eddie down and filled up the middle where he belonged. The trio format was what he was always intent on, and it was to stay that way. Still, Edward would admit lead vocals were not his strong point. He could and he can sing. But the power and tenor of his voice as would be required for the rather heavy responsibility of lead vocalist clearly wasn't there. He made up for it with his playing for the time being. "I used to sing and play lead in Mammoth, and I couldn't stand it. I'd rather just play," he said. In 1996, he added: "I never technically learned how to sing. So, I would kind of do a Kurt Cobain, after five songs and three beers my voice would be gone. You know, I would just scream it out and kind of waste my voice."

Jan suffered a horrific accident, particularly for a musician. Edward recalled that, in 1972, Jan "tried to lift up a trailer and it fell on his finger and just chopped his finger off." Jan essentially quit playing the clarinet. A critical component of his very livelihood had been severed.

Mammoth remained a relatively solid band throughout Ed's senior year, and upon high school graduation in 1973, he would follow his brother directly into Pasadena City College—a campus that became the gathering point for the original lineup of an act that changed the world. A fellow student, Michael Sobolewski (who later took the stage name Michael Anthony), started out studying psychology but quickly moved to music. Mike fronted a band called Snake on the same little circuit as Mammoth playing similar music, although with more of a boogie-rock focus.

Yet another Pasadena City College student was present amongst the backyard party circuit. This guy was also taking music classes. He was even in the exact same classes as the brothers. Musically, he was all about being up front and singing lead. His dad was a doctor, a rather highly regarded doctor at that. He entered into a signed contract with his father for a PA system which he was to work off. Having your own PA is like everyone asking you to help them move when you own a truck. If you have a PA, people come calling to use it. This guy charged though—ten bucks a night for it. He had an entrepreneurial streak. His name was David Lee Roth.

CHAPTER 5
"Van Halen" in the Third Person

Ten dollars per show ended up being a lot of money for Ed and Al to fork over every time they rented Dave's PA. "I figured it would be much cheaper if we just got him in the band," said Eddie. In quite a ballsy move, Dave went to the Van Halens home one day and knocked on the door. He said he wanted to sing with them. Alex and Eddie told him to learn "Crossroads" and a Grand Funk song and come back the next week. David came back the following week, and it did not go well. Eddie said, "It was terrible. He couldn't sing." The brothers simply did not believe that what they saw and heard that day was enough to overcome the rental fee for the PA. Dave's versions of their beloved Cream songs were not note-for-note, spot-on, Jack Bruce sing-a-like vocals. They were described as free-wheeling. Something about the whole situation weighed very heavy on Edward though, and he actually left the room so Alex could tell Dave it was a no-go. Eddie obviously couldn't bear Dave's reaction when told he wasn't what they were looking for. Ed maintained that Roth still holds a grudge against Alex for turning him down. In 1995, Ed said, "To this day that's why Roth still has a hair up his ass about Al, because he was the one who told him, 'Sorry, man. It ain't working.'"

Dave had already observed Edward from afar on the circuit. Dave had seen Mammoth "doing note-for-note, *verbatim* renditions of The Who, *Live at Leeds*, or Deep Purple, 'Smoke on the Water,' or shit from Woodstock, when Alvin Lee comes out and plays 'Goin' Home' faster than any known human being on earth, or at least up until that time—Edward could do *that* lick. You know. It was *amazing* stuff." Dave added, "I've always had a tremendous amount of respect for their musical ability—particularly Edward's. . . . I listened to him play, I watched him play, and I said, 'You know, what he does with his hands, I wanna do with my feet, I wanna do with my voice. He was kind of a mentor of mine."

Again, David was taking the same music classes as Edward, as well as Alex and Michael. Dave described their days at Pasadena City College as "treading water until a band got launched. I spent most of the time in junior college in music courses—theory and orchestration. I was not very good at it. Mathematically, I count to four and then start over. . . . The Van Halens were far superior to anything I could do in that area. So was Michael. They won all the awards."

Following his failed attempt to join the brothers, Dave formed Red Ball Jets, whose direction was similar to many bands at the time—vamped up seventies rock versions of fifties rock staples. Mammoth, Snake, and Red Ball Jets were constantly crossing paths on the tiny circuit. Dave said, "Playing those parties got competitive fast." Battle of the bands events would inevitably pit one of the bands against the other. Not everybody always won. Ed's vocals were not blowing anyone away and his stage persona was not yet hatched. He was bound to both the guitar amp and that damned microphone.

Before long, Alex reconsidered his and Eddie's earlier opinion of Dave and his peculiar style. Ed's vocal struggles and hindered front man abilities got Alex thinking about a band that had the whole deal—a trio plus a front man. The 1970s rock band template was a quartet (trio plus front man, that is): Sabbath, Zeppelin, etc. Dave's work ethic showed, plus he came with a PA, a rehearsal space, and transportation. Perhaps Dave's unique interpretations of the Mammoth cover song bible might just provide a nice segue into original music. Dave dryly noted, "Basically what I had to offer at that time was that I knew how to dance. I knew what was good dance music, and, hence, could get us into clubs." Eddie later maintained that he still considered what he was doing was playing in a trio, but just, in his words, "a trio with a throat." About Dave's vocal abilities at that time, Eddie said, "He got better—otherwise we wouldn't have continued on with him."

In late 1973, when Eddie was a freshman in college, David Lee Roth officially joined Ed, Alex, and Mark in Mammoth. The most important thing Dave provided Eddie was intangible. Dave gave Edward the freedom of movement and concentration that he had absolutely never had in his performance career to date. His playing style would shift to playing fills off the vocals rather than awkwardly playing around his own. Edward summed up the early college scene: "We played everywhere and anywhere, from backyard parties to places the size of your bathroom. And we did it all without a manager, agent, or record company. We used to print up flyers announcing where we were going to play and stuff them into high school lockers."

Mammoth played odd gigs, to say the least. One of which would no doubt be a traumatizing incident for anyone young or old. Edward recalled: "We did forty-five minute sets each night while these bikers drank and got crazy. One night, two bikers started arguing about whose motorcycle was quicker. One guy whipped out a hunting knife and stabbed the other one right in front of us while we were playing 'You Really Got Me.' The biker's guts were hanging out and he died the next day . . . The next night we moved our equipment about two feet from the wall so we could get out fast if there was any trouble."

David Lee Roth Names the Band Van Halen

Shortly after the New Year, the band would find out that their name was, again, already taken. It turned out that the use of the name Mammoth was indeed copyrighted. This warranted yet another name change.

David had a suggestion that sounded a little odd at first. He suggested Van Halen. Dave gets all due credit for settling on the band name that would not only dominate rock music, but would immediately raise Edward's, and his brother's, and their mother and fathers' profiles. Edward would take an enormous sense of pride in putting his family name on the line, so to speak. In no time, Edward was referring to the band "Van Halen" in the third person, as his family name was now indeed something bigger than just himself.

Dave said, "I figured if we named it after a human being, especially Van Halen, it sounds strong. It sounds like it has power to it. At the same time a classical piano player could be a Van Halen. Also in that way the band can evolve. But if you call yourself the Electric Plotz, three years from now you're expected to sound like an Electric Plotz." Dave later added the he felt the name Van Halen was essentially the same as Santana. It's just a name—it's not tied down to any one thing at all. And it was unique.

With the naming of the band Van Halen, Dave also ends up perpetually intertwined with the surname himself. Some could argue that at times, Dave would've been the first person one thought of when the term Van Halen was used in the third person. In fact, Dave was early on referred to as "Van" when doing business with club owners who thought Dave's name was actually Van Halen (first name-last name); this was specifically true about Bill Gazzari. It's a bit of the Jethro Tull/Marshall Tucker syndrome except that Van Halen is a *real* person's name. Yet Dave, literally by virtue of his center position on the stage, became the front and center representative for Van Halen (in the third person).

Dave was bearing the weight of representing Eddie and his family name as the band's unofficial leader. No one intended to fail. Between Dave's street smarts and the brothers' experience in music thus far—and their father's experience heaped on top—the marriage of David Lee Roth and Edward Van Halen was sown. However, their partnership would ultimately prove to be more complex than just any regular marriage—this particular relationship is not that simple.

On a more complex level, Edward turned over his fortune to Dave in many ways. There on, Edward handed over vocal responsibility to Dave almost one hundred percent totally and completely on both cover arrangements and lyrics and titles for original songs. What Edward wrote—what were just pieces of music to him—were given titles by David. These titles are synonymous with Edward himself: "Runnin' with the Devil," "Dance the Night Away," "Unchained," "Hot for Teacher" . . . The background vocals and harmonies that Edward would become famous for delivering came from the words and melodies crafted by someone else. It was a simple "I do the music, you do the words" arrangement.

When wondering just how different Edward and David were, David summed it up: "Right off the bat, two entirely separate record collections and everything." One was what the other wasn't and the other the same. One just wanted to concentrate on the music and the other wanted to systematically conquer the scene, and sing, too.

When the rechristened Van Halen hit the circuit, they were truly human jukeboxes able to play just about anything required or requested of them. Edward and the band wanted to play the clubs but their initial forays were unsuccessful, particularly at Gazarri's Teen Dance Club in Hollywood. With Ed all about the music and Dave all about show business, Dave laid it out: "They weren't getting the shows in the bars. They couldn't understand why. I explained to them one day, 'It's because you play all twenty minutes of 'I'm So Glad' by Cream, complete with drum solo, live, note-for-note, and it's very impressive, but you can't dance to it.' That's not 'Excuse me, do you come here often?' music. The club owners described it as 'too psychedelic.' The band couldn't get arrested."

Ed said, "We had to audition there at least three or four times. A guy would come running up in the middle of a song because I was too loud."

Henceforth, Dave vowed to "check every song for *danceability*." They stuck with rock obviously, but focused on ones with groove, like "Just Got Paid" by ZZ Top and "Walk This Way" by Aerosmith. Following Dave's lead, the band did finally land a regular gig at Gazzari's starting in April of 1974, where they made $75 per show. According to Dave, "We started working forty-five minute sets a night, running the dance contest and so forth." Looking to make a big impression, Ed once commandeered the stage with a new pair of platform shoes that required a little more lead time to get used to than he realized. Actually, the shoes were part of his following Dave's orders, the latter now the self-appointed fashion leader of the band as well. "He always told me I looked like shit," said Eddie. "So around the time we auditioned for Gazarri's on the Sunset Strip, I got some platforms and nearly broke my ankles." According to Michael Anthony, his first gig with band required him to wear a gold and silver lamè shirt, not his first choice under any real circumstance actually, much less a backyard Pasadena keg party. For the same show, Edward even wore a cape!

"Eventually we were a fixture at Gazzari's," said Dave. "We knew two-hundred songs by other people." To show how far the band went down the danceability route, they even covered "Twist and Shout." A 1974 live recording shows that it's not really the Isley Brothers or The Beatles. It sounds like Van Halen. Edward definitely packs in the guitar fills, but it is an excellent early example of how Edward and Michael's background dual harmonies worked so well against Dave's lead. This classic, gospelesque tune is specifically written as an old school call-and-response number for a lead singer with a background choir, if you will. It would end up becoming a songwriting/performance technique that Dave and Ed and Michael would perfect and become a signature of the classic Van Halen sound. Edward said that the unique VH harmony backing vocal sound stemmed from attempting to duplicate the horn parts vocally in the R&B covers the band so regularly performed.

Other recordings would take place that year. One was an original song called "Glitter"—obviously a nod to the glam scene. Ed's trademark bends are there, but overall his playing style is a tip of the hat to Tony Iommi, even though it still sounds like Eddie. In the eyes of some Van Halen purists, this song definitely has worthy moments and would have been able to have been altered and/or improved into a better track (which would become a common songwriting practice for Ed).

The Oldest Recordings

A great deal of what was captured on tape around this time shows that Edward's mind was in absolute musical overload. He pumped out easily over a dozen riffs during Van Halen's earliest few years that would be reworked or revived and eventually become some of the greatest classic rock songs of all time. Some original songs captured on tape at this time contained the bulk of what later became "Mean Streets," "Somebody Get Me a Doctor," and "Hang 'Em High." This is all in addition to having to learn hundreds of other peoples' songs to play the clubs.

A 1974 home audio recording of Eddie playing shows that his right-hand picking execution was already absolutely amazing. The nine minutes of audio also demonstrate a burgeoning mastery of mixing in bits of finger picking/plucking—a little known but quickly recognizable trademark of Ed's. He is working out a lot of different ideas during this recording which is clearly for his own posterity—there are pauses, starts and stops. A lot of it is heavy drone rock riffs with very distinctive/odd sounding changes. As an experiment he tunes his low E to low A and while noodling around he cranks out the main riff of "Somebody Get Me a Doctor." This experimental tuning style is a technique he would return to over a decade later for the *5150* song "Good Enough." The audio continues on and shows how Edward works fastidiously on cranking out the "Somebody Get Me a Doctor" riff.

This recording actually ends with some humorous audio of the band in a hotel room with some girls. The conversation is spirited and mostly revolves around Dave sending someone to get an extra room key. There is clearly flirting going on with the girls. Edward is quiet for the most part, until near the end, he clearly says, "Why don't you make . . . make sexy noises for him?" after which there is a pause and someone in the background points out, "They're recording you." Ed is then heard replying to a query, "Nah, man, I can't make that noise myself . . ."

As the band, and Edward himself as a player, became more popular, they set their sights on the Starwood. The difference, which presented a rather pressing challenge to the band, was that the Starwood was an all original club. As Dave bluntly put it, "You didn't play cover tunes at the

Starwood." Fortunately, Edward's relentless creativity gave Dave a well of material to choose from to add lyrics and melodies to. It would take them until mid-1976 to pull it off.

DeVry or Rock Music?

Eugenia attempted one more serious attempt to dissuade Edward from following in his father's footsteps and being a "nothing nut" musician. She attempted to persuade Edward to enroll at DeVry in Phoenix to take computer classes. Jan on the other hand supported the boys and "Van Halen" all the way. Edward had done well in school, and he got into and did well in college. One wonders what gave her the inspiration that DeVry held the keys to Edward's future. Possibly a television commercial? Nevertheless, Ed carried on as he had been, although his and Alex's both still living at home was likely getting awkward. Who knows what shape the tree house was in. Or if it was still there, and it was being used, what was it being used for?

It was well past the time that the boys had come into contact with a little more than Schlitz, vodka, or Pall Malls. As blunt an introduction to the topic as can be given comes from Ed himself: "Back in 1972, I OD'd on PCP, thinking it was cocaine." There aren't a whole lot of people that went through something like that at seventeen.

The band had an operation in place for whenever the backyard parties would inevitably get raided by the cops. After pulling a "we're just the band" routine, they'd be free to collect their gear and leave. When the cops had everyone cleared out, the guys would get down and their hands and knees with flashlights and collect ditched joints, booze, and what-have-you. "After combing the grounds, we would just sit up on that stage until four in the morning just samplin' everything," recalled Dave. The times, the place: L.A., Hollywood, Sunset Strip—mid-70s. Edward in his late teens, early twenties. The Schlitz were the steady old friends, but now, anything even found on the ground was fair game.

Nevertheless, Edward continued on with his classes at Pasadena City College and found kinship with a professor. Dr. Fisher apparently instilled in Edward a trait that would benefit his creativity for the rest of his life. According to Gordon Mathews:

Dr. Fisher made it clear to Eddie that that were rules to music but that those rules were meant to be broken. This actually got him into trouble with another teacher, who felt an arrangement Eddie had done on an assignment was incorrect. In a show of personal conviction, the normally shy musician addressed the class, asking them to decide whether or not the piece he had written (sic) was good. As legend has it, Eddie played the piece on piano, and when he was through, the class burst into applause.

Later, in 1982, Edward said, "You know, I think it's funny. If there's something that, that I wanna do, I won't give up until I can figure out some way to make it sound similar to what I really can't do. Does that make any sense?" It definitely makes sense to a musical rule breaker.

CHAPTER 6
Critical Years

By 1975, the Van Halen engine was already chugging at full speed. And the vehicle was not just too terribly far from what it would eventually look like three years later. The band played practically non-stop at Gazzari's all year long. To truly give an idea of the band's work ethic at the time: they played Gazzari's alone fifty-eight times in 1974 and forty times in 1975—nearly 100 times in just two years at the same Hollywood club.

Existing recordings from this period include an original called "Brown Sugar"—not a cover of the Stones song. Ed's riff is played with a phaser throughout. It is essentially just a vamped up blues riff. Ed has a very lengthy solo that highlights many features of his playing that would become signatures of his playing style throughout his career (fast right-hand picking and tremelo dive-bombing). Dave's vocals are reminiscent of his delivery on "Atomic Punk."

Mostly though, the band waded through covers performing live, including "Waiting on the Bus" by ZZ Top. Existing audio reveals an extremely vamped-up version—it is loaded with fills by Edward throughout—the song is simply a vehicle for his fills. At the right times, he is dead on doing the riff note-for-note, but then goes into totally and completely uncharted territory and is just absolutely killing. His right-hand attack and vibrato are over the top.

Another amazing recording from this period is a version of "Man on the Silver Mountain" by Dio-era Deep Purple. Dave starts out the song saying "The very gentle, the very delicate . . . Van Halen." Ed then launches straight into the mean-ass riff and they fucking *murder* it. Dave and Mike both sound great on vocals. If it weren't a Deep Purple song, it would be an absolutely excellent candidate for any of the first three Van Halen albums. The pre-chorus and choruses are excellent. The solo pulls out every jaw-drop inducing trick in the arsenal. From start to finish, their version is just absolutely over the top kick ass. Another cover recording that exists from around this time is The Edgar Winter Group song "We All Had a Real Good Time." Ed's solo is quite impressive and specifically features some intense right-hand picking.

In February of 1975, the band played the first of their own self-promoted mini-concerts at Pasadena High School, the brothers' former alma mater. Michael Anthony's band Snake was also on the bill and when Van Halen's PA went kaput, Mike stepped in and let them borrow his PA for free. Shortly after the show, Ed, Dave, and Al sat down with Mark and let him go. Mark was a straight-A student who was headed elsewhere in life. "He was going to school to be a pharmacist—swear to God," said Edward. "He spent more time at home building LSD molecules. We were playing parties with a repertoire of a hundred songs, and he wouldn't remember stuff." Michael Anthony was given the business during an audition but was ultimately given the job as bass player and back-up vocalist.

The fully-formed Van Halen returned to Pasadena High School two months later in April. Both shows were held in the auditorium of Pasadena High School. Recordings of both of these shows include seminal versions of the *Women and Children First* classics "Take Your Whiskey Home" and "Fools." Thrown in is a simply killer version of Joe Walsh's and his James Gang classic "Walk Away." Ed basically holds the same few chords together while the verse vocals are going, but otherwise completely dominates the song with over-the-top fills and solos.

One listen and you can already hear that he is completely ready to go the distance. The casual listener would not necessarily know immediately that Michael Anthony was *not* present at the February gig, but is quite obvious he *was* present at the April show. For the rest of 1975, only one other non-Gazzari's gig took place in June at the Pasadena Hilton Hotel.

Determined to succeed, Edward continued his high creative output over the next year, coming up with as many killer riffs and parts and pieces he could muster. In spring of 1976, the band played their first non-Gazzari's club gig of their career at Walter Mitty's Rock and Roll Emporium in Pomona, and they also opened for UFO, a high-profile gig, at Golden West Ballroom in Pomona. Finally, in June, Van Halen scored their first gig at the Starwood. Upon a return to the club later that year, a twenty-one-year-old Eddie and his band played a seemingly regular gig in November. Except that it wasn't a regular gig.

Thanks for Nothing, Gene

A competitor of Van Halen's was a band called Boyz (beating N.W.A. to the whole "boyz" thing by about fifteen years—in L.A., nonetheless). Two members of Boyz, George Lynch and Mick Brown, would later be half of Dokken in the 80s. Boyz played a Halloween gig at Gazzari's where the majority of the costumed crowd arrived dressed as members of KISS, whose popularity was absolutely soaring at the time. Specifically, that very Halloween, the band was guests on the *The Paul Lynde Halloween Special*, which was the biggest national television exposure they had gotten up to that point.

To appease the crowd, Boyz closed their set with "Firehouse" (a KISS song also covered by Van Halen). After the show, out of the crowd walked Gene Simmons. He was impressed by the band and told them that their record label Casablanca was looking for new artists and asked when their next show was. The following week, Gene brought some label reps out to the Starwood and Boyz completely stilted. However, Van Halen was on the bill completely kicking ass, and Gene's interest turned.

Edward was absolutely gleeful. Gene Simmons of KISS liked his band. Eddie said, "He's goin', 'You guys got a record deal? You guys got a manager?' We're going [acting stupefied and awestruck, scratching his head] 'No. What's a manager?! What's a record deal?!" Gene moved quickly and booked the band into Village Recorder Studios in Los Angeles off of Santa Monica Boulevard. Ed's songwriting over the past year paid off and they were able to lay down a dozen-plus original tunes. Four of those would go on to be classics: "On Fire," "Runnin' with the Devil," "Somebody Get Me a Doctor," and "House of Pain." Additionally, a track called "She's the Woman" would be reworked first into "Voodoo Queen," and then eventually into "Mean Streets." The former three tracks were reworked significantly before they finally appeared on early VH albums.

These tracks show that Van Halen certainly had their identity down by 1976—hard-driving guitar, incredible fills and solos, thumping bass, "end-of-the-world" drums, high-harmony backing vocals. The only thing about "the Gene Simmons demo" that might throw off the classic Van Halen fan is Dave's voice; it sounds as if it had not yet filled out completely and at times comes across a bit thin, and was, in fact, not well mixed or produced. Also, the guitar sound on these recordings is layered with a slap-back echo rather than a huge reverb; the latter would be a signature of the *Van Halen* album soon to come.

Following the Village Recorder sessions, in an attempt to wow the band, Gene funded a group trip to New York City. The first thing they would do upon arrival in Gene's hometown was take the tapes to Electric Lady Studios—the famous studio built to Hendrix's specs which opened just weeks before his death in 1970 (it is still run by Jimi's engineer Eddie Kramer). Edward would record only a few overdubs in the studio. These overdubs come across as extremely un-Van Halen. There are parts where Ed attempts to play a guitar harmony line with himself over a pre-written solo (as opposed to improvised which would be the only way he work from there on out). It sounds awkward and cluttered. Since Gene was 100 percent at the controls, it's possible he wanted to see how Ed would sound playing along with a second guitar. After a few overdubs, the session was mixed and completed.

The most important reason for coming to New York was not to throw a few overdubs down at Electric Lady; it was to play a showcase performance for Bill Aucoin, KISS's manager since their start in 1973. Bill passed on signing Van Halen. This has gone down in rock music lore as the equivalent of Decca passing on The Beatles and has followed Aucoin to this day. The truth is that Van Halen in late 1976 would simply not be the same Van Halen in late 1977. A lot of the songwriting was still a bit disjointed, the lyrics were not great, and Dave's lower timbre wasn't quite there (it sounds as if he couldn't yet pull off the Elvisesque "to satis-uh-fy" line at the end of "Ice Cream Man").

During the final "big meeting" with Bill, which took place on the top floor of a Madison Avenue skyscraper, as Bill had his shoes shined he told them, "Guys, I think the music is great but the vocals don't hold up. I just don't hear the melodies." He suggested to the band, "Maybe another vocalist would work. But otherwise, Gene has his own career, and barring any other permutations, I don't think I can work with you." This clearly left Edward and Alex reeling back to their original dismissal of Dave as a singer, and Dave embarrassed and guilty.

Not long after the debacle in New York City, Gene called up Eddie and Alex to have them back him on three tracks he was demoing for the next KISS album, *Love Gun*. Working as a trio, Ed and Al played with Gene on the tracks "Christine Sixteen" and "Got Love for Sale," both of which ended up on *Love Gun* (another track, "Tunnel of Love," was shuttered for a Gene solo record). According to Gene, "I liked his [Edward's] solo for 'Christine Sixteen' so much that when the band recorded it for *Love Gun*, Ace pretty much copied Eddie's solo note-for-note." *Love Gun* was released a few months later in June of 1977.

Dave was highly suspicious of Gene's activities from the start. According to Dave's autobiography *Crazy from the Heat*, he claims that Gene came to check out Van Halen based on word of mouth, and that it wasn't just a chance meeting as implied by the boys in Boyz. He also asserts that the whole Gene-scenario was an attempt to get Eddie, and possibly Alex, into KISS one way or another given the ongoing problems with Ace Frehley and Peter Criss. Upon Gene's demo-cutting invite, fiercely protective and possibly fighting for his life, Dave showed up with Edward at the studio. He said, "Simmons would look at me with horror. *Horror*. 'Cause I was on to his game way early." In August of 1977, Dave also claims that Gene invited the band to the KISS show at the Forum in L.A.—that is, everyone but Dave. "The Van Halens would be inside, comfortably ensconced in the back room with Gene and his pals," said David.

Gene Simmons is an interesting person, to say the least. Dee Snider recently claimed that Gene still thinks Elvis owes *him* for inventing rock and roll. It is common knowledge that Gene loves to take credit for "discovering" Van Halen. In fact, all he did was mix them a demo tape of debatable quality, fly them to New York City, and inject disharmony into a group that already came with conflict and tension as part of the main course. Ed called the recordings "the world's most expensive demo tape." Gene did take some bands under his wing—like Rush (perennially managed by their high school friend Ray Danniels) who toured with KISS during much of 1974 and 1975—and others he discovered, such as Casablanca label mates Angel. Gene's involvement in Van Halen eventually petered out.

Finally Getting Signed

Van Halen shared the bill with The Ramones at the Golden West Ballroom on March 13, 1977. Joey Ramone was later photographed for *Creem* magazine wearing an original, black Van Halen logo t-shirt. That May—the same month as the release of *Star Wars*—the band was playing what was a fairly crappy Monday night show at the Starwood complete with rain. Through their Starwood shows, they got noticed by Marshall

Berle (indeed, the nephew of the late Milton Berle), a well-connected talent scout who would become the band's first manager. Marshall convinced Ted Templeman to come out. Ted said, "I thought David was the first singer since Jim Morrison to have that kind of attitude." Ted in turn then convinced Mo Ostin to come out. Ostin was then the president of Warner Brothers; and Ted's studio production credits to that point included five Doobie Brothers records, as well as Carly Simon, Van Morrison, Little Feat, and Montrose. Ted was especially impressed and urged Mo to sign the band.

Edward told Jas Obrecht: "We were playing the club one rainy Monday night in 1977, and Berle told us that there were some people coming to see us, so play good. It ended up that we played a good set in front of an empty house and all of a sudden Berle walks in with Ted and Mo Ostin. Templeman said, 'It's great,' and within a week we were signed up. It was right out of the movies." As a result, Dave would be sticking with the band or Van Halen was stuck with Dave, however you want to look at it. To Edward it was a thorn in his side. But the album Ed and Dave delivered on would eventually sell *10 million* copies and counting.

Edward went to the Rainbow and had an interesting brush with fame when he met Ritchie Blackmore, who had been a significant influence on Ed, particularly with regard to the tremolo bar. The band of course had played several Deep Purple and Rainbow tunes. Eddie told Obrecht, "I met him once at the Rainbow with John Bonham when we were just playing clubs. You know, I grew up on him too, and I ran over and said hello, and they both just looked at me and said, 'Who are you? Fuck off.' And it pissed me off."

By 1977, Van Halen had left the Starwood behind and played almost exclusively the Whisky a Go Go playing at least once per month, often doing two-night stands. They continued to promote their own mini-concerts as well, most importantly at the Pasadena Civic Center. They played the center three times throughout the year, with their triumphant December 20 show caught on tape. Every song they played would be on either *Van Halen* or *Van Halen II*.

CHAPTER 7
Van Halen and the Guitar-Making Artist

In no uncertain terms, Ted Templeman is ten million times the producer Gene Simmons could ever hope to be. The band turned themselves over to him completely. He has been referred to openly as the "fifth member" of Van Halen.

The first day in the studio, they went straight in and captured twenty-five songs on tape as quickly as possible. After evaluating the material, they whittled the list down to nine total songs plus "Jamie's Cryin'" which was completed in the studio (Ed noted, "I already had the basic riff for that song"). Edward: "The album is very live—there are few overdubs, which is the magic of Ted Templeman."

During the recording of the album, Ted was also producing Nicolette Larson's debut album. She is most famous for the 70s soft rock song "Lotta Love" that went to #1 on the adult contemporary chart. Ted drafted Edward to play on one of her tracks. Dave objected: "When we made our first album for Warner Brothers, Ted Templeman, the producer, approached Edward and said, 'I'd like you to play on the Nicolette Larson album.' I got right between them, I said, 'No way! You're not going to run off with bits and pieces of the scenery before the play starts.' Ed wanted to play on it. I said, 'Great. But you got to put a question mark on where your name goes. Got to keep it all in one camp.'" Playing outside of Van Halen was considered a no-no as a *spoken* rule. It was the first but far from the last of such squabbles.

Ted produced Larson's debut album *Nicolette* and it also came out in 1978. It went to #15. "Lotta Love" was written by Neil Young, and another song on the album, "Last in Love," was written by Glenn Frey and J.D. Souther. Other artists that contributed to the album included James Burton (Elvis for starters), Michael McDonald and Patrick Simmons of the Doobs, Linda Ronstadt, Albert Lee, Klaus Voorman (of Plastic Ono

Band and The Beatles' *Revolver* album cover fame), and . . . Edward Van Halen (who went uncredited).

The track was called "Can't Get Away From You" and, for the most part, could easily be an ABBA song. Edward played on the entire track contributing a tight, driving rhythm guitar complete with his trademark flourishes. The guitar solo is almost completely in a major key and features Ed's wild bends, but sounds a bit hokey, especially given the backing music. What is slightly shocking is the outro of this somewhat limp soft rock throwaway—the outro sounds like it could have been straight off of *Van Halen*. It is nearly identical to the endings of "You Really Got Me," "Ice Cream Man," or "I'm the One." It ends with a one hundred percent Eddie Van Halen uninterrupted solo flourish that spans a full nine seconds of the three minute track.

As for the recording of *Van Halen*, Edward said, "I would say that out of the ten songs on the record, I overdubbed the solo on only 'Runnin' with the Devil,' 'Ice Cream Man,' and 'Jamie's Cryin'.' The rest are live. . . . Because we were jumping around, drinking beer, and getting crazy, I think there's a vibe in the record."

"Eruption"

In referring to the "ten songs" on the debut, Edward clearly did not consider one of the eleven tracks to be a "song" per se. It was not his intention to include a guitar solo instrumental on the album. During an interview conducted by Billy Corgan for a 1996 issue of *Guitar Player*, Edward said: "The whole story behind 'Eruption' is unusual. It wasn't even supposed to be on the album. I showed up at the recording studio early one day and started to warm up because I had a gig on the weekend and I wanted to practice my solo guitar spot. Our producer, Ted Templeman, happened to walk by and he asked, 'What's that? Let's put it on tape!' So I took one pass at it, and they put it on the record. I didn't even play it right. There's a mistake at the top end of it. To this day, whenever I hear it I always think, 'Man, I could've played it better.'"

Never before on earth or in the nether reaches of the universe had there ever been a track like "Eruption." For Edward, it's "easy" to play. This last-minute addition, all 1:42 of it, changed the approach to the electric guitar forever (some sources say it was one single take; others say it was two or three takes). Quite simply, you've got pre-"Eruption" and you've got post-"Eruption." If one was knowledgeable and had to pick just the top two (relatively unaccompanied) guitar solos, you'd be hard-pressed to pick anything but Jimi's "Star-Spangled Banner" and "Eruption." It is full of bluesy and classical sections, extreme tremolo bar dive bombs, and the ridiculous right-hand picking technique of death.

The man's right-hand picking style was established as unique on two fronts. First, his standard picking attack using his wrist is one of a kind. The accuracy and speed of his attack—his *attack*—no one had reached that before. Another incredibly unique aspect of his picking technique is a move which involves locking his elbow in position and rapidly rotating his tibia and fibula while holding the pick between his thumb and middle finger. Using the latter technique, he hints at his over-the-top musical vocabulary toward the end of the first half of "Eruption" when he throws in a tongue-in-cheek nod to his violin days by quoting *Etude No. 2*.

But of course, the big pay-off in "Eruption" is the neo-classical two-handed tapping section near the close. At some point, every single person that has ever picked up an electric guitar that had any sense of curiosity has attempted to learn that section. Not one day goes by at any Guitar Center in the world where someone is not overheard playing the tapping section of "Eruption" at least a dozen times per day every day for the last several decades. At the time, Eddie said, "A lot of people listen to that and they don't even think it's a guitar. 'Is that a synthesizer? A piano? What is that?'"

The rest of *Van Halen* was recorded in a live manner—with guitar, bass, drums, and even sometimes vocals all recorded absolutely live. The entire album was completed in three weeks time. The very first sound you hear on *Van Halen* is a slowed down and reversed tape effect of car horns that Edward cobbled together. The first time the horns were used on a Van Halen recording was the 1976 demo of "House of Pain" when they were utilized as a brief sound effect.

Hands On

Edward had a hardcore creative and deconstructive/constructive streak in him. You hear car horns; he hears a sound effect. You probably don't know the first thing about how to make such a device; Edward ripped out four car horns and got to work on it. "We took the horns out of all our cars," he said, "my brother's Opel, my old Volvo, ripped a couple out of a Mercedes and a Volkswagen—and mounted them in a box and hooked two car batteries to it and added a footswitch. We just used them as noisemakers before we got signed."

Ed had already been doing his own thing with his instruments for a while at this point. Every off-the-rack guitar had a perceived problem from Edward's point of view. They were either too thin sounding, not intonated correctly, frets too small, pickups in the wrong position, too many technical accoutrements, and, almost always, a tremolo bar that just didn't work like he wanted it to. For all intents and purposes though, Eddie basically wanted a Strat-style guitar that sounded like a Gibson (common today, but theretofore unheard of).

He went straight to the Charvel guitar factory and bought a Stratocaster-copy body and neck for less than $200. He put in a modified Gibson PAF humbucking pick-up in the bridge position. Go into a guitar store and you'll see countless variations of Strat-style guitars with humbuckers—but before 1978? Not so much. Edward's unique mind conquered not only music, but the tools he used to make his music. Through his own bouts of trial and error, he figured out how to build a guitar to do exactly what *he* wanted it to do, to play exactly the way *he* wanted it to play, to sound exactly the way *he* wanted it to sound. Therein lies a major point of distinction between Edward and his oft referred to "competitor" as king of the electric guitar, Hendrix. Edward didn't sing lead and write lyrics, but Jimi was perfectly content to take any Fender Stratocaster just exactly as it was made, no questions asked. To make it all the more simple, Edward's guitar had just one knob, a volume knob—no tone knob. "I don't use any fancy tone knobs," he said. A tone knob on a guitar?! Fancy? The ability to adjust the difference of the output between treble and bass? Reiterated on yet another occasion: "No fancy tone knobs here!"

If anything was *fancy* about this particular guitar, it was Edward's paint job, a seemingly random pattern of lines (and a little squiggly thing). Ed brushed it off, "Painted it up, you know, with stripes and stuff. I guess that's my thing." Again, Jimi did paint his guitar for Monterey, the one he burned, but when you think of Jimi, the guitar in his hands is bone white. Ed's guitar looked completely like his and his alone. He used tape to make the lines in various widths, lengths, and directions. He preferred Schwinn bicycle paint: "It's acrylic lacquer, like car paint. It's good paint." At first, this guitar—known as the Frankenstein—was just black and white, but it is the exact same guitar he is so famously known for (he added the red paint a little over a year later).

The "striped art" concept, if you will, was completely original in the world of art ("I love stripes," he said). His unique design is as instantly recognizable as the American flag. The mouse pad on my office desk is an official red, black, and white striped pad. The photo of Eddie on the cover of *Van Halen*, taken at the Whisky, shows him proudly brandishing his creation. The black and white stripes on his guitar make the whole cover. It is iconic. Arguably, it's as original and unique as a Jackson Pollock work.

The getting-to-be-not-so young man, twenty-three years old as of January 1978, was a legitimate artist, even punk rock in his approach—he didn't even need tone knobs! "A lot of bands keep hacking it out and doing so many overdubs and double-tracking that their music doesn't sound real. And there are also a lot of bands that can't pull it off live because they have overdubbed so much stuff in the studio that it either doesn't sound the same, or they just stand there pushing buttons on their tape machines. We kept it really live." Punk rock. Not Fleetwood Mac.

He built his own guitar. He inadvertently cast himself as an immensely successful graphic designer by painting his guitar in an extraordinarily original way. And he played the thing like no one had ever played one before. But damned if he wasn't still a bit naïve.

The Release of *Van Halen*

So proud of the *Van Halen* recordings, Edward took a tape of the album to play for the members of Angel at the home of drummer Barry Brandt. Angel on Casablanca . . . Angel discovered by Gene Simmons. Totally and completely without ill intent, Eddie played them a tape of the record. Shortly after, Ted called Eddie. Ted was furious. Ted informed him that Angel was in the studio trying to rush-release a copycat version of Van Halen's take on The Kinks' "You Really Got Me." All's fair, apparently. Of course, the VH version would be unbelievably superior to Angel's version, so Angel (and Bill Aucoin, and Gene, and Casablanca) would have only succeeded to confuse the market. Somewhere, alone with his thoughts, he undoubtedly referred back to the money disbursement at the wedding and Jan's "welcome to the music business" remark. Bill Aucoin looked Edward straight in the eyes, knowing how bad he wanted to make it—a kid flying all the way from Los Angeles to New York for his shot at the big time—and told him no. Then he tried to pull the rug out from under him. It was personal.

Because of Ed's mistake, *Van Halen* was in turn rush-released in February to beat Angel to the sucker punch. There wasn't a whole hell of a lot of time for build-up publicity, and, in the scurry, Dave convinced the band to all shave two years off their ages—age fabrication being a longstanding entertainment industry tradition, no doubt. Because of this, Ed's age would constantly be reported incorrectly for years. Many years later, Edward said, "I should've known when Roth said, 'Let's say we're two years younger than we really are.' And I'd say, 'Why? I'm only 22. What's the difference?' That still causes problems for me to this day."

Within a month, *Van Halen* was #19 on the U.S. album charts. March 3, 1978 marked the dawn of a new era in Edward's life. He became Edward the worldwide touring musician. Although he and Alex technically lived with their parents, the road would become home. It was definitely fun at first.

The very first iconic photograph of Edward Van Halen from my own original, well-weathered *Van Halen* album cover. Photograph © Elliot Gilbert (fair use)

CHAPTER 8
Around the World

The band immediately hit the road with Journey and Montrose blanketing the U.S. in two months time. Edward and the other guys took to life on the road with enthusiasm. Sex, drugs, rock and roll, and competition was their way of life. Edward admitted, "In 1978, I walked around squeezing everything that walked." In a 2009 Black Sabbath documentary, Eddie said, "It was our first tour. It was 1978. We were doing anything and everything we ever read about and then some."

Sammy Hagar had long since departed Montrose, and Ronnie Montrose mostly befuddled Ed with his ridiculously complex set-up. Edward said, "I see Montrose with his $4,000 studio rack with his digital delay and his harmonizer and everything else, and I swear to God, I can't tell he's usin' it. And then he laughs himself silly looking at my stuff. And then later on he's going 'Whoa, how do you get that sound?'"

Journey, though, was a whole other thing. Van Halen *hated* Journey. Alex once said he made one of them cry, and that he couldn't say his name "but *he sings like this*!" (in a mocking high-pitch tone). Steve Perry had only joined Journey about six months prior to the start of the tour, and Journey's *Infinity* album (with "Wheel in the Sky") came out just one month before *Van Halen*. Steve's somewhat sissy ways brought the wrath of the macho Van Halen down upon him. His penchant for wearing scarves supposedly to help his throat led to the band and their crew appearing on stage during a sound check wearing scarves tied around their dicks. How long did it take Eddie to get cocky? "When we first started touring, we were third bill. We opened for Ronnie Montrose and Journey. And within two months, they were begging us to stay," he said.

Early on in the tour, the band acted out their rock star fantasies of hotel destruction in Madison, Wisconsin at the Sheraton, reportedly destroying the seventh floor. Dave and Al ripped out the screen of the window in Ed's hotel room and sent his chairs and tables smashing down to the ground below. Very sneakily, Edward went to the front desk and, giving his name as David Lee Roth, secured a key to Dave's room. While Alex and David hid away waiting for their time bomb to go off, Ed quietly and quickly moved all of the missing furniture from Dave's room to his. The police arrived to find Ed's screen gone but all of the furniture missing from Dave's room. All in all, Edward said, "We were wild, man. Oh, God. We had fire extinguisher fights. There was like a foot of water in the hallway and it seeped through the floor to the other rooms down below us, so the people had to check out."

The Unofficial First Interview

During the tour, shortly after the New Orleans show April 16, Ed gave his very first interview ever as a professional to *Guitar World*. Much to his chagrin, however, the article was not published until 2010. He tells the story about his dad being a musician, moving over from Holland, taking piano lessons, him and Al switching instruments, the Teisco, building his own guitar, his effects, his modified amplifiers, the condensed version of the Gene Simmons story—the works. About learning the guitar he said, "I enjoy playing. That's the main thing. It's not like I was forcing myself. I wanted to be a rock and roll star." This would be possibly the only time ever that Edward admitted to wanting to be a rock star—from there on out, he would insist that he was "just a musician" and not a "rock star," usually in a very dismissive fashion.

When asked about album sales, Ed had all the figures at hand, and went on to bash Journey:

> We've sold about 350,000. We're like 29 with a bullet next week in *Billboard*. So we're kickin' some ass. When we started out with Montrose and Journey, we were brand new; I think our album was only out a week at the start of the tour. And now we're almost passing up Journey on the charts and stuff. So they're freakin' out. I think they might be happy to get rid of us. We're very energetic and we get up there and blaze on the people for 30 minutes—that's all we're allowed to play with them. They won't let us use any effects. For my solo, "Eruption," I do that every night live and I have this old World War II bomb which is six or seven feet tall and I put some echo boxes

> in it. Usually the thing blows up at the end of my solo with all the smoke bombs, but they won't let me use it. We don't get soundchecks; we don't get shit. But we're still blazin' on the people, man—we're getting a strong encore every night.

Amazingly, he mentions exploring keyboards as early as April 1978: "Who knows what lurks in the future? Me and my brother both play keyboards, too—I've been thinking about getting a synthesizer. But who knows? I might not." In the interview, he also refers to having just bought a new Les Paul in New Orleans. During one funny exchange, the interviewer asked if Ed played acoustic, to which he responded: "I have never in my life owned an acoustic guitar. . . . I guess one of these days I'll buy one. I don't know anything about acoustics. I know what I like in electric guitars, but acoustic I'm lost. I don't know what's good."

Edward's answer to one particularly innocent question would eventually lead to much more serious questions later in his life. When asked what picks he used, he replied, "Fender mediums. What I used to do was use a metal pick. A friend of mine worked in a machine shop and he always used to make me metal picks. And they were really cool—but hard to hold onto when you're sweating. They'd fly out of my hand and I'd be bummed out." In early 1978, Edward stated that he simply used Fender mediums, that he had tried metal picks but no longer used them.

Touring with Black Sabbath

At the beginning of May, Eddie and Alex returned to the Netherlands as professional musicians, exactly like their father. Considering the difference in the weather, it's funny to note that they added "Summertime Blues" to their set for a show at The Paradiso in Amsterdam. After playing a few more shows in Paris and Hamburg, Van Halen finally met up with Black Sabbath, a band they truly loved and admired. They embarked on a one-month U.K. tour that is legendary for its crazy partying. There is a well-known picture of both bands mooning the camera at some point on the tour—likely par for the course. Edward recalled, "When we toured with Black Sabbath in 1978, they scared the shit out of us. I'll tell you a funny story that I'll never forget. I walked up to Tony and began to ask him, 'Second song on side two of *Master of Reality* . . . ' Tony looked at me and went, 'What the fuck, mate?' By that time Black Sabbath had several records out, but we had only one album out so I knew where every track on our first record was. A few years later somebody asked me a question in the same way, and I was going, 'Oh, you've got to be kidding me.' The first thing that popped in my head was that incident with Tony! At first I thought it was odd that he couldn't remember what was on his records, and then it happened to me."

Black Sabbath was at its lowest point when Van Halen—fellow label-mates on Warner Brothers—joined their tour. Because Van Halen was so fresh and riding so high and Black Sabbath was so tired and riding so low, the joint tour eventually sunk Black Sabbath, who kicked Ozzy out of the band and later hooked up with Ronnie James Dio. Warner Brothers shifted its promotional focus to Van Halen and away from Sabbath. Edward recalled, "We were kind of double-edged sword to them, I guess, because we forced them to have to rise to the occasion, so to speak, to follow us." A live recording of the May 28 show in Ipswich reveals a rising Van Halen absolutely on fire. Their short set included nearly every song from *Van Halen* except "Jamie's Cryin'" and "Ice Cream Man," and they closed with "D.O.A.," which Dave promised would be on their next album.

In mid-June, the band went straight from the U.K. for a string of solo dates in Japan, some of which was captured on video including an interview with Dave. While in Japan, Ed had his first encounter with endorsements. He said, "When we were in Japan, some company wanted me to endorse their stuff. They gave me this guitar that's got like 20 knobs on it; I couldn't figure out how to work the thing!"

Upon their return from Japan, the band—barely even four months on the road—flew straight into Dallas for the then-annual Texxas Jam festival at the Cotton Bowl on July 1, 1978. The only thing that didn't fly straight into Dallas was Edward's amplifiers. "On the way back over," said Eddie, "all my good shit got ripped off. Got lost in air freight—by [shouts into microphone] Pan Am, ya fuckers!" Fortunately, about six months later, Ed got his amp back. He said, "Thank God, I got it back. This is the one I bought when I was a kid. I didn't even know what I had until now. . . . It used to be the house amp at the Pasadena Rose Palace; whoever played there has played through it."

For the Texxas Jam, Edward would have to play on borrowed equipment, but nonetheless completely rocked and floored the sweltering crowd in excess of 60,000. After the Dallas show, they headed south for a gig in Austin and then out to Long Beach for their own shows (they drew over 8,000 people at Long Beach). They then headed to New Orleans to open for the Rolling Stones and the Doobie Brothers; Superdome attendance was over 80,000. They played a few more festivals that summer, concluding with a monumental day at Bill Graham's Day on the Green show at Oakland Coliseum on July 23, 1978 with AC/DC, Foreigner, and Aerosmith. Here, Edward would famously give his first *published* interview with Jas Obrecht of *Guitar Player Magazine*. These days, Obrecht is one of the single-most respected and admired rock guitar journalists in the field.

Edward's First Official Interview

Jas originally went to the show to interview Pat Travers, but Travers dismissed him immediately, too busy cleaning a mirror and entertaining a few women to grant an interview to a punk kid. Jas was pissed. "I'm a hothead from Detroit at that time. 24-years-old, what do you expect? And I didn't wanna go back home to the magazine and my buddies empty-handed." Jas stumbled upon a backstage quarter-length basketball court and started taking a few shots. In 2009, Jas recalled:

> I went over and picked up a basketball and started to shoot. And a couple minutes later this kid comes over and he goes, "Hey, man! Can I shoot with you?" And I'm like, yeah, sure. So we play a real spirited game of one-on-one for about 15 minutes. I remember he whooped me. Uh, muscular, wiry, pimply faced kid a couple of years younger than me. So we get all finished shooting basketball and we sit down at the side of the court and he says to me, "Hey, man, what band are you in?" I said I'm not in a band and he goes, "What're you doin' here?" Well, I said I was here from *Guitar Player Magazine* and I was supposed to interview Pat Travers but Travers blew me off, and he goes, "Why don't you interview me? Nobody ever wants to interview me." I said, well who are you and he goes, "My name's Edward Van Halen." I was like whoa! Because his new album *Van Halen 1* (sic) had just come out and there was a song on there called "Eruption" which was about to redefine rock and roll guitar in a significant way. Eddie introduced a new way of playing, which was like hammering on the frets, which nobody

> was doing in rock and roll. And so, um, we sat down and that was Eddie Van Halen's very first interview (sic).

The article would appear in the November issue (released in October) of *Guitar Player* and was titled, "Heavy-Metal Guitarist from California Hits the Charts at Age 21"—thanks to Dave's age-trimming scheme (indeed, Edward stuck to the plan and gave Jas the incorrect birth year of 1957 rather than 1955). This was now the first time all of his early stories were actually published. Again—his father being a musician, emigrating from Holland, taking classical piano training, he and Alex switching instruments, the Gene Simmons demo. He revealed that Eric Clapton was his "main influence . . . I realize I don't sound like him, but I know every solo he's ever played, note-for-note, still to this day." He was also very complimentary of his vocalist: "Dave, our singer, doesn't even have a stereo; he listens to the radio, which gives him a good variety. That's why we have things on the *Van Halen* album . . . like John Brim's 'Ice Cream Man.' We are into melodies and melodic songs. You can sing along with most of our tunes, even though many of them do have the peculiar guitar and the end-of-the-world drums."

But in reference to Dave, Eddie dramatically over-simplified his joining the band, saying only that, "He used to rent us his PA system. I figured it would be much cheaper if we just got him in the band, so he joined." For positive publicity, it's a good idea to condense things down into easy-to-repeat stories, but certainly this is a white-wash over his struggles with lead vocals and Dave's first failed audition, as well as the showmanship and lyric and melody writing that Dave brought to the band.

He also said, "By the time we graduated from high school, everyone else was going on to study to become a lawyer or whatever, and so we stuck together and started playing in cities in California—Pasadena, L.A., Arcadia." The board of regents of Pasadena City College sure missed out on their big publicity moment. This was before it was cool to be a rocker and a college student.

About the band, he said, "I do whatever I want. . . . Everyone pretty much does whatever they want, and we all throw out ideas, so whatever happens, happens." He also tells the story about getting signed, about building his own guitar, and his amplifier modifications. Critical of some of his fellow compatriots, he said, "I know a lot of people who really want to be famous or whatever, but they don't really practice the guitar. They think all you do is grow your hair long and look freaky and jump around, and they neglect the musical end." With Edward, you got the whole package: practicing guitar and keeping up the musical end—*and* long hair, looking freaky, and jumping around. One thing he said that was not published at the time was about jamming, and remembering those jams: "Most of the time I'm so high I forget them!"

Something else Obrecht revealed in a 2009 interview was that Edward called him up after the original article had been published and said, "Hey man, if you put me on the cover, I'll tell you all my playing secrets." Edward desperately wanted the recognition, his face on the magazine cover, and even bartered to make it happen.

Early Success and Domination

In late August, Van Halen and Sabbath hooked back up for string of American dates that ran through November. On September 22, the band played a one-off headlining show in Fresno that was captured on film. The footage shows a band making a triumphant return back to California to stand on their own. Edward is fully engaged in his showmanship, leaving his G chord to ring open while raising his arms over his head to lead the crowd along with the "Hey! Hey! Hey!" part of "Ain't Talkin' 'Bout Love."

Their rise over 1978 was meteoric. By October, *Van Halen* was platinum. Edward spoiled himself with a sports car, a Porsche 911e Targa. Earlier in the year he bought himself a modest CJ Jeep Renegade. His taste changed as sales increased.

The band made a huge decision to fire Marshall Berle before the year was out. According to Eddie, "We got rid of our first manager because he had a heavy ego problem. He wanted to be the big manager, in control of everything. We'd say, 'Hey, don't do that. For better or worse, we want it our way,' and he couldn't handle it. Went through a big lawsuit. It's just fucked. This is all stuff that I never imagined I'd get into. I just figured, 'Hey, I can make my music—period.' But I'm handling it. I've learned things you can't learn in any book or any school." The band hired Noel Monk as their new manager. Noel was a stage manager at Woodstock and the Fillmore East. He was well-seasoned and would manage the band up until 1985.

Van Halen played Oakland and San Diego to end the year's live shows and returned to the studio with Ted to begin work on the follow-up to their absolute ass-kicking smash of a debut. Just before the year was out, Edward was named Best New Talent by *Guitar Player Magazine*; the first in a long line of awards to come.

Several aspects of Eddie and the band set them apart from both the bands of their day and the bands that inevitably followed in their footsteps. For one thing, the band was always smiling rather than scowling and looking mean or forlorn. Ed's smile is a trademark one—it is infectious and endearing. They jumped around and put on a show—they were by no means shoe-gazers. Dave as well as Eddie engaged the audience directly. And for another thing, they were all well kempt, good looking guys; tough but not ill-tempered. By virtue of the latter, they would draw far more women to their shows which would in general give the band a much larger audience than that of their peer group at the time.

CHAPTER 9
Van Halen . . . Again

Work on *Van Halen II* commenced on December 10, 1978, and would go fast. The formula that worked for the first album would not be tampered with, and the band would tap a well of already tried and true live hits like "Somebody Get Me a Doctor," "Bottoms Up!," and "D.O.A."

The tour of 1978 was essentially a ten-month long bachelor party times twenty. Following the tour, the band celebrated with a five-day vacation in Balise, an island in the middle of the South Pacific. Getting back into the studio presented some challenges for the band and it was Edward himself who stepped in and took action to get the band prepped and ready to knock out studio tracks. He said, "I was trying to wake the guys up, saying 'Hey guys, we've to chill out a little bit, because we've got another record to do.'" Again, like *Van Halen*, the album was recorded almost completely live with very few overdubs and a little extra time to get the vocals right.

The first three Van Halen albums were recorded in that exact manner. Ed, as well as Dave, used the pace of their studio recording time as a bragging right. They knocked bands that spent months and months recording, overdubbing and overdubbing to get a highly polished product. However, the way Van Halen recorded was anything but easy. It's true it was simple; simple in the sense that you are capturing three instruments live all at the same time which prevents wasting time on overdubs, retracking, and double-tracking (the latter rarely utilized by VH). So, in that sense, it was simple. But was it *easy*?

With sketch artists and painters, it is fairly simple to determine the quality of raw hand skill that any given artist has. It is possible to produce a great piece of art without excellent hand skills; it simply takes a lot of time and patience. On the other hand, a sketch artist can look at a face or a skyline and in minutes produce a near photographic rendering. Both can be great artists and produce great pieces of art, but, honestly, which is more impressive? Many artists are notorious for never being satisfied with their work, constantly tweaking a piece and struggling to find a suitable endpoint to call the work finished. Even heralded filmmaker George Lucas is now somewhat infamous for never being completely satisfied with his work, having re-edited and added new scenes to his incredibly famous and successful films. The ultimate artistic argument is not completely based upon the final product, necessarily. The step to deeper appreciation of any artistic work is to understand the method of its creation. Such discovery inevitably adds to or even takes away from its artistic relevance or importance.

Ed bragged about how "easy" it was to record the first few albums. Edward said, "We finished the music in six days, and the whole album took eight. I don't understand how people can take any longer." The truth is that Edward (and Alex and Michael to an extent) had excellent hand skills, using the apt analogy. Songs like "You Really Got Me" were recorded all in one take, from the intro through the guitar solo to the outro. Could anyone else have done so? All in one take? Anyone that has spent a decent amount of time in a recording studio will tell you, simply, "No."

The recording of *Van Halen II* went fairly fast and the album was similar to *Van Halen* in many ways. However, two songs were *very* different, indeed.

First Sign of a "Pop" Mentality

The second album opens with a cover of "You're No Good," a song written by Clint Ballard, Jr. and originally recorded in 1963 by Betty Everett, but was a huge 1975 hit for Linda Ronstadt—one of the principles of the Avacodo Mafia of Southern California. The Van Halen version is no doubt a rocking track, but at heart it is a heavy take on what was essentially a soft rock hit. As good as it was, Linda's hit was pure soft rock, adult-contemporary. Alex blamed Ted Templeman for the inclusion of the song, saying it was "somebody else's idea of a hit single." Once again, the band redid another established hit to ensure a hit of their own, but this was no "You Really Got Me." It should be noted as well that "You're No Good" begins with a *bass* solo.

Song two was a whole other ball of wax. Late 1970s. Disco. "Dance the Night Away." Get it? At its roots, the song is reggae-inspired; the I-V-IV-I-IV-V progression is pure reggae. Throughout the song, Edward utilizes his "false harmonics" technique where he hits the fret board with his right hand exactly one octave above the note he is fretting with his left. The melody and pattern he comes up with, combined with the naturally percussive sound of the false harmonics, intentionally or not, approximates the sound of steel drums. The attack and delivery is unique, but the set-up is pure pop. Dave came through with catchy pop lyrics and melodies. The song is void of a guitar solo if you don't count the phased false-harmonics passage before the final chorus. Otherwise, there is not a single bend or any vibrato in the entire song. Edward also layers a second guitar throughout—apparently no problems at all with overdubbing this time around. The first chorus and from the second chorus through the end of the song, there are two distinct guitar lines that interact with each other quite beautifully.

This was without a doubt a blatant attempt to secure a pop hit. It was about face from commercially *unfriendly* tunes like "On Fire," "Atomic Punk," and even "House of Pain"—which continued to be a live staple of the band in its original form up until 1977. "Dance the Night Away" is positive, it's in a major key, and it's about dancing. It was the only song that wasn't written before the band entered the studio, with Edward apparently stopping to test the musical waters at that moment and "Dance the Night Away" is what happened. It likely would not have been as big a hit if they had gone with Dave's original chorus lyrics and title "Dance, Lolita, Dance"—it was Edward's idea to dance *the night away.*

It worked. The single was released on April 2, 1979 and peaked on the chart that July at #15. *Van Halen II* was platinum by May thanks in no small part to the hit single. Oddly, there was a Cream song on 1967's *Disraeli Gears* also called "Dance the Night Away," but that was never an issue. There were over a dozen songs on the charts in 1979 alone with the words "dance" or "dancing" in the title. During the last year of the decade that was the 1970s, Van Halen had a hit on the singles charts.

"Dance the Night Away" also marked the moment that Van Halen first entered my life. The song was in the top 40 when my seventh birthday came around in April 1979, and my grandmother routinely bought my brother and I all of the Top 40 singles —"45s"—at the time of our birthdays and Christmas. "Dance the Night Away" was in there with "Sailing" by Christopher Cross. Both acts were on Warner Brothers, so the 45s looked exactly the same to me. So, being seven, I initially wasn't sure if it was the same person or not. I also remember being absolutely certain that Van Halen was a person—first name-last name—just like Christopher Cross. I loved "Dance the Night Away" then and still love it today. It makes me happy.

Van Halen II opens with a bass solo that segues into a cover of a soft rock song, followed by a pop song about dancing. It was a clear attempt to soften the band's edge and steer their image. Fortunately, the majority of the rest of the album was considered amongst my peer group, and the world at large, to be either the ultimate summer album or the ultimate party album of all time. Either classification will do.

For Edward's follow-up to "Eruption," he went acoustic. Ted Templeman hosted a New Year's party at his home, and Ed came across an acoustic guitar and played some passages that once again caught Ted's ear. With Ted's encouragement, Eddie came up with "Spanish Fly," a flamenco, nylon-string acoustic workout that features false harmonics, extended tapping sequences, and absolutely unbelievably fast right-hand picking. It's a short segment, but elements of the track remain a part of Edward's spotlight solo to this day. Once he proved he could do on acoustic what he did on electric, though, he didn't record another instrumental guitar track for three years.

In his estimation, the second album fell short of the debut. "We didn't spend as much time getting the sound," he said. "I like the guitar, but I'm not particularly pleased with the drum sound. I like the drum sound on the first album much better."

The 1979 Tour

Following the release of the album in February 1979, the band embarked on their first ever headlining tour. Their behavior on the road was the things legends are made of. The common things are all there—trashing hotel rooms and throwing TVs out of windows. Not so common, and little discussed, is the fact that the band engaged in production of their own pornographic films. They first started out with 8mm film and later purchased one of the first home video recording machines. The guys dressed the girls up in nurse costumes and schoolgirl outfits, while the crew that would film the band dressed as nuns. One can only hope that these films are secured away somewhere safely in a deep, dark vault . . .

Edward was regularly using cocaine, alcohol, and pot. The latter is hardly controversial, but coke and alcohol abuse, especially when combined, leads to dangerous places. Cocaine causes irritability, paranoia, mood swings, restlessness, and auditory hallucinations. Excessive use of alcohol damages nearly every vital organ, including the brain. Hardcore alcoholics suffer a variety of medical and psychiatric disorders including avascular necrosis (loss of blood supply to certain bones, including the hip) and degeneration of cognitive and brain function, confusion, panic attacks, and depression. Abuse of either drug affects you socially—and destroys families. Unfortunately, Ed was destined to become addicted to both, as well as nicotine. In 1985, Dave proclaimed to *Rolling Stone*, "Drink as well as cocaine—those are the two big ones. They kill your creativity and your spirit."

Guitarist Adam Brenner, who later went on to front Adam Bomb, followed the band for ten shows during the summer of 1979. Adam was only fifteen when he first met Edward backstage in Seattle. Adam described Edward at the time as, "The absolute coolest, most beautiful person, let alone rock god, I'd ever seen." Ed spent nearly three hours with Adam and his friend, signing autographs and talking about guitar licks and techniques. Adam recalled watching Eddie snort a bump of coke off of a guitar pick right in front of them. Ed told them he would have shared with them but he didn't have enough—a standard line used by many a cocaine abuser. Edward also had some pot that he said he used to help him get to sleep at night. Ed spent nearly three hours with Adam. Upon reflection in 2010, Adam said, "He was the nicest rock star I've met still to this day."

CHAPTER 10
The End of the Beginning

As Van Halen's career arc projected, Edward began encountering lots of problems the average person would never even conceive of. Right at the closing of the decade, Ed gave another interview with Jas Obrecht of *Guitar Player* on December 29, 1979. His response to Jas's very first question "How you doing?" was "Feeling a bit zombied."

There was a hell of a lot going on in Ed's world at the time, and not all of it was good. For starters, Edward talked about other top-of-the-line guitarists copying not only his tapping technique but also publicly performing the tapping section of "Eruption." The first such instance was in August of 1978 when Rick Derringer opened a pair of shows for VH in West Texas. Ed had admired Rick for years for his work with the Winter brothers Edgar and Johnny as well as his own solo material—Van Halen had previously covered "Rock and Roll Hootchie Koo" as well as other tunes Rick had played on. Rick incorporated the "Eruption" tapping sequence into his own guitar solo. "He did my exact solo," said Edward. "After the show, we're sitting in the bar, and I said, 'Hey, Rick. I grew up on your ass. How can you do this? I don't care if you use the technique—(but) don't play my melody.' And he's goin', 'Yeah, yeah, yeah.' The next night he does my solo again, and he ends the set with 'You Really Got Me,' which is exactly what we do. So I hate to say it, but I just told him, 'Hey, if you're going to continue doing that, you ain't opening for us.' So I kicked him off."

The same thing happened in June of 1979 in North Carolina when Van Halen played a stadium bill with Boston, who top-billed at the time. Tom Scholz did the same thing Rick Derringer did—he incorporated the "Eruption" tapping sequence into his own guitar solo. Edward was livid. "It was real weird, because it was a daytime thing, and I was standing onstage and the whole crowd was looking at me like, 'What's this guy doing?'" Eddie said. "I was drunk, and I got pissed. He never comes around. He doesn't say 'Hi.' He doesn't do anything. He just kind of hides out, runs onstage and plays, and disappears afterwards. So I started talking to the other guitarist, and I told him, 'Hey. Tell him I think he's fucked!'"

About exactly a month after the Boston incident, Adam Brenner had his fantasy hang-out with Edward in Seattle. Adam said, "He told McCrae [Adam's friend] I was better than the guy in Bad Company and I should start a band, but whatever I do, he told me, 'Don't just copy me like every asshole in L.A., take it somewhere further, somewhere else.'"

By the mid-1980s, the tapping technique would be common not only to nearly every single rock or metal release, but the technique also extended into the jazz realm with players like Stanley Jordan. It took a few years, but there would eventually become a marked distinction between guitarists whose careers were already established when *Van Halen* was released, and those who came onto the scene or had albums released starting around 1980 or so. Randy Rhoads, for example, came into national prominence in 1981 on Ozzy Osbourne's first solo album *Blizzard of Ozz*. Randy's solos and fills were chock-full of tapping and other techniques similar to Edward's, but Randy proudly named Eddie as a huge influence on his playing. When Randy and other newcomers used tapping, it then became part of the general lexicon of electric guitar playing. But in 1978 and 1979, when it was new and it was the signature sound of a singular guitar player, it was different. Edward deserved a grace period of ownership of his technique, but the lure of it was too much to resist for established guitarists like Derringer and Scholz, which, in retrospect, should be an embarrassment to both of them. Ed had every right to stake his claim.

"I guess they always say that imitation is the highest form of flattery. I think this is a crock of shit," Edward said. "I don't like people doing things exactly like me. Some of the things I do I know no one has done . . . . What I don't like is when someone takes what I've done, and instead of innovating on what I came up with, they do my trip! They do my melody. Like I learned from Clapton, Page, Hendrix, Beck—but I don't play like them. I innovated; I learned from them and did my own thing out of it. Some of those guys out there are doing my thing, which I think is a lot different."

Ed also expressed frustration about the jealousy of other guitarists and asserted that people outright hated him. "Other musicians, they're jealous," he said. "The more they hate you, the better you are. I mean, no other guitarist is gonna hate another guitarist if they're no good. You're no threat." Eddie added, "There's a lot of people who don't know me who hate me, because they think I'm some egoed-out motherfucker, but I'm not at all. That's just one thing that I never expected." Eddie specifically noted a sour encounter with Joe Perry of Aerosmith: "I walked up to shake his hand, and he looked at me and walked away."

Edward's love of Charvel guitar parts turned sour when the company began marketing a copycat version of Ed's Strat-style body with a humbucker and a tremolo. Edward had been close to Wayne Charvel, the company's founder, but Wayne sold the company in November of 1978 to Grover Jackson. Grover proceeded to produce the copycats and sell them for a thousand dollars. "It's my guitar design that's keeping them in business," said Eddie. Of his original guitar concept, he said, "It looks like a Strat, but it only has one pickup in it, one volume knob, no tone, no fancy garbage. . . . I'm not saying my guitar is 'Wow, the new guitar,' but it is a guitar that you could not at the time buy on the market." With regards to Grover Jackson, Edward said, "This guy kind of exploited my idea, so I'm suing him. See, I feel kind of fucked doing that, but all I want him to do is stop. I don't give a damn about the money." He added, "Here I am just a punk kid trying to get a sound out of a guitar that I couldn't buy off the rack, so I build one myself and now everybody else wants one."

Even Eddie's paint job was being copped. He said, "Just the other night, Christmas Eve, I went to the Whisky. A band called Weasels was playing, and the lead guitarist had a guitar exactly like mine. I just don't understand how someone could walk onstage with my guitar, because it's my trademark. You know, when people see a freaked-out striped guitar like that, with one pickup, one volume knob, they obviously know it's mine." Striped guitars would be a common sight at any guitar retailer in the 1980s.

The "flattery" didn't stop at guitars. Pickup maker Seymour Duncan also raised Eddie's ire. He told Obrecht: "See, I've rewound my own pickups before, and a guy named Seymour Duncan, I got pissed at him too. He called me up and said, 'Can we use your name for a special pickup?' And I said no. Next time I pick up *Guitar Player Magazine*, there's a special Van Halen model customized Duncan pickup. I called him up and said, 'What the hell's goin' on?' So he stopped finally. It's just kind of weird you know."

He even figured out he was getting fleeced at guitar shops. At one particular store, Eddie said, "I was smart, and I had my roadie go in and get a price list. They didn't know that I knew the price list, so I walked in with him. I go, 'How much do you want for this?' And they quoted me a price a grand above what it said on the paper. I said, 'Wait a minute, man, it says right here that it's . . . ' And they said, 'Oh, oh,' and tried to make excuses. I hate dealing with people like that. That's another reason why I build my own."

Interviewers were also getting under his skin. "I hate doing interviews. I just can't stand it," Eddie said. "They always fuck me over. They always write things that twist and bend what I say." His complaints were mostly about the teen-scream mags like *Creem* and *Circus*. But when a *Guitar World* interviewer asked him what he thought about other high-profile guitarists, Eddie snapped, "I hate doing this because you're going to make me come off like an asshole. Enough people hate me already."

Ed was open in his admiration for Obrecht as well as journalist Steven Rosen, who wrote for almost every rock and guitar magazine around. But Edward also talked about how awkward radio interviews were for him, saying, "I remember once I did a radio interview in the beginning—and I'm not much of a talker, really . . . Dave's real good at it. You're excited when you're listening to him . . . I can't do that. So here's Dave motor-mouth getting the guy all jazzed up, and then he turns to me and goes, 'I understand you and your brother are from Amsterdam, Holland.' And I go, 'Yeah.' That was it! Big long pause. I just wasn't ready for a big long story. It's like I'm not an entertainer with my mouth, but everyone expects you to be."

As far as touring goes, Edward stated that 1979 "will probably be the last ten-month world vacation," noting that he'd prefer the band slow down a little and play fewer gigs. This notion would return to him several times over the next few years.

The Birth of Frankenstein and Retiring Jan

There was a silver lining in all of this, however. Because Charvel was copying his guitar design and others were copying his paint jobs, Edward decided to modify his original black and white guitar from the first album. He said, "I really went to town painting it all freaked out, and I put three pickups back in, but they don't all work—only the rear one works." This was the birth of the famous red, white, and black striped Frankenstein guitar—Edward added the red paint at that moment. He said, "I just did it to be different, so every kid who bought one like that model would go, 'Oh, man he's got something different again.' I always like to turn the corner on people when they start latching on to what I'm doing." The repainted guitar made its first appearance on the *Van Halen II* tour. From there on, it would forever be associated with its creator. Eventually, it has become renowned as one of the single most important musical instruments in recorded human history.

In December 1979, no longer available for the Best New Talent poll—Edward was named *Guitar Player*'s Best Rock Guitarist, edging out his one-time idol Jimmy Page. His feats had earned him his first major accolade, and definitely not his last. After winning the award, Ritchie Blackmore's Rainbow played a show at Long Beach Arena. Edward went down there to finally give Ritchie a piece of his mind after being dissed by him years earlier, but the meeting actually went well. Edward said, "I went down there, in a way, with a vengeance, you know. I just felt like saying, 'Hey motherfucker, remember me? About three years ago, when you treated me like shit?' But I didn't. I just said hello, and he knew me just through records and radio, and he complimented me."

Still pining, Eddie ended his interview with Obrecht directly asking him, "When are you gonna do a cover story on me?" Jas responded, "In 1980, I hope." Ed replied, "Yeah, that'd be great. Tell him [the editor] you want to do a cover story on me. Shit, Best Rock Guitarist, you know. And I see clowns on the cover . . . Being on the cover would be like a dream come true for me."

In November of 1979, the film *Over the Edge* starring Matt Dillon was released. The film seriously resounded with the teenage youth at the time. The movie focused on the growing national trend of newly developed suburbs designed with adults in mind but not teenagers, who thus had nothing much to do but party and raise hell, when all they really needed was parental attention. The film featured several rock bands of the moment including Cheap Trick, The Cars, The Ramones, and Little Feat. Van Halen's "You Really Got Me" is featured during a prominent party scene in the film and the result was a fairly widespread introduction of Van Halen to many kids.

After two years of touring and two platinum albums under their belts, Edward and Alex retired their father in 1979. Earlier in April, regarding money, Edward told *Guitar Player*, "The first thing I'm going to do is get my dad to retire. Even just the weekly checks out of our corporation we're making more than he is in a week. So Al and I said, 'Quit your job.' He's been working seven days a week ever since we came to this country and we're gonna buy him a boat and retire him so he can go fishing." After the retirement, Eddie said, "On my dad's birthday . . . we retired him and bought him a boat. I want to make my people happy." It was a beautiful gesture to their father for all his years of hardship, not to mention the devastating psychological effects of the loss of his finger.

The final date of the 1979 tour on October 27 was huge for Edward and the band: it was their first time to ever headline their hometown arena, the Forum. However, the triumph was completely marred by night's end. "When we played the Forum, my mom and dad came," he said, "and when my mom came home, the house got ripped off for about twenty gold and platinum albums, which is real fucked because playing the Forum is like a dream come true. I've seen everyone play there. It was a hell of an event for me, and I come home and the back door is smashed in and all the records are gone. It's such a drag. To tell you the truth, I'm not into the star bullshit at all."

"Welcome to the music business, boys." Surely, Jan never could have imagined any of this. He knew full well the potentials and pitfalls of the industry, and he had definitely seen the best and worst sides of it firsthand. But early retirement? Gold and platinum albums? Headlining the Forum? Burglaries? For better or for worse, their profiles would only increase in part due to continued album and touring success, and in part based on personal decisions.

CHAPTER 11
Women First

And so the cycle continued. As soon as the *Van Halen II* tour was over, it was right back into the studio for the third album. *Women and Children First* was made in eight total days, including vocals. The songs "Fools" and "Take Your Whiskey Home" were reprised from their 1975 days, although with new arrangements and updated lyrics. However, when asked by Jas Obrecht if the songs for the third album were "All new ones?" Edward said yes. Also, when asked about the lack of an instrumental on the new record, Eddie said, "'Eruption' was the first one and then the second one I did was in flamenco style, but it was still the same type of thing. And what could I do this time? I didn't want to do one just for the sake of doing another solo." Additionally, there was pressure mounting to eschew the instrumental solos from Dave who wanted Van Halen to present itself more as a succinct band/unit.

Although it was little noticed or acknowledged at the time, *Women and Children First* marks the first use of keyboards of any kind on a Van Halen album. The signature sound on "And the Cradle Will Rock" is actually a Wurlitzer electric piano played through Ed's standard guitar set-up. Beneath the piano track is a beautifully orchestrated guitar track, and the music behind the guitar solo is all Edward's keyboard line. Clearly, he was now comfortable playing to tape and orchestrating overdubs.

"Everybody Wants Some!" became an instant party classic and was later featured prominently in the 1984 cult-classic teenage film *Better Off Dead* starring John Cusack. Behind the slamming chords during the "jungle part" of the tune, Ed overdubbed a number of absolutely wild sounding harmonics, tremolo dives, and various odd scraping and feedback effects. He was becoming more experimental.

The only true instrumental break is between the introduction and kick-off of "Fools" where Edward plays an extremely brief but extremely fast lead break before kicking into the actual start-up of the "Fools" main riff. The "Tora! Tora!" sound effect track that leads into "Loss of Control" is simply a backwards tape effect of a tremolo dive bomb—nothing terribly spectacular. One particularly clever track was "Could This Be Magic?," a Delta blues-sounding number featuring Dave on rhythm acoustic and Ed on lead slide acoustic with the band members singing in harmony. This was definitely a first for the mighty VH (the introduction to "Take Your Whiskey Home" is also acoustic). The most notable first, though, was the fact that *Women and Children First* was cover-song free.

Like clockwork, the band set out on yet another world tour to support the album. Shortly after the start of the tour, Edward told *Circus Magazine*, "I'm in rock and roll because I don't like being told what to do" (a statement stemming from his piano and violin days, or perhaps something more than that). *Women and Children First* had enough variety of tunes to avoid being as pigeon-holed as say Judas Priest or Black Sabbath. The album was released in March 1980 and was certified platinum by June (with two songs pulled all the way back from 1975). That made three records selling over one million copies in a row.

Ed gave another *Guitar Player* interview to Jas Obrecht. Finally in April 1980, Edward got the cover article he had been bargaining for for nearly two years. In the article, ironically, Pat Travers—who had turned down his chance at a star interview with Obrecht back in 1978—lauded Edward saying, "I don't think there's anybody better for saying more, getting a better sound, or just taking advantage of the straight Stratocaster-style sound." Other top name guitarists, like Rick Neilsen of Cheap Trick and even Ted Nugent, showered Ed with accolades.

Edward said that he played extremely loud both on stage and in the studio and doesn't wear ear plugs, adding, "I'm surprised I'm not deaf yet." He noted that his live set up included eighty—EIGHTY—twelve inch speakers! Eddie also claimed that in the studio he used four 100-Watt Marshalls cranked all the way up. "I like to feel it, you know," he said, "make my arm hairs move."

When asked if he would ever do a solo album, he said, "All of my energy goes into Van Halen; it's my family. I'm not going to leave my family until one of the members passes on. . . . If I ever do a solo album, which I don't see in the near future, I'd have plenty of ideas." As far as his personal progression in his playing, Edward said, "How much can you progress? I'm as fast as I can possibly get. I can't picture myself being too much faster. I mean, you can only hear so much. What I'm trying to do is be weirder and different" [a la "Tora! Tora!" and "Could This Be Magic?"]. Additionally, he noted that he was constantly getting asked to guest on other people's tracks, saying "'Will you play on my record?' . . . And I go, 'No, Van Halen is my family. I'm not gonna wash your dishes. I'll wash dishes for Van Halen alone." He seemed to have forgotten his work with Gene Simmons and his guest spot on Nicolette Larson's album, the latter who actually sang along with the rest of the band on the backing vocals for "Could This Be Magic?" Dave was especially perturbed that Nicolette was allowed to participate on *their* album.

Pulling back from his previous comments about touring, Ed stated that he'd sell his guitars just to go out on tour. "It's a world vacation, a way of life." He noted that experiencing different cultures was the biggest kick he got out of touring, specifically mentioning France, Germany, and Japan. He also said that, "Sometimes I'll pass on the party and take a day and go out and trip around," sight-seeing completely on his own.

"I don't even consider myself a rock star. I enjoy playing guitar, period," Eddie told Jas. "I'm considered a rock star because kids label me as one." He noted he had begun to have difficulties relating to people socially, saying if he was too outgoing, people would think he had a huge ego, and if he was normal, people would say, "That's all he is?" Frustratingly, he stated, "I don't show my face too much. I'm pretty much a loner. I just can't get along with people; they don't understand me." It wouldn't be too much longer before his days of being a real "loner" would be gone.

Touring in 1980

The 1980 *World Invasion* tour kicked off in March and it was business as usual on the road. Edward himself was the chief participant in an incident in his room that went down as "The Famous Ketchup Kaper" (no real description other than that is really necessary). The tour was also marred several times. Dave innocently told the crowd in Cincinnati to "Light 'em up!" during "Light Up the Sky!"—which is actually a lyric in the song. He was subsequently arrested and later acquitted of "inciting others to violate the fire code." About a month later, Dave jumped face first into some low hanging lights in Italy for television show and sustained some pretty serious injuries. Going against doctor's orders, they went ahead with their next show, in Geleen in the Netherlands, no less. Ed and Al backed up Dave on the radio repeating that Dave had said, "Fuck the doctor!"

The guys also threw out the suggestion that they film their adventures on the tour—aboveboard, of course—as a *Magical Mystery Tour* or *The Kids Are Alright!*-style documentary of their trips around the world. The band insider/filmmaker went by Snade Krellman (krell being loose code for coke). The project was abandoned, but footage does exist. Part of it shows the guys in the Netherlands and actually shows Ed and Al speaking Dutch—showing that they never lost their native tongue. The likelihood is fairly high that the project was abandoned because it likely would've turned out like *Spinal Tap* before *Spinal Tap*. Ironically, Eddie later told *Guitar World* that he didn't laugh at all when he first watched *Spinal Tap* later in 1984. He said all of the other guys were cracking up and laughing themselves silly, but Ed did not find it quite so funny. "It was so close to home, man," Edward said. "The whole lifestyle of it. Everything in that movie had happened to me. The record company parties with all the execs, and nobody showing up for things, and the guy who couldn't get out of his pod. All that stuff is real. So the first time I saw it, everyone was laughing, and I was sitting there thinking, 'This isn't funny.'" He later admitted, though, that *Spinal Tap* is a "classic flick."

During the early summer trek through Europe, Edward had an altercation with the most unlikely of rock and roll peers, Geddy Lee of Rush. After a show in Leicester, UK in late June, Rush and Van Halen were staying at the same hotel, their paths just happening to cross while on their separate tours. Any previous interaction between Rush and Van Halen is unlikely given a rundown of their historic touring schedules up to that point (the only exception being Gene Simmons mutual involvement in both of their careers). One of the bits of information that has been given about the incident is that Geddy had a portable tape recorder and played a track for Eddie—the same thing Eddie would often do himself for other musicians or interviewers. Rush had released their album *Permanent Waves* the same month as *Women and Children First*. Rush's album featured their biggest FM radio hit up to that point, "The Spirit of Radio." Rush had actually successfully worked a great deal of synthesizer support lines into that song specifically as well as their music overall, something Edward had been wont to do more and more. Behind the scenes, down at the fan level, there has always been a "Who's better, Rush or Van Halen?" thing going on. Geddy Lee was certainly the Eddie Van Halen of the bass; bass just isn't as sexy as lead guitar (nor was Geddy quite as sexy as Eddie in really any sense). [A December 1983 *Hit Parader* "dream band" reader's poll put

Ed on lead guitar and Neil Peart on drums (Steve Harris of Iron Maiden took the bassist category, which also cited Geddy).]

Unfortunately, this prime gathering of the potentially respective reigning kings of the six—and four-string guitar went downhill fast. While playing this track, which could potentially have been a song off of *Moving Pictures* (1981), Geddy purportedly "whispered" something into Edward's ear. Why would Geddy have to whisper something? And if he whispered, what was it that he whispered? In any case, Edward's response to whatever comment Geddy had made was to take his beer and pour it into Geddy's tape recorder. That's actually quite a spectacularly dramatic end to a conversation. Most likely, there was intoxication involved to some extent. It's doubtful that whatever Geddy said was put out there to elicit that kind of reaction; he's simply not known for that. But their paths would cross again. And even yet again.

Van Halen spent July and August wreaking havoc across Canada and the U.S. While Dave was mocking music critics for liking Elvis Costello "because he looks like most of 'em," Eddie was already lamenting that his adherence to the Van Halen format, as it were, was already limiting him. "I'd hate to fall into a slam-bang rock and roll thing and never get any farther than that," he said. A *Circus* article acknowledged that Edward had indeed brought keyboards into the mix for the first time on "And the Cradle Will Rock," and synthesizers would end up playing a fairly critical role on Van Halen's next three albums.

Meeting that Girl on TV

During the band's stop in Shreveport, Louisiana on August 29, 1980, Ed met his future wife. Valerie Bertinelli was extremely famous at the time. She was the super-good looking cutie on *One Day at a Time*, and this was back when there were three, maybe four or five channels to watch on television. An incredibly huge percentage of Americans would instantly have recognized her anywhere at any time, where as Eddie was still very much under the radar outside of the rock world. Valerie was visiting her parents living in Shreveport during an actors' strike in California. Her brothers Patrick and David—Van Halen superfans—were friendly with the local radio station who knew they were Valerie's brothers. They had concocted a scheme wherein Valerie was to be photographed handing out bags of M&Ms to each of the band members, and they'd all get in for free and get backstage passes. [The "no brown M&Ms" contract rider was simply a clause cooked up by Dave to ensure that the promoters and the venue had read all of the fine print. If there were brown M&Ms—you have to go back to square one and start all over. It was actually quite brilliant.]

Valerie had only recently familiarized herself with Van Halen, having heard the debut album and then just before the show *Woman and Children First*. She recognized "Everybody Wants Some!" from the radio, a song that never charted, but was growing into becoming the penultimate representation of Van Halen. Valerie also recognized that she found Edward attractive—his pose on the back of the album cover really captured her attention.

Backstage before the show, she posed for pictures and gave the M&Ms to Alex and then Michael. She was waiting for Eddie and Dave but was told they were "prepping for the show." Eddie came out and stopped to give her a glance, but just smiled and waved and headed for the stage. Valerie watched the show from Ed's side of the stage and he flirted with her throughout the show. After the show, she gave Dave his M&Ms. Valerie claims she semi-flirted with a charming Dave for several minutes. Dave's version is that he had "no idea who she was. Had no interest at all, so she fixed her eye on the door to Ed's dressing room." She was then taken to meet Ed who was in the middle of a conversation with his brother. Valerie said that they politely brought her into their conversation. Eddie asked her if she like *Women and Children First* and she told him that she loved it, but admitted Elton John was her main thing.

After talking for a while after the show, the party moved to the motel where the band was staying where Valerie and Ed and the entourage sat around the pool smoking and drinking the night away. During their conversation, she was surprised to learn that Ed and Al did indeed still reside at home with their parents when they weren't on the road. Before long, without even a kiss, Ed boarded the bus with Valerie's number and promised to give her a call. Valerie was shocked and mystified that Ed did not call for three days. But when he finally did, he invited her to join him in Oklahoma for their next show. She hopped on the next plane out and was there.

She again watched him from the wings of the stage and Ed admitted she made him nervous. Given that Ed was also performing for thousands of other people, Valerie was sure that was a fair sign something was definitely brewing. After the show, they finally started to really share their stories and Eddie told her all about coming to America and his mom and dad. Valerie prodded Ed more about the revelation that he and Al still lived at home. Eddie essentially just admitted that they were on tour for ten months a year, so it was just easier for the time being. But he also confessed to Valerie that his mother Eugenia continually had no faith in the band and still expected Ed to continue his education as soon as possible. Like a gentleman, Ed had gotten Valerie her own room that night, and even though Valerie made overtures, Edward, for reasons of his own, chose not to bed her until he got to know her better.

Valerie continued to travel on the road with Edward through most of the rest of the tour, often sleeping on her own private bunk on a tour bus. A solid month into their blossoming relationship, Ed revealed to Valerie that at some point earlier in his life, a long-term girlfriend cheated on him with a supposed close friend. That apparently burned him on opening himself up to any woman seriously, and also explains his sexual rampages on the early tours. After a brief break, Valerie joined back up with Eddie on September 15 in Phoenix. Yet again, Eddie had gotten Valerie her own room, although it was adjoining. Valerie opened the door between the suites and found Edward in tears. *Guitar Player* had just named him Best Rock Guitarist yet again, and apparently, for whatever reason, it set Dave off and Dave gave Ed a really hard time during sound check that afternoon, allegedly making claims that Ed thought he was "hot shit." Obviously, it was a textbook case of jealousy and rivalry. This one seriously hurt Ed and belittled him. As he wept with Valerie, they told each other they loved each other and made love for the first time.

After the band played a two-night stand in September in L.A., Valerie officially met Eugenia and Jan, who treated her very sweetly. However, Jan originally highly objected to the affair when he first heard about it, telling Edward he disapproved because Valerie was only 15. Ed humorously explained to his father that he had been watching reruns, and assured him that Valerie was actually 20.

In Valerie's autobiography *Losing It*, she revealed that Edward had to handle an ugly paternity case from "a girl from his past." The suit ultimately proved false, and the budding couple finally had a brief amount of time to spend with each other one on one. Ed finally moved out and into Valerie's place, which they were sharing with Valerie's brother Drew and his girlfriend. While Ed and Drew generally got along, Valerie did once come across them in a full-blown fist fight outside of the house. Nevertheless, they were enjoying a bit of domesticity and privacy at Valerie's estate, although they were often besieged by groupies on the prowl for Edward.

The two extremely young, famous people had fallen hardcore for each other and there was no turning back. Marriage was being discussed openly and not so subtle trips were made to jewelry stores. They even decided upon the exact $8,000 ring they would buy if they were to actually get married. Ed tricked Valerie into thinking he hadn't purchased the ring only to break it out on December 8, 1980. He proposed to her on one knee. Ed said, "By the way, I bought the ring. Will you marry me?" Valerie immediately accepted and they began to celebrate only to experience a very rude interruption. A runner from *One Day at a Time* was bringing a script to Valerie and walked into their glee with the question, "Did you hear?" He broke the news to them that John Lennon had just been shot and killed. They began talking non-stop about John and The Beatles and stayed glued to the TV for information. Valerie experienced her first pangs of anxiety about the groupies that followed Ed and the band incessantly.

CHAPTER 12

"Does it seem cold in here to you?"

After the proposal, Edward sunk himself into the creative process for *Fair Warning*. Often characterized as Van Halen's "dark" album, it really is Van Halen's first "serious" album. As per Valerie, Ed was working with his faithful engineer Donn Landee around the clock capturing ideas and experimenting with different studio tricks until Edward "ran out of booze, coke, energy, inspiration, or all of the above." Valerie admitted that Edward's nocturnal schedule and her daytime shooting schedule simply did not mesh, and she kept up with Eddie by drinking and doing cocaine through the night. The couple went to the priest who was to perform their ceremony for the typical Catholic Church pre-marriage compatibility exam. According to Val, "As we filled out the forms at home, we each held a little vial of coke. If you ask me, these aren't two people who should be making decisions about the rest of their lives."

"Between 1980 and 1984, I did a lot of blow," Edward told *Rolling Stone*. "And drinking. . . . I always got hammered to be able to cope. I have zero social skills." Consequently, he said that he would get drunk and make an ass out of himself.

Nevertheless, they plowed on and began planning the wedding. Apparently, the guys in the band suggested that Ed slow down, after all, they had only known each other for four and a half months. Dave especially urged him to hold off and later admitted being surprised when Ed went through with it. The wedding planning caused the first real friction between the couple when Ed once yelled at Valerie to just leave him alone. Apparently, Edward then went off to the studio and composed the hauntingly beautiful, psychedelic, dark, groundbreaking synthesizer masterpiece "Sunday Afternoon in the Park." When Ed told her that he came up with the track after a fight they had, she replied that she was flattered to "inspire cheerful songs." Whatever the inspiration, the rock world was better for it. It is simply one of the most amazing pieces of aural art ever captured.

Unfortunately, during the creative process for *Fair Warning*, Dave and Edward's relationship became more complicated than ever, most likely over petty jealousy over who was getting more attention from where. In fact, Eddie said that Roth was really pissed off about the marriage. "I think it pissed him off because all of the sudden I got a whole other side of the limelight he wanted. The tabloids and *People Magazine* kind of shit." On the other hand, a poster of Dave—and Dave alone—was included inside the album jacket along with the record when *Women and Children First* came out. It is a now famous image which was captured by world renowned photographer Helmut Newton. That poster went up on the wall of every girl's room that bought the album. In January 1981, *Guitar World* featured Edward on the cover with the tagline, "The World's Greatest Guitarist?" Dave alone was on the cover of the May 1980 issue of *Circus*. The deal certainly went both ways.

Dave had also just returned from a solo journey through the jungles of South America and eventually had a heavy life experience in Haiti where he had been absorbing the colorful life of the Third World until he came across a man who was literally starving to death and it changed him. Almost immediately, Dave was done with everybody wanting some and was moving onto walking these stinkin' streets past the crazies on his block. That was another element of the "darkness" of *Fair Warning*.

During this window, things apparently got so bad that Edward, clearly not in his right mind, approached Gene Simmons about joining KISS in some capacity. Ed apparently showed some of the synthesizer material he'd been working on (possibly "Sunday Afternoon in the Park") and suggested he join and bring in the keyboard and make a change to KISS's makeup. Possibly not taking the whole situation seriously, as it shouldn't have been, Gene pointed him back to Dave and told him to work it out.

Fortunately, things did work out and the band produced their greatest work to date, and possibly of their career. "Mean Streets," with its mind-blowing instrumental introduction that literally came across as simply *impossible* to play, to the pre-eminent Van Halen stadium rocker "Unchained," *Fair Warning* was a *masterpiece* from start to finish. The album was full of great variety with out and out stompers like "Sinner's Swing!" and the smooth "Push Comes to Shove" to the incredible—and finally realized—synthesizer work on "Sunday Afternoon in the Park" and its companion piece "One Foot Out the Door." The album is a landmark in rock history. The album took longer to record than any other Van Halen LP because, as Ed later told Jas Obrecht, "I did more overdubs, and it just took more time. There were more things on tape that had to be mixed. You know? I did so many different guitar parts and stuff, that the mixing took longer."

At that exact same time, Ed and Val were still trying to plan a wedding. Apparently, Ed was upset that Dave turned down his request to be a groomsman; who knows what had been going on that particular day. But Dave made up for it by buying Ed's white tuxedo that he would wear during his exchange of vows.

The day of the wedding, April 11, 1981, Ed had a bout of nerves and ended up drinking a bit too much, nearly fainting several times. However, he pulled it together in time for the ceremony, which went off without a hitch. Alex was his best man. The wedding ended up becoming a huge event, with over 400 people invited, mainly because Ed and Val didn't want to leave anyone out. The ceremony was a Catholic affair, reflecting both Eddie and Valerie's background and upbringing, and took place at St. Paul the Apostle Church in Westwood, California.

But the wedding day partying level was slightly out of control. Dave recalled, "Cut to the upstairs at the reception, the Beverly Hills Hotel, and Ed and I are doing blow and taking turns holding each other around the waist so we don't plunge head first into the toilet from dry heaving." Valerie claimed the night ended with her passing out on the bed still in her wedding dress while Ed fell asleep in the bathroom. On their way home the next morning, Ed was pulled over for speeding and the officer noticed an open bottle of champagne in the car. The cop recognized Ed and let him off.

Two weeks after the wedding, *Fair Warning* was released and went to #5 on the *Billboard* charts. Even though the album was an artistic masterpiece, there was not a single track Warner Brothers deemed worthy of release as a single. Worse yet, in purely numerical terms, each Van Halen record had been selling slightly less and less. Of course, it is hard to consider that a problem when the albums are still going platinum. But pressure from above started creeping into the situation which only served to further heighten tensions between Ed and Dave, and Ed and Dave and the record company.

The *Fair Warning* Tour

The five-month *Fair Warning* tour that started in May of 1981 would be their shortest yet. The following month, their Oakland shows were filmed which produced the live "Unchained," "So This Is Love?," and "Hear About it Later" videos that became staples of very early MTV. One of the earliest iconic images of Eddie was from these videos: shaggy black hair, shirtless, white half-pants, and red-striped stockings performing his classic trademark bent-legged jump. This was the first time a great deal of people got a glimpse of what Ed looked like while actually playing. I was only nine and I remember coming away from those videos thinking, "Man, those guys are tough." Three out of four were shirtless, which, around 1980, was about the toughest an older guy could look to a little kid, not to mention the gong being on fire. They reminded me of the gang members I had seen when *West Side Story* came on TV.

That June, Edward would cross paths with Geddy Lee yet again. Almost exactly a year later, Van Halen and Rush were booked at separate venues in Las Vegas. For whatever particular reason, Rush put it out there that Van Halen was officially banned from their show. Who knows if VH asked to be invited or if Rush was just preemptively telling them to stay the hell away. Most likely, this was all the work of their handlers. Unwittingly, one of Edward's bodyguards made a bad situation a whole lot worse. Geddy was passing through a casino and by coincidence came across Edward. One source claims that Lee attempted "to mend ways with Edward," but Ed's bodyguard wasn't letting Geddy have anything to do with Ed at all. Roth told *Creem* that Geddy "puts up his hand to shake hands. Now one of our security guards didn't have the vaguest idea in hell who he was and body-tackled him . . . threw him out." The Rush family and the Van Halen family would continue to cross paths for years.

The short tour came to a close on October 24, 1981 at the Tangerine Bowl where they opened for the Stones. Their ceremonial final bow and celebration was photographed and used for the back cover of *Diver Down*. At one point during the tour, *The New York Times* gave the band a positive review, but their reference to Edward as Dave's "right-hand man" could not possibly have gone over well with Ed in any way whatsoever. In fact, they were absolutely determined to spend time apart from each other, and even came up with a plan to spend as little time together as possible. But it backfired on them.

"Does it seem cold in here to you?"

Enter the PR Machine

Edward was yet again named *Guitar Player*'s guitarist of the year in 1981, now for three years running. Valerie's shacking up with a rock god forced some higher-ups somewhere to put an awkward PR spin on their relationship. In a November 9 issue of *People*, an article appeared titled "*One Day*'s Sweetheart: Valerie Bertinelli's Happily Over the Deep End About Her Rocker Husband, Eddie Van Halen." The article included the ridiculous line, "So the question remains: What's a nice girl like that doing with a guy who plays guitar with his teeth?" Apparently, Edward had morphed into Jimi Hendrix in the interviewer's mind. Valerie was defending Eddie with statements like "He's not the typical rock star" and "It shocked me that he was so normal."

For tawdry shock value, the article mentioned that Dave had taken out paternity insurance with Lloyd's of London. This is another one of those salacious tidbits of VH lore which, like the brown M&Ms clause, was taken out of context. In comparing Ed to Dave, Valerie said the public perception of Eddie's image was "by association only," referring to Dave. The factual irony is that the only reason Dave had purchased paternity insurance was explicitly related to what Edward had been through—not Dave. In a *Rolling Stone* article several years later, Dave explained: "What happened was that, about four or five years ago, a guy in the band had a suit from a woman claiming her kid was his. All the tests proved conclusively that that never was his kid. So I took out insurance in order to make someone think six times before she does anything." The "guy in the band" was Edward.

The goofy *People* article closed with what some might call famous last words. "We're both monogamous people," Valerie said. "I trust him, he trusts me, and there's no way anything would ever happen."

Late that year, Michael Anthony was interviewed by Jas Obrecht for *Guitar Player*. "There's a lot of time when I'll get frustrated because I can't play what I want to play," he said. "The other guys'll say, 'Why don't you just sit back and play this,' and I'll kind of grit my teeth and go, 'Well, okay.'" He added that "It's a little restricting playing behind a guitarist like Ed, but it feels good because of who he is." The days of "everyone pretty much does whatever they want" were essentially over. Dave and Ed ran the show even though their relationship was becoming ever more fractious.

CHAPTER 13
Take Cover

To satisfy Warner Brothers, as well as the market, the band decided to record and release a single for the new year to tide everyone over before they took the proper amount of time to write and record a brand new album. According to Edward, "When we came off the *Fair Warning* tour, we were gonna take some time off. You know, and spend a lot of time writing and this and that, and uh, we—Dave came up with the idea of 'Hey, why don't we start off the new year with just putting out a single?'" Dave was pushing for "Dancing in the Street"—made famous by Martha Reeves and the Vandellas in 1964—but Ed could not figure out a decent interpretation. Frustrated, he said that initially he just could not get any kind of handle on the tune. "So I said, hey, look, if you wanna do a cover tune why don't we do 'Pretty Woman'?", Edward said. "And it took one day, we went to Sunset Sound, recorded it. And it came out early, right after the first of the year."

Infamously, there is an entire section of the song missing. This is because Edward and Dave were needling each other about learning the song correctly, they were so at each other that of course they ended up recording it incorrectly. And even though they realized their mistake on playback, they simply left it as it was. Quite possibly, it was simply a musical happy accident.

Dave had developed grandiose ideas for promoting the track and set about filming a quasi-mini-movie for the video age. The set-up was ludicrous. The description of the video is just supposed to sound so crazy that it would've had to have been great. These are Ed's actual words he used when describing the video to Jas Obrecht:

> We had a transvestite tied up and two midgets, like uh, you know, harassing her, squeezing her ass and doing this and that, and uh, and uh, Dave was Napoleon, Mike was a samurai

> warrior, Alex my brother was Tarzan, and I was like a gunslinger wearing leather pants and twirling the gun and stuff. And uh, I guess the plot was that, umm—and a hunchback was in it. He was up in like a bell tower looking down at these two midgets harassing this supposedly pretty woman. And he would hop on the phone and call each one of us. And I'd hop on the horse and come to the rescue, and so would Al, and Dave and Mike. And at the end, Dave pulls up in a limo. You know, he's always the one that's got the classy, crazy shit. You know, so he pulls up in a white stretch limo. And looks at her, and she starts running towards him like he's her hero and she pulls her wig off and you see that she's a dude.

The description is accurate. The video took 40 hours to film and was not even filmed with the timing or rhythm of the song in mind in any way whatsoever. Once it was all edited down and they put the song over the "movie," they realized the video was longer than the song and that they were short of music to fit the final edit.

Thus was born "Intruder"—one of Van Halen's classic instrumental works. David himself wrote the music on a synthesizer in about an hour and played it himself on the recording along with Alex providing the powerful drum track. Edward swooped in and really brought the track to life with some of the most amazing and outrageous sounds that anyone ever made with a guitar or any instrument. What started as a throwaway is now considered one of the most experimental and grinding brief rock song intros of all time, and it is a pure Dave-Edward combination. In fact, it is a beautiful piece of musical irony that something so dark (with its E and B flat bass notes on the synthesizer) leads into something well-known and old-fashioned, yet updated—as if going forward and in reverse at the same moment. It was something as darkly beautiful as "Intruder" that made all the potential hell they went through with each other worth it.

Once the video was finally released to MTV, they promptly banned the video for featuring a transvestite. The banning of the video gave the band some great controversial press, but it was in reality a dear favor to them. Dave's first big video out of the gate was experimental, but it was comically bad, and not in a funny way. Back in the 80s and most of the 90s, there was virtually no way for anyone to see the actual video. In fact, the only clip of the video I myself ever saw as a kid was at the very tail end of the 1983 Us Festival video on the Showtime cable network. But the video is now at your fingertips here in the 21st century. Upon review, it is amazing that Edward agreed to even participate in such a project with Dave at the helm at that time in their career. Fortunately, Dave would eventually improve upon his video making skills in a massive way.

Around this time in 1982, Edward made a seemingly random phone call to Frank Zappa simply out of mutual respect and later ended up producing a single for Frank's then twelve-year-old son Dweezil. In 2010, Dweezil wrote on his website about the events after the phone call:

> Twenty minutes later Edward Van Halen was at our house. He had a new guitar with him. A purple Kramer with a piece of tape covering the logo. Frank called Steve Vai and asked him to come over. What followed as the coolest night a 12-year-old guitar player could ever imagine, or perhaps any guitar player. Edward Van Halen, Steve Vai, and Frank Zappa all passed around this new purple guitar. Occasionally I would fumble around on it as well. Many things were played and discussed. It was amazing. Of course I asked Edward to play "Mean Street" and "Eruption." He did and I got to watch it up close. The techniques he employed were burned into my brain forever. This jam session/discussion went on into the wee hours of the morning. Somewhere around 3AM. I had a little league game at 7AM. Even though I had pitched a no hitter the week before, I knew that night that baseball was no longer that important to me.

Edward said, "Yes, we had the milk and cookies sittin' there, you blow a good solo—you get some milk and cookies." He said that because of Frank's off-meter material, Dweezil had a lot of trouble playing in regular time. "It's really funny because his dad's music, he couldn't quite tap. He couldn't count to four. . . . It wasn't 'Get Down Tonight.' Dweezil had a rough time playing to a regular beat. So he just played, [I] captured it, put it together and it worked." Edward told Jas Obrecht:

> I met Frank Zappa right before he left for a European tour and he has a 12-year-old kid how plays guitar. And he called me up from Europe and asked me if I wanted to produce a

single for him, you know, for his kid. So Moon sang on it, and Dweezil, is the kid's name, plays guitar and Donn Landee and I produced it. And it cooks! It's called "My Mother is a Space Cadet." And the flip side is called "Crunchy Water." It's in the Zappa tradition. But uh, it's funny because, oh, the guitar parts really sound like me. Like I played it. But the only thing that I did play on "Space Cadet" was the intro.

Obrecht: Is that the first thing you've done outside the band since Nicolette?

EVH: Oh, yeah. That's the only–I mean, you know, this was a production thing–I spent about month doing it.

Obrecht: Too much!

EVH: Hey, the whole band was fucking twelve years old. They couldn't play for shit! You know? But when you hear it it will blow you away. Man, his guitar solo was a composite of about nine different takes after we sifted out the other eighty takes. It took about three days of five hours a day trying to get him to get his solo together.

Where's the Album?

So that "(Oh) Pretty Woman" could have a B-side, the band sang "Happy Trails" a capella. Again, initially considered an absurd throwaway, it is a Van Halen classic. All four band members were singing in four-part harmony all together live in the studio and cracking up while doing it. It became a huge part of their live act. Edward said, "Hell, we're even doing it in the show, man, and people go nuts for it!" It showcased a completely different side of the band.

Fortunately or unfortunately—mostly unfortunately relationship-wise—"(Oh) Pretty Woman" was a smash hit upon its release. The song was only the second Van Halen tune up until that point without a guitar solo, and it was their biggest selling single. Eddie said, "It almost makes me feel bad. It shows you how much guitar solos mean to people . . . 'Pretty Woman' is like our only legitimate hit." The track hit #12 and was the highest charting Van Halen single to date at the time.

That song they threw together to appease the record company; that song they didn't even record correctly; that song they made a horrible video for that never got played—that song was a *huge* hit.

This had the opposite effect than was intended. Instead of putting out a single and having Edward take his time writing a new record and spending time apart from David, the fact that the song was a hit had Warner Brothers putting the heat on them to deliver the album that they felt that song was supposed to be on. Edward said to Jas Obrecht, "We're going, wait a minute, we just did that to keep people, to keep us out there, so people know we're still alive. But they, you know, they just kept pressuring—'We need that album. We need that album.' So we jumped right back in without any rest, you know, without any time to recuperate from the tour, and started recording."

The process of recording *Diver Down* was completely different than anything Van Halen, or any other band for that matter, had ever done. Every single song was recorded one at a time. Whereas on the earlier records, they would lay down the bed tracks and go back later and add vocals and solos. For *Diver Down*, the band would not move on to the next track until the one they were working on was completely finished. Eddie said, "Instead of going into the studio and doing ten basic tracks, we would do one basic track, come back the next day, or the same day later on in the evening after dinner, and do the back-up harmonies and the lead vocals. And then that one was gone. You know? That one was in the bag. And then we'd record the next basic track and sang, and do leads and whatever. So we took each song, you know, one at a time as opposed to doing ten songs all at the same time."

The album was recorded in twelve days and released on April 14, 1982. Of the twelve tracks, three are instrumentals that are all less than two minutes long. Of the remaining nine, five are cover songs. In the open, he was defensive of the cover-heavy record. He told Jas Obrecht, "The fucking critics having been giving us shit about that. But uh, I think it's a bunch of crap." He continued, "I mean like say 'Dancing in the Streets,', 'Pretty Woman,' uhh, 'Where Have All the Good Times Gone?', you know, stuff like that, it's not like the original. . . . Whenever you do a cover tune, like say on the second album when we did 'You're No Good,' uhh . . . Whenever you redo a cover tune, I don't think you should do it like the original. And I don't think any cover tune we've ever done has been like the original. You know? And uh, it takes almost as much time to make a cover tune sound original as it does writing a song. . . . So fuck the critics." At the time, Eddie said his favorite track was "Secrets." Ed told Obrecht: "You know, like 'Secrets' to me is the first ever real mellow thing we've ever done, you know? That's why I like it so much, because it's still Van Halen. It's not like Journey, purposefully you know, doing fucking tear-jerking pop tunes to make money."

Valerie said that *Diver Down* was "one headache after another for Ed." The inclusion of "Where Have All the Good Times Gone?" doesn't require a lot to work to read into. Valerie didn't have a complete handle on what exactly was going on with Ed and Dave, but she just knew that Ed came home unhappy and "dazed and distraught" during the recording. Valerie noted that Edward's drinking had become increasingly worse during this period. They had only been married about a year before Valerie had her first thoughts of intervening to take care of Ed, but she did not, ultimately deciding that Ed was a grown man.

In the mid-1990s, Edward reflected upon it with Billy Corgan for *Guitar World*. "Half that album was damn cover tunes, and I hated every minute of making it," Eddie said, "David . . . had the idea that if you covered a successful song, you were half way home. C'mon—Van Halen doing 'Dancing in the Streets'? It was stupid. I started feeling like I would rather bomb playing my own songs than be successful playing someone else's music."

Jan Gets His Due on *Diver Down*

Despite everything that was going on, the search for tracks for *Diver Down* led Dave to bring a song to the table that dated back to 1924, and gave him the idea to do something truly special for the album. Dave stumbled across "Big Bad Bill (Is Sweet William Now)" and brought it to the band. As a beautiful gesture, Dave then suggested that Eddie and Al get Jan to play clarinet on the track. Edward told Jas Obrecht in detail:

> You know, it was actually Dave's suggestion. He said, "Shit dude, listen to this, man! Get your old man to play it!" We said, "Sure!" It was so funny, because, uh, I tell ya, I couldn't play the song for you right now. I had to read—excuse me one second. I had to burp. Umm, there's so many chords—ding ding ding—you know, stuff like that, that I don't know, I just

> couldn't remember it. So, here's my father sittin' to the left of me, with, you know, sittin' on a chair, with a music stand and sheet music in front of him. I'm sittin' next to him with a chair and with sheet music and a stand. And Mike too—he's playing like an acoustic bass. I don't know it's kind of weird, it's just like an acoustic guitar—you know like when you go to a Mexican restaurant and, you know, they come up and play in front of your face and aggravate the shit outta you—you know the kind of bass guitars they play? He played one of those. And uh, I don't know, it was funny as shit, we had a great time. It looked like an old 30s or 40s session

Jan Van Halen was finally getting his due. But he wasn't entirely comfortable with the prospect at all. Edward said, "He hasn't played his clarinet in 10 years. Because he lost his left hand middle finger about 10 years ago. . . . He was nervous as shit. And we're just telling him, 'Jan, just fuckin' have a good time. Man, we make mistakes, that's what makes it real.' Um, I mean, I love, I love what he did." Despite his appearance on the record, Jan had absolutely no plans to join the band onstage. Ed said, "I asked him if he would when we played L.A. and he said 'NO WAY!'"

The highlight track of the album is "Little Guitars." For the intro, Ed had come up with an amazing flamenco acoustic piece for which he "faked" traditional flamenco finger-picking. "I came up with 'Little Guitars Intro'—the Spanish sounding thing—and I bought a couple of Montoya records, and I'm hearing, you know, I'm hearing this guy going 'dadadadadada' finger-picking!" Eddie said. "And I'm going like, god, this motherfucker is great. I, I can't do that. So what I did is kind of listened to it, to that style of playing for a couple of days and I cheated." Instead of finger-picking, he used his unique trill-picking style on the high open strings while hammering on with his left hand. When his pal Steve Lukather of Toto first heard it, he said, "How the fuck did you do that? You overdubbed that, huh?"

The main track was written by Ed on an actual little guitar. It was a miniature Les Paul copy given to him by a fan. Because of the string length, the guitar is actually tuned to G instead of the standard E for guitar. The end result is that Ed came up with a very unique riff that actually used finger-picking to an extensive degree. The song is a brilliant combination of styles and has a pop-edge to it, but is still very unique. The little guitar itself did become a bit of a gimmick. The pictures of Ed playing the guitar were always greeted with a bit of a laugh, and unfortunately for Ed, there is indeed a scene in *Spinal Tap* that shows Christopher Guest's character Nigel Tufnel playing a little guitar—a direct parody of Edward himself.

Dave's influence was high on *Diver Down*. He had written and played the synthesizer part on "Intruder," he conceived and created their first real "video," he brought Jan into the fold by bringing a song especially suited for the brothers to perform with their father, and he played the acoustic guitar intro and harmonica solo on "The Full Bug." The album sold well and hit #3 on the U.S. charts. After its release in April, there would be no new Van Halen music for over a year and a half. The interim between albums would be an extremely interesting, exciting, and wild period of time.

CHAPTER 14
Public Relations

The *Diver Down* tour, nicknamed the "Hide Your Sheep Tour," was the biggest tour of its kind to date with over 170 tons of equipment required to put on the stage show. The tour didn't kick off until July—much later in the year than on previous tours. On July 30, while in Louisville, Ed gave an hour-plus long interview yet again with Jas Obrecht who was still writing for *Guitar Player* at the time. The full, unedited audio tapes of those interviews reveal some astounding examples of where he was at the time. The tapes were actually stolen from Obrecht, the only such seizure in over 800 interviews he has conducted. Edward and Obrecht were both very unhappy that the full tapes made their way to the internet. Jas has successfully had the interview removed several times, but it simply will not go away, not in the 21st century.

Via my correspondence with Obrecht, he has allowed me to use a bit of the bell that cannot be unrung. Part of the transcribed interview addressed growing problems with Dave with specificity in a way that was never publicly revealed for 25 years:

> EVH: "Cathedral," I've been doing for, you know, over a year and I wanted to put it on a record. . . . It's just that, uhhh, Dave said . . . "No more fucking guitar solos." You know?
>
> Obrecht: He's crazy.
>
> EVH: No, I mean, you know, he's, he's got—he's on an ego trip. He has always been. . . . But uh, he just, you know, he just said, "Fuck this, man. No more guitar solos." And uh, you know, Ted didn't know that that's the way Dave felt. And uh, so one day when Dave wasn't there, I said, Ted, what do you think of this? And what do you think of that? You know, I played him "Little Guitars", the intro, you know, the little flamenco sounding thing, and, uh, and "Cathedral" and he's going like

> "God! Why the fuck didn't you show me this earlier?!" And I explained to him, Dave just said, "Fuck the guitar hero shit, you know, we're a *band*." So Ted just said, you know, "Fuck Dave." So we put it on anyway.

That seems to match up with Valerie's story of how Dave belittled him after winning his 1980 guitarist of the year award. If Dave was worried that Ed was going to be doing things on his own, in retrospect he had every right to fear just such a thing.

Before they set out on tour, Edward received a late night phone call from famed producer Quincy Jones who was producing *Thriller* throughout most of 1982. Ed originally thought the call was a prank and hung up the phone. Eddie's friend Steve Lukather was the principal guitarist on the track "Beat It." At some point, the idea was born to bring in the all-star Edward Van Halen to add a unique touch to the hard-hitting Michael Jackson anthem. Jackson himself set out to write what he described as "the type of song that I would buy if I were to buy a rock song . . . That is how I approached it and I wanted the kids to really enjoy it—the school kids as well as the college kids."

Edward was originally given what was called a sketch of the song and suggested rearrangements that were made to suit the solo section. Ed was truly out of his element in the legendary Quincy's studio—the quintessential opposite of the Van Halen approach. God only knows how many individual tracks there are on the final version of "Beat It." Again, like so many times before, it has gone down in lore that the solo was done in one take or two takes or pieced together from two or three takes. Regardless, surely no one knew the impact Ed's solo, all of thirty seconds, would have on the music world at large at the time it was cut. For the mean time though, Ed's stepping out would remain in the closet for about a year. He told no one about his participation. At the time, Eddie claimed he simply thought nothing of it.

Whose Band Is It?

Throughout the tour during the fall of 1982, Edward absolutely felt that his control over the band was slipping permanently away to Dave. A photo shoot for *Life* magazine that September was proclaimed wife-free by David, and the married men complied. For Dave's guidance, the spread was littered with images of sexually-charged excess and rock and roll mayhem. It was the standard Van Halen image that the band had started out with, except now half the guys were married, so the image did not necessarily match the reality of the situation. But Van Halen was an extremely valuable brand, and Dave knew exactly what the public wanted.

However, Edward's wife was not an unknown. She was an extremely high-profile celebrity at this point in time, and her good-girl image was being tarnished by the Van Halen image. Somewhere, this was not sitting well with someone, and Ed and Valerie were trotted out on *Entertainment Tonight* to salvage Valerie's image by obviously softening Edward's. The opening voice-over gave a clear indication of what was to follow: "The odds of Hollywood marriages lasting are pretty slim these days particularly considering the long working hours and time apart. . . . They seem to come from different worlds. So when these two teen idols decided a year ago to marry, many of their fans and friends said it wouldn't work."

If ever there was a clearly obvious PR move, the interview featured Eddie and Valerie sitting in nearly matching white sweaters on a couch in front of a fireplace. Additionally, the interview featured an obviously fake cut of Edward actually flipping a pancake in the kitchen while Valerie awkwardly laughs along. They're also shown cuddling with a set of tiny, white kittens. Stars go on *Entertainment Tonight* for public relations purposes, especially if the only angle is the state of their marriage. The interview featured the following transcribed exchanges:

> Interviewer: The two of you seem to be so different. Valerie, you're kind of the goodie two shoes and the rock world is supposed to be so insane.
>
> Valerie: That's it—you just said the key word—supposed to be. I mean I've seen more insane people in the TV world than I have in his world. I mean, you know.
>
> EVH: I'll verify that.

The interviewer suggested that their lifestyles were fairly incompatible and that reports were flying that their brief marriage was already on the rocks. Valerie was exasperated that some magazines and journalists went so far in an attempt to simply take down the seemingly happy couple. She stated that they were such normal people as far as they were concerned, which was a notion that she didn't think others believed or could process.

On another tabloid television program, *PM Magazine*, the couple again went on the PR defensive about their marriage in an interview with Maria Shriver. Valerie again expressed frustration that she felt forced to repeat over and over that they were a happily married couple. Their potential incompatibility was reinforced by referring to the couple as the "all-American Valerie" and the "all-electric Eddie." Edward said that he was much happier being married and having a home than he was constantly living on the road with hotels as his permanent address.

When Shriver noted the general belief that a "rock star's life is groupies, drinking, late hours, and hard drugs," the following exchange took place:

> Maria Shriver: But does it apply to Edward Van Halen?
>
> Edward: Take a guess? No.
>
> Maria Shriver: 'No. None of it.' . . .
>
> Edward: The late hours and drinking, maybe, yeah.
>
> Maria: But the groupies . . .
>
> Edward: Of course, not! I'm married. I wouldn't do that.
>
> Valerie: I hope not.

This was part of a calculated effort to soften Ed's public image, but also part of an effort to portray Valerie not as a young 15-year-old sweetheart, but a 21-year-old married woman in order to placate the tabloid criticism of their "incompatibility." Edward appeared edgy and defensive (and shown on television both smoking and drinking).

As the tour rolled on, tensions ran high as Dave's circus-like partying ways clashed Edward's attempt at a softened image on behalf of his wife's career. A family friend of the author named D'Lesa attended their September 24 show at the Summit in Houston, and managed to take several classic, here-to-fore unpublished photos, most of which show a band with an audience that worshipped them aggressively.

Van Halen at the Summit in Houston in 1982. Photograph © D'Lesa Plunk

Busting a Few Things

The entire tour was sold out—every single arena they played. The record company wanted to capture the band live on both video and audio for a potential live album and/or VHS release. A two-night stand in Largo, Maryland was filmed and recorded on October 11-12, and the band played in Uniondale, New York immediately following on the 13th. The footage from Largo was never publicly released, but is widely available for review online. The video shows the band a tad sloppy and even featured some weak choreographed moves. However, the band is incredibly well-received and absolutely adored by the crowd. The video is also fully edited from multiple camera angles, obviously at a great expense.

During "Unchained," Dave stopped the song during the breakdown part to say the following: "We got some . . . we got some good news here tonight! He's a little bit . . . he's a little bit shy about this kind of thing and he's gonna get on my case about it later. But ladies and gentlemen, we received word about half an hour ago that says for the fifth year in a row [sic], from *Guitar Player* international magazine, the guitar player of the year—EDWAAARD!" Ed did not smile. He just tersely saluted the crowd. He stood there for a moment, took a brief bow, but turned to Alex to get the song going again as quickly as possible. It is likely that Dave's gesture was an attempt to make up for the previous years of jealousy. It is also possible that Dave would boast with pride in front of a roaring crowd, but not in private.

Regardless, things bubbled over in Pittsburgh immediately thereafter on October 14. Edward fractured his left wrist. Originally, this went down on record as the result of "fooling around in his hotel room". Ed told the press, "I was lucky that the break was to my left hand instead of to my right. If it had been the other way around I probably would have been sidelined for a couple of months . . . The accident has made me more aware of how quickly this can all come to an end." Acknowledging that it was not horseplay, Ed later admitted, "I hit walls when I get mad. I'm obsessed with music, and sometimes things don't go right." It is possible that an immediate review of the tapes from Largo were deemed unfit for release for one reason or another or something that night in Pittsburgh set him off. Whether it was Dave or himself he was mad at, the fracture landed Eddie in a New York hospital and three subsequent shows were canceled and had to be rescheduled.

Impossibly, Ed was only down for five days as the tour resumed in Philadelphia on October 19 and he played through the pain. Reaching new heights in popularity, the band played three straight sold-out nights in a row in Worcester, Massachusetts, with October 25 being officially declared "Van Halen Day" after circulation of 25,000-signature petition by a local Worcester radio station. The overly successful tour carried on through early December and took a one-month break before a South American and European tour planned to start in January of 1983.

CHAPTER 15
1984 Minus One

Eddie had been with the band around nearly the entire world, but had never been to South America before. According to Dave they were "treated like national heroes." Even though the South American way of doing things was adventurous, to put it lightly, the guys truly enjoyed their one month romp through Venezuela, Brazil, Uruguay, and Argentina. The band added a handful of fun, old-school covers to their sets, including "Heartbreak Hotel," "Beer Drinkers and Hell Raisers" by ZZ Top, and "Summertime Blues." Eddie played the final show in Buenos Aires, Argentina entirely from the right side of the stage for the first and possibly the only time ever. His to desire to just do something *different* was starting to show itself in a number of ways.

Valerie accompanied Edward on the tour and the two spent time with Alex and his fiancée Valeri (no "e"). She noted in her autobiography that they had been warned to leave their jewelry and other such valuables at home, so Valerie replaced her diamond wedding band with a cheap gold ring. In Rio, the two couples returned to their hotel and were attempting to get on the elevator when Valerie was stopped by a manager. He was going to allow Ed, Al, and Valeri up, but not Valerie. When she demanded to know why, the manager said, "You are familiar with the rules. We do not allow prostitutes in the rooms in this hotel." She pointed to her wedding band and said, "I am married to him," only to be countered by the manager saying, "We see that all the time from the professional women." Eddie and Alex cracked up and then intervened and brought Valerie with them and afterward, according to Valerie, they "had a few drinks and passed out."

Archival footage of several of these concerts shows the band ebbing toward their peak. The band appeared to be getting along famously during this trek. During the Buenos Aires show, Dave gives Edward a big kiss right on the side of his head. Ed was genuinely touched by the enthusiasm of the Argentina crowd—their chants of "EH-DEE! EH-DEE!" was only met with Ed gesturing back toward the audience, as if they were the ones to be applauded.

However, someone back at Warner Brothers started doing the math and sent word down that the European leg of the tour was canceled and the South American tour would end much quicker than was originally planned. Warner insisted they have an album out in 1983. Once again, the band was pressured and forced to get back into writing and recording mode by their record company.

"Beat It" Comes Out of the Closet

The day after their last date in South America, February 14, that one-off solo he did for Michael Jackson and Quincy Jones without any forethought hit the radio, and the video hit MTV the following month. Dave was at a convenience store when he first heard the track. "I was in a parking lot on Santa Monica near Sweetzer, the 7-Eleven, there were a couple of butch Mexican gals with the doors open of their pickup truck and the new Michael Jackson song 'Beat It' came on," he said. "I heard the guitar solo, and thought, now that sounds familiar. Somebody's ripping of Ed Van Halen's guitar licks. It was Ed, turns out, and he had gone and done the project without discussing it with anybody."

When it was discussed, Ed eventually revealed that he had done it simply as a favor, for no money at all, for no points on the record at all. Eddie said, "I was a complete fool, according to the rest of the band, our manager and everyone else. I was not used. I knew what I was doing—I don't do something unless I want to do it." Dave actually speculated that Ed was cunningly exploited. Most likely, Edward had only done it as a favor to Steve Lukather, and for Ed it was likely just an interesting evening. About Jackson, Eddie said, "Maybe he'll give me a dance lesson someday." Years later, Valerie quipped, "Ed never saw a dime; nor do I believe that he ever thought to ask to get paid. That was Ed." In a 1990 interview, Ed said, "My brother still won't let me live it down."

As for the solo itself, writer Joseph Bosso claimed: "The solo would be Eddie's most popular and analyzed work of the Eighties. All fired up, whooping and swirling, growling and shrieking, it is the product of the heart meeting the mind and connecting with the unknown."

"Beat It" was beyond huge. It went to #1 all over the world and the video ran day and night on MTV. Eddie's participation, along with that of Paul McCartney, on the *Thriller* album is one of the main reasons that Michael Jackson had such a strong crossover appeal, and therefore one of the principal reasons the album became the biggest selling record of all time. Nelson George, a black music critic who wrote a Jackson book, said, "The lead guitar breaks on Shalamar's 'Dancing in the Sheets,' and Lionel Richie's 'Running in the Night,' to name just two, came from Eddie's work on 'Beat It.' You never saw that kind of heavy-metal rock guitar on black singles before that."

The door for racial musical crossovers was opened wide. Rap pioneers Run DMC made heavy guitar riffs a staple of their sound, and their subsequent collaboration with Aerosmith, which completely resurrected that band's soured career, would likely have never happened at all had Edward Van Halen not answered the phone that night. The song caused MTV to soften its stance against airing black artists and made way for the huge success of Prince and other artists in the early and mid-80s.

Edward's contribution definitely opened the door for the later rap-rock hybrid genre of the 1990s and early 2000s. The course of popular music was clearly changed in a significant way simply due to Ed's unintentional power. But according to Dave at the time, "He went in and played the same solo he's been playing in this band for ten years. So big deal!" But it was no wonder that the March issue of *Circus* carried the article title "Van Halen: Biggest U.S. Band?," as if it were up for debate.

The Kramer Endorsement

Despite Ed's potential loss of income from "Beat It," he began to endorse Kramer guitars in 1983—his first official endorsement deal of any kind. Ads ran in all guitar magazines and fanzines with Ed's quote: "It's very simply the very best guitar you can buy today." The endorsement and design collaboration deal happened by chance, but once Ed was sold on the instrument, he boldly stated that he would make Kramer the "number one guitar company in the world." Before switching completely over to the Kramer though, Ed actually just switched out the neck on his Frankenstein before he was completely satisfied with the Kramer guitar body and locking tremolo system that he had helped developed with

Floyd Rose, although Rockinger was making the tremolo systems now and paying a royalty to Mr. Rose.

A few years later, at the urging of my hero via the magazine print ads, I convinced my parents buy me the cheapest possible Kramer we could get. It was a Striker, but it said "by Kramer" really tiny underneath it. The guitar was so terrible that we actually took it back and got our money back. And to be completely truthful, buying a Kramer wasn't the only thing about Eddie that I emulated. Way too young, after reading an article about his early days, I bought a pack of Pall Malls and subsequently nearly choked to death, and snuck a friend's dad's Schlitz—the first time I had ever seen one—and promptly vomited. The truth is that when you have a hero before you are fifteen, you cannot help but to deliberately try and emulate them, for better or for worse.

In April 1983, Edward and Valerie took some time off to celebrate their two-year anniversary by taking a trip to the Netherlands. Ed finally had the chance to show Val where he had grown up and told her all of the stories along the way. They took in the historical sites, but the highlight of their trip was a long, solo romantic boat ride down the canals.

Building 5150

Immediately upon return from their anniversary vacation, Eddie began construction on his famed 5150 studio. Valerie's brother Drew was put in charge of the construction phase of the new building, but Ed and Val themselves demolished the old guest house taking turns on a Caterpillar tractor to make room for the studio.

Eddie's faithful engineer Donn Landee worked with him on all of the technical parts of the studio construction. But Donn's input was more critical to Ed than just his technical expertise. Ed said that Donn was "more than an engineer." The cathartic experience of building the studio was facilitated by Donn's desire to help Ed fulfill his dream and take control over his art. Edward said, "Donn did a lot to get me mentally healthier, and let all that stuff out and not worry."

What ended up happening with the construction is that they told the city they were simply building a racquetball court, period. At the time, Eddie said, "All I hope is that the city doesn't even find out about the studio. They don't even know it's here." He said the building was inspected and approved by the city as a racquetball court. Eddie said, "Then I put some walls up, though I never told them. No more racquetball court now. . . . They could make me tear the whole place down and start over."

5150 was where the entire *1984* album was recorded, and nearly every subsequent VH album as well. It was a huge dream for Eddie to have his own backyard recording studio and the subsequent amount of control he would have that came with it. The building would become much more than just Ed's studio—it would be his absolute sanctuary from the outside world where he would continually disappear for hours—*days*—at a time. From there on, the purely physical space in which Van Halen existed was 5150. Ed built everyone the ultimate backyard tree house.

The name of course, at least Ed thought, was taken from the police code for an escaped mental patient. "Name of my studio is 5150—that's police code for escaped mental case," Edward told *Musician* in 1984. In fact, though, 5150 is actually a section of the California Welfare and Institutions Code "which allows a qualified officer or clinician to involuntarily confine a person deemed to have a mental disorder that makes them a danger to him or her self, and/or others and/or gravely disabled."

The 1983 US Festival

The writing process was coming along, and Edward had a nugget or two of an idea already in the bag, namely a catchy keyboard tune in C that he had developed a few years earlier. Dave had disappeared on one of his Jungle Studs jaunts through South America when he got word that Apple Computers co-founder Steve Wozniak was putting together a second go at the US Festival (as in "us", not "U.S."). The Woz, as he is known, put together the first US Festival on Labor Day Weekend of 1982 with some of the biggest names in music at the time: Fleetwood Mac, Tom Petty and the Heartbreakers, The Police, The Cars, and even The Ramones. Wozniak was shooting to put the second one together for Memorial Day weekend, at the end of May in 1983. He intended Van Halen to headline one of the four days of the show—the day known as "Heavy Metal Day."

Edward was perturbed that the process of making the record was being interrupted, but $1.5 million dollars for a single show was a record-setting amount, and they were all in. About the preparation for the show, Eddie said, "That whole US Festival to me was like the world's quickest tour. We rehearsed for it like a tour. We had to design the amp setup, the lights, everything. It was like a tour except there was only one show. And after we got done with that one show I said, 'Well, where are we going after this show?' And it was home. You get yourself psyched up for a show and you want to do more when you're done. You're just getting warmed up after the first one." The entire US Festival would be filmed and condensed down to 90-minute encapsulations of each of the four days and was broadcast on cable. (The entire Van Halen performance was filmed and is readily available to resourceful fans.)

On May 29, Van Halen played before a crowd of 375,000 people. Dave got quite intoxicated before the show, and it showed on the program (Dave actually had to recut vocals in a studio to bring the broadcast version up to par). For those with cable at the time, especially hard rock minded youth of say age eleven, the Heavy Metal Day showing of the US Festival was a bit like a superhero movie. For the author, it was the first time outside of the *Fair Warning* era videos that we got to see the band in their full Technicolor glory. It was played ad nauseum in our house. We mimicked every single move, jump, facial gesture—everything.

After the show, Eddie told Steven Rosen, "The whole US Festival to me was a pain in the ass. The only thing it received in print was how much we made. All you hear about the US Festival was how many people got killed on our day and the money we made. I'm still wearin' the same pair of shoes and the same pair of pants. . . . For the amount of money that we made, we lost more than it was ever worth. A million-and-a-half dollars sounds like a lot, but what you can lose that much in return video-wise and every other way."

Ed considered the distinction of playing on Heavy Metal Day rather dubious. "I didn't really even realize what bands played with us, it didn't even hit me until I was over at Donn's house watching it on Showtime," he said. "I'm going, 'Now I know what they mean by heavy metal.' . . . I think the only way we really fit in was volume-wise. I don't consider Van Halen heavy metal at all. I don't even know what the word means." He added, "To me, heavy metal is just rock 'n' roll. I guess the more leather and studs you wear, the more heavy metal it is. So, I wear funny striped clothes. . . . I sure as hell don't see us as heavy metal."

With the festival out of the way and 5150 built, Edward tried to return his attention to the task of writing and recording the upcoming album, only to be interrupted yet again by a radio show. "The US Festival, again, hasn't stopped haunting us," Eddie said. "We were committed to do a radio show we didn't know about and in the meantime we're trying to do a record. We get a call, 'Hey, you're committed to a radio show,' and we go, 'Oh, God, not again!'"

Eventually, recording on the next record proceeded in earnest. Prior to the album's completion, Ed told Rosen: "I think this next one is going to be a hellified record. The majority of the solos will be overdubs. It just depends on how it feels right. There's a fast boogie called 'Hot for Teacher.' . . . Lots of overdubs. My dad might play an intro for a song. There's a song called 'Panama' with a live solo. And a song called 'Jump.'" The latter Edward played a rough demo tape over the phone for Jas Obrecht during their 1982 interview. The demo was merely a sketch at that time, but within it were all of the essential elements of "Jump."

When asked how fans might react to Ed's burgeoning fascination with synthesizers, he responded, "I think as long as I do whatever I do well, whatever they say, I don't really care. I mean they can't say that it sucks. If they don't like seeing me play keyboards, that's too bad." Another unique instrument Edward used on the album was a prototype stereo guitar built by Steve Ripley. "On this guitar you can pan each string to whatever side you want," he said. "And I have a super duper prototype which allows you to not only put each string to the left or right, but you can also add an effect to each string, left or right. It's a crazy sound." This guitar was used to record "Top Jimmy."

Early that summer, Eddie and Valerie rented a beach house in Malibu from composer Marvin Hamlisch where they spent their weekends trying to relax. Ed continued to work on music, though Valerie's only consolation was that he was at least within sight. Over the July Fourth weekend, Eddie heard a news report warning swimmers of strong riptides, and Ed, knowing Valerie was not a strong swimmer—nor he for that matter—warned her to be careful. A hairdresser friend of Valerie's, Jimmy, went out to the water with her and within minutes they were in serious trouble. Eddie noticed and leapt into action, yelling for Valerie to swim sideways and not fight the current, but she was too far out to hear. Panicked, Ed ran over to a group of volleyball players begging for help. The volleyball players were strong swimmers and jetted past Ed, who was still in shallow waters, to get to Valerie. The two Samaritans dragged Val out of the water passing Ed in the shallows. Eventually, Valerie and Edward stumbled together and hugged, both obviously quite shaken.

TV-Movie Music

While still at the Malibu beach house, Ed was roped into recording some music for one of Valerie's many made-for-TV movies, *The Seduction of Gina*. Eddie said he felt "cornered" in contributing to the score. "I went to pick Valerie up from the Burbank Airport after she had been filming up in San Francisco for a week and I saw her and she was all excited. And she said, 'Write a song to this,' and she explained the scene. As soon as I got home I started plinking on the synthesizer and came up with something. She heard it and said, 'That's perfect.' Donn and I went down and saw the dailies and it did fit. It's pretty much perfect for the scene, but the director wanted vocals."

The director soon wanted more and more out of Edward, pushing him for additional pieces and eventually asking him for a tape of ideas (which he refused to do) as well as pushing him to do the whole movie. In his response, Eddie let loose an innocent line that reflected volumes about his feeling about lead singers, and/or singers in general. "They're trying to get me to do the whole flick and I don't want to. There's too much pressure; I'm not mature enough to handle that kind of shit. I don't know how to deal with adults who want to sing."

Additionally, the tabloids were now targeting Eddie and Valerie every chance they got. They even wanted to purchase the Malibu house from Hamlisch, but an *Enquirer* story overestimating their net worth ruined their chances at getting any kind of a realistic price for the property. Every few months, one tabloid or another ran an article about the couple's relationship problems and that they were close to a split. While none of it was true, Valerie said, "If you read it often enough, or if others read it often enough and call to ask if it's true, as they did, it pollutes the air."

Alex was having his own marital problems at the same time. He had married his Valeri in June after two years of courting; however, the marriage ended in divorce only two months later.

In December of 1983, the January 1984 edition of *Hit Parader* hit the stands with a very happy looking Edward on the cover. The fan magazine proclaimed Van Halen—who had not toured for almost a year or put out any new material for a year and a half—to be America's number one rock band. This was just prior to the release of *1984*. The *Hit Parader* article was a clear example of exactly the kind of thing that the press twisted or conveniently got wrong on purpose. "Eddie VH," they wrote, "regarded by many as rock's premier guitarist, broke his hand in the midst of the group's tour, forcing them to cancel the European leg of their road jaunt." A more confused and discombobulated explanation could not possibly have been given.

CHAPTER 16
The Peak

Valerie put it bluntly when she said, "Ed was at the peak of his artistry as he worked on songs for the *1984* album."

1984 was officially released the first week of January, although the album itself features a 1983 copyright date. "Jump" was released as the first single back in mid-December, but it took a fairly slow route up the charts. However, by late February, it became the one and only Van Halen song in the band's history to hit #1 on the *Billboard* charts. It stayed #1 for a solid month.

I will never forget the first time I heard "Jump." I was out on the driveway shooting hoops when my older brother Brandon and his friend Steve pulled up in the driveway. I could already hear music coming from the car. Brandon opened up the passenger door and said, "Come here! It's the new Van Halen song!" I came over and instantly was perplexed by the synthesizer sound. Then I heard the guitar solo, which was familiar territory, and then the keyboard solo kicked in. I was amazed, in shock. Brandon and I were both giddy, but I will never forget Steve looking over at me with a smirk and saying, "I don't like it." Steve said it as if he knew he was going to have to live with it because, even if he didn't like it, he knew that everyone else would.

Again, "Jump" was written quite some time before. The song languished reportedly because Dave and Ted Templeman were both against incorporating synthesizers so heavily into Van Halen's repertoire. The building of 5150 finally gave Ed the license to record it alone with Donn's help. He said, "The first thing I did up here was 'Jump' and they [Roth and Templeman] didn't like it. I said 'Take it or leave it'; I was getting sick of their ideas of what was commercial." Furthermore, Ed claimed he was told "that people wouldn't like seeing me playing keyboards. I disagreed with that so this time around I just did it."

In 2009, Edward said that the reason he had even built his home studio in the first place was out of the driving desire to properly record the synthesizer parts for the song. An excerpt of his interview with Steve Baltin reads as follows: "It's like 'Jump': It was our only #1 single, and believe it or not I built my studio to put that song on our record 'cause everyone hated it . . . Alex and I tracked the whole thing, certain people didn't want to be a part of it . . . and all of a sudden it's like, 'Hey, yeah, great!' But it was like pulling teeth to get the person to sing the damn song. . . . But I was always up against certain people saying [about 'Jump'], 'That doesn't sound like Van Halen.' [I was told] verbatim, 'You're a guitar hero; nobody wants to see you playing keyboards.' Well, I didn't mean to ram it up their poop chute, so to speak, but it's our only #1 single. . . . It's a keyboard-based song. 'That's not Van Halen.' Well, what is Van Halen? Van Halen is whatever I write because I write all the music [*laughs*]. But I get outvoted because we are a democracy, so to speak."

On the surface, there is a simplicity to "Jump" that is universal in a way that transcends any culture around the world. But just beneath the surface is a hidden, meshed complexity that requires a critical ear to find. There are very subtle synth-note octave stretches throughout. The bridge of the song is layered with several synth lines and an arpeggiated guitar line, and the music behind the guitar solo almost defies comprehension. It almost seems to make no sense, and is of course lost to the beautiful guitar solo, but it is the epitome of the "fall down the stairs and land on your feet" Van Halen principle. When people first heard Edward's keyboard solo—and when they first saw it on MTV—they were duly impressed and immediately won over, if I may speak for a generation of American culture.

Ted was actually squeezed out for the most part for the recording of *1984*, which Ed and Donn Landee did primarily by themselves—obviously a result of the bond they had developed, particularly in building 5150. A September 1984 *Hit Parader* article chronicled an ugly episode in which Ted and Eddie actually came to physical blows. The article said: "Reports emanating from Los Angeles describe an alleged fight between Edward and the band's long-time producer Ted Templeman. Evidently Templeman . . . criticized Edward's increasingly egotistical attitude. This forced the axe-slinger to retort with verbal and physical force. . . . Ted wasn't thrilled with being left out of the recording process and . . . there was a bit of hostility on of their parts." In fact, the article said that Ted's name was included in the *1984* credits solely out of a "feeling of commitment" based on all the work they had done together in the past.

Of course, Dave relented on "Jump," wrote the lyrics and vocal melody as always, and the song skyrocketed. Dave in turn took heat for initially pooh-poohing the song, although he didn't necessarily apologize. "I don't remember from two years ago," he said, referring to the fact that the song had been in demo form since 1981 or 1982. "Maybe it wasn't right for two years ago. . . . We can't possibly put everything on the album. 'Jump' made it there eventually." Of course, without Dave's concept and lyrics, no one knows where the song may have gone. That is impossible to know. What is known as that it became more than just the number one song from the early spring of 1984; it is a song that endures, a song that will be around forever.

Dave assumed the director's chair for the song's video—a straight-ahead mock stage performance all for reputedly "$600." This was likely Dave's reaction against video like "Thriller" that cost millions to make. Whatever the actual cost, the simple idea was colorful and effective and was a huge hit in heavy rotation on MTV. Ed is seen mostly playing guitar, but there are several shots of him on keyboard (hilariously covered in studio dust). Ed smiled for almost the entire video, and even hammed it up quite a bit singing the "Jump!" refrain with good humor. Dave performed a standing back flip for the video (reversed to look like a front flip) that took him three takes to nail. Dave's overall improvement as a music video director would have him at the same helm for two more songs on the album.

"I'll Wait" was the other synthesizer-driven masterpiece of the album. The combination of Dave's dark lyrics and Ed's moody keyboard lines made for an absolutely classic rock song. No one knew it at all, much less now but especially not at the time, that Michael McDonald of The Doobie Brothers and solo fame was a co-writer on the song. The extent of his input is not known, but he is clearly listed as a co-writer in the ASCAP database. His songwriting credit has been left off of the American release of the album since the day of its first issue. The irony is that Edward was himself the uncredited guest on Nicolette Larson's debut, whereas Michael McDonald was a credited collaborator. It is likely that Templeman's Doobie Brothers connection led to this rather unlikely combination of talents. Nevertheless, the result was yet another timeless classic from the *1984* album. Dave contrasted the two keyboard-driven songs: "'I'll Wait.' Totally different feeling from something like 'Jump.' 'I'll Wait' has a very somber tone. Almost sad. But it still has a lot of torque. It gives the impression of being fast."

The *1984* Tour

The first leg of the *1984* tour concentrated on the southeast United States, kicking off on January 18 and wrapping on February 22 with an amazing twenty-six shows in just five weeks. Every single show was sold out, including a final two-night stand in Atlanta. Multiple-night stands would become common on this tour, as fans just could not possibly get enough of Van Halen.

As the tour started though, the final wedges were essentially in place between Dave and Ed. Summarizing the mood at the time, Valerie said, "Ed and Dave had basically had enough of each other. Onstage there was nothing but respect, but offstage they were like warring countries, unable to communicate." Dave continued to be bothered by the fact that Eddie had ventured out of the camp to do something as high-profile as "Beat It" and also that he had done work for Valerie's TV movie, which happened to air that January. As per his earlier comments, Dave must have felt like Eddie was now running off with bits and pieces of the scenery—that is, while the play was actually being performed, sold out, every night—on Broadway. All it took was for it to come up a few more times . . .

On tour, Ed's drinking worsened as tension behind the scenes of the band reached unbearable highs. About the *1984* tour Valerie said, "Ed had changed. He would breakdown physically, suffering headaches and stomach problems from all the fighting, and the stress and pressure he felt. Off the road, he sealed himself in the studio." He was feasting on alcohol and cocaine. Valerie could no longer keep up with his usage.

That spring, the Roth-directed video for "Panama" hit MTV. The video was an absolute classic workout of on-stage performances littered with fun little cameos of the band backstage and elsewhere. Dave's work behind the camera had come full circle. One could not flip on the channel in the spring of 1984 without seeing "Jump" and "Panama"—as well as "Beat It." The videos were run almost non-stop. "Jump" was on the radio constantly on every station: rock, pop, and even R&B (now even Van Halen was crossing over). Every single fanzine had Van Halen on the cover in one way or another; in fact there was not a single *Hit Parader* in 1984 that did not feature an article or photo spread on the band. The tour sold out at every single stop. Despite what was going on behind the scenes, Van Halen was absolutely on top of the entertainment world, period. All of the attention was fairly disconcerting for Eddie, even though one could argue it was all he ever wanted. A decade later, he noted, "When 'Jump' went number one, I was almost embarrassed."

The pace of the *1984* tour was nearing the ridiculous. The second leg, which ran thirty days from March to April, included twenty-three shows. Of note is that fact that of those shows, seven cities got two, or even three, shows: two nights in Cincinnati, two nights in Providence, two nights in Philadelphia, two nights in Landover, two straight back-to-back nights at Madison Square Garden in New York, two nights in Detroit, and three consecutive nights in a row in East Rutherford at the Meadowlands Arena. Fan demand was insatiable. The third leg was similar: from mid-April to mid-May, twenty-four dates including multiple night stands in San Francisco (three consecutive nights at the Cow Palace), Los Angeles (two nights in a row at The Forum), Phoenix (two shows), and San Diego (three nights in a row at the San Diego Sports Arena).

While on break in April, Eddie spent two nights in the studio with Brian May just jamming on three songs. Two were very offbeat Brian May compositions—something along the lines of a cheap anime cartoon's opening credits music. One other, "Blues Breaker," was a tribute to Eric Clapton. Because one song was called "Star Fleet," Brian dubbed the jam session group Star Fleet Project.

Brian May sent the "Blues Breaker" song to Eric Clapton who reportedly found the song to be not terribly bluesy. Ed was greatly disappointed. On top of that, Eddie had finally met Clapton the previous year. *Rolling Stone* reported that Edward "was so nervous that he got drunk and blew the whole thing." Later, Eddie elaborated: "I've met him, and we've talked. But he isn't really an easy guy to talk to, and I'm shy. It was just a backstage-hello kind of deal."

Can It Last?

In May, the June 1984 issue of *Musician* hit that stands. The front cover featured a smiling Edward leaning back with his head on Dave's shoulder while Dave has his back to him and his pulling a full "pose" for the shot. The prophetic title of the cover on the article was "The Oddest Couple: Can It Last?" The article that ran was at the time taken as an indication of just what incredibly disparate personalities combined to make a whole so much greater than they were as individuals and that was the magic of the band—the four different personalities. Hindsight, though, shows just how thinly veiled Ed and Dave's comments about each other were. They were interviewed separately.

Eddie was out to recast himself in a new mold of his own definition—and to shed any attachment to Dave or to the band at large and prove that he was only out to please himself and no one else. He wanted to make it clear that he was "different"—a word which he pronounced with an exaggerated American accent to the point that the interviewer, Charles M. Young, wrote the word as "diffirnt" repeatedly throughout the piece.

Young may have been the first writer to make the suggestion: "Anyone so blessed with talent—so goes the equation—is going to be equally cursed." Edward's following rant would be the subject of much debate: "It's an obsession. I'm not saying I'm better than anyone else. I'm diffirnt. I play diffirnt . . . I'm totally into . . . I'm obsessed with music. I'm selfish. I'm a sick fuck. . . . I'm not saying I'm an unsocial asshole, but I don't need humans a lot. I got my wife. I got my brother. I got my parents. I got Donn. That's it, concerning deep humans."

When people read the list, the obvious question was "What about Dave?" Ed mustered a left-handed compliment for Dave, saying "He's good. A complete motherfucker, man. Okay, so he's not an opera singer." Edward added, "Kids come because they want to live the fantasy of Dave. That image: fuck all night and get wasted. But that's Dave and not me."

For the first time on record, Ed openly questioned his songwriting arrangement with the band in terms not terribly flattering. "Ten years ago, we sat down at Dave's father's house and said, 'Well, what are we going to do if we make it?' I said, 'Split it four ways. There are four people, right?'" Edward said. "That was before we found out I'm the only one who writes. I made my own bed, so I'm sleepin' in it. It's like bein' married. You find out things about your wife later on, but you're still married, so what the fuck. I could be an asshole about it, but it would just create problems." The marriage analogy couldn't have sat too well with Valerie.

Finally, though, Ed delivered a very terse response that shocked most Van Halen fans. When asked if his mother would be offended by some of the lyrics to the songs, Edward said flatly, "I don't know what the lyrics are."

Such blatant disinterest in just exactly what it was that his musical counterpart was bringing to the table to make Van Halen what it was is as shocking now as it was then. Dave later responded in veiled jest that he didn't know how to play Ed's solos either, although it was clearly a pointed jab. On the other hand, Dave belittled the idea of building a backyard studio—one of Ed's biggest dreams. "He's got a great new studio. How many tracks is it? Nice microphones. Pretty floor. All those little pieces of wood that fit right together all the way to that big door." Dave added, "Edward adores the studio. He'll spend the rest of his life in one, I expect."

It was in this article that Edward referred to his tone as "brown." Eddie was making reference to the color of wood and comparing and contrasting the more pleasant sound of wood than the sound of metal. The more pleasing tonk of a wood block versus the harsh clank of metal pipes. Thus was born "The Brown Sound"—an oft-repeated reference to Edward's tone that he later said he regretted even saying it because every single interviewer for years would inevitably ask him to explain it over and over again.

Taking Control of MTV and America

Early that summer, the video for "Hot for Teacher" hit MTV and was an immediate, absolute instant classic; a timeless bit of rock and roll film. The character of Waldo was voiced by Phil Hartman, and the cast featured little kid look-alikes of the band members. Eddie completely played along to the point of lip syncing a line of the verse, all the way up to-or down to—participating in choreographed dance sequences with Dave out in front of Ed, Alex, and Mike. The sequence, of course, is famous for the irony of the band in smarmy suits doing ridiculous dance moves, and the fact that their choreography is off only makes the sequence that much more endearing. But how Eddie felt while dressing up for the scene was likely a whole other issue.

Ed's walk down the library tables is a legendary sequence in and of itself, forever capturing him at his coolest. The close of the video shows Eddie in a mental hospital bound in a straight jacket with his guitar leaning up against him as he gazes hypnotically at a television set. The caption reads: EDWARD VAN HALEN IS TEMPORARILY "RELAXING" IN BELLEVUE MENTAL WARD AND MAKING PROGRESS. Dave set a new standard for rock videos with "Hot for Teacher," and it joined the other two videos that remained in heavy rotation. Their profile was as high as it could possibly be.

Alex married his new girlfriend Kelly Danniels in 1984, less than a year after breaking off his marriage with Valeri. One thing that makes Kelly Danniels interesting—other than the fact that she is an intelligent, beautiful model, and *SCTV* alum—is the fact that she is the sister of Ray Danniels. Ray was high school friends with Alex Lifeson and Geddy Lee of Rush. Ray dropped out of high school right along with Alex and Geddy serving as Rush's manager from day one until this very day—Ray is the only manager Rush has ever had, since before their debut record came out in 1974. Under Ray's management, Rush has sold 40 million albums and has the third most consecutive gold or platinum album records of any rock band (trailing only The Beatles and The Rolling Stones). With Alex marrying Rush's manager's sister, Ray would later enter the picture as manager in the mid-1990s, subsequently twisting Van Halen eight ways from Sunday.

The fourth leg of the 1984 tour would end up what no one ever thought it would be—the last few shows of the original incarnation of Van Halen. Starting in early June and wrapping on July 24, the band logged an incredible thirty shows, with no less than nine cities having multiple-night stands.

On July 11, 1984, this author attended his first ever Van Halen concert obviously knowing very little that it would one of the last of a handful of shows ever played by the original line-up of the great American rock band Van Halen. [See the appendix for the full story.]

That night, something was wrong with Ed's wireless set-up, so he actually played with a guitar cable and his mobility was thus limited. Yet seeing him on stage right at the moment was truly hard to comprehend. It was almost too bizarre to be real. He played amazingly—we were one million percent blown away, our expectations completely shattered. I remember I had no idea that he played "Cathedral" on guitar rather than on a keyboard until that night. It was also astounding when he played the guitar solo for "Jump" on the keyboard so that he could simply go right into the keyboard solo. This would be the only brief window in which Ed would ever actually play the keyboard parts to "Jump" live—he would afterward simply play his guitar along with the band to pre-recorded backing tracks.

During "(Oh) Pretty Woman," I recall that the band actually broke down and had a small train wreck. Dave stopped the band cold mid-song and made a funny comment about screwing it up. Rather than booing, the crowd completely ate it up. It was blood on Superman's brow—a reassurance that they truly were human. They launched right back into the song to outrageous applause. (Years later, I had convinced myself that the "(Oh) Pretty Woman" shtick was planned—but a review of several 1984 live recordings proved me wrong.) The other highlight that I will never forget is when Dave came over right in front of us during "Ain't Talkin' 'Bout Love" and sang, "I been to the edge / There I stood and looked down / I lost a lot friends there, baby / Ain't got no time to *fuck* around . . ." I'll never forget the slight shock, which was then followed by a feeling of "We're playin' with the big boys, now!" It was practically the very next day that Mike and I started playing music together (we had both been learning guitar but never actually played together). Again, it's almost thirty years later, and Mike and I still perform together. That's how inspired we were that night.

But one of the greatest things is that my sister's friend D'Lesa was a hardcore concert photographer of the every single rock show that came to Houston. She was not a professional and she simply used your basic point-and-shoot camera. But D'Lesa had a knack for getting up close and getting incredible shots—some of which have been published in this book for the very first time ever. Amazingly, she was able to capture of photo of Edward in Houston at the Summit that night from about the third row on the right side of the stage. D'Lesa used to make collages of all of her classic concert photographs and she literally cropped this incredible photo with a pair of scissors! However, the photo remains mostly intact and captures Edward at the peak of his classic bent-leg jump shortly after the beginning of the show. In fact, based on Ed's fingering, the photo may have been snapped during "Unchained."

Edward Van Halen at the Summit in Houston, Texas in July of 1984.
Photograph © D'Lesa Plunk

The *1984* tour closed out in the U.S. with three sold-out nights in Dallas immediately following the three-night stand in Houston. Van Halen crossed paths with The Jacksons on their Victory Tour in Dallas on July 14, and Ed made a special trip over to their show at Texas Stadium to sit in on "Beat It"—his only public performance the song ever. The event was indeed captured on video. Eddie then raced over to Reunion Arena for the first of the three Dallas shows—the final U.S. shows of the tour.

The band went on to play the Monsters of Rock Festival at the Castle Donnington Raceway in Derbyshire, England on August 18, 1984. The final shows were in Stockholm on August 25; Winterthur, Switzerland on August 31; Karlsruhe, Germany on September 1; and finally Nuremberg, Germany on September 2, 1984.

That was truly it. It was the last time Edward Van Halen, David Lee Roth, Alex Van Halen, and Michael Anthony would ever perform together live on stage. Subsequently, everything finally unraveled.

CHAPTER 17
Dave Steps Aside

Over the course of the *1984* tour, on his breaks at 5150, Ed, along with Donn as his right-hand man, had been composing and recording material for Cameron Crowe's follow-up to *Fast Times at Ridgemont High*. Starring Eric Stoltz and Christopher Penn, *The Wild Life* hit the theaters in September. The opening credits list Edward Van Halen as the musical director for the film. Ed used tons of little pieces of his own music recorded at 5150 for the film, much of it would be recycled for use later on mostly during the Hagar years. Ed's touch on the film, though, was brilliant. The movie didn't fare as well at the box office as its predecessor, but it certainly has valid cult status.

The soundtrack only featured one song of Edward's from *The Wild Life*, a funky six-string bass track called "Donut City." Shortly thereafter in October, Brian May officially released the Star Fleet Project jams as an actual album. Edward had played first on Nicolette Larson's album, then on "Beat It," he recorded soundtrack music for one of Valerie's TV movies, he recorded with Brian May, and he scored a major motion picture on which he had a solo song on the soundtrack.

What had Dave done outside of Van Halen? Nothing yet. But that was about to change. At the same time Ed was working on *The Wild Life* soundtrack, Dave, along with Ted Templeman, began production on an easy-going and fun four-song EP of classic cover tunes. Dave's first solo single would be "California Girls," for which he continued to improve upon his very highly visible video production prowess (along with Dave's partner in crime, Van Halen lighting specialist and all-around key player Pete Angelus). Beach Boy Carl Wilson even contributed backing vocals on "California Girls," and Brian Wilson himself has stated openly that it is his favorite Beach Boys cover that he's heard. Dave had the idea of redoing some classic songs for a while now, and with the fall fairly wide open, he jumped right in.

In an early 1985 interview, Dave said, "I just wanted to put out some of my favorite tunes, something that had nothing to do with rock 'n' roll. The only thing that held me back before was that the band was in full swing. Once I saw the opportunity to go after it, it took me about a month to put the project together and about four or five days to actually record it." Dave also noted that Ted, Van Halen's faithful producer, was a huge driver behind the EP. "Putting together the backing team was sort of Ted's responsibility, since I'm not overly familiar with session musicians, especially the A Team of session musicians," Dave said, "so he put all the very best characters together." In addition to bringing in an actual Beach Boy, he also recruited Edgar Winter on keyboards and Christopher Cross to provide additional backing vocals.

Dave ended up approaching his *Crazy from the Heat* project as a holistic promotional vehicle—although it didn't necessarily start that way. It wasn't just singles, it wasn't just an EP, and it wasn't just videos—they were singles promoted non-stop on MTV by videos which in turn boosted EP sales. The "California Girls" video, which hit MTV in early 1985, was followed by Dave's most outrageous video yet for his version of "Just a Gigolo/I Ain't Got Nobody," which was a big budget send-up of most of his mid-80s contemporaries. This new video featured an extensive introduction before the start of the music that was extremely entertaining and very funny. Dave's image of himself as a leading video director was mirrored on the cover for the "California Girls" single—he is sitting on a beach with two video-editing machines in front of him. The single eventually went all the way to #3 on the Billboard charts.

Dave came out swinging publicity-wise—he was David Letterman's first guest of 1985 on New Year's Day. His megawatt personality was on fire. He spoke fondly of Van Halen while promoting his own album, but he lightly mocked Alex for "forgetting the concept" of the Van Halen videos.

Toxic Sessions and Selective Memory

Initially, Edward publically expressed what appeared to be great pride in Dave's solo effort. He said, "I think it's great he's actually doing it. . . . He did four cover tunes . . . yet managed to project his personality through them. . . . I've heard it all and it sounds real good. . . . I don't think he's out to prove anything. I know it will be good for him personally and his own self-satisfaction when it takes off the way I expect and hope it will. I seriously want the best for it, in the same way he'd want the best for me or Al or Mike if we did anything outside the band."

It only got more perplexing from there. Dave claimed that the only reason he made the videos for his solo record was because of the constant delays coming from the other side of the fence. In his autobiography, Dave noted that he and Ted waited endlessly on Edward. "I'm sitting with Ted Templeman outside of Ed's backyard studio for four and five days in a row . . . . We would sit on this little bench for hours waiting for Ed to pick up the phone in his bedroom, knowing he was in there but he wouldn't pick up," he said. Dave quipped, "He had been up all night working on his own version of a mix for a song or working on a tune for one of Valerie's TV movies." In fact, Ed only worked on one of Valerie's movies, and that was a full year before, so it was simply a bitter complaint from Dave based on the fact that Eddie had done so much work outside of the band. Dave's comment about working on his own mixes revealed bitterness toward Ed over the newfound control he had gained by constructing 5150. Dave also reported that "Mr. Fingers couldn't get out of bed for four days in a row." Edward had also developed a large ulcer.

Dave said that the plan all along was to reconvene Van Halen after New Year's, and they did. Ted Templeman confirmed that the new VH album was his "number one priority. All the time we were doing that EP, he kept saying, 'Whatever you do, Teddy, don't put any fucking guitars on there. I don't want this to get in the way of Van Halen.'"

Dave recalled a conversation he had early in 1985 in which Eddie, in tears, claimed that Dave never told him he was going to release "California Girls." Dave replied, "Well, yeah, I did, Ed. Why else would I spend that much money and recruit that much stellar talent?" Dave claimed Ed retorted, "Yeah, but I don't remember. . . . We don't remember you telling us about this." Dave claimed it was a case of Eddie's "selective amnesia" from heavy drinking. And Dave held the line: "I made sure—goddamn sure—that everyone knew. And I also knew that memories were short when diluted, so I repeated my plan, again, and again." Dave also holds that his solo project all fell in an interim between the end of the tour and the start of work on a new album.

The sessions at 5150 were untenable once they finally got together to start recording the follow-up to *1984*. About the material, Dave said, "The music was turning morose. Probably because of individual personal habits more than anything else." He also added, "My choice was to commit poetic felonies, wind up doing melancholy power ballads. *No way.*" As far as the actual sessions, Dave noted that "the chemistry had turned rotten. . . . The arguments became more and more vehement, loud and venomous, with threats, hands balling into fists." Dave also claims to have often asked what the timeline of the album was, only to be told repeatedly by Edward to give it a year.

This whole time, "California Girls" and "Just a Gigolo"—like the three videos from *1984*—were in heavy rotation on MTV (one even might have called it "Dave TV" at the time). Sensing an opportunity to take it to the next level, Dave started kicking around the idea of developing an Elvis-esque summer movie around the style of his five extremely successful videos. He very much wanted Van Halen to provide the music. After all, Prince had just had a smash with his *Purple Rain* film. Dave developed a loose script, but had no company backing him at all. It was still just an idea. Eddie said, "He wanted to make a movie—and he actually asked if I'd write the music for it."

But another critical issue came up yet again on the subject of touring. Edward had always thrown around the idea of touring less, and his idea was to do just two or three months of stadium shows rather than ten months of 15,000-seaters (of which they were routinely selling out three nights in a row on the *1984* tour). This was completely counter to Dave's plans, which were to keep the show on the road as per standard procedure. Dave loved life on the road while Ed was getting tired of it and wanting to spend more time with Valerie and in his new studio. In March, Dave laid it all out during an interview on French television:

> Dave: I like to dance, you know? I like to, you know, go out on the road, man, and go in front of a camera, and go in front of a microphone, go on the stage, go under the stage, I wanna be doing, you know? I says what's the pay off, he [Edward] says, "Well, we don't wanna go on the road anymore for these big six-month tours, you know, it's been five, six, seven years." You know? Like that. "We figure we'll go play stadiums in the U.S. for two-three months . . ." You know? Stadiums?! You need to get 50,000, 90,000 people in there? Yeah, you make a lot of money but you can't hear my jokes in between the songs.

> You can't see my shoes that I paid $300 for, you can't see the lights, you can't see—it's a rip-off. I mean in three months I don't even get to the right weight. You know? What's the story? I said, "You wanna do the soundtrack for the movie?" He goes, "No, the movie'll probably stink." Yeah, like the last three videos. . . . There will be a soundtrack for the movie, whether or not it will be Van Halen is really in question at this time.

Also that month, Dave went on *Good Morning America.* Kathie Lee Gifford's introduction stated: "For the last eleven years, Van Halen has been a hugely popular, yet widely unheard of band, but the year 1984 changed all of that with the album called *1984* giving the group their first #1 pop hit and directing the spotlight squarely on the flamboyant face and physique of David Lee Roth." Again, Dave spoke stridently about the band, saying, "I think Van Halen can go down to the beach with a sword in one hand and a torch in the other and still inject a sense of humor." When asked why some people are so bitter within the music industry, Dave said, "I think a lot of people enter this business with a lot of problems already. It's just they're just couched and they won't dish them—certainly won't dish them up to you in an interview. They come in with a lot of bitterness, they come in with a lot of problems, and then only compound it through drug use, drinking, the stress in terms of hours and responsibilities that are heaped upon them, or that they heap upon themselves through excess, laziness, sloth, egotism . . ."

Maybe Dave Didn't Actually Quit

In his autobiography, Dave said, "Somewhere around March, it came to a head." According to *Rolling Stone,* "[Ed] went to the singer's twenty-room mansion in Pasadena, California, to settle matters once and for all." Dave had bought his father's house from him—the house with the basement where the band's greatest tunes were born. "Ed and I hugged each other and cried at my father's house," said Dave. "I said, 'Ed, your brother is up to two six-packs a day. Maybe if we get ourselves square, down the line we can reconvene, and I would love nothing more than that.' I don't think he understood. We went our own ways." By calling out Alex's drinking, he was likely hinting to Edward that alcohol had become a real problem for the band.

Ed's version was that Dave said, "I can't work with you guys anymore. I want to do my movie. Maybe when I'm done, we'll get back together." And according to Edward, his reply was, "I ain't waiting on your ass. . . . See you later. Good luck." Ed also admitted, though, to crying and being very upset.

Valerie came home from shooting a film to find Ed "totally defeated and bleaker than I'd ever seen." According to Val, Ed said, "Dave doesn't want to come back. I don't know what the hell I'm going to do." Later Edward said that he never thought Dave would actually quit. "The things he said were so weird," Eddie said. "He asked how long the album was going to take, his attitude was, 'Hey, man, I've got better things to do, how long is it going to take?' I told him to count on about a year from starting point to album release—writing for a couple of months, recording for three months, and then all the red tape crap of mastering, album covers, T-shirts and all that. And he put it in the press like I just wanted to rot in the studio for a year."

Yet another part of Van Halen lore is that Dave announced he was leaving the band on April 1, 1985—April Fool's Day—when in fact all he did was tell *Kerrang* the familiar quote, "Eddie's not happy unless he's unhappy." The truth is that there was no real formal announcement of any kind at that time. In fact, Eddie had said the thought Dave would "wake up." The following month, on May 16, just six weeks after his last face-to-face with David, Edward sat in with the *Late Night with David Letterman* band. Letterman did a week of shows from Los Angeles—thus Eddie's presence. Eddie's hair was short—a very different look than the past seven years (he had shorn his hair after Dave departed). Edward played songs during the commercial bumpers including "(Oh) Pretty Woman," "Sunshine of Your Love," and "You Really Got Me."

This night was a triumph for Letterman as he landed Johnny Carson's first ever late night talk show turn as a guest rather than an interviewer. Immediately upon the conclusion of David's huge interview with Johnny, as Carson walked off to huge applause, Ed was poised at one of Paul Schaefer's keyboards and started "Jump" as soon as the camera hit him. After the first bar, the drums and bass came in wrong and Edward looked up with a slight scold and opened his mouths is of to say "Ahh!!!" to the other musicians. After the commercial break, Ed moved to guitar and Paul has taken over the keyboards. Edward delivered a spectacular improvised solo over the main riff of "Jump."

After Paul called the song for Dave's next segment, the crowd gave a huge ovation. Letterman said, "Very nice! Very nice! You know, Eddie—Eddie . . . you could lose those other guys. These, these are the ones." The audience claps as Ed smiles quite uncomfortably, given that the world didn't yet know what had transpired over the previous month and a half. Letterman followed that up with, "Does . . . does David get on your nerves?" Eddie laughs quite loudly and he jokingly lifts his guitar up to cover his head, but visibly nods 'uh-huh' with a smile. But he turns away and purses his lips tightly, choking back great discomfort. Letterman goes on to ask Eddie if he'll come back for the Monday show. Eddie says back, "I don't think you'll be here Monday," to which Letterman replies, "Oh yeah, that's right!"

Feeling a bit redeemed after standing on his own, Ed returned to the Letterman show the following month, the same night his wife would be on as a guest promoting her latest TV movie. The interview with Valerie was simply awkward, especially when they brought up the fact that Paul Schaffer had dated Valerie when she was sixteen—right in front of Eddie. Even though it was late June at this point, nothing at all in the interview acknowledged the fact that Van Halen was broken up or that Dave had left in any way. The only tidbit that Valerie allowed to slip was when she said, "He doesn't go out on the road any more"—a comment that was left untouched by Letterman. Edward even performed "Panama" with the Letterman band, with Paul providing the vocal line on the keyboard—which came off awkward.

Dave's departure simply didn't become public knowledge until CBS bought Dave's movie deal for $10 million and Sammy Hagar officially joined Van Halen. Personally, I only remember hearing about it through the grapevine at our local guitar shop. Sammy would ultimately make the declaration publicly from the stage in September 1985.

With Dave went the entire road crew as well as Noel Monk, the band's manager since 1979. Noel was loyal to Dave. Edward said flatly, "Noel Monk was Dave's goddamn puppet. . . . We wanted a manager that managed the band—not someone who did only what one person said." After being let go, Noel promptly filed suit against the band.

That summer, "(Oh) Pretty Woman" was featured in a prominent mall scene in the cult classic *Weird Science* starring Anthony Michael

Hall. Also, Steven Spielberg's massive summer hit *Back to the Future* had a pivotal scene that centered around Eddie himself. Marty McFly, played by Michael J. Fox, attempted to scare his 1955 father into asking his 1955 mother to the dance. To shock him from his sleep, Marty takes a Walkman and inserts a tape that says "Van Halen"—but above it to the left it says "Edward" in smaller letters. When Marty hits play, it is a sound bomb of whammy-bar dives and harmonic screams which then leads into an extremely short but incredible segment of a thundering tune he had leftover from *The Wild Life* soundtrack. Michael J. Fox also mimicked Edward's patented finger tapping during another scene. Since the movie itself was set in October of 1985 and we saw the movie in July, I myself was personally positive that it was a track from their new album that they had leaked to the film company as a tie-in. We were sure of it, yet that was simply hopeful teen logic gone awry.

CHAPTER 18
A Tabloid Marriage and a Random Phone Call

At the end of the *1984* tour, Valerie brought Eddie out to see the band Scandal led by Patty Smyth. The video for their pop-rock hit "The Warrior" was running non-stop on MTV. Patty, Valerie, and Eddie all really hit it off together, so much so that they even went on tour with the band for a few days. Ed sat in on several live songs alongside Scandal guitarist Keith Mack. But it was Patty that really caught Edward's attention.

Patty was actually pregnant at the time. She was married to musician-poet Richard Hell, and they were having a tough go at marriage. Patty, Valerie, and Eddie made a nice little team for a while, but Valerie noted that Patty and Ed "gravitated toward each other through their mutual experiences in music." Valerie admits she was naïve. "I had such trust in Patty that I had no qualms about her staying at our house with Ed when I went out of town," she said. "Likewise, he palled around with her on an occasion when he was in New York. Eventually I heard him talk about Patty did this or Patty said that or Patty likes this designer one too many times, so that I asked if anything was going on between them. He said no."

When Dave left, Patty was the first person Edward asked to replace him. Patty—at eight months pregnant—says she declined because she knew it wouldn't work, although she did have some regrets later on. Most Van Halen fans could not or would not believe it, and it wasn't published or publicized at the time at all. "It was like an urban myth, but it was true," said Patty. "It was just not the right time for me . . . I was a New Yorker, I didn't want to live in L.A. . . . and those guys were drunk and fighting all the time." Looking back, she added, "I would have liked to have done one record with him."

About Patty joining the group, Valerie said, "The other guys vetoed that idea, but it didn't end Ed's friendship with Patty. His infatuation with her seemed to intensify after she had her baby, and soon I was listening to him compare my hair and makeup to Patty's." Valerie admits that at that point she was essentially determined to even the score with Ed.

During a trip back to Shreveport to visit family, Valerie's brother Patrick took Ed and Val to see a band called Private Life led by a vivacious female lead singer. Ed took a liking to the band and offered to produce a record for them at Val's urging. In the process, Valerie developed a deliberate crush on Private Life's drummer Craig. During a band trip to Japan in August 1985, Valerie and Craig had an affair, leaving Valerie only with incredible guilt. She chose not to tell Eddie anything about it, and, as she has made a small industry out of publicizing, she turned to overeating to cope.

No Idea What to Do

Following the ill-fated and ill-advised invitation to Patty to take Dave's place, Ed's next idea was to do a project with Pete Townshend. Ultimately, that did not work out and Pete was none too pleased. "I feel really bad about that," Edward said. "I think Pete Townshend is really pissed off at me. We talked—actually he never called—but he sent telegrams. I tried calling him back, and he telegrammed to say he doesn't like to work in the States, that he wanted to work in England. That kind of threw me for a curve, because I was kind of planning to do it in the studio at home." Eddie continued, "But that wasn't the main reason. He wouldn't have been able to start until November . . . I was tired of waiting to do something. Also, here are Alex and Mike, who I love . . . I couldn't exactly just leave them out. I just hope he's not mad at me because I never got hold of him to tell him, 'Sorry, I can't do it.'"

Warner Brothers even put pressure on Ed to take some time off from the band and make a solo record of his own. Hoping that the original band would ultimately come back together, the idea was to satisfy Edward's personal musical appetite, but he was completely disinterested. "No way," he said. "If they think I'm going to experiment and futz around, doing a solo project as opposed to what I really want—just to wait and see if Roth comes back—they're off their nut."

Eddie had yet another other idea to do an album featuring several different lead singers including Joe Cocker, Phil Collins, and Mike Rutherford. "But Alex talked me out of it," he said. "He said that would just be a one-shot project, and it made me realize, yeah, I want a family, I want a solid thing." Oddly, it would take a high-end auto mechanic to bring together a new Van Halen family—rocky marriage number two.

Among the many things Ed is famous for is his car collection—a normal habit amongst the high-earning rock celebrities. He had a special penchant for Lamborghinis, and as per usual, his Lamborghini was often in the shop. His auto shop of choice was a high-end place in Van Nuys run by an Italian car dealer named Claudio Zampolli. Sammy Hagar was such a regular at the shop that Claudio was even featured in Sammy's "I Can't Drive 55" video for MTV. That summer, Edward was in Claudio's shop: "He's a friend. I hang out at his shop to talk about cars. And I told him, 'Hey, man, our singer left, he quit.' And he said, 'Hey, well, I just talked to Sammy and he's coming to town.' So he gave me Sammy's number and I called him up."

Enter Sammy Hagar

In more detail, Eddie told an interviewer in Canada: "My car broke down. OK? And it just so happens that Sammy and I both buy cars from the same dealer . . . I was bummed out, you know, my car broke down . . . *and a few other reasons*. And uh, his name's Claudio Zampolli. And he goes, 'Hey, I just spoke to Sammy today?' I go, 'Sammy Hagar?' He goes, 'Yeah!' And I told him, you know, our singer just quit the band. He goes, 'Why don't you call Sammy? Call Sammy!' I called him right there from the shop, and, um, three days later he came down. And that was it."

That one phone call changed everything. The band Van Halen, fueled by the creative friction and passion of Edward and David, took at least a ninety degree turn at that moment—if not a complete one-eighty. Sammy took the call excitedly, but decided that an up-front formal meeting was a better idea that to just dive in and play. Ed called it a business meeting. "He wanted to come down to meet us first and see what kind of condition we were in. Because he'd heard some horror stories about my being . . . way out there, a space case." Ed had relished at being a "5150"—and referred to himself and Donn both as "5150s". But he went on the defensive about him being called weird, even though he'd called himself weird and "diffirnt" quite often (not to mention "a sick fuck").

With Sammy came his manager, Ed Leffler, who would play a major role in Van Halen's career until his death, and who summarily replaced Noel Monk. When Sammy and Leffler felt assured that Van Halen was looking for a permanent member—not just a one-shot deal, they went ahead and held a jam session. Edward said, "He came down the next Monday and we jammed, and that was it. The first tune we did was 'Summer Nights.' And from then on it was just straight up. In twenty minutes we had a complete song." The music tracks for "Summer Nights" and "Good Enough" from the *5150* album were both two tracks that the band worked on with Dave just before his departure, with Ed noting that "we rehearsed [with Dave] for maybe a total of a week within a month's time."

When it came to the keyboard ballad "Dreams," Eddie said, "We never even got to work with Dave on that." It clearly was the tune that Dave had described as a "melancholy power ballad" over which he would have been forced to commit "poetic felonies." Obviously, with Dave, it surely would never have been called "Dreams," but that is clearly beside the question—Dave likely would have never agreed to work on the track. While Dave's departure was in fact a perfect storm of many years of complicated issues, the timing of the introduction of that tune with Dave's departure must certainly be included as one of those issues. It is obviously not the sole reason, but could clearly have been the back-breaking straw for Dave.

Sammy fell in immediately like a long-lost brother. Sammy Hagar is a nice guy, a friendly and honest fellow. As the lead singer of Montrose, Sammy and Ronnie Montrose couldn't get along, even while producing classic tracks like "Rock Candy" and "Bad Motor Scooter." Sammy had a fairly successful solo career and made his own videos for MTV, including the aforementioned "I Can't Drive 55" video, which was, in fact, completely in the style of Dave's video vignettes. Sammy, in effect, didn't have much to prove and entered the project as a new challenge for himself—to be a consummate band member, not for it to be the Sammy Hagar Show, or the Eddie Van Halen Show, for that matter. Ted Templeman had, in fact, even produced Sammy's 1985 album *VOA* immediately after working on Dave's *Crazy From the Heat* EP.

Edward characterized Sammy's joining the band as bit like hitting the reset button. He discredited the notion of friction causing passion by pointing out how well he and Sammy got along, saying "Sammy and I are in tune with each other . . . The theory that opposites attract is not valid in this case." Even with a few contractual obligations to settle on Sammy's part—some that would return at the worst possible times—the band forged ahead with the recording of the new record in Ed's backyard. Valerie said, "Ed became completely occupied with work. Recording of Van Halen's *5150* album filled our driveway with Lamborghinis and Ferraris and the studio with music. I enjoyed the harmonious atmosphere as the guys began referring to themselves as 'the real Van Halen' and devouring chips and beer and cigarettes all house of the day and night as if they were a troop of grown-up boy scouts."

CHAPTER 19
5150 and the War of Words

Psychologically, Ed felt so much relief. He and Sammy jammed joyously on stage on September 22, 1985 at the Farm Aid benefit concert, jamming through Zeppelin's "Rock 'n' Roll" and "Wild Thing," as well as an unaccompanied solo by Edward. The broadcast of their performance was cut part way through "Wild Thing" because of "Hagar's constant verbal obscenities" (also noted: "Hagar started joking about his dick"). What was not broadcast, though, was Sammy's announcement at the conclusion of Edward's solo that he had joined Van Halen. That was essentially the unofficial-official announcement. The September 26 edition of Rolling Stone carried the following excerpt: "Of Sammy Hagar, the man most likely to succeed Roth in Van Halen, Dave says, 'Sammy Hagar's been making good records for years, but Van Halen's been making history.'"

When Dave said, "Eddie's not happy unless he's unhappy," the timing indicates that Dave made the remark following their tearful March 1985 departure, period. Rumors during the late summer seeped everywhere, all the way down to the fan level. Shortly thereafter, the Dave bashing began. The first real remark from Edward came in the December 19, 1985 *Rolling Stone*: "Twelve years of my life . . . putting up with his bullshit." He said this well after Sammy had officially joined. Additional remarks by all of the members about Dave ventured into uncharted territory.

Alex specifically made two analogies about Sammy versus Dave. One, that original Van Halen was like a Volkswagen, and the new Van Halen was like a Porsche. Secondly, he said it was like getting a rotten tooth pulled and having it replaced with a gold filling. This was after the band came off the most successful year in their history. The new act was often fond of calling themselves "the real Van Halen." Alex said, "People know that Van Halen is now the real Van Halen; a rocking band that hasn't jumped into a volcano because Mr. Roth has left the band."

Eddie gave several interviews in which he lobbed his most pointed words. He said, "I think he started believing the attitude he was copping, the 'Hey, I'm God' syndrome. To the point where his hat wouldn't fit his head anymore." He also added, "I don't know if this is slandering Dave, but Sammy is just a better singer... Dave is kind of limited, vocally—range-wise and stuff." He said, "I'm a musician, he's a star. A musician doesn't want to go star, direct, and write his own movie. . . . Trying to live with him on tour . . . you ask anybody that's gone on tour with us and he'd yell and scream for his apple in the morning. Or ransack people's rooms for the *Playboy* somebody borrowed the night before." Edward intimated that David was jealous of Sammy Hagar. He dismissed Dave's million-plus selling EP as a novelty. He also lightly threatened, "I could write a book about the stuff that went down, and none of it had anything to do with music. The guy just did not treat anybody like a human. He was like Idi Amin or Muammar Qaddafi."

Dave stayed silent for months and months. But finally, he'd had enough and he held a press conference in Toronto in October 1986 and laid it all out:

> Just like any band—*any band*—we're having a career difference here. We're having a musical difference. And we're gonna go our own ways. And we cried, and we hugged, and we split and two weeks later I'm reading in *Rolling Stone* what an asshole I am [NOTE: The reader has to assume that Dave meant two weeks after Sammy officially joined Van Halen in September of 1985]. And how poor little Eddie was forced to spend the last twelve years of his life living a lie, like the fuckin' *National Enquirer* or something. And here comes his wife, you know, to back it up, you know [laughter from press corps]. And on and on and on. So, I stayed quiet for six months, seven months. And I'm just reading diatribe after harangue, after this, after that, you know, again and again and again. And I still believe there's no—it's not necessary to make a comparison. I don't think you have to make a choice. But Van Halen *demands* it. Van Halen is *demanding*—for some bizarre, retarded reason—for the audience to make a choice. 'You have to either love us and hate him' or vice-versa. They demand it; they demand it. *Well*, I'll rise to the challenge. If we have to have a comparison, fine—I

> eat you for breakfast, pal [laughter]. I eat you and smile. . . . I don't talk about Van Halen not once on my stage during my show and I haven't on this tour. I think we're on our 50th gig. I only started talking about Van Halen in the last several months after six, seven months of silence. And they have taken it upon themselves to attack me every single opportunity they have. I don't know, have they played here, yet? They played here? [NOTE: Van Halen played Toronto on August 18, 1986.] Then I'll bet you five bucks they made a big production of cheap, low shots—make a scapegoat. That's German mentality. You know? Just go and go and go. They've got nothing better to talk about. We're beginning to see this now. Regardless of the music, regardless of their stage direction, they've got nothing better to talk about. I do.

When he said "pal"—he was clearly referring to Edward specifically. Being Jewish, Dave's comment about "German mentality" was especially pointed. About VH's future, Dave was notably unenthusiastic. He said, "I don't know if there's a Van Halen without David Lee Roth. But I know that nobody cares about Van Halen without David Lee Roth." In the short term, it turned out that Dave was not right at all, to be sure. But in the long run, Dave would ultimately be proven right, even if it took a few decades to be vindicated.

In 1992, in a radio interview with Howard Stern, Dave ended up claiming that drug and alcohol abuse was actually the main reason he left the band. Stern asked, "The reason you left Van Halen was why?" Dave responded, "Because they were completely stoned all the time. How do you make music with someone who has a hangover or is copping a buzz on a regular basis? . . . You've got kids, right? . . . Would you like your daughter to spend any amount of time with somebody who's constantly hung over or constantly coppin' a buzz?"

Eddie's story about the details of the split suggest that Dave stopped coming to the studio, again, quite possibly after hearing the demo for what became "Dreams." "Personally I didn't know there were going to be any changes until Al, Mike and I were out here in the studio making music and Roth wasn't showing up," he said. "So we called him up and said, 'Hey, do you want to do a record or not?' And he said he wanted to do a movie. . . . But we want to make a record and go on tour." Ted also said he never saw the split coming at all, and he was essentially the fifth member of the group.

Edward told MTV, "When Dave quit the band, Alex, Mike, and I were just . . . pretty devastated, really. We were just sittin' there going, 'Now what?' You know? I mean, we've worked with the guy for eleven years, so to speak, and he just kind of, like, walked—took off." Alex added, "At that point, Ed and I didn't know what the hell we were going to do."

Edward later admitted, "I said a few things about him in the beginning, you know, that I might not have—I shouldn't have said. But . . . I was bummed out. I was pissed." He also confessed to saying things in anger that warranted an apology. He also directly addressed his feelings when Dave left that day in March. "I cried, I was bummed . . . I slagged him in the press because I was pissed and I was hurt. The thing was, Dave is a very creative guy and working with him was no problem. It was living with the guy. And that's what I meant by all the years of putting up with his bullshit. I didn't mean musically. But, boy, it just freaked me out. He left us hanging." But with Sammy, "This will still be the Van Halen band," Edward said, jokingly adding, "Even though we're still going to do everything my way!"

Recording *5150*

Edward's individual guitar talents were recognized on November 13, 1985 when he was inducted as a member of the Rock Walk outside of the original Guitar Center on Sunset. For Ed, the honor was extremely special as he was inducted right alongside Les Paul—the father of the electric guitar (Ed and Les would eventually form a genuine friendship). A photo of the event shows a beaming Edward with he and Les each with one hand in the other's cemented hand prints in the sidewalk. That same month, recording began on the album *5150*.

Ted Templeman would not be around for this record at all. He instead went to produce Roth's album, *Eat 'Em and Smile* (CBS was bought out and Dave's movie deal was axed, so he formed a supergroup with guitarist Steve Vai, bassist Billy Sheehan, and drummer Greg Bissonette). Donn and Ed would do the engineering and producing themselves, until Warner Brothers brought in Mick Jones of Foreigner to help. Jones noted that Edward and Alex were "going through a particularly charged emotional relationship at the time, and there were some crazy situations that went on there." According to Sammy Hagar, "When they were both drinking, they'd fight at least once a week. I mean, go at it. Fistfights. Mike and I would try to pull them apart." He continued, "The next day we'd come to the studio, the windshield would be busted out of the car, the trash can turned over." Sammy also noted that when they brothers screamed at each other in Dutch when they did not want anyone to know exactly what they were saying to each other.

With Ted out of the picture, *5150* would have a drastically different sonic quality than albums one through six. The change in the sound can only be described as less live sounding—the crux of their previous approach—and far more polished and slick. Audiophiles would describe the new sound as "compressed" and "chorusy" (as in similar to the sound of typical stereo chorus guitar pedal). Ed himself described it as "a little more polished, a little shinier." [The technical root of this sound change was Ed running a single guitar track through an Evantide harmonizer detuned to 98 which in turn created a simulated double-tracked guitar sound.]

As per usual, the record company was a never-ending source of headaches of Edward. Lenny Waronker of Warner Brothers strongly urged Eddie and the band to adopt a new moniker and retire the Van Halen brand name. Incredulous, Ed and Al flatly refused the bizarre suggestion and turned to focus on writing and recording.

During the midst of the recording of *5150*, Edward and Valerie began to try to have a child. She became pregnant in January 1986 and she and Eddie were ecstatic. Horribly, Valerie would miscarry just two months later in March. "I went through the necessary procedures, and, at home, Ed brought me tea and soup while I recuperated in bed. He was sweet and tender." Awfully, though, her upbringing led her to be wracked with illogical guilt. She said, "I was convinced that God had taken the baby as punishment for my affair in Japan."

Shortly thereafter, Valerie had her first ever asthma attack, and Eddie rushed her to the emergency room. The same thing would happen a few weeks later. Valerie described herself as "choking emotionally." It was also upon one of these return trips to the emergency room that she angrily told a lurking reporter inquiring about her pregnancy status, "No, I'm not pregnant. I just had a miscarriage. Thanks for asking."

Edward was already occupied with the release of *5150*, which hit in March, the same month as her miscarriage. In just three weeks, the album was the first ever Van Halen record to hit number one on the album charts (*1984* had been perennially blocked at #2 by *Thriller*, of course on which Ed also appeared). Edward felt completely vindicated. *5150* was a record on which he felt he had complete control over the music and that he was the most satisfied with. Ted Templeman said, "Frankly, I think they did a better job without me. They made a pop record. They picked up a new audience that they didn't have before." Three songs, though, were new territory—sometimes predominantly musically, and sometimes predominantly lyrically. Just these three songs would create the division between party lines that fueled untold millions of musical arguments for years to come.

Pop Power Ballads Are, in Fact, a Major Shift in Direction

The first single off of the new album was the not-terribly-tough titled "Why Can't This Be Love?" A completely keyboard-driven tune, the song is considered a pure pop song by most music critics. The basis of the song, for example, revolves around a very common progression in popular music—C-A-F-G—which is most well known as the progression for the classic piano duet "Heart and Soul." These four chords have been used repeatedly throughout pop music history. Additionally, Edward's main keyboard melody line is purposefully simplistic—not quite approaching the complexity of "Jump" or "I'll Wait."

But the biggest change made clear by the first single was the lyrics provided by Sammy Hagar. "Why Can't This Be Love?" was essentially about a guy declaring that his love for his girl was so strong that he dared her to contemplate why what they had couldn't possibly be love. This song, and a subsequent multitude of Hagar-penned songs, did not poetically leave much to the imagination ("It's got what it takes / So, tell me why can't this be love? / Straight from the heart / Oh, tell me why can't this be love?"). This was a *gigantic* change in Van Halen's music, which made the subsequent label "New Halen" applicable—but the phrase most often used to describe the sound was, without argument, "Van Hagar."

The songs "Dreams" and "Love Walks In" only further cemented the serious change in direction. Just as Ed had worked with pop specialist Michael McDonald on "I'll Wait," Mick Jones helped work on writing and arranging "Dreams" with him and Sammy (Jones was fresh off his own quite sensitive hit, Foreigner's "I Wanna Know What Love Is"). The lyrics to "Love Walks In" suggest that love is possibly nothing more than some divine being—possibly an alien from outer space—simply pulling a string and dropping love into someone's life at random. That's what love is all about. Some of the lines include "There she stands in a silken gown, silver lights shining down / And then you sense a change, nothing feels the same / All your dreams are strange, love comes walkin' in." Dave had foresight—he knew the only thing that would fit over such keyboard-laden soft rock chord progressions would be "poetic felonies."

"Dreams" said, "Baby, dry your eyes / Save all the tears you've cried / 'Cause that's what dreams are made of." Lyrically laughable, and at best incoherent. Yet there I was, fourteen years old, singing out those trite lyrics with all my heart. I was an adolescent and fell for it hook, line, and sinker. And the truth is that *Edward* was my hero. My youthful lack of ability to process cognitive dissonance disallowed me from believing that Van Halen Mach II wasn't all it was cracked up to be, even though there was no badassery in those lyrics—there was no fun in those lyrics—there was no sense of humor in those lyrics. The words were either so direct that reflection was simply not necessary or so disjointed to the point of being nonsensical.

Edward's old decision to turn over the lyrical responsibilities for his music 100 percent to someone else had been a huge sacrifice of control. Dave took the job very seriously. He pulled out witty and original classic and timeless lines, including simple quips like "I don't feel tardy" and "One break . . . coming up!" His lines left room for the listener to fill in the gaps in their own imagination. A classic song like "Panama," the listener isn't always exactly sure if he's talking about a girl, or a car, or the country Panama—there was some guesswork left there, and everyone loved it.

In his place was a lyricist without a sense of genuine innuendo or mystery. Sammy's lyrics were what-you-hear-is-what-you-get. *People* even said Sammy's VOA was for "rock fans that don't demand a whole lot of subtlety." Clearly though, his approach appealed to a great many unsophisticated, young American rock fans, which at the time included me, my brother, and all of our friends.

The *5150* album opens with "Good Enough" with Sammy belting out "Hellooooooo, baby!" Sammy obviously did this as a nod to The Big Bopper and his classic "Chantilly Lace," but that was completely lost on anyone under 35 at the time. Instead, it was Sammy's big introduction to the fans. "Good Enough" was already in progress with Dave, and it succeeded musically. Ed even pulled out one of his oldest unique tunings by dropping his low E to a low A—this gave the music a very heavy groove. The music for "Good Enough" and the title track "5150" was proof that Ed was, for the most part, still at the top of his game musically.

CHAPTER 20
Van Hagar Hits the Road

The *5150* tour started in late March in Valerie's hometown of Shreveport. There were a few warm-up gigs scheduled, but those were canceled while Edward, Donn, and Mick Jones finished mixing the album. On the way to rehearsal for the tour one day, Eddie ran into Dave in traffic. "I saw this black Mercedes, I pull up to it, and I'm going, 'Goddamn, that sure looks like Dave's car.' And it was. I honked and waved." He said Dave gave him the cold shoulder. "His classic look," said Edward. "It's like he basically flipped me off. I thought he would at least wave and say hi, you know? He didn't roll down his window. He looked at me and drove off."

The first shows with Sammy were very well-received and clearly helped lift the sales of *5150*. By mid-April, the album was #1. The band celebrated to commemorate the occasion. *Guitar Player* writers Bud Scoppa and Billy Cioffi stated that "the boys in the band attribute a lot of those sales to mere consumer curiosity." Another important aspect to remember is that the backing vocals provided by Edward and Michael still sounded the same, and the guitar, bass, and drums were still the same. So most fans were satisfied that they still heard enough essential aspects of the Van Halen sound—especially the guitar solos—to swallow it.

One of the most bizarre aspects of the early *5150* tour shows was rampant Dave bashing both from the crowd and from the stage. Fans brought spray-painted bed sheets emblazoned with "Dave Sucks" and "No Daves Allowed" and "David Lee Who?" During a May stop in Pittsburgh, Sammy brought up a kid out of the audience to sing "Jump." As per a *Rolling Stone* article: "Hagar ushers him offstage to a standing ovation and turns to a video camera in the photo pit that is recording all the action. 'See that, Dave?' he shouts at the camera, furiously poking his finger at the lens. 'That guy sings the song better than you!'"

Apparently, there was a line crossed there, and Edward took Sammy to task. "When he brought the guy up to sing 'Jump,' he said, 'That was actually better than the other guy.'" A band meeting was held after the show and Sammy was told to tone it down. "We all said, 'Come on, you don't have to go that far,'" said Eddie.

The shows were selling out, and they were even pulling two-night stands in several cities through the summer, and even some three-night stands as during the *1984* tour. In July, the new incarnation of Van Halen played three nights in a row at the Forum in Los Angeles, their first hometown appearance with Sam.

However, in May, during a string of shows in Michigan, Eddie and Alex received word that their father Jan had had a heart attack. Valerie said, "Ed's face turned gray." Ed, Valerie, and Alex took a private jet straight to Los Angeles and raced to the hospital. The heart attack had been severe and was worsened by Jan's non-stop drinking and smoking. His chances for recovery were slim and Valerie noted that "he was in and out of the hospital for seven months."

The tour continued through the summer and this author had one hell of a life experience the weekend of July 19, 1986 [see the appendix for the full story]. Me, two of my best friends, Dave and Chris, my brother Brandon, and his friend Gary all went to Dallas for the annual Texxas Jam. These festival shows at the Cotton Bowl were absolutely legendary. Van Halen had played several, including their first tour, and Sammy had the distinction of being the artist to play the festival the most times. The bill was Keel, BTO, Krokus, Loverboy, Dio, and Van Halen. We were only about thirty yards from the stage when Dio ended, so we figured we were in great shape for Van Halen's set.

We weren't. During the wait for VH to take the stage, the crowd surge was beyond what three 14-year-olds between eighth and ninth grade could handle, so we bailed back to the side sections near the stage, leaving Brandon and Gary, plenty capable of taking care of themselves. Dave, Chris, and I all ended up with great seats right at the bottom of the nearest seated section on Ed's side of the stage. We had an incredible view when the band took the stage.

The band was honestly on fire and had the crowd of 72,000 in the palms of their hands. It was easy to tell that it wasn't just an ordinary night for the band. Ten, fifteen, twenty-thousand people adoring you—that's amazing. But tens of thousands lighters going at the same time is a whole other thing. The electricity was incredible. I was transfixed by Ed's solo. He played Beethoven's "Fur Elise" with both hands on the fret board.

Ed Still Can't Stop Slagging Dave

The tour introduced entirely new elements into the Van Halen stage show, most notably Sammy Hagar taking on guitar duties while Ed played keys. They also jammed together on Sammy's tunes "There's Only One Way to Rock" and "I Can't Drive 55." The inclusion of Sammy Hagar solo tunes in a Van Halen set caught some by surprise. But acknowledging that Van Halen's audience had inherited a lot of Hagar fans, Eddie said, "I think Sammy's fans would be disappointed if we didn't play it ["I Can't Drive 55"]."

That July, Roth released his first full-length album, *Eat 'Em and Smile*—the title of which came from his retort to the challenge Van Halen laid out for him. Mr. Roth did not to do too shabbily. The album went to #4 and sold a million copies by September. Dave led fans down the trail that Van Halen had left off, where as the Van Hagar incarnation clearly went more pop. And Dave was back in the director's chair for his videos. Although his movie deal had fallen through, he ended up with two videos from his album that went into heavy rotation on MTV. Van Halen on the other hand made the deliberate decision not to compete with Roth on the video front.

Eddie slagged Dave's album, saying he "pasted together a junior Van Halen." In response, Dave said Eddie was an excellent guitar player but "a shitty human being." Edward's retort was almost exactly the same, verbiage and all: "I mean, hey, the guy's creative, okay? But he's a lousy human being." Eddie had also gotten over the pain of Dave's departure he once deemed "cruel", and was now calling it "a blessing in disguise." He added, "When we get nominated for a Grammy and win, I'm going to thank him. I'm serious."

In early August, at the Hard Rock Café in Los Angeles, the band held a celebration party for *5150* going double-platinum. MTV covered the party, the voice-over saying, "Eddie gave us his impression of a former bandmate [Eddie proceeded to bend over and shake his ass at the camera, immaturely mocking Roth] and gave MTV the Van Halen philosophy." Edward, bleary-eyed and obviously quite intoxicated, slurred the nonsensical line, "Whatever you do, where ever you go, there you are."

Dave made an appearance for an interview with Joan Rivers for her brief run on the late night talk show circuit:

Joan: What about the feud with Van Halen? Is that real? They have big banner at all their concerts that says 'Screw David Lee Roth' . . .

Dave: I don't know, there's been a battle raging on back and forth between myself and Van Halen. And I shook Edward Van Halen's hand over a year and half ago, we both had a tear in our eye and said, "We have a career—a musical difference like all bands—like *all* bands—and then several weeks later, I'm reading how he was forced to survive, to live a lie, you know. Twelve years after Maserati, after Rolex, after Lamborghini . . . and on and on, you know? And now it's reached proportions of a little bit comical proportions, so I just figure, 'Fellas—you keep on raining, and I'll still be the parade.'

"Pa" Passes Away

Van Halen's August 22, 1986 show in New Haven was filmed and released as the video *Live Without a Net*—the band's first ever official live release of any kind. On September 29, the band returned to Texas for another show at the Summit, which my brother and all of our friends attended. Still just fourteen, I remember very clearly seeing a banner that said "Drop Dead Dave"—a play off of "Drop Dead Legs" from *1984*. There was something about that that bothered me. Van Halen hadn't even been making records for a decade yet. They had seven albums at the time—six with Dave and one with Sammy. I loved *5150* at the time, but I also worshipped the six with Dave. Even at such a young age, the apparent dismissal of those first six albums from any source absolutely did not feel right.

Our seats weren't great, but one friend and I were determined to get as close as possible during Eddie's solo. There were two empty seats just ten rows from Ed's side of the stage. I watched his solo from just twenty-five feet away. I can only describe it as akin to a religious experience.

The night after the Houston show, the band played in Fort Worth. During the show, someone threw an 8x10 photo of Dave on stage that said "David Lee Who?" on the back of the photo. Sammy picked up the photo, went over to Eddie and borrowed his lighter. Sammy then lit the picture on fire. It would be unbelievable if there wasn't photographic evidence to back it up, but sadly there is.

The tour continued on through early November, wrapping with an astonishing four-night stand at the Cow Palace in San Francisco. Unfortunately, Jan's health had seriously deteriorated. After the tour, Eddie and Alex had the opportunity to spend some quality time with their father, but sadly, he died that December at the age of 66. Ed and Al went to 5150 and played together for reportedly ten hours straight. Dave, who had been a great admirer of Jan and who had personally recruited Jan for "Big Bad Bill," put the big feud on hold and called Edward to console him and express his grief.

One of Jan's last wishes for his sons was that they quit drinking before they encounter the same alcohol-related health issues he had brought upon himself via his addiction. Valerie said, "When the doctor made a point of saying that alcohol had contributed to Mr. Van Halen's weakened health, my thoughts had naturally turned to Ed and his health. After his father's death, every day seemed to become more and more of a battle." She noted that Ed had "retreated to his comfort zones: work and alcohol." In another interview with *Redbook*, she said, "He [Edward] doesn't abuse me, but he hurts himself . . . He's got a problem I'm not happy with, but I bring stability to his life." In her autobiography, Valerie said, "After his dad's passing, I think he relied more heavily on alcohol than before, even compared with the bust-up with Dave."

CHAPTER 21
A Spiral Begins to Take Shape

In early 1987, after the conclusion of the successful *5150* tour, the entire band was interviewed by Leeza Gibbons for *Entertainment Tonight*. Leeza didn't exactly give Edward or the band the softball interview they were probably hoping for. After Sammy went on a diatribe about how it's okay for all of the guys in the band to be married—including Sammy himself, who was married for eighteen years at that point in time—Gibbons asked if that policy was not that way when Roth was in the band. A flustered Edward started to answer but abandoned the question, saying he just didn't want to talk about it.

Gibbons, likely not intentionally, absolutely incensed Edward during the interview:

> Leeza Gibbons: With this last album, it seems that Van Halen has been able to really broaden its audience and reach more of a, more of a pop audience.
>
> EVH: What do you mean by "pop audience"?! [NOTE: Edward became visibly angry and removed his sunglasses.] . . . To me, you know, pop, if you make good music and more people like it all the sudden you're pop?! You know? If you're a punk band and nobody buys your records then you're cool, or something, I don't know. I don't get it, you know? As soon as you start selling a lot of records, you're pop. . . .
>
> Leeza Gibbons: You don't see any change in the music?
>
> EVH: Oh sure, there's change in the music. If we kept doing the same thing, you know, why not just buy our previous record? Why buy the new one if it's not different?

It's not clear why Edward would get so defensive about the use of the word "pop" in describing specifically the songs "Why Can't This Be Love?," "Dreams," and "Love Walks In." They are not thrash metal or country or smooth jazz. "Why Can't This Be Love?," as analyzed, uses a very common chord progression in pop music. To deny that that song was in fact a pop song is a confusing aspect of Edward's perspective. It certainly wasn't "Unchained."

He didn't soften his position on the semantics. The following year, in an interview with Alan di Perna for *Keyboard World* magazine, an otherwise soft interview turned as follows:

> ADP: The synth work on *5150* tends to be on the more pop-oriented songs.
>
> EVH: I hate that term. If a song sound good and people like it, all of a sudden it's pop. What do you mean by pop? I don't understand.
>
> ADP: Van Halen's more pop-oriented songs are different melodically.
>
> EVH: They're better melodically, that's all.
>
> ADP: They're perhaps less riff-oriented; based more on chord progressions.
>
> EVH: Yeah . . . well . . . to me they just sound better.
>
> ADP: You don't make a distinction between the more metal side of what you do and the more pop side?
>
> EVH: No, it's all rock and roll to me. . . . I'm not into labeling anything. It's all music to me. . . . Like the Sex Pistols. They were a band just learning how to play their instruments. And people called that punk. But if you listen to it, it's just a bad rock and roll band. . . . Punk would be bad, rock and roll would be good, pop is better—if you want to put it that way. Pop is something more people can hum along to and enjoy. Like a Christmas carol or something, is that pop?
>
> ADP: Based on sales, yes.

First Attempt to Get Help

In February, Valerie hosted *Saturday Night Live*, and Edward was a musical guest, as a solo artist, and performed with G.E. Smith and the *SNL* house band. They played an instrumental called "Stompin' 8H" in reference to the NBC studio in which the show is filmed. Valerie and Eddie actually appeared together in a skit together called "Dinner with the Van Halens" in which Kevin Nealon, Dana Carvey, and Dennis Miller played roadies securing a restaurant table for the couple. Ed was clearly out his element during the relatively weak skit and appeared uncomfortable. During the news segment of that episode of *SNL*—knowing that many a VH fan would be watching—Dana Carvey parodied Roth in an unflattering manner.

Shortly thereafter, Valerie was walking out to see Ed in the studio when she stopped short and overheard him on the phone saying that "he wanted out of the marriage." Valerie was sure it was Patty Smyth. Patty, however, has continually denied any romantic involvement with Edward and said she was only trying to help him get sober. However, her eavesdropping led to their first separation. Valerie said, "I stayed in the house, and he moved into the studio and wherever else he landed. To be honest, I don't really know where he went, but it wasn't like I'd seen him that much before." The separation lasted only three weeks.

Valerie then got extremely serious. "I insisted that Ed get rid of his coke dealer and quit drinking. Period. As I told everyone—and this was justified—I worried that Ed was going to kill himself with these habits." Alex had finally quit drinking permanently in April of that year, and taking some inspiration, Valerie staged a formal intervention. It was ugly, but it worked and Ed checked into the Betty Ford clinic for thirty days—his first attempt at rehabilitation. Valerie was stressed beyond belief and slipped and had a wine cooler before going to visit Ed in rehab. When he asked if it was alcohol he smelled on her breath, riddled with guilt, she had to lie and told him no.

Sadly, Eddie immediately relapsed. Lamenting his failure and recalling his father, he said, "I tried to quit for him. I tried to do it for my wife. I tried to do it for my brother. And it didn't do any good for me. After I got out of Betty Ford, I immediately went on drinking binge and I got fucking drunk-driving ticket on my motorcycle." Ed later said, "I got one drunk-driving ticket ever, and I was on my motorcycle leaving an AA meeting. I'd just had it up to here with everyone's shit and stopped at a bar for a couple of shots." However, Ed did manage to get back on a decent track and worked earnestly with Sammy on his solo album that he owed Geffen.

Working on Sammy's Album

They worked in both Los Angeles and in Mill Valley north of San Francisco. Valerie drove up to spend some time with Ed but she ended up by herself most of the time as Ed and Sam worked away on the record. While doing Sammy's solo record, Ed contributed the bass line to the title track of the god-awful Sylvester Stallone arm-wrestling vehicle *Winner Takes It All.* Sammy is even seen in the video arm-wrestling Stallone.

When initially asked about Sammy's album, Ed insisted that he would only produce and that he would not play even a single instrument. Before going headlong into the project, Edward said, "If I write and play, it would sort of sound like Van Halen. And it's not a Van Halen record. I don't want anyone to have the impression that it is." Ultimately, Eddie played bass on all the tracks, as well as a small piece of uncredited guitar work, and contributed backing vocals.

Not being a bass player, it was an odd role for Ed to assume, but on the surface it is clearly a power-balance act. Sammy surely had his best interest in mind working with Ed as a team, as a duo, rather than Sam working all alone. The producers on the album are listed as "Sammy Hagar & Edward Van Halen." Both appeared on the cover of the October 1987 issue of *Guitar Player*—Eddie almost humorously holding a bass while gesturing toward a screaming, leaping Hagar. For Michael Anthony, it must have felt like Ed's attitude was "anyone can play the bass."

The recording of the album took ten days. Two of the songs, "Give to Live" and "Eagles Fly," made their way into Van Halen's live set on their next tour; both were pure power ballads. Originally untitled, an MTV contest was drummed up allowing a fan to name the album. Ultimately, the album was titled *I Never Said Goodbye*—as if in reference to his fanbase. It also reflects a willingly ignorant naiveté that he'd be with Van Halen forever given the ups and downs with Roth. Possibly, it was a gesture of good faith on his part. Ed, along with Al and Mike, appeared in the video for the song "Hands and Knees," although the video did not get much airplay. My brother Brandon bought the *I Never Said Goodbye* cassette the day it came out and listened to it non-stop. It was part of his soundtrack of 1987, no question about it.

Sammy's solo record for Geffen was also timed in such a way that there would be no competing Van Halen/Warner Brothers product in the market. "We *definitely* didn't want a Van Halen record out there while his record was too," Edward said. "People would really go, 'Huh? What, is he in Van Halen or what, now? Who's gonna be the *next* singer?'"

About this time, the band's admiration of Hank Williams, Jr. led to the country singer calling out the band by name in his song "Young Country." Waylon Jennings is shown singing the line "We like ol' Waylon," followed by Hank Jr.'s declaring "And we know Van Halen!" That line was followed by a brief, mock tapping section. The entire band was featured in another of Hank's corny videos, "My Name Is Bocephus." A short-haired Ed stole the show at the end of the bit by getting so into miming the track's guitar solo that he fell down on his back on the stage pretending to wail away on his Kramer.

Rebuilding and Relapsing

With Sammy's project out of the way, Eddie finally turned his focus to writing and recording the next Van Halen record, one that would be important in psychologically validating his work with Hagar, and one that could not rely on curiosity buyers. There was tension between Valerie and Edward as the making of the new album loomed. "At first, his sobriety lightened the mood at home," she said, "but as time passed, I saw it get more difficult for him, and I remember having the sense of walking on eggshells. I also remember knowing that the question wasn't will he stay sober but how long will he stay sober?"

At that time, Eddie and Valerie had gone ahead with plans to build a new, much larger, much nicer house on their estate—a 9,000 square-foot dream house. The construction started in 1986 would take four years. It was a never-ending source of headaches for them. Valerie said, "Entire shopping centers are built faster than our house." Edward said, "The thing's taking twice as long as it was supposed to, and it's costing six times as much!" They found respite in Colorado that winter, beginning what would become an annual ritual vacationing in Aspen.

"By spring Ed was drinking again," said Valerie. She was partially satisfied that he kept his drinking at a moderate level, but she said, "I was really pissed off and frustrated. We couldn't seem to break out of the same old patterns." In April of 1988, Ed and Val retreated to the Fiji Islands for an attempt at a romantic adventure to celebrate their seventh anniversary. Valerie called it "the eight-day getaway honeymoon we never took." At one point, in this remote paradise, they were being serenaded at dinner by a group of musicians. One recognized Ed, gave him a smile, and attempted to do finger tapping on a beat up acoustic. Ed confirmed that it was the weirdest place he had ever encountered his own music. They enjoyed their stay, although Valerie was still fostering anger about Eddie's drinking, so much so, in fact, that upon their return from Fiji, Ed woke up in the middle of the night with severe vomiting. Valerie's response was to ask, "What the fuck did you take this time?!" Turned out Edward had contracted dengue fever in Fiji and ended up hospitalized for three days, his temperature at times reputedly reaching 105 degrees.

CHAPTER 22
Who Ate What

Work on next Van Halen album began in September of 1987 and was not completed until the following April. Ted Templeman's relationship with Edward was far too strained to consider using him to help with the recording. In the end, no one helped at all on the album which was exclusively produced by Eddie and Donn themselves. Ed stayed sober as recording started, but lapsed about half-way through production.

Musically, Ed returned to his well and pulled two tracks back from *The Wild Life* soundtrack, one of which became "A.F.U./Naturally Wired" and the other the keyboard-driven "Feels So Good." All in all, the overall batch of tracks reflects a continuing softening of Van Halen's once edgy sound and image. Certainly, Edward was no longer in his early twenties, and at the age of 32 it was obviously natural for him to write music that sounded less like barely restrained reckless abandon and more subdued. "Feels So Good" was one of those tracks, which in fact was not liked by either Alex or Michael for going so far down the pop-rock road. And in the vain of the ballads of *5150*, out came another doozey.

"When It's Love" was a piano and keyboard driven power-ballad that was pure Journey. Ian Christie, author of *The Van Halen Saga*, referred to the record and its featured ballad as "an album of prom themes." "When It's Love" is so far musically from what made Edward's songwriting and playing exciting as to give one pause. Just like "Why Can't This Be Love?," "When It's Love" used a familiar chord progression in pop music, and, again, Sammy's poetic felonies warrant a life sentence in songwriter's hell. The refrain repeated "How do I know when it's love?" asked by the backing voices with Sammy answering as the wise sage, "I can't tell you, but it lasts forever." The technique is repeated for the line "How do you feel when it's love?" to which Sam answers, "It's just something you feel together." Things like Metallica and some other heavier bands started to become more appealing—I can certainly attest to that by my own observations of the sheer numbers of jean jacket back patches worn at school. Edward cannot be blamed for writing the lyrics but only for letting them pass.

During the recording, *Guitar World* interviewed Edward at his studio. Writer Bud Scoppa rubbed Edward the wrong way by suggesting that Van Halen's sound was now "more polished"—in reference to both the synthesizer aspects of the new album and to *5150*'s "Why Can't This Be Love?." Eddie defensively snapped, "It's more pop-popular right? If more people like it, it's pop, right? What's wrong with that? I would love to have written a Christmas carol. What's wrong with that?" When Scoppa wondered if Ed would share any of his "secrets," the interview turned openly contentious:

> EVH: There ain't—not that I know of. What do you mean? What kind of secrets?
>
> Scoppa: I don't know. If there was a secret to it and you could unlock it for people, they still wouldn't be able to play it like you do.
>
> EVH: I already explained to you how I came up with the idea of how to *do* it, and I just *did* it. . . .
>
> Scoppa: I [met] you once before, but it was wholly different circumstances, and you seemed like a regular guy to me at the time—
>
> EVH: Oh, and I'm not now?
>
> Scoppa: Gimme a chance, for chrissakes! There's such an intense interest in you . . . How do you deal with that? . . .
>
> EVH: Maybe I *don't* deal with it . . .

When Scoppa returned a few days later to listen to rough cuts with Donn, Ed happened upon the writer running his tape recorder while listening to tracks. "Hey, what's this?" Eddie said. Scoppa deadpanned, "I'm makin' a bootleg . . . Actually, I forgot to turn it off." Eddie said, "Hey, you'll get yer free CD soon enough." Then he took Scoppa's tape machine, rewound it to the top of where the music started, and ensured that the tape was eaten up with conversation. Scoppa wrote, "Fair enough, Ed."

Eddie wanted to title the new album simply *Rock 'n' Roll.* He said, "That's what it is. It ain't heavy metal, it's not hard rock—it's rock 'n' roll." In his interview with Scoppa, he said, "I dunno why in that press release they put *OU812.* Probably Ed Leffler just thought, since that was the latest one we bounced off of him, that's the one we decided on. *Rock 'n' Roll*—I think that's classic."

Oh, You Ate One . . . I Get It

In the end, the album was called *OU812* as a direct retort to Dave's album title *Eat 'Em and Smile.* The "oh, you ate one, too" acronym had been around for years, and Sammy was the one that actually brought the title to the table. The fact that Edward agreed to go along with the title is a shame as it became a permanent symbol of the childlike name-calling and feuding that had gone on with Dave. He'd already told the press Dave was a lousy human being, that he was like Idi Amin, that he had a limited vocal range, that he put together a junior Van Halen—but it's one thing to put spout it off during an outpouring of honest conversation with an interviewer, and quite another to permanently cement the feud via the official title of a Van Halen album.

Just a few months earlier, Dave released his second solo album *Skyscraper* (production was credited to "David Lee Roth & Steve Vai"). Just before VH slagged him with their album title, Dave recorded a plaintive and reminiscent tune called "Damn Good." An excerpt of the words shows it was clearly an open-letter to Edward:

> Those were good times, damn good times
> Hey, take a look at this picture! Can you believe that was you?
> And who's that standin' there in the corner? Not me! Ahh, the crazy things we used to do

The mixing of the album continued right up to April, until the last possible minute. It was sign that something was possibly amiss. Nevertheless, the album was released in May and two weeks later became the second Van Halen album to go to #1 on the *Billboard* charts with Sammy on vocals. The success of the album is attributable to the band's extremely loyal fanbase at the time, but the album was immediately deemed below par for Van Halen standards—and not for just the songwriting and lyrics either.

All one has to do is bring up *OU812* on a standard sound system and put it up against any of the previous albums and you immediately notice a major lack of well-rounded fidelity. Ted's absence was obvious. Ed and Donn had done their best, but even Eddie later admitted, "Sonically it was shit." Ian Christie noted that the guitar level was "largely subdued" the bass so low that it was "as if the band was trying to hide its animal impulses," that is to say, to purposefully try and sound more mature. Michael Anthony let loose on the record down the line, saying "I probably didn't even have to play on that album. . . . Because of the production, you could barely hear any bass."

The opener, "Mine All Mine," was an attempt at serious political reflection, a first for Van Halen. Unfortunately, it comes off lyrically like a junior high school essay attempt at tackling world affairs. "You've got Allah in the East / You've got Jesus in the West / Christ, what's a man to do?" asks Sammy. Bringing religion and world politics into Van Halen's music just absolutely does not work—then or now or at any time. Van Halen is not U2. Reportedly, Sammy agonized over the words, going through revision after revision with Donn until Donn simply put his head down on the console while Sammy tracked his vocals. Upon completion, Donn told Sammy it was his best work ever. All producers are forced to lie to their artists at one point or another just to keep their spirits up.

The lyrics were printed inside the album cover, something that was never done when Dave was in the band. The song "Source of Infection" clearly showed that that was not a great idea:

> Hey! Alright! Woo!
> How 'bout 'cha now, come on!
> Oh yeah! Dig it! That's right
> Is everybody ready? Let's go!

The music itself is actually incredibly similar to "Hot For Teacher," utilizing the same familiar shuffle-style beat with incredible guitar solos and even an extended tapping intro to match. As a 16-year-old, my focus was still on Edward and his guitar playing. It wasn't until a friend of mine actually said to me, "Did you read the lyrics for 'Source of Infection'?" I actually hadn't, and we looked at them together and I'll never forget his comment: "If those are the words, why would you print them in the album?" By now, the cognitive dissonance was really growing inside me—and obviously, lots of other fans of the band and of Edward's.

Another *OU812* track would eventually lead the band into a business venture south of the border. Sammy owned a condo in Cabo San Lucas, Mexico where he frequently vacationed soaking up the sun and the beach. He penned "Cabo Wabo," an ode to the easy-going, fun-loving, beach-bumming paradise. Critic Chris Willman of the *L.A. Times* took aim at the song, his comparison mirroring my own contention that Sammy writes "what you hear is what you get" lyrics. "Roth might have turned the paradise resort of 'Cabo Wabo'—where there are 'pretty girls coming by the dozens' ready to 'make love in the sea'—into a parody of male fantasy," he said. "But with Hagar it's just male fantasy." Musically, it's a strong track from Ed; the solo could arguably his best since *1984*.

One night, while Ed and Sam were both staying at their Malibu homes only two doors down, Eddie knocked on Sammy's back door at 2am and asked him to come down. Sam was on the verge of getting amorous with his wife and told Ed it was too late. Eddie said, "The old lady kicked me out. Come on, man, let me in." Sammy wouldn't let Eddie in because he was smoking, so they sat on his deck and Edward showed Sam a fun and different type of song for VH—a blues and country mix that became "Finish What Ya Started." Featuring nothing but finger-picking and "chickin' pickin'" by Edward, Sammy contributed an acoustic guitar track. Musically, it is fresh and fun. Lyrically, it is of course juvenile (Sammy's ode to "blue balls"—or "unfulfilled sex" as he referred to it). While recording the tune, Eddie recalled how Alex played alone in the main room while he, Sammy, and Mike played to him from the other side of the studio glass. "Sammy and I were in here direct, and Mike was in here, too, playin'. So we three are standing here wavin', goin', 'Hey Al, havin' fun out there?'"

Lyrically, there was nothing nearly as biological to match "Black and Blue." The foundation of the song is a groovy, funky, dirty riff with amazing dynamics between Ed, Mike, and Alex. But on an album that took a shot at determining when your relationship has indeed reached the status of love, as well as pontificating upon world affairs, "Black and Blue" would stand out on *any* album as some of the most corny and immature lyrics ever recorded. Sammy Hagar penned the lines: "The wetter the better (the harder the better) / Do it 'til we're black and blue!" It wasn't even blush-worthy. It was banal. And "Sucker in a 3-Piece" was yet another great riff ruined by juvenile, sexist lyrics. The irony of such graphic, low-brow words in the same forty-minute swath as confused politics and trite notions of true love was enough to catch the attention of *Good Morning America*, who read the lyrics to both songs on the air—raising the specter of Steve Allen reading the lyric sheet to "Bee Bop-a Lula." Author Ian Christie noted, "The would-be censors raised an interesting point—why Van Halen would go to the trouble to make music designed to rock the masses and then dent their commercial appeal with blatantly artless songs about fucking." In 2011, Sammy admitted, "The songs were not my best stuff lyrically. 'Black and Blue' . . . the lyrics were a little too eighties." Also, Sammy addressed the "Source of Infection" lyrics upon reflection only with the word "ugh."

Just before the album came out, Ed addressed some personal issues for the first time ever, really, in *Rolling Stone*. Acknowledging his stay at Betty Ford, Eddie said, "You reach a certain age where you just can't party as hard as you used to. . . . I've cut back on the booze, and I'm starting a workout program."

Keyboard World?

In July 1988, Edward appeared on two magazine covers at the same time. His *Guitar World* cover story was the contentious one with Bud Scoppa. The subhead "What Next?" on the cover wasn't particularly positive. But his image on the cover of the premier issue of *Keyboard World* was definitely different. The cover read: "The Big Switch? Edward Van Halen: The Making of a Keyboard Hero." In the article, Eddie said, "I was so deep into getting a sound out of these things that I totally forgot about playing guitar. Sammy, Al, and Mike said, 'Hey! We need some guitar tunes too you know!' Because I had written four songs for the album—all on keyboards. I tend to go a little overboard when I dive into keyboards. I get tunnel vision and forget about guitar."

One bizarre tidbit out of the *Keyboard World* article concerned the storeroom at 5150. Writer Alan di Perna called the room "a true equipment arsenal. It also houses Eddie's guitar collection—which is even more extensive than his keyboard collection—*and* his guns. He picks up an Uzi and holds it out with fatherly pride. 'Y' into guns? This one's a bad motherfucker.'"

Evidence of the impact Edward's new songwriting, keyboard, and production work showed up in the form of Billy Joel that spring. Joel approached Edward to produce his upcoming album *Storm Front.* Ian Christie noted, "Drinking excessively, disorganized, and overwhelmed by Van Halen's plans for a major summer tour, Eddie turned down the piano man."

Also, in July, Ed gave one of his most revealing and direct interviews ever to Steve Pond of *Rolling Stone.* He said, "I started working out about a month ago. I've been trying to clean up my act, you know, stop drinkin' and everything. I went to Betty Ford and the whole bullshit, because it worked for my brother. He's been sober a year in April. . . . My dad died a year ago December, from drinking, and he asked if we'd stop drinking and shit, and partying, and I tried to do it for him." He also said his hospital stay for dengue fever had a pretty serious impact on him. "That kinda made me look at things a little different, imagining being there for an OD or alcohol, like my dad died from."

He said that he had been sober for twenty days at the time of the interview and that he was starting to feel better. "The last ten years of my life, I don't think I've been truly sober. I probably had half a heat going round the clock, all the time. I'd wake up, crack open a beer before I'd eat anything. . . . But if my brother can do it, I should be able to do it." Valerie said, "He was never a mean person, but he's gotten nicer . . ." For all of their well-known alcohol antics, Eddie claimed that Sammy and Michael Anthony weren't really even drinkers. "They're not alcoholics, let's put it that way," he said. "Alex and I are. We come from an alcoholic background and everything. We've got that X factor."

OU812 was dedicated to Jan, the liner notes including "This one's for you, Pa." The tour to support the album would be monstrous, literally.

CHAPTER 23
Monsters On the Road Again

When I first heard "Cabo Wabo" and the line "I've been to Rome / Dallas, Texas / Man, I thought I'd seen it all"—I immediately *knew* that Sammy was referring to their triumphant Texxas Jam show I had attended in the summer of 1986. Turned out I was right. Van Halen's manager Ed Leffler teamed up with Texxas Jam promoter Louis Messina to take the Texxas Jam on the road and deliver it to the rest of the country.

The tour name, Monsters of Rock, was taken straight from the spate of similar festivals in Europe (and elsewhere), one of which Van Halen played in England at the very end of the *1984* tour. This was also the resurrection of the old idea to tour by playing stadiums, and therefore fewer dates. The lineup was the Led Zeppelin clone band of the day Kingdom Come, Metallica (on pace to a meteoric rise), Dokken (on pace to disaster), The Scorpions (the same Scorps you'd always gotten and you'd always get), and headlined by VH. The scope of the tour was enormous and the shows would last an exhausting nine and a half hours each. The *L.A. Times* called it "one of the most ambitious concert packages ever mounted." Running from May to July, it included twenty-seven dates in twenty-two different cities.

The show came to Houston on July 2, 1988, and, of course, my brother and all of our friends were there. It was a scorching hot Texas afternoon, and Rice Stadium was filled to the upper decks. To appease Texans, the show was co-billed as an unofficial Texxas Jam (the very last Texxas Jam was held the following year—after that, it was gone forever). The Scorpions played just before Van Halen. I suppose I felt a certain excitement during their set because of the 2,000 times I had watched The US Festival video from 1983 when The Scorpions immediately opened for Van Halen.

Now that I was sixteen, my testosterone-fueled buddies and I were tall enough and strong enough to brave the stadium floor and nothing was going to stop me from getting as close I possibly could to the stage on Ed's side. We pushed, shoved, and cursed our way to within twenty to thirty yards of the stage directly in front of Eddie. Any further and we'd have been crushed.

The band came out slamming and played a great set—no P.A. problems. However, I will never, ever forget the look on Eddie's face when one of his sequencers nearly failed. It was a first for Van Halen to play to recorded tracks—Edward had partly abandoned playing keyboards onstage live and nearly all of the keyboard and synthesizer lines were sequenced in. During one song, the sequencer cut out for at least five full seconds. Because of the fact that I watched Edward the whole time, I saw his face the moment it cut—he went from a smile to sheer horror in microseconds. Since Al was wearing headphones to play along with the track, Ed turned to him to give him that "What the hell do we do?!" look, and right about the same moment, the sequencer kicked back in in perfect time, as in it was only briefly muted and didn't skip or start over. The band continued on and Ed looked back toward the audience after shaking his head in disbelief and giving the "Whew!" expression. Technology has its drawbacks.

I don't recall Sammy's voice having any problems at all, but the next night in Dallas, his voice was 100% completely gone and he could not perform. Without forethought, Sammy announced from the stage that the band would come back and play a free show in Dallas to make it up to the fans. "We cut the show short, and the brothers went nuclear on me afterward," said Sammy. "They crucified me for that. It was three years before we made good."

Honoring Les, and Taking a Break

During a break following the three-month Monsters tour, Edward paid tribute to Les Paul on August 18 along some other musical big wigs. Ed and Les had by now formed a genuine friendship—a humble apprentice and an equally humble master. Les's presentation of Edward went as follows:

> Les: What are you doing here?
>
> EVH: It's just a goddamn honor to be here. I wanna ask you a question. That little black box you have—yeah, yeah,

yeah—where can *I* get one? [NOTE: The "little black box" was the very first ever magnetic tape echo device]

Les: [Riotous laughter] Listen, that was in 1944. Now a lot of time has gone by since 1944-1988 . . .

EVH: I wasn't even alive yet!

Les: Yeah—your old man was just thinkin' about it, right?

EVH: Yeah! [laughs]

Les: Here it is, 1988, I would like to go down and sit in the front row and watch what you got to do now. And you've changed things a lot.

EVH: I just want to say one thing. That without the things that you have done, I couldn't do half the things that I can do—now—including, the echo stuff . . .

Les: Well, forget your married life . . .

EVH: No, no, no . . . ! [much laughter] Hey, we wouldn't be able to make records like we do if you didn't invent multi-track recording.

Les: Thank you, thank you. [Ed kisses him on the cheek for a second time]

Eddie—go get 'em!

Playing a Kramer, Ed performed a brilliant unaccompanied solo that started out with sound effects before he launched into "Cathedral"—which of course he would not be able to perform without an Echoplex device or similar pedal which Les laid the groundwork for. Edward then wrapped it up with a killer, and totally revamped instrumental version of "Hot For Teacher" with Jan Hammer on synth, Tony Levin on bass, and Bill Bruford on drums. After the performance, Les returned to the stage with Edward saying, "See what this guy started!" Les replied, "Fantastic . . . fantastic. And the people love you. Thank you very much—Eddie Van Halen, everyone!"

For the second leg of the *OU812* tour, the band played smaller venues as per usual from late September 1988 to early February 1989, wrapping with a short string of shows in Japan and Hawaii. For the opening act, they brought along Ed's pet project band Private Life out of Shreveport.

When VH returned to Texas, they only played El Paso and Austin, so we did not get a chance to see them a second time that tour.

At the behest of Sammy, who specifically requested an extended amount of time off, the band entered their longest hiatus period of their career thus far and would not enter the studio again until March 1990 and would not perform a concert until August 1991.

During the break in mid-1990, Edward indulged his increasing love of golf when he played the T.J. Martell Rock 'n Charity tournament. His playing partners were his golf instructor Ron Del Barrio, Steve Lukather, and Motley Crue drummer Tommy Lee. Ron christened them the "alcoholic foursome." "The way we played, it should have been called the Jägermeister Celebrity Open," said Ron. "Eddie says he doesn't remember that day. I believe him."

That year, my band members were all juniors in high school, and, as usual, the school talent show was our biggest show of the year. Proving my devotion, we played "A.F.U."—note for note (video exists). However, the shift away from Edward as the premier guitarist of the day resulted in me being specifically targeted at school. In my Spanish class one day in eleventh grade, someone actually left a note on my desk for me to find when I got to class written on behalf of the other big guitar player at school. This guy was as good as Yngwe Malmsteen—and I am 100% serious when I say that. Turns out he was actually cool and had nothing to do with it. We ended up becoming friends and actually performed some Metallica songs together doing all those crazy tandem guitar lines.

The note on my desk said things like "Eddie Van Halen sucks" and "You can't play shit without a stupid whammy bar" and "Yngwe Malmsteen and Tony MacAlpine blow Van Halen away," as well as "You suck!" for good measure. Good lord, I was pissed. I'm not a big guy per se—and was certainly not a very big teenager—but I wanted to find out who wrote the letter and absolutely let them have it. I brought it home and showed all of my friends. But they all completely laughed it off and essentially told me to take it as a compliment, and to screw that—Edward was the king and those other guys were jokers. And of course, just like any ridiculous nonsense like that, it always has the opposite effect—I never wanted anything to do with guitarists like those bozos and it only strengthened my devotion to Ed and Van Halen and learning and performing their material to the best of my ability. I suppose I won out in the end. As a graduating senior, I was voted "Most Likely to Become a Rock Star."

CHAPTER 24
Filling Time and Getting Help

One of the first things Edward did during his time off in 1989 was to double the size of 5150. Having recorded three million-selling-plus albums there, he proceeded to knock out walls, add an isolated drum room, replace most of the equipment, and even added on a little pinball arcade. To match his personal style, he had a golf cart customized with red, white, and black stripes for getting back and forth between the studio and the main house.

Always having feared he'd be discovered by the city for his "racquetball court," Los Angeles mayor Tom Bradley called Edward on the phone one day. Apparently, an outfit known as the Hollywood Association of Recording Professionals had called for a crackdown on home studios, claiming they were hurting their business and that fidelity of recorded music was ultimately suffering. Turns out the mayor had called to hold Ed up as an example to counter the complaint and would thus not have to go about enforcing the zoning ordinance. Edward does not rent his studio out to anyone. "I like keeping it all to myself," he said. "I don't want people recording in here, putting a mojo on the vibe." According to author Ian Christie: "For his celebrity testimony in this political squabble, he was given the proper zoning variance to legally make music at his house"—thereby acknowledging that the other three albums were recorded "illegally."

Things for Valerie were not going well that spring, and she decided to take drastic measures to get her weight under control. She went to the Pritkin Center which, according to Valerie, is "the Santa Monica weight-loss clinic you checked in and ate three low-calorie meals a day based on the famous Pritkin low-fat, high-fiber diet." Following a return trip from Aspen, Valerie checked in and Eddie went with her, suggesting that he might stop drinking again as well to show support. She said, "My hopes were dashed when I saw him bring a six-pack of Schlitz into the room." In April, Ed was pictured in *Rolling Stone* with a cigarette between his teeth standing alongside a cross-eyed Billy Idol. Ed was referred to as "Idol's biker pal."

However, Valerie said that it was a good period for them overall. The video for "Finish What Ya Started" won an MTV award, and they were nominated for three American Music Awards in the categories Favorite Heavy Metal/Hard Rock Artist, Favorite Pop/Rock Band/Duo/Group, and Favorite Heavy Metal/Hard Rock Album. Although they didn't win an AMA, the nominations were certainly nice (even though Ed likely bristled at the "heavy metal" tag). MTV even asked the band to give a go at its *Unplugged* series. Noting they were not an acoustic band, they denied the offer.

While watching Ed onstage accept the MTV award, Val reflected, "Well done. He'd worked hard, made great music, and earned the accolades. I hoped he found satisfaction in it. Such moments sometimes didn't register with workaholics like Ed."

Near the close of 1989, Ed was interviewed by *Guitar World* and was named their Player of the Decade. The studio and the house were both still under construction. When asked what his wildest printable touring memory was, he named the Sheraton incident on the second tour. When asked what his favorite *unprintable* touring memory was, Edward said, "The chicks, man. The chicks on the road. That first and second year—oh, God, man! I can't . . . [breaks down in laughter]!"

Valerie dove back into commercial television with the sitcom *Sydney* that started production that September. The following month, reflecting his growing interest in charity work, Eddie and Michael Anthony participated in the First Annual World Music Invitational Pro/Am Celebrity Golf Tournament in Dallas. In mid-November, Ed and Valerie were spotted out at the Roxy attending a gig by Steve Stevens' Atomic Playboys.

Worst. New Year's Eve. Ever.

However, the stress of her marriage, her weight, and her television show was too much for Valerie and she suffered yet another asthma attack in mid-December. To make things worse, she subsequently scalded herself with soup and had to return to the hospital for treatment of third-degree burns. On top of all of that, she noted that Ed had started drinking excessively yet again. On New Year's Eve, Edward and Valerie went to celebrate the evening at the beach house in Malibu with her parents. In her autobiography, Valerie said:

> Ed was drinking Jagermeisters and getting progressively drunker and angrier for no apparent reason. Pissed off at everyone, he decided that he wanted to leave. Everyone knew that he was too wasted to drive—everyone, that is, except for Ed. As he got up, I grabbed the car keys, and the two of us tussled as he tried to pry them from my hands. My dad stepped forward and yelled at Ed to take his hands off of me.
>
> "Daddy, I'm OK," I said.
>
> "Stop it, Ed," my dad ordered.
>
> "Daddy, he's not hurting me," I said. "Don't worry about it. I'm just going to hide the keys."

As she was attempting to do away with the keys, Edward suddenly lunged for them violently and Valerie's father Luke—who had boxing experience—clocked Edward directly to the side of his face. After things settled down, Ed went to blow his nose and, and according to Valerie, "the whole side of his face blew up. His cheekbone was cracked." She took him to the emergency room. Upon hearing of the altercation, the doctor assured Edward that his face would be fine, but said, "You might want to check yourself in someplace and get help."

On January 1, 1990, Edward once again checked himself into a rehabilitation facility, this time for twenty-eight days. With work on *Sydney*, Valerie was struggling with being an actress in a sitcom during the day and trying to save her husband and her marriage at night. After shooting, she would drive to the hospital to spend time with him. She said, "On Wednesday nights . . . I sped to the hospital for couples group. I would constantly check my watch on those nights, because I couldn't be late." She even started attending Al-Anon meetings which she could not stand. She said, "Supposedly anonymous, there was nothing anonymous about those meetings for me, and I feared people would talk about Ed and me. After a couple of meetings, I stopped going."

As soon as Eddie checked out of rehab, Valerie checked herself in to Overeater's Anonymous (OA). She said, "Looking back, it's so transparent: I really wanted help controlling my life, not my weight. But the OA meetings were beneficial. I related to them much better than Al-Anon, perhaps because they were about me and my problems rather than Ed and his."

Making great strides in his battle with alcoholism, Valerie began feeling more emotionally connected to Ed as she had in a long time. She said, "The proof was in the bedroom. We made love more over a month than we had in the past year." Blowing whatever potential sex hype befitting such a high-profile couple, Valerie said, "Ed was a tender, caring lover. That's what made it so painful when he we was off in his own world."

For Valerie's thirtieth birthday in April, Eddie bought her a white Jaguar XJE. Knowing that her favorite car of all time, though, was a Chevy Nova, Ed followed up by delivering one to her shortly thereafter. According to Valerie, "It was bright orange and all tricked out." Ed was there for her when the network pulled the plug on *Sydney* during the filming of its thirteenth episode in May.

Valerie decided that she and Ed needed a new project. She said, "This one involves diapers, cribs, and formula. I figured we'd gone through the tough parts of marriage, a miscarriage, so why not finally get to the good stuff and have a baby? He agreed. It was time for us to start a family."

CHAPTER 25
One on the Way

The band's joint business venture—the Cabo Wabo Cantina—was opened on April 22, 1990 with a loosey-goosey performance by the group from the club's small stage. The opening was pushed by MTV with a contest and full weekend coverage called "Viva Van Halen Saturday." It was an important media coup for the band that had been inactive for over a year.

The MTV feature was at best lightly funded and showed the band hanging out on the beach and Ed in white overalls rolling through town on an ATV. Ed rocked his classic Kramer on stage for the show and sweat his ass off. Sammy performed with a drink in his hand. There is an excellent clip of the band sitting around in the town square with Eddie cranking through "Cabo Wabo" on an Ovation acoustic guitar. Sammy starts with the lyrics, "*I've been to Rome!*" Ed retorts, "Hey! When have you been to Rome?" Sammy replies, "About 1982. *And Dallas, Texas!*" "OK, Dallas, I know. We've played Dallas," Ed joked.

There are a few hard and fast rules in business, one being "Don't go into business with your friends." For all its initial grandiose glory, the club became a financial disaster far before its eventual long-term success, and Edward and the others eventually sold their shares to Sammy giving him full ownership. This would eventually become amongst the absolute sorest of subjects in the band's history.

Andy Johns Teams Up with Ed

Around March, work actually started on the new album—their third with Sammy Hagar. By 1990, Hagar had been in Van Halen technically for five years, and the original Van Halen's reign following the release of the first album was roughly seven years (although they were technically together for twelve years). With the revamped 5150 studio ready to go, apparently having learned his lesson on *OU812*, Edward solicited legendary Led Zeppelin producer Andy Johns to help engineer and produce. He was going to make damn sure the album was going to *sound* good. Musically, it would be a much more experimental record than the previous two.

In an interview, Eddie said they hoped to enjoy the luxury of being able to come up with a stockpile of material and release it when they were ready, which would have been a first for the band had that actually happened. "With *5150*, you know, everyone was wondering what was going on with Van Halen so we released it," Ed said. "And with *OU812*, we were already committed to the Monsters of Rock tour before the record was even done. We would have preferred to finish the record, put it out, waited a bit, made sure we liked the record, and then booked a tour. That's what we're going to do this time." However, it would turn out Ed had too much on his hands to create a body of material from which to cull new music.

Eddie's relationship with Andy was an important one. Not only did they get along on a professional level, but on a very personal one as well. Andy wanted to bring in a second engineer but Ed told him straight out that the studio was too small. He came alone and on the first day just spent time setting up microphones and getting to know each other. "What I really appreciated about Andy was that he gave me space when I needed to develop an idea," Edward said.

Donn wouldn't be around for this one. "We weren't unhappy with Donn," Eddie said, "but we've done eight records with him and felt it would be nice to get a different spin on things. It wasn't any big deal." Ed said that the band spoke with him about wanting to get a different sound for this album—which is a practical no-brainer considering the fidelity of *OU812*. However, during the discussion, Donn replied, "If you want something else, get someone else." Edward later said of *OU812*, "In hindsight, I wouldn't mind re-recording it."

In comparing Donn and Andy, Edward said, "This is kind of a touchy subject. In the old days, Donn Landee kind of monopolized 5150. He was the only one who really knew how to run anything. It was his gig, so he was very protective and didn't want anyone else touching the knobs. Andy is just the opposite. He showed me how to run the console and seemed more than happy to receive my input. It was a real relief to finally know my way around . . ." Although Edward was certainly a grown man, Andy had a fair amount to do with Edward resuming his drinking around the end of the year.

When Ed first contacted Andy and got him on the phone, it happened to be Andy's birthday. He was smashed and said he'd call back the next day, and he did. About Andy's personality and propensities, Edward said, "He sounded like Dudley Moore in *Arthur*. . . . Andy is so rock and roll it's ridiculous. We're pretty stiff competition in that area, and he makes us look like lightweights."

The Best News He Ever Got

In May, Ed and Valerie caught Madonna's show at the Forum and Sinead O'Connor's performance the following week. That June, the two traveled to Big Sur, and then to Mississippi for Edward's business meeting with Peavey. When they checked into the hotel in Mississippi, Val let Ed know that there was some work to be done. "I was obsessive about keeping track of when I was ovulating," she said. "You could set your clock by me. During those months, Ed learned more about a woman's reproductive system than he ever cared to know." By the end of June, their new project was proving successful. Valerie was pregnant.

"At home, I jumped up on Ed and gave him a big hug," she said. "He was over the moon—as he should have been." She openly counted the blessings of their careers, their dream house and studio, and now a child. Valerie said, "I hoped Ed would be able to use that as motivation to keep healthy. It seemed he might. In the early stages of my pregnancy, he was nearly as excited as I was and pretty much stayed off the booze." At first, Valerie struggled with nausea and even lost some weight, but she bounced back and was soon healthily pregnant. Later in October, she recalled that she and Eddie caught *Phantom of the Opera* and had a romantic dinner afterward. "Driving home, I rested my hand atop Ed's as he navigated the dark roads," Valerie said. "He turned up the music on the stereo to make sure the baby inside me could hear it. . . . It seemed like we might have finally got our life together in gear."

Build *His* Guitar and Amp

Ed had another baby on his hands—a newly designed guitar done in conjunction with Ernie Ball. He was ready to move on from his Kramer endorsement and wanted to design a unique sounding two-pickup electric guitar. Edward struck up a relationship with "Biff" Sterling Ball, first on the development of 5150 brand electric guitar strings. Biff in turn approached Eddie about designing a guitar. Ed had two qualifications: he wanted a company that worked out of the U.S. and one that wouldn't put out the guitar until he had recorded and toured with it first. For the design of the body, Edward said, "I wanted to get away from the whole Strat thing. I wanted my own body. I sat there and drew up things and had Dudley Gimpel computerize it. We collaborated on the whole thing and felt that it looked good."

To get the guitar neck exactly right, Eddie said they simply copied the neck shape from his original Frankenstein neck. "We took measurements and built the neck. It wasn't quite right and finally said, let's digitize the thing and find out what's going on." What they ended up doing adapting an ergonomic approach based on how Ed's hand's had naturally shaped the neck over years and years of hard playing. Prototypes of the Ernie Ball Music Man—or Edward Van Halen guitar—were built in January 1990. Ed first saw the guitars in April and worked with the company until November before he was satisfied with the final working model of the guitar. He introduced the guitar at the National Association of Music Merchants (NAMM) convention and production began in 1991. The print ads for the guitar said, "I endorsed the guitar I used to play. I designed this one . . . Big difference.—Edward Van Halen." Production was limited to only 1,000 per year and they sold for $1,600.

As for the Peavey venture, Edward said, "Hartley Peavey flew me down to his factory in Medirian, Mississippi, with the intention of getting me to use one of his guitars. I told him I didn't need a guitar, but it would be cool if they could design an amp for me. They agreed." Peavey flew engineer James Brown out to California to work with Ed for a few weeks. "He'd tinker away, then ask me what I thought. 'I'd say, 'That's not quite it, how about adding another tube.' And so on." Edward said. The research and development of a new amplifier was something that he took extremely serious. And with all of the technical, scientific equipment at his disposal, the only thing Ed used as a point of reference for the development of the amp was his own ear.

The real question a lot of purists were asking was why he would change from his classic Marshall set-up. "I'm not sure whether it's that my tastes have changed or if the amp has changed, but I think that my Marshall is starting to fade—it just doesn't sound like it used to," Edward said. "Even Donn Landee started noticing it. So I guess it was time to start looking elsewhere."

Recording the Album with the Dirty Title

Once Andy was finally in the studio, he basically set up the microphones for the drums in the brand new isolated drum room at 5150. While it is a niche category for sure, if there is a single person on earth that is the absolute greatest at knowing just exactly how to tune and position drums and set up microphones in the most exact, precise, optimum way, it is Andy Johns. *Led Zeppelin IV* . . . and dozens of other masterpieces. Alex played along with the "live out your Zeppelin fantasy" and played purposefully as Bonham-esque as possible on the tracks. The studio was outfitted with a brand new, warm-sounding mixing board as well.

Just as Andy was possibly the greatest rock engineer of all time, he noticed that something in Edward that few others had. Andy said, "Eddie has this part of his brain which you would call semi-genius. He recognizes things very quickly that would take you or I some time to ponder on, or someone would have to show us, or we would have to go to school." The truth is, there's no such thing as semi-genius any more than there is semi-pregnant or semi-dead. In fact, Nuno Bettencourt of Extreme was featured in a column called "In the Listening Room" in *Guitar for the Practicing Musician* in March 1992. His one-word first response to "Unchained" was simply "Genius?" He added, "Whoever just thinks he was a solo player and only inspired a generation to solo missed the whole light on what Eddie's all about."

Once they had Ed's guitar set up, there was just one problem. He hadn't prepared, written, or salvaged a single song. At the end of the day, Edward said, "The guys were asking me, 'Hey, Ed, you got any licks?' I said, a little panicky, "Hell no! Give me . . . uh . . . give me until *tomorrow*." So he plunged in deep overnight and came up with the first track that became "Judgment Day." The song only truly came together after extended jamming in the studio.

And so it went, one song at a time, exactly like *Diver Down*. One difference, though, was that *Diver Down* was recorded in about two weeks. The album that became known as *For Unlawful Carnal Knowledge* would take a year to record. However, another difference is that this album would have an incredible variety of instruments, instrumentation, effects, and recording techniques. "The whole record was done one song at a time," Ed said. "We'd completely finish one track before moving on to the next one. That's why there are so many textures on this record."

The first song on the album, "Poundcake," featured one of Ed's most interesting experiments yet. Ed's guitar tech Matt Bruck was using a drill when Edward had a brainstorm and noticed that the drill channeled through the pickups at a specific tone. As Ed's assistant, Bruck said, "Working for Ed is great because he's a fine human being and he cuts right to the bone. There's no bullshit. He's also a great role model, because if Edward doesn't have a 'tude, no one should have one."

About the experiment, Ed said, "The motor of the drill got picked up by my guitar pickup just like a microphone. I turned my volume on and it sounded like kick starting your engine. . . . It was just a goofball little thing." What's more though, is that instead of just using it as a stage gimmick, Ed actually played off of the tone that the drill produced, almost like playing two instruments at once.

My lifelong friend and bandmate Mike and I were in college in Austin when the album came out in mid-1991. We were returning from playing an indoor soccer game when we heard "Poundcake" on the radio. I remember wondering what that crazy effect sound was—another "How in the hell did he do that?!" moment. I just thought the sound was huge, although a little compressed and chorusy like the other Hagar albums.

The artistry of Ed's music, once again, was sullied by juvenile lyrics. There's innuendo, and then there's tragic, failed attempts at innuendo. "Poundcake" is the latter. One could go through the song line by line and attempt to find a nugget or two of a hint of something that might suggest something along the lines of genuine love for your partner, but the refrain "I sure love my baby's poundcake" is as blunt and disposable a line ever penned. It's because of that that "Poundcake" doesn't have the timelessness its music deserves—Sammy's contribution was the bad apple in the barrel that spoiled the whole bunch.

The rest of the album followed the same pattern. Ed came up with amazing licks and riffs using a Danelectro six-string bass for "Spanked" only for the song to be ruined by lyrics about 1-900 sex numbers. Two phrases that don't go together: timeless and classic, and "Call me up on the spank line." Even Sam's attempt at capturing the irony of having to pay to born and pay to be die (via the funeral, etc.) was completely marred by the title "In 'n Out." It is a sexual play on words any way you look at it, and reading the title on the back of the album titled *For Unlawful Carnal Knowledge* was enough to make even the most diehard devotee of the band just roll their eyes.

Drinking before Lamaze

In mid-November, the house was finally finished, all but the electricity, but Ed and Val moved in anyway. Valerie said, "It looked magnificent, like a fairy tale castle, and I was ready for my fairy tale to begin." The house was incredible, but at first they felt like it might have been a bit too much. Valerie said they couldn't even shout across the house to each other—they had to use the phone.

That Thanksgiving would be far more pleasant that the last family holiday gathering. The Van Halens and the Bertinellis all came together for dinner at the new house. There was a combination of Indonesian and Italian food cooked and served to accommodate everyone's heritage. Valerie said that with everyone there and football blaring on the television, it finally felt like home.

Yet, Valerie recalled that Ed went back to drinking approximately "three-quarters of the way through" her pregnancy, which would put it right around the end of 1990 or early 1991. While Andy Johns was no doubt a contributing factor, it was just a simple fact of falling back into old habits, a more and more familiar pattern. In January 1991, Ed and Val were taking Lamaze classes prepping for Wolfie's birth, and Eddie was showing up with alcohol on his breath. "(He was) behaving in ways that drew stares from the other couples. Those sessions could be horribly embarrassing." Ed tried to keep her happy with jewelry and other presents, but Valerie said "I would have traded all of that for a sober week of his time."

Finishing the Album with the Dirty Title

In the studio, Sammy said, "Andy Johns was a disaster. With Al sober, Eddie needed a new partner in crime and that was Andy." He claimed that Andy was intoxicated almost perpetually, and Eddie eventually ended up getting trashed along with him. So Ted Templeman re-entered the picture.

Ted arrived in January, and as Eddie said, "He cracked the whip and pulled everything together." Ed admitted that between himself, Andy, Alex, and Michael, they could've spent years experimenting without ever finding a stopping point. Ted was a "very organized cat," as per Eddie, "he came in to save the day." Ted rarely grants interviews out of his belief that producers should remain behind the scenes, but offered one up to *Guitar World* that year. After years apart, Ted said, "It was a little awkward, in the beginning, because it was a new studio environment. But in terms of the band, it's like we'd never parted." As far as his role on the album, Ted said that Edward and Andy had built the car, and that he just painted and polished it.

Sammy insists that he brought Ted in himself after Andy accidentally erased one of Sammy's vocal takes. "That was it," said Sam. "I wasn't working with the guy anymore. I stormed out of the studio." Ted ended up doing all of the vocals with Sammy, and Ted had the final word on the mix of the album.

One track on the album would be called "316"—named for the date of Wolfie's birth. The beautiful, clean solo guitar piece was an older piece Ed had used to slow down his solo spot a bit with something bluesy and jazzy as far back as the *5150* tour. It was one of the songs Ed played acoustically against Valerie's belly. In a critique of the song, former Watchtower and powerhouse solo guitarist Billy White said, "He's gotten past the point of trying to impress people. He just plays exactly what's right without having that kind of guitar hero thing hanging over his head. . . . You can hear it in his playing."

CHAPTER 26
Another Van Halen Production

Valerie's March 3 due date came and went, and she was none too pleased. She was bedridden, and Ed's drinking drove her so crazy that she couldn't stand the sound of him playing guitar or piano. As the wait progressed, Ed again showered her with lavish gifts, this time a Chevy-Nomad with personalized plates that read SHESMAD. Eventually, Valerie ended up at the hospital where they had to induce labor via a Pitocin drip. The whole family was there, but Val's labor went on for a good ten hours. She wasn't allowed to eat and was starving. Edward left the delivery room for a breather and grabbed a candy bar. When he came back to the room, Valerie went ballistic. "You had a Payday bar, didn't you? And you were eating it while I was sleeping, weren't you?" Ed was wracked with guilt and said, "I ate it outside. While you were sleeping after the second epidural. . . . Honey, I was so hungry. I'm sorry."

Wolfgang entered the world on March 16, 1991. Ed was overjoyed, sometimes incredibly overcome. "I caught Ed staring at Wolfie with a look of disbelief, as if he couldn't have helped create something so miraculous," said Val. Ed was doting right off the bat—he eagerly changed diapers and loved feeding Wolfie in the middle of the night; he even kept a bottle warmer at his bedside. Being a first-time mother and having suffered a miscarriage, Valerie was a nervous wreck for the first few months after the birth, even terrified of walking down the spiral staircase.

Finally, the Album with the Dirty Title

Out in the backyard, work on the new album continued. Ed's drinking toward the end of the recording escalated to 12 to 15 beers per day. He admitted, "It's completely ass-backwards. And the only reason I keep doing it is because it works, believe it or not. It just breaks down the inhibitions. And I'm too inhibited, ordinarily—I get real nervous." The same nervousness he felt as a six-year-old who couldn't speak English hiding behind his bigger brother, watching him get beat up for being different. The nervousness that Jan cured with a lick of Vodka. Pondering the frustration of why he was wired to be nervous and why he had to rely on alcohol, the same thing that killed his father and was potentially going to kill him, had to have been a source of great distress. As he himself said, he has that X factor. He didn't ask to be born with it, he just was. Then he ends up in the Catch-22 of "alcohol: the cause of *and* solution to all of life's problems" cycle.

While the new album was free of sap-soaked power ballads, it did feature a bit of a dramatic pop classic, the song "Right Now." It is singular in that the sound is not that of a heavy synthesizer, but of a straight grand piano. The rapid-fire, delicate, haunting melody countered by the heavy underlying bass chord changes was effective and extremely successful. Lyrically, the idea of living for today—the idea that you could get hit by a bus tomorrow and not wanting to ever die with regrets—it is certainly and admirable subject and worthy of reflection. It's just that when Sammy Hagar gives it a go, without the least bit of surprise, it's trite. One line from the *Van Halen* album captured the entire essence of the song more than a dozen years before: "I live my life like there's no tomorrow." In fact, that's the opening lyric on the very first Van Halen album, period. Eddie told Sam, "I played this for you on the last album and you didn't dig it." Interestingly, Edward originally composed the song with the notion that it would be perfect for Joe Cocker's voice.

The crux of the song, though, is the opening and closing piano refrain. It has that feel that makes it *perfect* for brief interludes at major sporting events. As a Texas Longhorns football season ticket holder, I have heard the song over the PA at least once at every single game for nearly two decades. That riff goes out to a stadium of 100,000 people and the feel of that melody sweeps them all. Every time it happens, without fail, I bump my uncle and say, "That's Van Halen, by the way." It's the opening piano part they play—not the vocal part.

The album is rounded out with the recycled tag from the end of "Jump" becoming "Standin' on Top of the World." Musically, it's a decent pop-rock composition. Lyrically it is cliché after cliché after cliché. "Let's give it all we got." About the song, Eddie said: "I almost didn't want to put that on the record, because everything else seemed so new and fresh.

Andy forced me to put it in. . . . To be honest, we had five other tunes that I would've preferred to use."

Finally, the album was in the bag. The title *For Unlawful Carnal Knowledge* was Sammy's idea, but Eddie went along with it. They chose to test the bounds of censorship, and ultimately, they did on several occasions, a few somewhat serious. There may have been another factor, though, driving the band to do something outrageous or something that potentially pitted one generation versus another. By 1991, the music scene had changed. Drastically.

An Alternative

Here they came: Nirvana, Pearl Jam, Soundgarden, Ministry, Nine Inch Nails, Jane's Addiction, Red Hot Chili Peppers, Smashing Pumpkins, Alice in Chains, Pantera. And there they went: Bon Jovi, Ratt, Warrant, Poison, Motley Crue, Def Leppard, Dio, Iron Maiden, Skid Row. Long, big hair became ridiculous. Tight clothes became absurd. A brightly painted guitar with a tremolo bar became uncool. The biggest change though was in the lyrical content of the new wave of music. Specifically, the song "Cherry Pie" by Warrant was the absolute breaking point for anti-intellectual, base and banal garbage lyrics. It was The Beach Boys gone porno. It had reached its end. Lyrics with more of a Dylan-Morrison-Lennon bent were back in style big time. People wanted to listen and stop and think and talk about the lyrics. A complete 180 from "Do it 'til we're black and blue."

Sadly, of course, when everyone turned their back on the 80s, David Lee Roth was among the very first to go. His antics in the "Yankee Rose" video alone would have him indicted as the definition of exactly what was no longer cool at all. As a member of Van Halen and for his first EP—Dave's videos are classic. Right at "Yankee Rose"—he pushed it too far, period. His 1991 solo album with guitarist Jason Becker was really a collection of some fairly outright plaintive songs, and it did not fair well commercially at all. Sadly, Becker was stricken with Lou Gehrig's Disease and was given only a few years to live. He is alive to this day and communicates by blinking his eyes via a system developed by his father. Edward reached out to Jason and established a friendship with him completely on his own.

In 1991, through the strength of Ed's songwriting, Van Halen was able to transcend both the rising and the falling bands of the day and stay in the mix. A controversial album title was a relatively good move. The only thing is, past its first year of release, the title lost all of its impact. Because of the changing music scene, in an interview in September, about finger-tapping—not done at all in the 90s, period—Edward said, "Sometimes I almost feel embarrassed for coming up with that shit!"

In the end, the title was just another one of Hagar's "how much more blatant can you be?" personal challenges. Eddie Vedder drew a hanger on his arm on *Unplugged* to illustrate a pro-choice stance. Kurt Cobain made the tortured individual a hero. Sammy's response is "let's call the album *fuck*." Again, initial giggles all around, followed by guffaws. Followed by silence and an ahem. And right at the same moment they are trying to re-establish their credibility; they took a $2 million dollar check for using "Right Now" in a Crystal Pepsi commercial. Although somewhat commonplace now, it was theretofore relatively unfathomable.

Still in the Game

The album referred to as *F.U.C.K.* came out in June 1991 and for the third straight time in a row, the album went to #1 on the *Billboard* charts. Three up to bat with Sammy—three number ones—no *Thriller* to run blocker. The new album was definitely an improvement over *OU812* sonically and musically, but not lyrically. As far as the lyrics went, writer Jean Rosenbluth noted, "There's not a ballad in the bunch, and the group abandoned its short-lived pretention of including a lyric sheet with the album." By mid-July, after three weeks, the album was still the biggest selling in the country.

The fact that the album succeeded despite the lyrical movement of the day truly speaks to Edward's remarkable ability to write, compose, and arrange compelling, new and interesting material. Ted Templeman said, "Edward, who's been struggling to synthesize his role as a serious songwriter and a guitar hero, has managed with this record to bring both sides together."

The tour started in August. Boosting their credibility by embracing some of the new kids in town, Alice in Chains was the opening act on the tour. The only Roth-era songs in the set were "Panama," "You Really Got Me," and "Jump." Eddie's drinking escalated and his behavior worsened. The tour proceeded almost non-stop from August until a brief break in mid-November.

In September, in Costa Mesa, California, a review of the show suggests it was a pure love-fest. Sammy told the crowd that Edward was "my best friend in the world." Ed returned the sentiment. That same month, the band kicked off the 1991 MTV Video Music Awards with a live performance of "Poundcake." Edward was 100 percent on his game and played flawlessly, utilizing the drill as both a performance and musical jaw dropper. MTV was instrumental in ushering in the new wave of alternative music, so opening the award show that year was a hell of a coup for the band.

Shortly after their performance, the band was interviewed briefly backstage. Pee Wee Herman was a few months off of his porno theater bust and had introduced the opening of the award show in costume saying, "Heard any good jokes lately?" Kurt Loder was interviewing the band and asked what they thought of Herman's situation, Eddie said "I tell you, though, there are people out there that do a lot worse things than what he did, you know? Like, like *preachers*. You know, man? Give me a break. He's cool."

Valerie ended up in North Carolina on location for another one of her TV movies, and Ed joined her during the band's first brief respite. It did not go well. It was a virtual repeat of the infamous New Year's Eve of 1989, only without a punch to the face. Val said, "He proceeded to drink his way through the entire time we spent together." As per Valerie in her autobiography:

> The four of us had gone out one night, and Ed exploded in a rage. He yelled at my mom and then destroyed our rental car, breaking the windshield and kicking the rear until it dented. My poor mother was traumatized by Ed's verbal assault, while my emotions ran from embarrassment at having to call the producers and lie about what had happened to the car, to hurt, to outrage, and anger. . . . Ed struggled with his own issues, too. Every so often, he'd fly a girl out to meet him on tour. Everyone knew but me.

In January 1992, Alice in Chains left the tour to be replaced by no-names Baby Animals. That month, I was just shy of my 20th birthday, in a band, and I was a torn individual musically. I was completely into the new music—I was in college. But you cannot separate yourself from a band you've been following since you were seven just because they were in danger of falling out of fashion. My old buddy Mike and I decided it would just be dumb not to go see them on January 29 at the Frank Erwin Center in Austin. We bought tickets just before the show, but ended up with fairly good seats on Ed's side. It was a bit of a last-minute decision. Not like the time we camped out for tickets six months in advance of the *1984* show.

This was my fifth Van Halen concert. It was the one I was the least excited about, but I was thinking *"If Eddie Van Halen is in my town playing, how could I possibly not go see him?"* I remember that the show was pretty good, but a tad lackluster because of Sammy who continued to ramble on about how he drank too much the night before in Dallas. I remember thinking to myself, "You are here in front of a good 12,000 people or so—be a professional. Don't address the audience by wryly implying that you can't put on a decent show for them because you partied too hard the night before." I didn't pay good money to hear that crap. Of course, Sammy was playing the "everybody likes to party a little too hard—and, hey, I'm just like you, I'm just a regular guy" role. I would say this is particularly egregious when your voice is your instrument.

I was very satisfied with Ed's playing whether or not he had been drinking, and pulled my old trick of walking around to the section closest to him for his solo and got to observe him from within fifty feet. He was incredible and played a lot of new material I had never heard him do before. I walked out of the concert with the feeling that Ed put everything he had into it—any emo guilt I felt about still being a VH fan was completely wiped out by Edward's playing and performance. I also walked out thinking Sam came off as a pathetic, hungover "performer" that barely even moved around on stage the entire night.

Some time after that show, the *band* Van Halen, sadly, fell from the top of my totem pole of awesomeness, although I had not turned my back on Edward at all. My own band was starting to make waves in Austin, and I consciously cut myself off from listening to any music besides The Beatles—old or new. I entered a phase where I was afraid that too much exposure to any outside music would compromise my ability to write tunes that were as original as possible. The funny thing is, that's exactly what Ed did. He claims to have purchased two albums in all of the 1980s: a Brand X album and Peter Gabriel's *So*. Grunge was so hot at that moment, I was openly mocked for my VH dedication, given a Jane's Addiction tape, and told to get with it.

Just four days after seeing the concert in Austin, my brother Brandon and his wife Susan saw them in Oklahoma City. Brandon was attending flight school in Tulsa learning to become a pilot, and Susan was well into an extremely successful career as a DJ. Through Susan's radio connections, she managed to get on the meet-and-greet list for the February 2 concert. Brandon called me when they got the news and said flat out, "I'm going to meet Eddie Van Halen." He said the words, but I wasn't sure I heard them. My emotions flashed. Shock. "Are you serious?" Desperation. "How can I get myself in Oklahoma City in one day to join them? I can't!" Anger. "Why does he get to meet him and not me?!" Then jealousy, which was ultimately followed by pure awe.

There were three others in their group for the meet-and-greet, but for the photo that was taken, Brandon put himself square between Eddie and Sammy with his arms around both of them. At 6' 2", Brandon kind of dwarfed both Ed and Sam. In the photo, Brandon is leaning way down and Sam is on his tip-toes. Edward was dressed casual with a big smile. It was brief, your standard meet-and-greet. About a week later, I got a photocopy in the mail of the picture. Brandon had labeled the photo—"I think you know who these guys are!" Then he noted each person's name—"Eddie, me, Sammy . . ."

Over the following years, almost every time I'd talk to my brother on the phone, I'd ultimately end up saying, "Man, I can't believe you met Eddie . . . What exactly did you guys say, again?" I wanted to know every single thing that was uttered. Around 1985 when Brandon was 17, he told us all how badly he wanted to drive all the way to Los Angeles and find Eddie's house in the hills. We all thought he was crazy, and of course it was just superfan talk. But I'll be damned if his dream didn't eventually come true. Honestly, Brandon was such a massive Eddie and Sammy fan, I thought he might blow it somehow. But it was very casual. As far as specifics, I can only recall Brandon saying that he told Edward how big a fan he was and how much he admired him, Ed replying with a cool, "Hey, thanks, man. Thanks a lot."

Edward Van Halen, Brandon Dodds, Sammy Hagar, Susan Dodds in February 1992. Photograph © Susan Wise

The Timeless Refrain of "Right Now"

While sales of the new Van Halen album proved that the band still had enormous economic potential, a virtually inevitable decline of various sorts was about to begin. The tour had caused Eddie to miss Wolfie cutting his first tooth and having his first real laughing fit. The road stretch that started in August lasted all the way until May 1992, with only a few minor breaks.

The band made MTV videos for "Poundcake" and "Runaround," but it was the video for "Right Now" that became a huge hit on MTV. It was a quirky, commercial-esque interpretation by director Mark Fenske. The video was mixture of text and images, some bizarre and some poignant, depending on how you look at it. A microscopic visual of sperm is accompanied by the phrase "Right now people are having unprotected sex;" an image of a man running is overlaid with "Right now opportunity is passing you by;" and simple text saying things like "Right now, blacks and whites don't eat together too much," etc. The video doesn't reek of Van Halen necessarily. There's no vibe to it that says "this is classic VH." It is a decent video (as proven by the multiple awards it would gather), yet it could've just as easily been applied to almost any other heady song at the time. Edward and the band are not featured prominently in the video at all, and in fact, Sammy was so disapproving of the video concept as to become uncooperative during shooting. The final shot of the band heading toward the dressing room was completely unplanned. Sammy had enough, so Ed, Mike, and Al headed off, followed by Sammy looking angry and disgusted as he slammed the door. The camera then incidentally zooms in on the word "MEN" on the sign on the door.

It turned out that Edward's piano riff and Sammy's "right now" theme—"What are you waiting for?"—along with its advertisement-like video led to new territory. In 1992, there was a brief phase when beer and cola companies figured out a way to remove all coloring from the beverage and make it clear, like Sprite or 7-Up. This was the "crystal fad." Pepsi paid the band $2 million to use the song to promote Crystal Pepsi—a short-lived product if there ever was one. Eddie agreed, just like the others, and the commercial started airing regularly for a solid month or two. At the time, you were not only hearing the song on the radio (or listening to the CD—or tape) in your car and watching the video on MTV, you would hear it during commercial breaks while watching football or *Seinfeld.*

Well into the 2010s, a band having a song on a national commercial is pure gold. It's possibly the only remaining avenue in which you can reach so many people at the same time. Nearly every single rock band of any acclaim, old or new, has played a central role in advertising over the past ten to fifteen years. It is a prime spot for bands from The Beatles and the Stones to Stone Temple Pilots to even Rush and Van Halen (yet again in 1996). Back in 1992, it was sort of as if Ed was standing right there when a certain artistic dam broke, especially during the peak of the somewhat faux artistic integrity of the grunge movement with its arguably hypocritical anti-corporate stance.

The truth, though, is that Pepsi simply informed the band that they were using the song, period, which they had every right to do. All they had to do was pay the royalty and have the song re-recorded by session players. "Pepsi told us that they were going to do that . . . that way all they have to do is credit the artist and pay the studio cats," said Ed. So the band relented and just charged a high fee for using the actual song. "I ain't that proud, you know. I'm not going to say—'No, go ahead and rip us off. And keep the money, too!'" he said.

When it comes down to it, it was that piano riff of his. It was just hypnotic, and it still is today. Eddie got half a million dollars for allowing a company to use his song for a 15-second commercial—that is completely separate from all album and singles sales, on top of the overall songwriting royalties. The main piano refrain is one of Edward's most identifiable pieces of music, played repeatedly during football and basketball games, and chances are 98% of the crowd knows the melody, but only 10% know it's Van Halen. It's not a guitar scream, or finger tapping, a tremolo dive bomb, or an Echoplex trick—it is Edward at a grand piano playing a haunting, psychological musical refrain. Straight off of the man's fingertips rolled a riff and a song that was suitable for a socially-conscious video, a national ad campaign, and major sports events. It was absolutely the closest Ed had come to writing something virtually timeless during Sam's stint with the group.

The tour wrapped in May with two dates in Mexico City and closed with a three-night stand in Hawaii. After the tour, Ed took some well deserved time off to spend with his two-month old baby boy.

CHAPTER 27
Awards and Live Overdubs

Once again, MTV would play a large role in maintaining Van Halen's profile and career. On September 19, 1992, the "Right Now" video won three awards including no small one: Video of the Year. It also brought Mark Fenske an award for Best Director and one for Mitchell Sinaway for Best Editing. The video was nominated in three categories in which it did not win, one being Breakthrough Video. Grunge was white hot at the time, and Nirvana's "Smells Like Teen Spirit" was also up for Video of the Year, but ended up taking home only Best Alternative Video (a new category) and Best New Artist in a Video—fair enough.

Ed was wearing a dark red tuxedo jacket with an AIDS ribbon, a white shirt and slim bow tie, jeans and cowboy boots. Upon winning the Video of the Year award, all four band members took the stage. Sammy spoke first and had to be bleeped out, then Alex thanked a few people in management. Ed got up and the auditorium burst into applause. He simply said, "I should say somethin'! I . . . Yo! Thank you!" Ed then grabbed the MTV award off the podium and walked away with it off stage while Michael Anthony was giving his thanks to the fans. Host Dana Carvey—who had parodied Roth a few years earlier on SNL—spoke immediately after. "Alright, Van Halen. Way to go Sammy," he said. "For those of you at home he just said 'clucking.'"

In December 1992, Edward and Valerie attended a Bill Clinton fundraiser. Their photo was featured in *Rolling Stone* with Edward looking intelligent in eye glasses. Ed had never gone public with his politics before. Valerie is admittedly a liberal Democrat, and although Ed had never said it explicitly, his attending a Clinton fundraiser might give an indication. Sammy Hagar is known to be a Toby Keith-type conservative and admitted to donating $2,000 to the George W. Bush campaign.

Ed's close friend Toto drummer Jeff Porcaro passed away in August from a heart attack triggered accidentally from inhaling too much pesticide around his home. Edward performed in a memorial show for him on December 14, 1992. "Jeff was the groove master. He was a buddy," said Ed. Porcaro was also responsible for the drum beat on "Beat It," along with Steve Lukather's rhythm guitar, and, of course, Edward's solo. The list of all of the artists on the bill for the Tribute for Jeff concert was over-the-top. Along with the entire band Toto came George Harrison, Don Henley, Donald Fagen, Michael McDonald ("I'll Wait" collaborator), Boz Scaggs, and David Crosby, amongst others. Eddie and his pal Steve Lukather held a head-cutting session and jammed on "Ain't Talkin' 'Bout Love" and "Hold the Line" with Steve. A fantastic photo of Edward with George Harrison appeared in *Rolling Stone*. Eddie played side-by-side with a Beatle! Ed's grin in the photo can't be beat.

A "Live" Album and Serious Tension

Ed Leffler had finally convinced Eddie and the band to release a live album, something Edward had fought against vociferously for years and years. Ed had often said he simply didn't see the point in releasing a live album. "I've never heard a tape that I've been completely satisfied with, something always goes wrong during the course of a show," he said in 1991. "Anyway, there's really no such thing as a true live album. I don't know of any live record that hasn't been doctored in some way . . . Even Cream doctored their stuff." And damned if that isn't exactly what they ended up doing. "They re-recorded everything," said Sammy.

Sammy's personal life was in major upheaval at the time, and it spilled into the VH camp. He finally left his wife Betsy of two decades in December 1991 for Kari Karte. At the time of their first meeting, Kari was the girlfriend of NFL quarterback Jim Kelly. She was half Sammy's age. Sam was spent mentally from his personal battles and so worn out by Van Halen that he simply became defiant. After the tour wrapped in August 1992, he retreated to Hawaii with Kari and wanted to be left alone. He thought the live album would be a no-brainer, but he said, "The dumb-ass brothers decided to take the live album, because they were so bored, back in the studio."

The bulk of material for the album was recorded and filmed over two nights in Fresno in May 1992 and was originally edited for broadcast on the Westwood One radio network. But Ed and Al went back and started to fix the tapes—every spot that the guitar was out of tune, every place that the beat was off. When Ed fixed his tuning—Sammy's live vocals were out of tune. When Al fixed the tempo—Sammy's live vocals were off the beat. All of these edits required Sammy to redo his tracks to suit the edits. "Now I had to go back in the studio and redo all my vocals," Sam said. "I wanted to kill those guys." He was not happy about it all. After weeks and weeks of re-tracking, fixing, and remixing, an agitated Sammy flew in, recut all of his vocals in just three hours and took off. Eddie and Alex were peeved by the lack of time and effort Sam put into it. They proceeded to comb through every single syllable and then called Sammy back for more fixes which he again did reluctantly and angrily. "When they found something," he said, "I went out and fixed it. Fuck you."

After two months, Eddie and Alex reached the end of what they could do and were burnt. Andy Johns came in to save the day this time. Ultimately, he would pull the best versions of some of the songs from as far back 1986 and 1988 which required some pretty heavy lifting on Andy's part as far as mixing and editing went. The album and DVD called *Right Here, Right Now* was finally released in February 1993. The title recalled the outro of their smash video, but was anything but an accurate reflection of the material within—which ranged from brilliant to horrific butcher jobs.

The version of "Right Now" on the album is one of the few goose bump-inducing moments on the record—the best of all of the original songs. But the absolute peak was a cover of The Who's "Won't Get Fooled Again." Edward had transposed Townshend's classic keyboard parts into a delicately brilliant finger-picking guitar part. Once the listener realizes that Ed is actually playing those classic lines on his guitar, you're simply left with the feeling that "Damn . . . he did it again." And much to Sammy's credit, his voice is perfectly suited Roger Daltrey's, and his screams on the VH version certainly do justice to Roger's original performance.

On the other side, Sammy Hagar completely and totally ruined "Panama." First off, he either refused to or simply did not learn the correct lyrics, period. Instead of "Don't you know she's coming home to me," Sam sings "home *with* me." Instead of "Got a feel for the wheel, keep the moving parts clean / Hot shoe burnin' down the avenue / I got an on-ramp comin' through my bedroom," Sammy sings "Got a feel for the *road*" and "I got a *freeway runnin'* through my bedroom." During the quiet mid-section after the solo, Sammy launched into a non-lyrical diatribe that was as out of place, off-point, and as wildly nonsensical as one could possibly dream up. He said the following over a brutal three full minutes:

> I tell ya . . . We been lookin' forward to this show. We were off last night, sittin' around here in Fresno with nothin' to do. So all I was doin' was thinkin' about tonight, you understand. But what happened was I was sittin' around thinkin' about tonight, the boys in the band were having a party over at the hotel. They had about fifteen fuckin' chicks up there and I was sittin' in my room watchin' TV. And if that ain't a bunch of bullshit, I don't know what is. See, the problem is, and learned my lesson real quick, because I was worrying about tonight last night. Last night, I should've been worrying about last night. And the night before that, I should've been worrying about that night because worrying about tomorrow is a bunch of shit. Because tomorrow may not never come. Tomorrow—there's no guarantee about tomorrow. Fuck tomorrow! You dig what I'm sayin'? Because yesterday, shit, yesterday, that's history. That's dead and gone. Yesterday ain't worth nothin', man, that's gone, man. 'Cause all you got to worry about is . . . right here, right now. Right now! Right now!

"Fifteen fuckin' chicks?" Alex? Married with children. Michael? Married with children. Edward? Married with a child. "May not never come?" Double-negative—makes no sense. So, what are you supposed to do? Party every single day of your life all day? I can only wonder how many people in the audience had to get up and go to a regular job the next day who were legitimately concerned about "tomorrow." And while yesterday is indeed history—you are bound to learn from your past to make for a better future. So, yesterday is not "ain't worth nothin'" in my opinion. Lastly, what in the hell does this diatribe have to do with "Panama?!"

As Edward, Alex, and Michael were performing, one can only imagine what ran through their head when Sammy claimed that they were partying in the hotel with "fifteen fuckin' chicks." Was he implying they were having an orgy? Or were the fifteen chicks in the room their collective wives, sisters, and daughters? Probably not. And before he met Kari, Sammy claimed that he was with a different woman every single day.

Staying consistent, Sammy destroyed "Jump" by butchering the lyrics and melody throughout. Instead of "I've got my back against the record machine / I ain't the worst that you've seen / Can't you see what I mean?", Sammy sings "I've got my *ass* against the record machine" and "*You know* what I mean?" Edward, Alex, and Michael didn't butcher their parts. Bringing "Jump" back into the set rubbed Sam the wrong way. In his 2011 autobiography, Sammy Hagar—of all people—mocked the lyrics to "Jump"—lyrics he couldn't or wouldn't even learn correctly.

Runnin' into Dave and the 1993 Tour

Just before the February release of the album, the most unlikely of strangers bumped into each other at random on the streets of New York City: Ed and Dave. "I was walking down the street in New York, and literally just bumped into him," said Eddie. "I said 'hey' and 'good luck' and I think he was really shocked that I said anything at all to him." Ed added: "He was kind of hesitant. I shook his hand. I asked him how he was doing, and he looked kind of shocked." Dave recalled the meeting very clearly in his autobiography:

> I'm heading down Madison Avenue, it's nine in the morning, and somebody walks by and goes, "Hey, Dave." And I think, that sounds very familiar. I turn and I look and a full block away on the corner is a fat guy waving his arms, he goes, "It's Ed, Dave." I didn't recognize him, he's gained thirty pounds, you know, and a dozen years gone by. . . . I walked up, I said, "Ed"—I remember I said the exact same sentence that my grandma said to me when I saw her at the hospital when she was eighty-eight years old. She said, "All my life in front of my eyes, and look who's here now." Just popped out. So I said, "All my life in front of my eyes, and look who's here now. Ed, how are you?" . . . He says, "Oh, I hear you're playing with Terry . . . how's it going?" "It's going good. I hear that you're a dad now, congratulations."

And the two parted. Dave had been working on his latest solo album in New York with Terry Kilgore—an old mutual acquaintance dating back to Van Halen's club days. The two hadn't spoken to or seen each other in eight years. Their next communication gap wouldn't be quite so long.

Prior to kicking off a world-wide tour to promote *Right Here, Right Now*, the band returned to its club roots (although in a different incarnation) by playing a one-off madhouse show at the Whisky a Go Go club in March 1993. It had been a solid fifteen-plus years since VH played the Whisky. Three-thousand fans clamored for just 250 tickets and caused a major traffic jam and escalated police presence.

Following the Whisky show, Ed and the band packed up and returned to Europe for the first time since 1984. They toured for the entire month of April. According to Ian Christie, European fans blamed the "uber-American Sammy for keeping Van Halen away from Europe so long—especially in Holland, where a thirteen-year absence had strained family ties." In fact, the major European singer Nan Mouskouri was quoted as saying, "I just love Van Halen and David Lee Roth." The band added lots of fun covers to their sets during the European jaunt including "Won't Get Fooled Again" (The Who), "Born on the Bayou" (Creedence Clearwater Revival), "We Gotta Get Out of This Place" (The Animals), "Norwegian Wood" (The Beatles), "Waitin' for the Bus" (ZZ Top), "Crossroads" (Cream), and "All Right Now" (Free) as per *The Van Halen Encyclopedia.*

Following their April 29 show in London, the band took a break until resuming the tour in the U.S. on June 25. For the American leg, Motley Crue lead singer Vince Neil—then a solo artist—joined the tour as the opening act all the way through to the end of August. In Motley Crue's biography *Dirt*, Vince said that he and Sammy struck up a friendship. Sam took shots with Vince before his set and then they had margaritas before Van Halen's set. "He ended up with the short-end of the deal because he was always wasted before he hit the stage," said Neil.

In early July in Boston, Edward had a bug lodged in his ear which came close to causing serious damage. In a March 1995 *GUITAR* interview, Edward told writer HP Newquist:

> We were playing outdoors in Boston, and there were all these bugs flying around; June bug type things. I didn't think anything of it, and after the show I went to the hotel and went to sleep. About six in the morning, I get this excruciating fucking pain in my ear. At first I thought it was part of a dream, and I slapped myself around the ear, and it stopped. So I think

> that I must be crazy and I go back to sleep. An hour later, same thing. *Aaaaagghh!* I wake up again. I've always had nasal problems, and I have this saline solution spray, so I spray it in my ear, thinking, 'There's got to be something in there!' After I spray it, I whack myself on the head a couple of times, and out comes this bug almost an inch long! And it's still alive! There's this fucking June bug from my ear in the sink! I didn't think anybody would believe me, so I put it in a matchbox and took it up to my brother's room, and said, 'Look what crawled out of my ear.' It was amazing. Then the doctor said it was real close to my eardrum and could have actually wasted my ear.

Rolling Stone reported that the insect was a beetle. Also while in Boston, Edward met a brain surgeon with whom he had a running joke for about a year at the time. Ed quipped to MTV in early 1992 that playing guitar wasn't brain surgery. Dr. Jim Schumacher, an actual brain surgeon at Massachusetts General Hospital in Boston, spoke out claiming that playing guitar was harder. Schumacher wrote Edward telling him he'd trade him a day of neurosurgical lessons for a guitar lesson. Whether they met before or after Edward had an insect lodged in his ear coming at his brain isn't clear.

On August 6, at the Cynthia Woods Mitchell Pavilion in Houston, Ed's limo broke down. Obviously in a care-free mood, Ed abandoned the car on the side of the road as smoke plummeted out of its hood. He started thumbing for rides from concert-goers leaving the show and made quite a public scene and caused a traffic jam. He was so heavily hounded by autograph seekers that he was eventually rescued by Michael and Sammy in their limo that was following nearby.

CHAPTER 28
A Friend Lost, and Some Ugly Scenes

Tensions between Sammy and Eddie worsened during the last month of the tour centered around issues regarding Sammy's divorce and the health of their manager of nine years, Ed Leffler. At the outset of the tour, Leffler was diagnosed with throat and lung cancer and his condition continued to worsen. He went to the hospital immediately upon the conclusion of the tour at the end of August in 1993. Also, Sammy was working to put out his own greatest hits album with new solo material.

Hagar's divorce with his wife Betsy was being finalized and she played some serious hardball. For Betsy to give up all of her rights to any material that Sammy had written during their marriage, they negotiated a settlement for one substantial lump sum payment. Geffen lured Leffler who lured Sammy—they set up his deal so that the album would *exactly* pay for his divorce settlement.

Edward was not pleased. In just January of 1992 in *Rolling Stone*, Sammy discussed the free makeup show that Van Halen finally played in Dallas. "For a while they were joking 'You can go and do it by yourself' and I said 'Sure,'" said Sam. "Then they say 'We'll go, too. No solo shit.' Because they know I've been chomping at the bit to do a solo show." Edward's point of view was to stick to the plan—*I Never Said Goodbye* was to be the last Sammy solo album, period. It is also highly likely that Sammy had the money to pay Betsy, but jumped at the chance to knock it out lickety-split and conveniently making it his excuse to do some solo material. But it would put a competing product in the marketplace.

When Sammy went to meet with his lawyer to sign the papers on the deal, Ed and Al were sitting there in his office waiting to see exactly what it was all about. "They didn't want me to do the album," Sammy said. "They argued and argued. They said it would be bad for the band." Ultimately, Ed and Al had to capitulate, but it was the first step toward complicating all of their business matters. This time, Edward certainly did not contribute in any way to Sammy's new solo material.

The band closed out the tour with a three-night stand in Costa Mesa, during which, according to Hagar, "All Eddie's bad-news friends showed up with the drugs and the women, and he was wasted." During one of the Costa Mesa shows, Sammy played a solo-spot acoustic ballad for Leffler, during which Edward came on stage an adjusted his amplifier set-up seemingly oblivious to Sammy's performance. "I'm out there doing this song and Eddie's over there panicking, taking his equipment down behind me," said Sammy. "[Edward was] fucked up out of his mind."

As far as Ed's level of intoxication, Vince Neil had already confirmed his drinking routine with Sammy during this leg of the tour. On top of that, an August 30, 1993 *Los Angeles Times* article featured the following: "Singer Hagar was only affirming the obvious when, a few songs into the show, he told the near-capacity crowd that the antic, L.A.-based quartet had already been partying for hours with a horde of fans backstage."

When Sammy's spot ended, he came offstage and grabbed Eddie to confront him physically, but Ed Leffler—in his horrific condition—separated the two. After the encore, Sammy claims he was ready and waiting to throw down with Edward. Leffler forced him into a car and away from the arena.

The next day, Eddie apologized to Sammy. "He was like that," said Hagar. "He would do the worst shit you could ever imagine, and the next day he'd be humble, whiny, crying and hugging you. It was easy to forgive this guy, because he went all the way to the ground with his humility. Next day? Whole different guy."

Ed Leffler Leaves a Void

Sammy had big plans for his annual birthday party in October at the Cabo Wabo Cantina—then on its way to becoming a regular spring break-style destination draw. Michael Anthony joined him. A few days later, Ed and Al called, Sammy said, "[They said] if I wanted to see Leffler alive again, I'd better get right back." Sammy called Leffler who assured him he was feeling fine, so Sammy chose to stay in Cabo and continue on with his birthday celebration.

Ed Leffler succumbed to cancer the following day, October 16, 1993. The funeral was held three days later. Hagar said, "I went to the funeral, and did a little speech for Leffler. When he died, they put a gram of blow and a bottle of J&B Scotch in his coffin. His friends were characters. They didn't take it lightly or unlovingly, but they did this crazy stuff. That was the end of Ed Leffler."

The whirlpool began almost immediately after the funeral. The band did not have a manager. Edward sensed it was time to take the reins of his band once and for all. Marshall Berle had screwed him; Noel Monk was Roth's "puppet"; and Leffler, though beloved, came from Hagar's camp. The search for a new manager was ultimately a no-brainer as it was right there in the family, but was arduous, stressful, and difficult all the same.

Sammy brought over Shep Gordon (manager of Alice Cooper) and Johnny Barbis (an all-around well-connected industry mogul). "We met with them," said Sammy. "The brothers didn't like them." Via David Geffen, Sammy then suggested Elliot Roberts, manager for Neil Young. "The Van Halens blew him out in about five seconds," said Sammy.

Of course, Alex was married to the sister of Ray Danniels, the manager of Rush for their entire career (still to this date). It was an obvious decision for Edward and Alex, but Sammy objected highly. "The second Ray Danniels entered the picture, everything changed," said Hagar. According to Ray, "Sam was distant and made it clear that he had his own guy in Ed Leffler, who had managed him prior to joining Van Halen. He felt a loss of control." Once again, Rush and Van Halen's paths crossed in a curious manner.

During the dark period following Leffler's death, Eddie made his way out to Neil Young's Bridge School Benefit Concert with Sammy on November 6, 1993. The main act was a reunited Simon and Garfunkel. Sammy and Edward performed together just three songs. Sammy said, "We didn't go over as well as you might have expected, but it wasn't our crowd." Edward ended up performing as a guest with Simon and Garfunkel on the classic "Sound of Silence" contributing a guitar solo. According to Sammy, after his and Ed's performance, they went back to their trailer and did a few lines. Paul Simon's trailer was right next to theirs, so Sammy struck up a conversation with him. Sammy said:

> Paul Simon invited him to play on a song. "Do you know 'Sound of Silence'?" he said. "No, I never heard of it," said Eddie. Simon took him to the trailer and tried to show him the song. . . . Eddie couldn't get it. I guess he was too

> wasted. . . . Eddie's a great musician, but very methodical. He doesn't simply jam those things.

During Simon and Garfunkel's performance of the song, Eddie came out on to the stage to a burst of applause and played an improvised solo over a bit of music that doesn't have a solo over it as originally recorded. Ed had twenty minutes to prepare to wing it. It was definitely a unique combination—Paul Simon, Art Garfunkel, and Edward Van Halen. Sammy claims Ed "butchered the song." Reviewer Dave Sigler said Ed provided "an OK solo." Eddie did fine. It's a complicated piece of music, it's not a jam song—the chord changes are delicate. They asked for an Eddie Van Halen guitar solo over "Sound of Silence" and that's what they got. The show finished with a jam of Neil Young's "Rockin' in the Free World" during which Edward and Neil had a guitar dueling session.

Eddie made it out to the Rock Walk in Hollywood to help celebrate Jimmy Page's induction on December 7. Unfortunately, later that month would be one of Ed's worst personal moments, only to be followed by yet worse.

The Nirvana Thing

On December 30, 1993, Nirvana—at the absolute peak of the music world—played the Forum, which was by now practically Ed's home away from home. A highly intoxicated Eddie made his way backstage intent on confronting this Kurt Cobain fellow and to insist on letting the L.A.-native Edward sit in with the band. In an interview with The Germs and Nirvana guitarist Pat Smear (also with Foo Fighters) conducted by student journalists at the University of California, Santa Barbara, he recalled the incident in detail:

> Pat: Can I tell you my Eddie Van Halen story? I actually met him. He was backstage at the final Nirvana concert at the Forum, which for me, was like, "Oh my God, I'm playing on the SAME stage as [Queen's] Brian May!" I was dying. Anyway, Eddie Van Halen comes backstage drunk out of his fucking mind, and he started begging Kurt to let him play with us. It was so disgusting.

Interviewer: I heard he was running Mennen Speed Stick deodorant all over his face. Is that true?

Pat: Yeah [laughs]. Kurt had this deodorant, and he sniffed it or something like that, and it got on his face. It looked like he had cocaine under his nose.

Interviewer: I heard he was asking Kurt to let him come on stage and play "Eruption," but Kurt said, "No," and Eddie said, "C'mon, let me play the Mexican's guitar," referring to you.

Pat: I told Krist [Novoselic], I thought we should let him play with us. But he said no because we'd never get him off the stage. When I walked up to Eddie, he was talking to Krist. I just saw the back of his head so I didn't know who he was. And Krist goes, "Oh Eddie, you haven't met Pat. He's our new guitar player." Eddie turns around and sees me, but he doesn't say hello or anything. He just says, "Oh no, not a dark one." At first I thought he was kidding. But he kept asking me, "What are you? Are you like a Raji or something? Are you Mexican?" Then he kept saying to Kurt, "C'mon let me play the Mexican's guitar." I was horrified! . . . Eddie Van Halen is the perfect example for me of not wanting to meet your heroes 'cause you'll be disappointed. I hear he's sober now. I blame that incident totally on the alcohol. I've done a lot of bad things when I was drunk, too.

Interviewer: I don't think you're coming from a judgmental place at all.

Pat: I was just shocked. I was thinking, "God, Eddie Van Halen hates me."

A *Mote* magazine article provided additional detail, noting, "Filmmaker Dave Markey, who was videotaping the show that night, witnessed the entire incident and turned off his camera in disgust, thus saving future generations from witnessing this fiasco on YouTube." In the Cobain biography *Heavier Than Heaven* by Charles R. Cross, Markey simply said, "It was surreal." The book chronicled Cobain's final reaction: "'Actually, you *can* jam,' he promised. 'You can go onstage *after* our encore. Just go up there and solo by yourself!' Kurt stormed off." Cross noted that Edward was Kurt's "one-time idol."

The Edward Van Halen that showed up to the Forum that night was in pain. It wasn't just that Van Halen was a fifteen-year-old band now and Nirvana was the top new act of the era, impeding on his turf, and Ed wanted to throw his weight around. The loss of Leffler, the strife with Hagar, and the current uncertain future of the band was certainly enough to push Edward to extreme states of anxiety and depression coupled with binge drinking. Ed may have, in fact, also been suffering ill effects from two extremely significant medical conditions that were not yet diagnosed.

Secrets Exposed

No one else but Edward and one other person knew about a secret he had been trying to keep quiet but had steadily lost control of. Feeling extraordinary guilt, Ed took some extreme measures.

In early 1994, Valerie overheard Edward speaking quite seriously on the phone in his private bathroom inside the bedroom of the main house. Valerie said:

> Ed was telling a woman . . . that he was through paying her to keep her mouth shut. He was tired of being blackmailed, and if she wanted to go to the press with photos that proved they'd slept together, that was her decision. He'd given her enough money over the years.

She waited downstairs for Edward and, as Val said, "what ensued was an extremely unpleasant confrontation." Apparently, exercising obvious poor judgment, Ed had allowed this woman—one Andi Remington—into their home, and into their bedroom over a period of two years, but had cut off the affair. Remington was ready to sell some of her horrifically embarrassing photos to a gossip rag. The photos were taken by Remington from inside of Ed and Val's bedroom, and showed a nude Edward wearing only a guitar and holding that MTV award. Ed's attempts to keep her quiet reveal a private panic and a desperate act to make an awful mistake go away.

Valerie left, but cooled off after a few days, and given Ed's assurance that the affair was long since over, she decided for the sake of the family that they would try and work it out through therapy. For weeks and weeks in a row, they would both alternate sessions as well as take part in sessions together. "At some point, Ed, who felt awful, came clean about other affairs," said Valerie, "including the wife of a guitar company executive, another woman in St. Louis—and other women."

She felt the time was right to come clean about her affair in Japan with Craig, the drummer for Private Life. She felt great getting it off her back, "but Ed flipped out." Valerie said that he truly felt he had never done anything to her on that level, and she felt, like most men, he clearly had a double-standard when it came to the issue of fidelity.

After all of the sessions, the two decided to stick it out and keep trying to make a go at getting the marriage together. Valerie said, "'Look,' I told Ed. 'You fucked up. I fucked up. Let's just get this behind us.'" For now, Remington was keeping quiet, so all they could do was go about their lives as best they could and just ignore her altogether.

At one point afterward, Valerie received a phone call in her hotel room from a man Valerie referred to as a business associate of Ed's—that "guitar company executive" Val had previously referred to. The man was screaming at her on the other end of the phone that Edward was sleeping with his wife, as if Valerie had actually given it her blessing and was partly to blame. Val, of course, shot back with the rather obvious retort that *his* wife was sleeping with *her* husband! Strange days.

Production of the Ernie Ball Music Man Edward Van Halen signature guitar came to an end for reasons that are easily deducible . . . Their personal relationship ended. Of their business relationship, Edward said:

> The truth is, that I thought that since I designed the guitar, that I owned it. . . . I was sadly mistaken . . . And when I found that out, that Music Man also registered the trademark "5150" for string use . . . I mean come on, you know, the world pretty much knows the 5150 and the stripes is pretty much my thing. And they registered the trademark, so I just said, you know, fuck you guys. And the guitar was never really finished for me. The next guitar I wanted to build would have been the Wolfgang anyway. I wanted an archtop, and I wanted to experiment some more. I figured they were a small shop, but they couldn't keep up with the orders . . .

Northridge and a Norelco

On January 17, 1994, Edward and Valerie were at home when the Northridge earthquake hit. Eddie was pretty shaken by the whole thing. He bragged to *GUITAR* about how solid 5150 was built, "This place is like Fort Knox," he said. "Nothing happened to it during the earthquake in 1994. It's all two-foot cinderblock filled with cement. It ain't going anywhere." However, the main house was rattled, although the damage was primarily cosmetic. "Man, that earthquake scared the shit out of me!" Edward said. "I thought that Satan himself was underneath the house. The TV spit about five feet off the wall and I almost got nailed by that. It was hell, man. I'm pretty prepared, too; I've got my flashlight and boots next to the bed. But this one hit so hard that I had one boot on, my underwear half on, and I was falling on the floor. I couldn't do anything. In the meantime, Valerie's already in Wolfie's room grabbing him, and was back already. It was like she was on autopilot."

Dave's Pasadena home actually suffered rather extensive damage. His heat was out for much of that winter. His insurer attempted a $350,000 payout. Dave eventually returned fire with a $5 million suit.

That same month, Eddie played the annual Bob Hope Classic golf tournament with tour pro Payne Stewart as his one of his partners. Sportscaster Jim Lampley apparently mocked Edward throughout the broadcast—Ed actually claimed Lampley was "cartooning" him by making fun of his wardrobe as well as his game. "Maybe Mr. Van Halen should spend less time in the studio and more time on the driving range," said Lampley. Ed was not playing well that day, and Stewart was reportedly unhappy with the pairing. Worse yet, Ed beaned a spectator with a ball, although the man was not hurt and was delighted to have been hit by a wild Eddie Van Halen shot. The next day, Ed met up with his instructor Ron Del Barrio and began taking his golf game much more seriously.

Sammy's *Unboxed* solo album with two brand-new songs came out in March 1994. He went on TV to promote it on Letterman. But when he planned to bring Michael Anthony out to join him on *The Tonight Show*, Ed and Al were so peeved that Sammy ended up canceling his appearance altogether. Eddie was still mourning the loss of Ed Leffler and was reportedly upset at seeing the band's singer doing self promotion in the media. Ian Christie noted: "Memories resurfaced of another lead singer testing the waters with a solo record before abandoning Van Halen."

The spring of 1994 was not a good one for Ed at all. His grief over Leffler's death, the stress of the marriage counseling, and the strife with Sammy—all contributed to a bout of prolonged heavy drinking. "I reached a point . . . where I was absolutely at wit's end, and drinking wasn't helping me," Edward said. "I was literally freaking out." Ed admitted that he literally starting pulling his hair out of his own head. Sammy claimed that Edward was so smashed that Valerie had locked him out of the house and wouldn't let him in. He grabbed a shaver and cut his hair. "I was so pissed off and frustrated with myself, I grabbed a Norelco and did a butcher job. Valerie freaked, obviously. . . . But that was the beginning of a new me." Eddie also said, "I walked down to the house, grabbed a Norelco shaver and just shaved my head. I looked like an Auschwitz victim. . . . I was losing it."

After he had shaved his head, the band went to Europe for a promotional trip. Ed's hair was still ridiculously cropped, and, again, it was a complete 180 from the image that everyone had ever had of him. "This one German journalist said to me, 'Now wait a minute. I'm no psychologist here, but nobody just does that to their head,'" Eddie said. He said that, at the time, he didn't feel like explaining what was going on, so spun it away from the truth, claiming he had lost a bet to Jim Kelly.

Eddie returned to a rehab facility late that spring, but did not finally make truly serious progress for several more months. The band actually played a gig that April at the Hard Rock in Los Angeles to launch Ed's new charity tournament Eddie's Celebrity Golf Challenge which was attended by stars including Bill Murray, Tommy Lee, Joe Pesci, Dweezil Zappa, Steve Morse, Jim Kelly, Neil Young, Bret Michaels, and Rob Lowe.

Recording *Balance*

Recording for the next Van Halen album started in May and would last until July. This time there would be no Ted Templeman, no Donn Landee, and no Andy Johns. Edward told HP Newquist:

> We met with a bunch of different people when we were looking for a producer. I talked with Mike Clink, with Bob Rock, with Andy Johns—they were all busy. Of all the guys we talked to and considered, Bruce Fairbairn was the one who worked out. We had already done a few albums on our own, but I prefer to

> work with somebody and bounce our ideas off of them. Just an outside ear, you know? But producing's a very elusive job. You're everything from baby-sitter to amateur psychologist and schoolteacher, and you're just trying to keep it all going in the right direction.

Bruce Fairbairn took over as producer for the album that would become *Balance*. With Aerosmith, Bon Jovi, and Loverboy on his resume, the man knew how to make platinum albums. Engineer Mike Fraser got the studio set up in May getting ready for Bruce's arrival. "I guess Alex and I were dicking around in the studio since October of 1993," Eddie said. "But we didn't start actual recording until June 1, and it took us four months to write and record the whole thing. That's very quick, especially for us, but Bruce was very on top of things—he doesn't let you get away with loafing. He has a schedule and he makes you stick to it."

Everything except for some lead vocals for *Balance* was recorded at 5150; some vocals were done in Canada where Bruce lived. The album was mixed at the Record Plant instead of 5150. "But we'd still come up to my house to make sure it sounded right," said Ed.

About the recording of the album, Sammy said, "Eddie was supposed to be sober, but he wasn't and he could be trouble. He couldn't drink around Valerie, and Ray Danniels was all concerned we keep Eddie straight." Sammy said that Edward was stashing cocaine and vodka—along with chewing gum and cigars—in the studio bathroom, where he was frequently disappearing to. Sammy confronted Alex about Ed's use and claimed that Alex was in denial. Sammy then confronted Eddie directly who told him flat out that he hadn't had a drink for months. Sammy said, "He'd break down and cry, bust up things. It got ugly."

Edward said he tried to temper his alcohol intake by drinking non-alcoholic Sharps with a few real beers in between. He had finally reached a point where his physiology was suffering. "All of a sudden my mind and body started retaliating," he said. "It wasn't fun anymore. I'd wake up in the morning and puke. . . . I'm realizing I'm a fucking alcoholic. I'd have to drink a six-pack to feel normal."

One of the most significant things that came out of the *Balance* sessions was Edward suggesting lyric changes for the first time ever in the history of the band. Sammy felt that Edward was so frustrated with him that he was using vocal criticism as a lever to wedge Sammy out of the band. Sammy claims that was the real reason he and Bruce went to Vancouver to finish recording the vocals. Second engineer Mike Plotnikoff said, "Sammy would only come between three and five, and he had dinner reservations at six, so you had to get what you could out of him in that amount of time, and that was it. I think that was why Eddie and Sammy weren't getting along."

Worse yet was the song "Amsterdam." While the city is indeed famous for its legal marijuana cafes, it just also happens to be the exact same city where both Edward and Alex were born. Sammy's focus was completely on weed, and it tweaked Ed and Alex. They asked him to rewrite the words, but Sammy refused. "I always hated the words to 'Wham, Bam Amsterdam,' from *Balance*," said Eddie, "because they were all about smoking pot—they were just stupid. Lyrics should plant some sort of seed for thought, or at least be a little more metaphorical." The band spent a ton of cash making a video for the song while walk the city's streets as well as showing Edward getting his famous Wolfgang tattoo. But MTV wouldn't show the video because of the song's blatant drug references. So Warner Brothers stepped in and insisted Sammy redo the lyrics—just as Ed and Al had done earlier—so that the video could air. MTV still didn't play it. Later Edward said, "'Wham Bam, Amsterdam' wasn't my fault! Blame the music on me, but not that other stuff."

Sammy's Club and Eddie's Sobriety

There was also the issue of the cantina. While Eddie was sinking tens of thousands of dollars into the place, it fell into shambles. Confident that the Cabo Wabo was an obviously unprofitable deal, Ed and the others gave up their shares to Sammy—gladly leaving him holding the bag, in a sense. However, Sammy's newfound independence caused him to refocus on the club—update it, get better management, and he Michael Anthony went down to jam as often as possible to raise even a few thousand dollars at a time.

By 1994, Sam had actually turned the club around, and now that Ed wasn't a partner in the venture anymore, there was open animosity on the subject that would last for years and years. Sammy was proud he sunk his teeth into the club, leaned into it to bring it back from the dead. Again, Ed's take had to have been that when he was a partner, it was a losing venture, and he lost a lot of cash. But now that Sammy's got it to himself, he's diving in and turning it around. The question was why didn't Sammy lean into it while Eddie was throwing money at it? What was originally a band venture was now a Sammy Hagar solo venture, for which he can now claim all credit for in the end.

Finally, Ed got much more serious about his alcoholism. "That's when I got sober, on October 2, 1994," Ed said. "And I started seeing this therapist, a Sikh woman. And she changed my life." Eddie's therapist was Sat-Kaur Khalsa. He had been seeing her for two years before he finally made a major breakthrough. He told *Guitar World*:

> I fought her tooth and nail, man. I said, "There's no way—I need a couple of beers to loosen up before I play." So finally, about a year ago last summer, she goes, "Just give me 12 hours to work with you." I said, "Okay." So she comes out from Santa Fe, New Mexico, and says, "Are you ready?" "Yeah, I guess . . . this is weird." So we do all kinds of intense mind-balancing things for a half-hour straight, and she tells me to sit down. I thanked her, because I was about ready to drop. She goes, "Close your eyes and just breathe. Now, go to that 'room' you go to after you drink. Go to that place, that feeling that you have after you drink." A couple of minutes go by. She goes, "Are you there yet?" I go, "No." She goes, "Go to that room." All of a sudden, this whole new feeling comes flooding in. I said, "I think I'm there!" She said, "Keep your eyes closed." She handed me a guitar. And I immediately wrote three songs. It took her an hour, not 12 hours. . . . And it was just like she'd been telling me. "You don't understand, Ed, you've been blocking the light." She was right, and now I can't stop the light coming through, and I don't want to stop it. . . . I was numbing myself because I couldn't deal with things. I was hitting the brake when I thought I was hitting the gas. And now it's wide open. Because that ego, all those neuroses and worries and fears, just isn't there. Those three little letters don't exist any longer. Not in the way they did.

This bout of sobriety would last longer than previous stints, but Ed was about to get sidelined with some serious medical news.

CHAPTER 29
Shot from the Hip

Balance was released in January 1995 and the tour started in March in Florida. It was noted that Edward performed "stone-cold sober as a recovering alcoholic for the first time in his career." The show was filmed by MTV for "Spring Break Rocks." He looked very different, too. His hair was extremely short and cropped and he was sporting a goatee. One would practically never recognize him. On a *Beavis and Butthead* episode, the characters "reviewed" the video for "Can't Stop Loving You" and at first they started out saying, "Alright, Van Halen! Van Halen kicks ass!" Then after a few moments, Butthead says, "Uh . . . uh . . . . oh boy . . ." Beavis says, "Is this Van Halen?" Butthead responded, "Yeah, but it's like . . . where's Eddie?"

When the album was released, Eddie and Sammy went on the *Jon Stewart Show* (his predecessor to *The Daily Show*). The entire band acted out a few comedic skits with Jon, and Ed and Sam sat down for an interview. The interview was pretty soft, but in retrospect reveals thinly-veiled jabs. Jon noted that they each drove pretty nice cars to the show. Sammy said, "Eddie's rich." Ed responded sarcastically with, "I'm rich? Yeah, you ever heard of General Motors? I own it." When asked by Jon what kind of a car he drove to the taping, Ed said, "It's a Ferrari. You know . . . putt-putt." Sammy responds, "*Putt-putt?!*" and breaks out in laughter at Ed's attempt to downplay the car. Ed says, "You should listen to this guy. You've got *three* of them."

In January 1995 (the month that Ed turned forty), hoping to redeem himself, Eddie played the Bob Hope Classic again. This time, one of Ed's partners was pro Tom Kite with whom he had a friendly relationship. "Hopefully I won't do any brain damage to the peanut gallery this year," he said to Kite. Ed's instructor Ron accompanied him on the course. "We walk to the first tee—maybe 10,000 people are watching, and I'm nervous as hell," said Ron. "I send Eddie a telepathic swing thought: Don't shank it and kill someone!" For the most part, Ed played absolutely excellent. On the twelfth hole, "Tom hits a 4-iron about 12 feet from the pin," said Ron. "Eddie looks at me. Eddie looks nervous. There are an awful lot of spectators around the green. The pin is 180 yards away. So figuring my guy is pumped up, I hand him a 5-iron instead of a 3. He knocks the ball three feet from the hole. The gallery goes nuts." How Ed played so well with his as-of-yet undiagnosed ailment was a mystery. About turning forty, Ed told *Rolling Stone*, "I feel 18. I don't feel any different, except now I'm having a hip problem."

At the beginning of the *Balance* tour, Ed started to experience an escalation of pain in his hip. At first, he thought he had probably just taken a bad golf swing, but it got to be so intense that he finally went in for an MRI. Eventually, he was diagnosed with avascular necrosis—a loss of blood supply often caused by excessive alcohol consumption. It essentially caused the ball joint of his hip to collapse. Ed at the time claimed that his hip damage was from jumping around on stage for years, which likely didn't help, but the number one cause of avascular necrosis is alcoholism. Edward said that his situation was exactly the same as athlete Bo Jackson, but that is not entirely the case. Jackson was sidelined by a major blow to the hip in one game, and only afterward was it discovered that Jackson had avascular necrosis. But Jackson was a lifelong athlete playing football and baseball both in college and professionally. The amount of wear and tear on Bo's hip does not quite equate to Ed's two or so hours of performing on a given night. Surely, for Edward, the fact that the condition was caused by alcohol must have been personally devastating, and a stark reminder of the warning his father had given him from his death bed.

Because of his hip, his performances on the tour were mostly stock still. Sam said that Ed seemed to be on painkillers. "Eddie walked with a cane," said Sammy. "He would walk up to the stage, put the cane down, and walk out. Every so often, he would sit on the drum riser or a stool to play a couple of songs, because his hips were killing him so bad." Ed would put off surgery—that had been recommended immediately—for almost five more years.

On Wolfgang's birthday, the family went to Disney World while they were in Florida. Ed was not drinking, and Valerie said, "We had several fun weeks together there—though Ed and Sammy were at odds for reasons I didn't pay attention to." In Dallas in late March, Wolfie walked out on stage to his first ovation (but not his last). He and his dad kicked a beach ball around to the delight of the crowd. Early the following month, the band was trekking through their home territory for shows in San Diego, L.A., and Oakland.

On the Cover of the *Rolling Stone*

The April 6, 1995 edition of *Rolling Stone* was the third time Eddie had graced the cover. However, this time, it was Ed and Ed alone. He looked completely different than the image that everyone had of him for the previous fifteen years. He had cropped, highlighted hair, and a smart goatee. He really looked great. The photographs throughout the article by Mark Seliger were exceptional and artistic. There was an excellent family portrait and a shot of Eddie holding his guitar walking through a field with his Dalmatian. The interview, conducted by David Wild, was incredibly revealing. The interview took place on Valentine's Day 1995.

Reflecting upon the Norelco incident, Edward said, "Cutting my hair off did come at the end of an unbelievably heavy time for me." He continued, "Our manager, Ed Leffler, died. Then Sammy Hagar was off doing his loony fucking solo career." The latter Sammy slagging was a sign of things to come. Ed also complained that the band was in the short term managing themselves and found that handling each and every call that came in was overwhelming. They had finally realized all of the crazy requests Leffler had pre-empted and declined for the band. Edward said he actually fielded a call from an agent wanting to know if he wanted to host *Star Search*.

At the time of the *Rolling Stone* interview, Ed had been sober for five months—his longest stint yet off the bottle. Valerie said she was confident that this bout of sobriety would last. "If I wasn't," she said, "I wouldn't be here. Fourteen years living with an alcoholic is my limit." Valerie went out of her way to say that you wouldn't know it just by simply talking with him for a few hours, but that "they guy has the biggest heart in the world." About his sobriety, Ed said drinking simply wasn't an alternative anymore. "Drinking does not work for me," he said. "I mean, I used to drive drunk. God, that's a fucked-up thing to do."

Edward also said that being a father had a profound impact on this sobriety stint. One night, Eddie had stayed up all night partying and stumbled in the house at 8am. A four-year-old Wolfie looked at him and said, "Are you all right, Daddy? What happened?" Ed added, "When your kid knows, it's time to give it up."

When asked what Roth had brought to the original Van Halen, Edward said was basically like "an emcee, a clown. I hope this isn't coming off as slighting him, because he was great at what he did." When directly asked if he would ever play with Roth again, Edward said it was only if they ever made it into the Rock & Roll Hall of Fame. "We're going to have jam together," Ed said of Roth. He went further and added, "I think it would be hilarious. Listen, I don't hate the guy."

"The Gun Thing"

It turned out April was not a great month for Ed. During a show at the Forum on April 5, he had technical difficulties during his solo and threw his guitar to the stage in frustration. Then, just two days later, he made the news with what he called "the gun thing." Edward was so used to flying charter that when he was preparing to fly United Airlines to Oakland, he forgot to take his fully loaded .25-caliber Beretta out of his carry-on luggage. Burbank Airport security saw the gun when scanning his bag on the x-ray machine. Eddie was immediately detained and taken to a secure area.

Ed then endured 90 minutes of good cop-bad cop. "One of the cops was like Barney Fife, a real young guy with one bullet in his gun," said Edward. "Thank God Andy Griffith showed up later on." Airport Police Chief Tony Lo-Verme said, "He was very cooperative. He stated he normally travels by charter, where you more or less do what you like. This time, he traveled by commercial aircraft and forgot to take (the gun) out." The gun was seized and Ed was eventually released.

By April 11—it was out. "Rock Star Van Halen Faces Charge of Carrying Gun Into Airport." "Van Halen Caught With Gun." "Rocker Van Halen to Face Weapons Charge: Burbank: Guitarist says he forgot to leave loaded gun out of carry-on luggage at airport, authorities say." MTV picked up the story. *The Los Angeles Times* carried the following:

> Van Halen Enters Plea On Handgun
> April 14, 1995—Vivien Lou Chen
>
> Rock star Eddie Van Halen pleaded no contest to unlawfully carrying a handgun into Burbank Airport and was fined $910 and placed on one year of probation, a prosecutor said Thursday. Van Halen, 40, of Studio City appeared at Burbank Municipal Court to enter his plea Wednesday, eight days before his scheduled arraignment. "He was advised of his constitutional rights, asked how he wanted to plea, and said, 'No contest,'" said Burbank Deputy City Atty. Robert W. Walters. "He's human."

The bottom line is that is was a simple mistake, period. An oversight—a rushed packing job. But it is definitely not the kind of press you want to get. Fortunately for Eddie, this was pre-9/11, otherwise, he could have been a lot worse off. Horrifically though, this wasn't the worst press he'd ever get. It wasn't even the worst press he'd get that summer.

Bad News

From late May all the way until the end of June, the band toured Europe opening for Bon Jovi on all but just a handful of dates. Ed's hip was causing him horrible pain, and on top of that, Bon Jovi was much bigger in Europe than Van Halen was. "It was a total disaster," Sammy said. "Van Halen had no place on a bill with Bon Jovi, who was huge over there. . . . It was total oil and water. . . . It was the worst idea ever for Van Halen. We got nowhere on that tour. I could feel the end coming."

Shortly thereafter, Andi Remington sold out Eddie Van Halen for a little bit of money to the glamorous black and white newsprint tabloid *The Globe* (which via deduction means that *The National Enquirer, People,* and *US Weekly* all gave a "thanks but no thanks" to her story). Remington did all of this just to make a little bit of money, but ultimately the publicity caused extreme embarrassment, and seriously hurt a family with a young child. Within the walls of your own home is one thing; on every newsstand in every grocery store check-out line is another. Once informed, Valerie knew what was coming and made Ed call her agent Jack and tell him exactly what was going on—they had managed to keep the whole thing a secret for a year. In Valerie's autobiography:

> "What were you thinking when you let her take pictures?" [Jack] said.
>
> "I'd had a couple beers," Ed replied.
>
> "But you're posing naked with a guitar. And you're smiling!"
>
> Ed sighed.

The story hit on July 4. Valerie was devastated. Eddie was devastated. Then the gossip TV show *Hard Copy* picked up the story. All Ed could do was go back out on tour from mid-July through all of August, September, and October, with the touring wrapping in early November. What a horrific few months.

The *Balance* tour was nicknamed the "Ambulance Tour" not only because of Ed's hip, but also because Alex was forced to wear a neck brace because of three vertebrae in his neck he damaged from innocently lifting up his son. They looked like aging, worn-out athletes.

In early August in Michigan, the band threw "Foxey Lady" and "White Room" into their set for fun, and later that month Leslie West of Mountain joined the band on stage for a rendition of his classic "Mississippi Queen." In Colorado in September, the band played an outdoor gig in Denver during a freak fall snow storm.

In late September, Van Halen came to Austin and I didn't go. I hadn't seen them since 1991. To be honest, I couldn't get past the song "I Can't Stop Loving You." I thought it was horrible, trite pop garbage. The lyrics could've been written by a twelve-year-old girl. Cliché after cliché after cliché—again. Writer David Wild referred to the song as "unapologetic power pop." *Balance* was the first Van Halen album I didn't buy. I was talking to my brother Brandon on the phone after it came out and he asked me what I thought about it. I told him I didn't know, that all I knew was what I had heard on the radio and seen on MTV, and I didn't like it, so I didn't buy the album. "What?!" my brother said. He put down the phone and yelled to his wife Susan, "Kevin hasn't even bought the new Van Halen album . . ." He continued, "What's your problem with it? It's still Eddie, man." I said, "That song 'I Can't Stop Loving You' is horrible! I cannot believe that's even Van Halen, man. It's awful." He said, "Man . . . that's like Susan and mine's song right now." Mine and my brother's musical taste didn't always match up.

The Twisted Breaking Point

Although the entire band was inducted into the Rock Walk of Fame on October 6, Ed and Sammy were at the breaking point as the tour came to a close. After finishing the stateside part of the tour in California, they flew separately to Japan for two weeks of shows starting in late October. They even stayed in separate hotels. Before heading to Hawaii for the last two shows of the entire tour, Sammy says that Ed called him at his hotel drunk and aggressive. Hagar said:

> "What are you going to do when we get back?" he said. . . .
>
> "I don't know," I said. "Take some time off. What are you going to do?"
>
> "I don't know yet," He said. "When I figure it out, I'll let you know. I've got some plans, but I'll let you know if it involves you or not."
>
> "Okay," I said. "Fuck you." I hung up the phone.

On the family front, Edward, Valerie, and Wolfgang spent Christmas alone in 1995. Sammy's now wife Kari was pregnant and Sam had plans to stay at their new house in Hawaii for an extended period of time. They had a solid birth plan—the baby would be born in April in Hawaii, Sammy would spend the first two months bonding with the child, and the band agreed to start work on the next album in June. The showdown was on. Sammy's personal life versus the demands of the band via Edward with Alex at his back. With a shark like Ray Danniels in the water—the pieces were in place. Just a few more songs, and off everyone ventured into bizarro world.

Ray came to the brothers with a proposal to cut two songs for the soundtrack of an upcoming film starring top-list actors Helen Hunt and Bill Paxton called *Twister* (ultimately, the movie would completely bomb with imbecilic lines like "Look at all that data!"). The idea was to use modern digital special effects to capitalize on the growing trend of storm chasing which had become its own cottage industry. The film was slated for a May release, so anything Van Halen was going to contribute had to be completed post-haste. "I thought it was the worst timing in the world," said Sammy.

Ed wrote a killer tune that became "Humans Being" for the film. Coaxing Sammy out of Hawaii to work on that song, and the second, titled "Between Us Two," was difficult. Sam had several objections. First, they had already agreed not to work until June at the earliest. Second, his wife was pregnant and he did not want to leave her. Third, the songs were destined for a soundtrack album, which Sammy viewed as ripping off the fans by making them buy a record with a lot of other acts that they may not even like.

Sam was sure that Ray was simply cooking up ways to make a lot of money fast for little effort—two songs on a soundtrack and a greatest hits collection. "Ray Danniels was always looking to make his cut," said Hagar. "The guys wanted to do it for some stupid reason." Sammy was most likely correct in his assertion that Ray's tacks here were pre-meditated. Ray was not an idiot. Ray is a consummate rock band manager. However, Sammy's contention was that Ray had a rather devious plan ready to go all along, but chances are that what ultimately transpired was not Ray's direct intention, but not that he had a problem with it either.

The recording of the songs proved to be the dissolution of Van Halen Mach II. Edward later admitted, "It got so bad I actually started drinking again." The first debacle was that Ed and Al insisted that the songs be completely free of tornado or storm imagery of any kind. Not communicating well, Sammy spoke with director Jan de Bont and picked his brain for tornadic references and came up with "Drop Down." Sammy claims he cut a quick demo for it and de Bont loved it. Eddie and Al were flabbergasted. They told Sammy they had specifically said not to write lyrics about storms and tornadoes, despite Sammy's claims that de Bont was satisfied with it (Edward said that de Bont actually called him to ask why Sammy was asking such questions). They didn't care (or believe him) and demanded he return to re-cut the song immediately. According to Sammy, Ray took it to the point of telling him on the phone point-blank, "If you're not back tomorrow, we're assuming that you've quit the band." Sammy balked.

"Yeah, I may have pulled a prick move by not showing up when Eddie told me to, but I had very good reasons," said Sammy. After some rather heavy encouragement by Ray, Sam returned for a band meeting on May 1. Sammy said, "I almost got into a fist fight with Alex when he jumped up and said, 'You fucking insulted my brother! He told you to come down here and you didn't come!'" Eddie said, "We had several band meetings with Sammy where we told him that if he wanted to continue with Van Halen, he had to stop running around doing all his solo shit and become more of a team player—and that might involve collaborating on a lyrical level." At first Sammy resisted. "The conversation went something like, 'Fuck you, I hope the guy can sing!'" said Hagar. "The second time, however, I told Eddie I might be open-minded to the idea."

Eventually, Sammy came up with "Humans Being" (with help from Alex), and a ballad, "Between Us Two." The latter was a collaboration between Edward and Sammy. Hagar considered his work done and was ready to return to Hawaii to be with Kari. But Sammy said Eddie stopped him at the last minute and said they were not going to use the ballad for the movie and instead needed just another minute and a half to lengthen "Humans Being." Sammy resisted greatly, but relented. Working with Bruce, Sammy said, "We wrote the lyrics, I sang the song in three parts in about an hour and a half and split." In the end, it turned out one additional song was added to the movie, but was credited to and performed by only Edward and Alex. It rolled over the film's end credits and featured Alex on piano and keyboard with Edward on guitar. It was an instrumental, but for all the bickering about not having storm-related lyrics, the title "Respect the Wind" is ironic, at least. The song is an epic-sounding, dark quasi-classical piano piece with underlying snyth strings overlaid with soaring lead guitar, feedback, and harmonic squeals. It was a huge first for the brothers, and ended up being the only song ever that Alex is credited on outside of the band.

In early June, Edward told Sammy that Glen Ballard had come up with some lyrical ideas for "Between Us Two." Sammy claims those that had heard the original version of the song thought that it would be "Van Halen's 'Stairway to Heaven.'" Eddie asked Sam to return to the studio to re-sing the song. The real problem may have been that Bruce Fairbairn was claiming that he, Sammy, and Edward had co-written the song together, and came telling Ray he wanted one-third. Ed and Sam called bullshit on Bruce and fired him. So Edward brought in Glen to rewrite the lyrics to the song. Sammy was incensed and called Glen. Sammy claimed Glen said, "Eddie and Alex asked me to write new lyrics. They're the ones that said they didn't like the lyrics you'd written to that song, and that you weren't happy with them either, so they asked me to take a shot at it."

But when Sammy learned that the revamped song would be featured on a greatest hits album, he went through the roof. "We're not a greatest-hits kind of band," Hagar said. "We do not need to rely on the past. . . . We spent eleven years trying to bury the past and make the music different and expand and grow." Sammy said, "I told them I wasn't doing any songs for a greatest hits record and split."

The earlier ultimatum was laid down a second time. Edward told Sammy that if he wasn't at the studio by six o'clock the following day, then that was it. Sam did not show. He changed his name at the hotel and didn't answer the phone. Ed called all night long until security came to Sammy's room informing him they had Edward on the phone and that he demanded to speak with him. Sammy's reply was, "Tell him to go fuck himself."

On June 16, 1996, Edward called Sammy. As per Sammy's *Red*:

> The phone rang. It was Eddie Van Halen. He had been up all night.
>
> "You've never been a team player," he said. "You never want to do anything when we want to do them. You always wanted to be a solo artist. You can go back to being a solo artist. We've been working with Roth on the greatest-hits record and it's going great." . . . "Fuck you, you fucking motherfuckers," I said, and hung up.

Eddie said that Valerie stood next to him for the entire conversation. "[She] counted eleven times that I said, 'Sam, all I ask is that you're a team player.'" Sammy spoke to Ray next who tried to calm Sammy, but he wasn't having any of it or any more of Ray. As Ray tried to talk him down, Sam retorted, "Fuck you. It's over." Ed later claimed that Sammy "was only into being in Van Halen for the prestige of it."

And as insane of a ride it had been so far, no one had yet to see the level of insanity that would follow. A screaming ride on the out-of-control *DLR Express*.

CHAPTER 30
The Reunion from Hell

In 1996, Dave had taken up temporary residence in Florida. On a stroll one day, as he told Kurt Loder, "I saw somebody take a face plant—went right over the handlebars of his mountain bike. And he landed on his head without a helmet, and I thought, boy, that'll sure knock 1982 out of the old memory banks! And I started to get a little nostalgic and I started to think, 'Hey, I think back through those years, let me make a little peace. You know, the battles that were between us, the feuding and fussing, it rings like off of your ear after a while. I made a call and said let's be at peace." In his autobiography, Dave said that as he was finishing up his manuscript, he called Ed. According to Dave, he said, "Ed, I want to be at peace. That's all. I have no agenda other than that. I'm not trying to get back in. You guys are solvent, no more of this quarreling." Dave said Ed responded with, "Yeah, I feel the same way."

Word of the greatest hits package made its way to Dave via Rudy Leiren. Ed said, "I'm playing golf with Rudy Lieren who's sometimes my guitar tech and also works for Roth. And I'm playing golf with him and he goes, and he goes, 'Oh, by the way, Roth wants you to call him.' I went, 'Oh! OK . . . *sorry*!' Like, you know? 'He's got my damn number, tell him to call me!'" After a few weeks, Ed checked his answering machine and found two messages from Dave. "I'm standing there with my wife saying, 'Should I call him back or not?'" said Edward. "She says, 'Go ahead. Call him back. What the hell?' It was a Sunday and we had just come in from the beach and Valerie talked me into it."

Dave had questions to ask about the construction of the greatest hits album. Of the first time they spoke, Ed said, "We both we basically apologized for the two-year-old mentality of mudslinging at each over the years. And we went on to discuss the, uh, packaging whether it's two discs, one disc, la-la-la-la-la-la. I told him I don't much of anything right now, 'cause Sammy just quit the band, and I don't know *where* it stands. And, uh, I'll let you know mid-week, you know, when I speak to Ray, what's going with it. If it's happening at all." Their follow-up phone call lasted a solid 45 minutes and was a very cathartic experience. Valerie said, "[That] call went so well, Ed said, that they had apologized for some crap they had said to each other when they were younger." Eddie said they apologized for things going all the way back to junior high school.

Shortly thereafter, Ed said, "I decided to drive over to his house." The two sat around and "BS'd" for a couple of hours. "He seemed like a different guy than the old Dave," Eddie said. They had a great time just catching up as friends. Ed said, "We hung out for about three hours and smoked some cigars." Edward said it was about two weeks later when he realized that they only had "Humans Being" to add to the greatest hits album, when he said he "came up with the crazy idea of having Dave sing on some new songs." Edward said that one thing led to another and he said, "I had this hare-brained idea, which I don't know if I should have ever brought up . . ." Ed called Dave back and asked if he'd do a few songs for the greatest hits record. Dave humorously answered, "Sure, I'm not doing anything."

It was a reunion that millions had fantasized about for years and years—Dave and Ed burying the hatchet and coming back together. Just the thought of the two of them sitting around at Dave's old Pasadena mansion shooting the breeze in the summer time of 1996 is just amazing to contemplate. "During the process," Edward said, "Dave and I were really becoming good friends." Any bliss, though, was short-lived. Tension ratcheted up immediately, on the first day in the studio.

Back in the Studio with DLR

Dave said that Ed approached him with the line, "No matter what happens, we're going to be friends, right?" Dave was uncomfortable from the get-go. He'd been out of practice vocally for six months and needed some time to break his voice back in. He suggested the band run through some of the classics so that they could no-brain it and fall back into place to get that old machine oiled again. As per Dave, Ed said, "No fucking goddamn fucking way. We're not going to retrace any fucking old steps. We're not going to do any old songs or anything that even remotely sounds like any old songs. We're going to write a fucking set of songs where it doesn't matter who the fucking singer is or how he fucking sings it, it's just going to be a good fucking song that anybody can sing."

Besides noting that not a single photograph was ever taken at all during the sessions, Dave said that when rehearsals actually began, he was placed in an isolated vocal booth, as in a soundproof room with no windows—a box. All Dave had was headphones and a microphone. Dave figured if he was going to be shut out in a closet, he was going to make it Club Dave. So he brought it potted palm plants, some lights, and an ashtray. Alex went ballistic on him. "We're motherfucking forty-year-olds!" said Alex. What is this fucking palm tree horseshit?!" Still, Dave didn't buckle.

He started showing up at 5150 with lyrics that he claimed were briefly scanned and immediately dismissed. What Eddie had started with Sammy was now in full execution on Dave. Edward brought in super-producer Desmond Childs, and Dave even gave it a go. Ultimately, Roth declined to sing what he called "sanguine, sissified, grew-up-way-too-close-to-mommy lyrics." Edward said, "Eventually we narrowed it down to a pop song, 'Me Wise Magic,' and a shuffle, 'Can't Get This Stuff No More' with a 'Panama' sort of groove. 'Me Wise Magic' has a line in it, 'I know what you're thinking,' which Dave felt uncomfortable with. He said, 'That sounds a bit angry; it's just not me. People want to hear Dave sing.'" Dave acquiesced and sang the line.

"Me Wise Magic" was one of the most progressive-rock sounding tunes Van Halen ever attempted. It was full of intense off-time changes and at least a dozen different sections. It made Rush look like a blues band. It's Dave with Van Halen again—which is amazing in and of itself. But Dave's voice doesn't really sound like Dave's voice—it's heavily effected. Upon my first listen, I thought that it sounded like Dave was trying to match Sammy's range and style and was slightly bewildered. But after about a hundred repeated listenings, it grew on me and I was in hog heaven.

"Can't Get This Stuff No More" was the real deal. The music was leftover from *Balance*, a song originally called "The Backdoor Shuffle" that Sammy had apparently written lyrics and a melody for. Dave wrote 100% new vocals for the tune, but when Sammy spoke up, Ray immediately wrote him a $35,000 settlement check over the tune.

Lyrically, Dave was back in the saddle for this classic song. Right off the bat: "Got me a date with a super model / I know, I know . . . I'm thinkin' fuck it / Dinner at the hotel—champagne bottle!" But the refrain, "Keep that in mind, when we say goodbye, that you can't get this stuff no more"—it was an honest open reading of the current situation. Dave snuck in a warning, as it were: it's this or else. "Can't Get This Stuff No More" is a song that with some imagination could have been on follow-up to *1984* if Dave had stayed. It was supreme and majestic. Their producer for this effort was Glen Ballard—who had recently sent Alanis Morissette to the top with other-worldly production.

But there were small, daily battles during the recording process. Edward said, "Every other day, I had to reiterate, 'Dave! We don't even have a *song* yet and you're pulling a hamstring gettin' ready to go on tour that is, that is *not* gonna happen.' You know?" Eddie added, "I mean, he, he just—I don't know. 'What don't you understand? The N or the O?' . . . I just kept telling him, 'Quit puttin' the horse in front a damn cart that doesn't even exist yet. Otherwise, we ain't doin' anything!'"

On June 26, 1996, the band put out the following press statement:

> SRO Management has announced that Van Halen is in the studio working with original lead singer David Lee Roth. Their collaboration will be included on the band's upcoming Warner Bros. Records *Greatest Hits* collection, scheduled for release this fall. It has also been announced that Sammy Hagar, Van Halen's vocalist since 1986, is no longer with the group. The band is currently considering a replacement.

It was the strangest damn press release almost anyone had ever seen. In one sentence it says they're back in the studio with David Lee Roth, and in another it says they are currently considering a replacement. Dave said he had approached Eddie to be sure that they weren't just going to do two songs, that that would be a rip-off for the fans. Dave claims Edward assured him they were just taking "baby steps." When Dave saw the SRO press release, he said, "Ed, what is this?" Ed said Ray was out of line with that and that he would talk to him. Dave said there were a dozen such incidents.

The 1996 MTV Awards Ceremony

There are bits of Van Halen lore that have been debunked so far. Most were from the early days—so they didn't actually parachute to the stage in Oakland. But the activities of one single day in Van Halen history—September 4, 1996—are well documented and everyone had a hell of a lot of opportunities to tell their side afterward.

The band was asked—or set up—to make an appearance on the annual MTV Music Video Awards show which they had appeared on many times before. Dave had reservations, but went along with the band to New York. At 6am on the day of the awards show, Ed called Dave at his hotel room. As per David:

> Let's just address this six o'clock in the morning. . . . He thinks he's going to wake me and ruin my day. Trouble is, I'm excited, I'm in great shape, I've been up since 5:30am, I'm drinking a cup of coffee and I'm about to go rock climbing in Central Park. I got James Brown on the stereo. I'm on fire. I'm ready. The phone rings, I casually reach for it. Ed, screaming, at me over the line. Screaming "Goddamn it, I'm sick of this fucking bullshit. I told them when they did that special tribute to you on MTV where they showed bits and pieces of your videos, I said to them, 'Fuck that. Fuck you. I ain't a fucking backup guitar player.'" . . . As if anybody in the fucking solar system thinks of Eddie V. as a backup guitar player. . . . He's screaming beyond real.

Dave said that when the limo came to pick him up to take him to the show that Ray, Alex, Eddie, Michael, and their security were all in the limo. Dave said Edward told him, "Look all we're going to fucking do is we're going to just fucking walk out there and fucking give away the award and when we talk to the press all we're going to fucking talk about is the two new songs and that's fucking it." Dave replied, "They're going to ask you about everything *but* those two songs." Ed said, "Fuck them. We're talking about the two songs and that's it." And then the limo arrived at Radio City Music Hall.

Although there was no official word that they would be coming out on stage, the rumors were flying loose and freely and we all knew to program the VCR and stay glued to the set. It was a ways into the show, when finally, Dennis Miller introduced Van Halen as the presenters of the next award. Dave said that Alex told him just before they took the stage, "Milk it, Dave. Milk it for all it's worth." Dave was a bit unnerved by the statement, but bounced on out.

"Runnin' with the Devil" came blaring over the PA. Edward came out first, followed by Al and Mike who both stopped to high-five a few audience members . . . finally followed by Dave, who the mere sight of brought the house down. Ed ignored Dave's moment by immediately approaching the microphone and saying "Hi, Wolfie! Hi, Hon." Then Mike, Al, and Ed moved off to the left of the podium and Dave stood there by himself on the right still basking in the response. Chris Rock was shown on screen clapping and yelling and the rest of the crowd went absolutely wild. Nearly a full sixty seconds of unadulterated applause went by before they took the microphone.

Eddie was so visibly uncomfortable, and appeared to stick to his plan to just present the award and bail. "I think we're here, uh, to present the Best Male Video of the Year award." Ed then stumbled and Michael pointed to the teleprompter with the pre-written dialog ready and waiting to go. Ed said, "Oh . . ."

Dave immediately jumped directly in front of Ed as he was attempting to read the teleprompter and boldly interrupted him saying, "No, no, no. Instead of the best of award thing, we have to make an announcement. We have to address this subject here." Ed leapt out from behind Dave and moved to the left as far away from him as possible and fumbled for his sunglasses that were tucked into the collar of his white overalls. Dave continued, "This is actually the first time that we've stood on stage together in over a decade." At one point, Ed had his back completely to Dave, but after Dave's statement, the house burst into thunderous applause and Ed spun back around to face the crowd. Dave sincerely shook Al's hand, and turned around to face Eddie and moved in to give him a hug. Dave used both of his arms; Ed only used one.

Eddie then cut the shit and leaned over in front of the mic and said, "I'll do it for Al. We're here to present the award for Best Male Video. Michael?" Ed gestured for Mike to read his lines. Dave jumped right in between them. "You noticed how things have changed a lot since the last time we were up here, really. No, really. It used to be 'I want my MTV', now it's like 'Give me my fucking MTV or I'll blow your head off, man!'" At that point, Ed grabbed Dave by both of his shoulders and physically moved him out of the way to the left of the podium as Michael scrambled to regain order. Before Michael could get a word out, Dave was off on his own on stage left shucking and jiving for the crowd. Michael finally said, "I got a line here. This year's nominees come from all over the musical map from Beck to R. Kelly and everything in between." Eddie said, "Let's take a look at them," and they went into a montage of the nominated videos.

Hoping to get this scene wrapped up, Ed stepped up and said simply, "And the winner is . . ." Dave jumped in with the envelope and said, "The winner is—ladies and gentlemen, a big blast of noisy, screaming, non-stop summit or plummet New York City-style applause for B-B-B-*Beck*!!!" Beck came up and was greeted by the band. Ed tried to pull Dave over to stand collectively with the band of to the left of the podium, but Dave drifted back to the right, directly into camera view behind Beck as he was giving his award thanks. Dave continued to dance to a few overexcited segments of the crowd, and clearly was a distraction during what should've been Beck's moment, not Dave's. Beck actually did thank Van Halen for presenting the award during his speech.

Ed stomped off stage and then they headed for the press tents. Dave was hesitant, "Guys, this is very, very dangerous. This is a minefield." As per Dave, Ed replied, "Well, we just say baby steps, we take it step by step and see how it goes." Dave came back, "By the way, I'm not real good with baby steps. My specialty is ass-kicking. Does that sound unreasonable?" With that, Dave said the brothers were furious.

Their first stop was with a friendly Kurt Loder. But the first real press tent was a semi-hostile environment. A question about Howard Stern came up, with whom Eddie reportedly had a bit of a feud. Dave jumped in and gave a classic word-packed response claiming Stern was the "spiritual glue of the entire United States." Follow up to Edward: "You like Howard, Eddie?" Ed shrugged off the question and said, "I got no problem with the guy." Dave said he was forcibly moved away from the mic and said that at one point one of them even put their hand over his mouth. The press hounded Edward about whether or not they were looking for another lead singer to which he said that was just rumor and gossip. Dave said the press corps shouted "Bullshit! Bullshit! It came from your manager and he's standing right there." Ray ducked out. "Now the Van Halens realize they are no longer in control," said Dave.

When asked about Sammy, Edward said, "Sammy wanted to pursue a solo career." When asked about Dave, a clearly frustrated Eddie said, "I asked him if he'd be interested in doing a couple of tunes for the greatest hits. And that's what we've done. And the next step is video. When we're done with that, we'll see."

Asked again, Ed, close to fuming, said, "We'll do a couple of videos. Beyond that—if we do tour, we have to write and record a new album. So, we're taking it, we're taking it–" Ed was interrupted by the press corps and snapped back, "Wait, wait, wait, wait, wait! We're taking it step by step, because, you know—*twelve years*. We're gettin' to know each other again. *Okay?!*" Ed added another hurdle to a reunion when he began telling the press that he was also scheduled to have hip replacement surgery that would take four to six months to recover from. According to Dave, the vibrating press room just went dead. Dave called it Ed's "'my tragic life' routine." Then again, Dave wasn't living with excruciating pain.

Dave said that between press tents, he stopped Edward and said, "Now is not the time to start addressing a whole lot of personal issues. We created a scenario, we have invited a whole lot of people to celebrate and now is not the time to bring everybody down and start talking about your hip. It's selfish." Dave said Edward replied, "Hey, man, this is my fucking life. I'll say whatever I want, all right? It's my fucking hip, I need fucking hip surgery." Dave retorted, "Fuck that, it's bad manners. You're also talking about things that I have no idea about. Don't put me up in front of the international press and start talking about plans I have no idea even existed." Edward said that Dave got up close and said, flat out, "Tonight is about *ME*!" Apparently, Dave's emphasis on the "M" in "me" caused moisture—either spit or sweat—to fly into Ed's face. Thus Eddie's later claim that Dave spit in his face.

Dave said Ed lit into him: "Nobody ever fucking talks to me like that. You ever fucking talk to me like that, I'm going to kick you in your fucking balls. You fucking hear me?" At this same moment, pain from Al's ruptured disk—and possibly the stress of the situation—caused him to collapse to the ground in the fetal position. Dave went over to check on Al only to be stopped by security. Al recovered after fifteen minutes or so.

In the limo on the way back to the hotel, Dave said, "Everyone's pissed, silent." Dave said Ed asked, "Say, Dave? Got one of those Cuban cigars?" Dave said they were in the other car, but went over and got one and handed it to Edward. Dave turned briefly and before he could turn back around, Eddie was already halfway to the hotel door, cigar in hand.

Dave went on to spend the evening at Alanis Morissette's party via producer Glen Ballard, and even after everything that had transpired, Dave suggested they call Ed and invite him to the party. When Dave returned to his room, there was a message from Ed. "Hey, man, we've got to fucking talk. This is bullshit, man. . . . If you ever fucking talk to me like that again I'm going to kick your fucking balls. I run into you, you better be wearing a cup. I'm going to fucking kick you in your nuts."

Two Open Letters

After all of this, three weeks later Warner Brothers approached Dave with a video treatment that he said had him performing on large screens while the three band members performed together in front of the screens. Dave said, "At that point, I said no, just no." And that was it.

Dave penned an open letter to the media, but Ray tried to talk him out of it. "Don't get excited, Dave, no need to go to the press," Ray said. "Ed's a little upset, but, hey, he hasn't made any decisions. So don't go to the press."

On October 2, 1996, two competing press releases went out. From David Lee Roth:

> To whom this may concern,
>
> You've probably heard rumors that Van Halen and I will not be consummating our highly publicized reunion. And since neither Edward, Alex, nor Michael have corroborated or denied the gossip, I would like to go on record with the following: Eddie did it.
>
> It's no secret, nor am I ashamed of my unabashed rapture at the prospect of resurrecting the original Van Halen. A "couple of songs" was all I knew for sure when Edward and I got together three months ago to write them. At that time, the band tip-toed around me sprinkling sentiments like, "this isn't sure thing, Dave; this doesn't mean anything long term, Dave; we're still auditioning other singers, Dave." I was cool. I was happy. I was in the moment.
>
> The next thing I knew, the four of us are doing surprise walk-on at the MTV Awards. I told Edward at that time that I didn't think it was a good idea for the band to go to New York half-cocked; and that I didn't want to imply by our presence

> that we were "back" if in fact it was just a quickie for old time's sake.
>
> Well ain't hind sight always 20/20 . . . Had I asked for something in writing, this wouldn't have happened. Had I acknowledged the occasional icy grip in my stomach, maybe this wouldn't have happened. But I didn't. Like I said—rapture. And, I love these guys. Do I trust them? That question never entered my mind.
>
> Then, a series of events last week led me to discover at about the same time the press did, that the band, along with their manager, had already hired another lead singer, possibly as long as three months ago. I wonder how he felt the night of the MTV Awards. It certainly explains why on that night Edward looked as uncomfortable as a man who just signed a deal with The Devil. I can't think of a reason Edward would lie to me about being considered for the lead singer when he had already hired someone, and then let me appear on MTV under the impression that there was great likelihood that Van Halen and I were reuniting. As I said, I told him in no uncertain terms that I didn't want to do the MTV gig as a band unless we were in fact, a band.
>
> And so I apologize to my fans and my supporters, and to MTV. I was an unwitting participant in this deception. It sickens me that the "reunion" as seen on MTV was nothing more than a publicity stunt. If I am guilty of anything, I'm guilty of denial. I wanted to believe it just as much as anyone else. Those who know me know that trickery was never my style.

Right back from camp Ed, Al, and Mike (and Ray) came the following:

> We parted company with David Lee Roth 11 years ago for many reasons. In his open letter of October 2nd, we were reminded of some of them. The intention all along was to do two new songs with Dave for the Best Of Volume 1 package. He was

> never lead to believe anything but that. When the four of us were asked by MTV and Warner Bros. to present an award at the 1996 MTV Video Music Awards, the four of us agreed.
>
> Dave was never an "unwitting participant". We appeared in public just as we do before releasing any other Van Halen record. For the last two weeks we have been working with someone who we hope will be part of the future of Van Halen, although no final decision can be announced until contractual considerations have been resolved.
>
> Van Halen will go forward and create the best possible music that we can.
>
> Edward, Alex, Michael

Later that month, Ed and Al opened up on a radio interview with Tommy Nast. Edward admitted that he was extremely depressed about the situation with Dave because in his heart he truly wanted to believe that Dave had changed and could be related to as an adult. Eddie said: Some excerpts follow:

> EVH: I'm gonna be 42 in January, I'm not a drunk 23-year-old who's easy to manipulate. I can read through everyone's BS now that I'm clean, you know? And I *really* wanted to believe that he had changed. And he had me fooled pretty good for a while, until MTV, when he basically spit in my face. And that was it as friends. And I was still willing to go on professionally and shoot a video with him, 'cause Warner Brothers wanted it. But two minutes of public adulation at the MTV awards and boom! Right back to old pure D.R.

Alex noted that Dave had simply declined to do a video, even though the video treatment offered to Dave was essentially unacceptable. Alex also claimed that the memory of and legacy of the original Van Halen with David Lee Roth had been romanticized and had gotten to the point where the perceived history no longer matched reality. And Van Halen fans were about to get a healthy dose of reality—no Dave, no Sammy . . . the boat was headed into uncharted waters.

Just two days later, Eddie and Alex went on the Mark & Brian radio show on KLOS out of L.A. on October 4. Eddie stated, "Gary Cherone, yes, 99.999% he will be in—there are some contractual things that need to be ironed out. And if those things happen, then he's in. But, contrary to any rumors or belief, I'd not even met Gary till after the MTV awards." Ed also said that his hip replacement surgery was scheduled for December 16, 1996, but he would put it off.

On September 4, mine and my best friend Mike's band had played a Saturday night show in Austin, and we missed the MTV broadcast. However, I had taped it and the whole band plus our friends raced back to my house after our gig to watch the footage. We feverishly fast-forwarded until we saw it. Upon the very first viewing, we were all exactly like the people in the audience. We were beyond floored. We were so adrenalized that we didn't even notice the obvious discomfort. We just saw Ed and Dave together, saw them hug, loved Dave's over-the-top comments. Then we started re-watching it repeatedly. Someone soon said, "Man, Eddie does *not* look like he wants to be there at all." Then someone else suggested, "I don't think Dave should've been doing that during Beck's acceptance speech." Then we watched the press tent interview segments they showed and were dismayed. I bought the greatest hits package the day it came out. I listened to the two new Roth songs about a hundred times in a row. It was bittersweet.

CHAPTER 31
Third Time's a Charm?

It didn't make national press, but the *Boston Herald* printed a rumor of Gary's audition on August 26, 1996. That was at least three weeks prior the MTV awards show (in Dave's open letter, he may very well have meant three "weeks" rather than three "months"). The short column also suggested that Gary was even staying at Ed's house for the duration of the supposed audition. Gary was already in close company—Ray Danniels' partner managed Extreme. With Extreme on hiatus, the leap to bring Gary in was not a very far one at all. The timing does indeed suggest that everyone either had Gary in mind already, or Gary was in place as a back-up plan should things not pan out with Roth. In 1998, Edward admitted outright, "The idea was not for [Roth] to be in the band again, but to try and help him get out of the Vegas trip he was in. Let him establish himself as a rock and roll singer again so he could put together a new band and do his own thing."

There are no major, big-time organizations, corporations, or what-have-you that goes into any huge venture without contingency plans. Van Halen was a big organization; Ray Danniels is a calculating human being—he didn't successfully manage Rush for more than two decades by winging it. As far as Ed's claim about never meeting Gary until after the MTV awards, the truth is that the *Boston Herald* story did not get national attention and was not noticed by hardly anyone at all. In doing research fifteen years after the fact, all one needs to do is line up the dates, or put Eddie's word against the *Boston Herald*. Or you can believe that the departure of Dave and the confirmation of Gary all within the course of a month was merely happenstance and that the fact that Ray co-managed Extreme was pure coincidence.

A full-blown interview with Ed appeared in the *L.A. Times* on October 26 and was conducted by Chuck Crisafulli. The first quote from Edward in the article is two words: "Utter lunacy." That's how he simply described the previous month's events. Exemplifying his depression, he said, "I've just been feeling sick about all this. . . . I thought we were taking the high road by not commenting on anything, but it got crazy." Eddie said that Sammy had straight up told him he wanted to be a solo artist again after Edward had begged him to be a more of a team player. "If he had wanted to be in this band, he'd still be here," Ed said. He threw out his personal diagnosis of both Sammy and Dave—that they each suffered from what he termed L.S.D., lead singer's disease. "But truthfully, it doesn't feel good to say bad things about Sammy or Dave," Edward said, adding, "They're both talented, we made a lot of good music together, and we had a lot of fun together. I still respect them both, but it's going to be hard to ever be friends again." Looking back and contemplating the future simultaneously, Eddie said:

> And despite everything we've been through recently, when I shut the studio door and start making music, I'm as pumped up about it as when I was a little kid. We've got 11 albums behind us, a greatest hits coming out, but frankly, I don't feel like I've done anything yet. I'm sober, I'm writing music every day, and I'm in a great band—I feel like I m just getting started.

On Halloween, while Valerie was on location shooting a movie, Ed took Wolfie trick-or-treating, bad hip and all. Valerie said he sounded "worn out from daddy duty." The very next day, *Van Halen Best Of Volume 1* with the two new songs with Dave hit the charts at #1—proof of the enduring interest in the band known as Van Halen. It was effectively the first DLR-related VH album to go to #1. Three days later, Sammy rush-released an internet-only single. On November 1, Ed and Al went on CNN to do more damage control over Roth's in-and-out departure.

Still Playing Incredible Music

On November 17, Ed performed at a benefit for Dave's one-time guitarist Jason Becker who suffers from ALS (also known as Lou Gehrig's Disease). Ed played the ALS benefit show in Chicago along with his long-time friend Steve Lukather, drummer Pat Torpey, as well as one-time Roth bassist Billy Sheehan.

That night Edward was somehow able to put everything that had been going on aside for one glorious evening. When asked how he became involved the day before the benefit show, Edward said, "We're in a position where we can help and raise some awareness and some money for [Becker's] family and . . . God, if it happened to one of us, I hope somebody would do the same. It's like he's very much alive. You look in his eyes, ya know, but he can't eat, he can't talk, he can't move, and there's no cure for it. It's like he's a prisoner in his own body." Eddie also added, "It's going to be a lot of fun tomorrow. I think we go on last. It's for a great cause and we've got a few surprises for ya."

The one-night supergroup was dubbed by Edward as The Lou Brutus Experience—named for a Chicago DJ—and it was magic. Captured video shows the tunes they covered were done in masterful fashion. Edward's playing on their ten-minute version of The Beatles' "I Want You (She's So Heavy)" is simply unbelievable—he played with such amazing precision . . . and *taste.* His adjustments to the many chord changes in the tunes were dead on. After he handed off the solo to Steve, Ed went and had an on-stage conversation with Sheehan during which Billy giggled as Steve soloed on. Eddie even contributed harmony vocals during the tune.

Other tunes they knocked out included "Wipeout," "Fire" and "Little Wing" (Jimi Hendrix), "Good Times/Bad Times" (Led Zeppelin), and "Ain't Talkin' 'Bout Love." For the Zeppelin tune—Ed performed a masterful mix of note-for-note Page licks as well as adding his own flavor all over it with tapping and bends to the heavens. When Ed launched into "Ain't Talkin' 'Bout Love"—the crowd burst into outrageous applause (Sheehan more than capably handled the lead vocals mimicking Dave's every inflection from the original recording). Steve and Eddie played the solo section in tandem to great effect and the crowd response after the tune was overwhelming. During "Fire," Steve said, "Oh, move over, Rover / And let Mr. Van Halen take over!" Again, Ed's perfect combo of note-for-note Jimi licks with his own trademark licks thrown in showed a man a top of his game musically. "Fire" went on forever and Ed wailed over every bit of it. The exact same can be said of their version of "Little Wing"—a far more delicate tune though, not a jam tune at all. Ed's contributions were beyond tasteful and beautiful. One could argue it was one of his finest live moments in years.

Dealing with Peavey and Taking Care of Eugenia

In late 1996, production began on a new line of Edward Van Halen custom guitars which he named after his son. The Peavey Wolfgang was clearly similar to the Music Man, but was tweaked a bit. Eddie said: "I held the guitar back a year—they showed it at a NAMM show, and I said, 'Hey, it ain't ready . . . ' So a lot of people got ticked off, you know, dudes that they put in their orders, and they didn't get the guitar till a year later. But, Hartley Peavey's a man of his word, you know, and I told him, hey, this guitar's not going out until I say it's ready, and he kept his word."

One of Edward's many patents and inventions was a device called a D-Tuna—a special lever for automatically dropping the low E string to the D note in quite an ingenious manner. "It's called a D-Tuna, and I've got a patent on it," Eddie said. "I've used it for quite a while; I just haven't marketed it until now. It's basically a cylinder that can be fined tuned and fits over the screw on the bridge. You just pull it out, and it automatically drops the low E down to a D—you don't even have to unclamp the nut. Push it back in and the D goes right back up to an E."

For Thanksgiving, Ed and Wolfgang traveled from Los Angeles to Park City, Utah along with Valerie's parents to join her for the holiday where she was filming on location. The family enjoyed Thanksgiving dinner together and spent the weekend skiing and playing in the snow. When Valerie's movie wrapped, she returned home hoping to ignite a spark in their marriage, but it failed to bring much fire. To make their domestic situation even more complicated, on Christmas Eve, Eddie's mother Eugenia fell and broke her pelvic bone and was hospitalized for several weeks. In early 1997, Edward and Valerie took care of Eugenia at their home. For several months, they were her 24-hour nurses. Valerie recalled how she found it especially odd that they could rise to the occasion so well in the face of some never-before encountered situations. They each would take the responsibility of taking off her clothes and bathing her delicate, damaged body by hand. Ed and Val also took care of her meals every single day.

Eugenia was feisty as ever, even at 82 years old. According to Valerie, one of her friends politely asked her how she was feeling and she responded by saying, "How the hell do you think I'm feeling? I broke a bone." Val said that Mrs. Van Halen complained vociferously about the price of groceries, and also had no filter when it came to Valerie's weight issues. Edward's mother was finally able to heal well enough to live independently again. Ed and Al bought her a brand new home in The Summit neighborhood near Beverly Hills. The house was barely 3,000 square feet, modest but plenty of room for Eugenia to stretch out. She was only two minutes or so away from Ed's house.

Recording *Van Halen III*

Upon Mrs. Van Halen's departure, the backyard started buzzing all over again. Recording of the Van Halen Mach III album started at 5150 in April 1997 and lasted until September. Gary's presence brought a completely new vibe to the camp in every sense. Gary was not "Look at me!" like Dave, and not Everyman like Sammy. Gary was a quiet but fairly intense fellow. He was a true metrosexual. Valerie said Gary played baseball with Wolfie while waiting for Ed to arise from a nap and that she enjoyed have deep conversations with him about the Bible (Gary had actually played the lead in a production of *Jesus Christ Superstar*). His band Extreme was temporarily disbanded, as they say. Originally a progressive, funk-rock band, Extreme became best known for two songs that were the only two that were, ironically, out of their comfort zone. Their best known hit was a simple acoustic guitar and vocal duet between Nuno Bettencourt and Gary called "More Than Words." The song was a #1 smash in the early 1991 and was an MTV staple. It was a pure love song ballad. There wasn't a prom in the nation that didn't play that song that year. Nuno was originally well known for his incredible shredding abilities, and then it turned out Extreme's biggest hit was a simple acoustic guitar ballad.

Eddie praised Gary's talent and personality. He said his presence with the band was magic, and said that Gary added "another flavor to the soup." With regard to their creative process, Edward told writer George A. Fletcher that it was important for a band and a producer to have the common goal of simply making a song the best it can be, no matter what it is. "Gary's that kind of player," said Ed. "He's into being part of that process, being part of the team. As oppose to, 'I want it my way, I'm gonna take my baseball bat and go home.'" Edward called him a brother and said, "He's a normal guy like Alex, Mike, and me."

As far as Gary being a "team player," at this point, the meaning of "team player" had changed. By 1997, Edward was the head coach with Alex as his loyal assistant coach with everyone else as the players. It turns out the brothers had been playing with a host of other players for a while. In April 1997, Sammy Hagar told David Huff, "I've just heard some pretty strong rumors that Michael Anthony is no longer in Van Halen." According to Sammy, the brothers were rehearsing with British female singer Sass Jordan as early as February 1996. She lived just doors down from 5150 and confronted Ray Danniels one day, telling him she thought they were seriously considering her becoming the band's new singer. He responded, "Of course, they were! Why the hell else do you think you were up there?" Also, singer Mitch Malloy had an up-and-down with the band. They had reportedly told him he had secured the position in early summer 1996, only to witness the MTV debacle and quietly back out of the deal. Whatever was going on with Michael Anthony during 1997 was not elaborated upon.

In March of 1997, Edward and Alex made an appearance in the famous "Got Milk?" print advertising campaign. Edward had a milk mustache and milk dribbling from his chin, and Alex had poured the entire glass over his head and milk was streaming down his shirtless body. The caption was written in Edward's voice: "Of all the lead singers we've had, most never got enough calcium. Typical. But not for Alex and me. Because every time we change singers, we have an extra glass of milk. That way we're sure to get more than the recommended three glasses a day. As you can see, sometimes all at once." It was an effective way of poking fun at themselves but reinforced that brothers-against-the-world mentality, with Edward doing the talking and the bigger Alex standing behind him with his arms folded.

The album that became *Van Halen III* was a collection of diverse material, although what is diversity to one is incongruity to another. At the outset of the project, Edward told Steven Rosen that he wasn't worried about what the fans would think about Gary. He said:

> You cannot please everyone all the time. No matter who sings, someone is not gonna like it. I'm sick and tired of being controlled, and I don't want to control. I just have so much music and I want to put it out. Gary's very talented and we work very, very well together. . . . I don't care. If it touches one person, then it's great. I don't care if it sells millions, I don't care if it sells a tenth of the records that we've sold. It's not about that, it's for the love of music.

Eddie also noted that if things ended up not working out with Gary, "That would pretty much be it for Van Halen. Al and I would just move on, score movies, whatever." Ed even joked that he'd take up the tuba if the project failed.

The producer for the album was an odd choice. Mike Post was a golfing buddy of Edward's who had originally been a musician (having performed the guitar part on Sonny and Cher's "I Got You Babe") and later a semi-super-producer who wrote and recorded some of the most famous TV soundtrack songs of all time. Post had little to no rock experience, but Edward was far more concerned that they be able to work well together by Ed's definition.

Edward recorded whenever—and where ever—inspiration hit him. Eddie had a special studio set up in the bathroom so he could record while sitting on the toilet, where he said "God gave him frequent inspiration." Edward was pumping out so much material that they at one point considered making a double album, however, the logistics had already proven detrimental with the live album. Nevertheless, the album run time of sixty-five minutes is more than any two of the first six albums added together.

Going Down a Path

Edward took the lyric writing very seriously. It was the first ever time that a singer had handed over piles of lyric sheets to edit or to provide a spark for writing music. "I've been making music for 37 or 38 years and never has somebody handed me lyrics to work with," Eddie said. "This record is the biggest milestone in my life because the lyrics came first, then the music. I finally had something to bounce off."

Ed was lying in bed with Valerie one evening reading over lyrics given to him by Gary when he came across what became "How Many Say I." Eddie said the lyrics struck him hard and hit a deep cord. He later hailed and/or defended the lyrics by saying that they were "not all about female body parts." This one song is arguably the single greatest departure ever taken on a Van Halen album in the entire history of the band.

The song is a nearly seven-minute piano and vocal duet with Ed playing piano and Gary singing falsetto harmony. Edward sang lead vocals. The first minute of the song is a slightly haunting yet delicate bit of piano work not terribly unlike "Right Now" or even a John Lennon song. When Ed starts singing, you can immediately recognize his speaking voice within his singing voice. The talking-style vocal delivery is something totally and completely different for Van Halen. It was more along the lines of Tom Waits or Roger Waters with very little melody at all. In fact, it feels a bit like a Pink Floyd song.

It was Ed's attempt to get very serious and very heavy. Unfortunately, an audience tends to take their seriousness and heaviness from someone that's already in that line of work. Ed was not, traditionally, a "heavy" person. He was Mr. Charming with a "pretty boy smile." His "brand" is not heady, but that was fine. This was his "OK! I've had it up to here with this whole fucking party thing!" He even slagged the classic Van Halen image, deriding the tag, in his words, that VH was "America's premiere party band."

With regard to "How Many Say I," it is hard to imagine a single person saying, "Oh man, I really want to hear that again. Play it again. One more time." It is surely scientifically measurable as the least re-listened-to song in Van Halen history. It is likely that the majority of people listened to the song once and never did again. The tune in and of itself could've been what sunk the album in some people's minds.

When Ed sings about hungry children and the homeless, it simply does not resonate. There's a line about denial that Ed really delivers with aplomb. As far as a vocal melody, there really isn't one, and what is there is very limited in range. Gary's falsetto does not mesh well with Eddie's voice on the track, and the repetitiveness of the chorus approaches grating. Where the song is posted on YouTube, where everyone's opinion is out there for the world to see, user AeroZach1029 posted the following comment: "Christ, those of you defending this song may need your heads checked. This is not only the worst Van Halen song of all time, this may be one of the worst songs I've ever heard in my entire life. . . . Just an abomination of both Van Halen and music as a whole."

The album's opener was a beautiful instrumental called "Neworld." It was a classical piece with Mike Post on piano and Edward an acoustic guitar. The song is exactly what those wishing for an Edward Van Halen solo album should have anticipated. Musically, it is a brilliant workout between the piano and the guitar—Post truly did an excellent job. If marketed properly, it could have killed on the classical music charts (surely those do exist). Another instrumental on the album, "Primary," fits the same EVH solo album category. The latter is a guitar workout with an extremely effected sound approximating a sitar with a supremely low bass sound.

"Without You" was the single. It was the first video and the first to hit FM radio. It had a slow, steady stomping beat in the "Poundcake" vein. Edward wrote the majority of the lyrics to the song. He said, "I wrote the first two verses and the chorus to 'Without You,' and Gary wrote the third." Edward explained:

> It is about the fact that we're all living on the planet, and in order to keep the light alive for our children, we've got to get together. "I can't do it without you." I certainly can't do it on my own. I picked up this book on Buddhism in Japan and it was so to the point of what we're talking about: all things are impermanent. Ego isn't real. "You" own nothing. If you surround yourself with impure people, you wind up with impure or toxic thoughts. Greed and being out of touch with what's real in ourselves is the basis for so much of what we've screwed up. Humans have only been around for a relatively minuscule period of time, and look what we've done to this planet just in the last one hundred years. It's like we're sawing off the limb we're sitting on. That's basically what "Without You" is about.

The guitar and bass work was classic Van Halen style—incredible riffs, chord progressions, and lead guitar work. Once Gary's vocals hit, there was an immediate reaction that each listener experienced. Either the combination worked for you or it did not. The main line in the chorus was "There must be some kind of way that we can make it right." Quite unintentionally, it expressed a kind of plea from the band to its fans. Sadly, the song tried but fell flat. Reaction was almost immediate and universal. It did not work. The formula was not the same without David Lee Roth or Sammy Hagar.

As history would prove, Edward Van Halen is at his best when he works with David Lee Roth as his creative partner. Their combination is magic, and for an entire generation, Dave Roth and Ed Van Halen were their Simon and Garfunkel, their McCartney and Lennon, their Plant and Page. There's no way of scientifically dissecting the unbelievable power they brought when they work together. The sum was much greater than the total of its parts. It could very well be that it was because of the fact that they went back so far together, they just had a common brotherhood-like bond that made them both better at what they did. They had put in all of that original hard work together as teenagers playing backyard parties and dance clubs. Ed and Dave had one of rock music's healthiest competitions. When David Lee Roth and Edward Van Halen come together, they can do what very few people in the world can do, and that is command an audience with pure authority.

There are some that surely believe whole-heartedly that Edward was at his very best with Sammy Hagar, and on *5150*, at the least, there's an argument to be made. But the balance falls to Dave. There's no real reason for it, it simply is what it is. Back in 1996 when MTV was covering the news of Dave's return the studio, Lars Ulrich said, "Seeing Van Halen with Dave again would be the ultimate. . . . And I hope they wanna do it. And more power to 'em and good luck." Jerry Cantrell of Alice in Chains, who actually toured with Van Halen in the early 90s, said, "I love Sammy and I don't know Dave. But I would have to say that I prefer Van Halen with Dave. I'm sorry to Sammy."

Van Halen with Gary Cherone would be a short-lived, ill-advised venture.

CHAPTER 32
The Crash

Production on *Van Halen III* was credited to "Mike Post, Edward Van Halen." The album was released on March 17, 1998 and debuted at #4 on the *Billboard* charts. "Without You" did very well on FM radio and was #1 on the *Billboard* Mainstream Rock Tracks chart, specifically, from March 7 until April 11. The song "Fire in the Hole" went to #6 on the same chart briefly, but "One I Want" peaked at #27, and that was it. The album did not sell well. By July, it was completely out of the top 200.

I did like "Without You." I never changed the radio when the song would come on, but that was possibly in part perhaps because I knew I was not going to purchase the album, so I had to hear it when I had the chance. I happen to be somewhat surrounded by more than half a dozen certifiable Van Halen superfans—both back in the day and still to this day. At the time, I was getting reports of bad news from the ones that had bought it and listened to the entire album, all sixty-five minutes worth. There were murmurs of "a terrible song" and "it just doesn't work" being exchanged frequently. I did not buy the album. It was not because there was an "I Can't Stop Loving You" on it. It was simply because I chose not to engage in what I was sensing was going to be an artistic failure. I just did not want it in my collection or in my head. My brother Brandon, on the other hand, ran out and bought the album the day it came out. He liked it. He was an extremely loyal fan.

That March, Edward gave an extensive interview to Vic Garbarini of *Guitar World.* He called *Van Halen III* the most important album of his life. "I'm very nervous about going out on tour with this record, but that's something I've got to deal with," Eddie said. "I don't know how many people are going to get it, how many people are going to be in shock. . . . People are either going to like it or they're not."

In Garbarini's presence, Ed was off doing phone interviews with Japanese and Spanish language reporters. It was noted that the interviewers were essentially focused on the history rather than the future of Van Halen. "Karen Moss, Ed's veteran publicist, is concerned," Garbarini said. "She asks if he's okay, it must be exasperating, she wants to make sure he isn't depressed. Depressed? Ed puts his arm around her and promises her that he's fine, no worries."

Dave's revealing autobiography *Crazy from Heat* had been released by that time. It was well-received and hit the *New York Times* bestseller list. It was one of the first ever texts to ever truly dish on Edward. When asked if he had read Dave's book, Ed said, "Why bother? I know the guy better than he probably knows himself." He did concede that he believed Dave was "an intelligent, well-read guy."

The Ill-fated *Van Halen III* Tour

When I heard that MTV was going to air an hour of one of the very first concerts of the tour on May 1, I was ecstatic. I had already read that songs like "Somebody Get Me a Doctor," "Unchained," and "Mean Streets" were in the set list, and I was as excited as ever to see what it was like.

I was alone at home with the VCR rolling when the broadcast started. It was cool to see Ed with long hair again—he looked like the old Eddie. When they kicked into "Unchained," I was fucking giddy. But when Gary's voice—and his showmanship—kicked in, I was experiencing extreme cognitive dissonance, as extreme as it can feel when it comes to art. Half of it was brilliant and half of it didn't work. I continued to give it a try as they plowed through other songs. "Why Can't This Be Love" was interesting in that Michael and Eddie both sang lead on the second verse, with Mike taking the first two lines and Ed taking the last two lines. Ed's voice was raggedy though, and he missed the vocal mark.

I was frustrated because I wanted Edward to succeed so badly, but I knew this particular lineup was simply not going to work, and it was difficult to deal with, to be honest. I was 26 years-old and had already been following him for two-thirds of my life. At the time, for the most part I just looked away and poured myself into my own music and my own band.

The Van Halen show that aired on MTV was filmed in Sydney on April 20, 1998. The tour started with two weeks of dates across New Zealand and Australia before an eight-show run in the U.S. in May. Ironically, the U.S. jaunt kicked off in my old hometown of Houston before heading to Dallas. Fan reviews were overwhelmingly positive with most praising Eddie for still being Eddie and giving Gary a pat on the back for a job well done. Some though came away saying they couldn't get used to Gary's voice. He was accused of having the wrong look and stage moves approximating a poor imitation of Freddie Mercury. After Dallas, they played in Chicago where Eddie sported one of his Wolfgang guitars with a Chicago Bulls logo on the body. The band continued on to Cleveland, Detroit, Boston, Madison Square Garden in New York, and the Spectrum in Philadelphia. They then traveled for a series of shows in Europe, but it would be a short-lived, cursed excursion.

On May 27, Van Halen played in Helsinki. On May 29 and May 31, they played two enormous festivals in Germany sharing the bill with Ozzy, Bad Religion, the Deftones, and others. They played one show in Berlin before heading to Hamburg, where the tour came to a sudden stop. During sound check, a piece of the ceiling at the arena crumbled and fell. The chunk of plaster hit Alex, tearing a muscle in his right arm and inflicting a debilitating bruise. With only four shows on this leg of the tour under their belt, the band was forced to cancel the remaining eleven shows due to Alex's injury.

Alex was ready to go by July and the band played twenty U.S. dates in that month alone. However, one July show in Sacramento drew an alarmingly low 1,600 people. "I heard they played for forty minutes and Eddie walked off stage," said Sammy. "I wasn't there, but Gary told me after we became friends." At a show in early August, Gary took a blow to the head from his mic stand resulting in a gash. Their August 12 concert in Montreal was canceled, and the band didn't make it fifteen minutes into their set the following night in Boston before Gary lost his voice in front of his hometown crowd. Eddie and Alex reportedly asked the crowd if they would come back the following night. During the makeup show the following day, Hagar claims Cherone told him that Edward walked offstage and disappeared for a full thirty minutes. The band played solid through the rest of August and into early September before their September 6 show in Wisconsin was canceled. They played only three more shows when their Puerto Rico date on September 20 was canceled due to a massive hurricane. To top it off, the next three Brazilian dates were canceled reportedly due to conflicts with a promoter.

In early October, Van Halen played two shows in Vegas and one each in Alaska and Hawaii before a string of ten straight shows in Japan. At the time, no one knew that it was the end of yet another era of VH.

Sadly, it was the end of something much larger for me. My brother Brandon had actually become a successful commercial pilot. He and his wife Susan had been living in Los Angeles for several years, and Brandon worked at the Van Nuys Airport. He actually ended up befriending Phil Hartman (the voice of Waldo in the "Hot for Teacher" video—just another thing that made it such a wild friendship). Brandon even got to fly Phil's plane to Catalina with Phil in the passenger seat. Brandon also went to his home and met his wife and his children. They were friends. When Phil was murdered by his wife in the summer of 1998, I was the first person that broke the news to my brother, and he broke down and wept on the phone.

On December 8, 1998, my brother went on a flight run and his plane was found eight days later underwater in Lake Okeechobee in Florida. Van Halen lost one of its most hardcore fans of all time that day. My life was never the same. Brandon was the one that really brought Van Halen into our household, into our lives, and into our brains. We were better for it. He only lived thirty years—but he packed them full of adventure, including having put his arm around Eddie Van Halen.

CHAPTER 33
Staying Conscious

In March 1999, the Recording Industry Association of America (RIAA) created a new record sales award: diamond status. This recognition goes to albums that sell ten million copies or more. Upon creation of the diamond award, *Van Halen* and *1984* were both honored. It is certainly one of Edward's biggest achievements—twenty million-plus copies sold of just two albums alone. The only test that matters—the test of time—has proven that those are truly *the* two albums. This made Van Halen one of only six rock bands that have had at least two different album releases sell more than ten million copies domestically. That put Edward and the band in good company with The Beatles, Led Zeppelin, Eagles, and Pink Floyd (Def Leppard is somehow also on that list). There is a clear distinction that the two albums on that list are the Dave/Edward albums.

The idea for 1999 was to focus on a follow-up to *Van Halen III*. But little actually took place, and there was certainly nothing outside of 5150 to show for it. In July, the band reconvened to begin work on a new record. Renowned producer Danny Kortchmar was officially named producer of the next album in August.

Edward's continued postponement of his hip surgery finally got to Valerie. "He continued to put it off until he reached the point where he could no longer manage the pain by drinking or doing whatever else he did," she said. "I offered little help with his discomfort and less sympathy. . . . My capacity for compassion was degenerative too."

For reasons known only to Gary Cherone himself, he used his place in Van Halen as a soapbox to counter Pearl Jam's Eddie Vedder and his pro-choice position on abortion. Gary penned a somewhat infamous poetic rant on his quasi-scientific pro-life/anti-choice stance on the issue. The poem/article was literally titled "An Open Letter to Eddie Vedder" and was published in June of 1999. Obviously an issue that divides people into one of two camps, Gary argued that a human being is a human being at the point of conception. Needless to say, some might argue against that notion, and some might even argue that that's not even the point. In fact, some might argue whether the third lead singer of Van Halen—who was coming fresh off the entire disaster that was 1998—should be opening his mouth about such a divisive issue in the media. There's also the angle of him being an unwitting representative of Van Halen—a then 25-year-old band—taking on the last man standing of the grunge movement, Eddie Vedder. Again, only Gary knows why he chose to pick such a fight.

In October 1999, Edward once again opened up to Vic Garbarini of *Guitar World* in an extensive interview during which Ed was extremely frank on nearly every possible issue. He minimized and deflected any outside diagnoses that he was suffering from depression in any way. "I can be perfectly happy and write and play," he said. "Put it this way: I don't like being bummed. I don't have to be depressed to play the blues. And if anyone begs to differ, well that's their way."

He faced the relative failure of *Van Halen III* head on. "I'm not hurt or angry that the record didn't do as well as we thought it would," he said. "I'm still very proud of it, just like every other record." He acknowledged that it was indeed different, and theorized that the range of emotions on the album may have simply been too much for some people. "It was over the top," said Edward. "This might sound arrogant, and I really hope people won't take it that way, but I had to play what I felt moved by and enjoyed. I can't contrive that. It's funny about guitar playing, because that's the stuff I can't remember doing at all. That came from my real self, which my ego can't take credit for."

Eddie defended Gary against the idea that his vocals on the album sounded stiff. "Yeah, he might have been a bit nervous," said Edward. He continued:

> If you feel there was any stiffness, then you really should blame me. Because he sang just about everything the way I asked him to. The fact that I was writing all the music and it wasn't his own, and he had to learn it so quickly, probably made a difference, sure. Now we know each other a lot better. Gary's working with me and writing some of the music himself, rather than just handing in lyrics. We're all a lot looser, and the new record will reflect that. But I'm very proud of that record. When

> we moved on with Sammy, I never looked back. And I'm not looking back now, because there ain't no "back" to go to.

Ed complained that the CD pressing plant that cranked out *Van Halen III* was the reason why the CD had poor fidelity. Upon hearing test pressings, Edward apparently leapt into action and went straight to the facility. "They have nothing at these pressing plants that measures sonic quality," he said. "They have nothing to analyze the full frequency range on the disk; they can only tell if there's a scratch error or if the disc skips. So when I went down to the pressing plant, I raised a stink. Well, you're talking about fighting Time-Warner, and I came away feeling like I'd stuck my nose where it doesn't belong."

Garbarini pushed Eddie into a corner and asked him which one single song he would put in a time capsule. After initially resisting, Ed finally answered with "Jump." Noting what a departure it was for Van Halen at the time, he said, "We had the challenge of using the synth and keyboards for the first time and integrating that with the guitar and melody line. It was also our biggest hit. And 'pop' comes from the word popular, which means a lot of people liked it. Now, 99 percent of the reason that I make music is to hopefully try and touch people with it. And that one touched the most people. So far."

At the end of October, Roger Waters of Pink Floyd released a song titled "Lost Boys Calling" for the soundtrack of the film *The Legend of 1900*. The song was a collaboration between Waters, legendary film composer Ennio Morricone, and Edward. The tune is a typical Floyd-esque quiet, English piano ballad. Ed's middle solo so incredibly understated, beautiful, tasteful, and spot on; it's almost a direct nod to Clapton. Ed also has a brief outro solo in which he beautifully incorporates his own trademark octave feedback notes with tremolo manipulation.

Van Halen Mach III Falls Apart

The band had indeed worked on a few songs over the course of the year, but eventually, the follow-up project was simply abandoned. Without too much surprise, Gary reportedly decided to leave Van Halen of his own accord on November 5, 1999. "Van Halen is one of the greatest rock & roll bands of all time," said Gary. He went on to lament that it was a simple matter of fact that hardcore Van Halen fans would never accept him or anyone else in the band other than David Lee Roth, or, for a different audience, Sammy Hagar. Alex said, "He was just the wrong choice, it's that simple. . . . The chemistry was just wrong." Pushing the idea that the departure was amicable, Edward referred to Gary as a brother, and proclaimed that they would continue to have a personal and musical relationship. That never did pan out. At the time of Gary's departure, an official Van Halen press release admitted work on the album they had been recording was only half-finished.

A few years later, Gary opened up a bit more about the split. "I always knew that, every time I stepped on stage, I didn't have to do anything [wrong] for people to hate me," he said. "Most of the fans were good, but some of the fans got in my head." Cherone said flat-out that he was in a no-win situation, period, but that he did not regret taking the job or the experience he took away. "I wouldn't trade it for the world," he said. "I wouldn't trade the experience. I made good friends, and I definitely grew as a singer. Eddie made me a better singer in the studio." Over a decade removed from the situation, Gary said, "My managers asked me to write my Van Halen story (my three years in the band), but I told them that that stuff is going to be taken to the grave." Typically, when something really great happens, or you have an awesome experience, you want to talk about it. For the most part, you don't take great experiences and memories "to the grave." Ray Danniels simultaneously departed and returned to devoting himself full-time to Rush.

Hip Surgery

It was over. There was only medical work to be done. Edward finally proceeded with his hip replacement surgery just two weeks after Gary's departure. The procedure took place on November 16, 1999 at Saint John's Health Center in Santa Monica and was performed by Dr. John R. Moreland, a bit of a hip replacement surgeon to the stars (his other clients included Liza Minnelli and Elizabeth Taylor). Ed desired to stay conscious during the entire procedure. Rather than general anesthetic, Eddie requested an epidural. Edward actually documented the entire ordeal on an audio recorder. Dr. Moreland said, "Maybe he'll use it on an album."

Ed came out of the surgery in severe pain. "He complained that the morphine they gave him made him high but didn't relieve the pain," said

Valerie. However, things settled rather quickly for Ed and he was walking on his own only three days after the operation. When they went home from the hospital, Ed hilariously brought a little souvenir with him—his hip bone wrapped in a plastic bag. "He put it in the freezer," said Val. "He wrapped the bag with tape, and in large bold letters he wrote: MY HIP BONE—DO NOT COOK!"

With a titanium hip in place, Eddie would eventually recover well. On December 1, Edward told *USA Today*, "I literally just saw my x-ray. It's perfect. This is really heaven-sent." The future would find him doing his trademark bent-leg jumps yet again. If things had only gotten better from there.

For Christmas, Ed gave Valerie a beautiful, understated ruby ring set. Valerie was overjoyed that it matched her taste exactly, but likened it to just another wad of jewelry to throw on the pile. She said it didn't matter because they weren't happy. "Part of me wanted to keep kissing Ed," Val said, "and part of me wanted to wring his neck and scream, 'Don't you get it?'"

Just three day before Ed underwent the surgery, my collective VH buddies and I caught David Lee Roth at Stubb's in Austin. [Note: This show would later become semi-famous in 2011 when a hilarious video called "Find the Mystery Rocker" featured pictures from the show went viral in an attempt to track down the person that lost their disposable camera at the show. The guy that lost his camera was found in relatively short order.] We got there early so we could be as close as possible. We had no idea what we were in for. The man came out swinging and had the capacity crowd at his command like no time had passed. Beautifully, other than "Yankee Rose," the set was nothing but classic Van Halen songs. From my perspective, Dave had something to prove. He came off the 1996 debacle looking a bit like a played chump. There was talk that he didn't have the voice anymore to be in the game. I can tell you that from where I stood, Mr. Roth was on fire. He belted out the outro of "Little Dreamer" like a consummate professional. I considered myself a pretty decent singer at the time, but after hearing that break at the end of that song, I remember distinctly thinking, "Damn, now *that* dude can really sing, man. Anyone that says he can't hasn't seen this."

After catching Dave's show, I called my brother's widow Susan. She was a bit taken aback by my call because, for one thing, we didn't talk that often beginning shortly after the plane crash, and also because my voice sounded so much like my brother's to her, it kind of freaked her out. I went on and on about the show and how Dave did such an excellent job carrying the classic Van Halen torch and that there was absolutely no reason he couldn't handle the job on a much larger scale. After a bit of awkward silence, I just blurted out, "I don't know . . . this would be a phone call I would usually make to Brandon, so I just wasn't sure what to do, so I just called you." It was bittersweet, to say the least.

CHAPTER 34
The Diagnosis

Kicking off the millennium, Ed did an exclusive interview with *Guitar.com* in January 2000. About Dave and Sammy, he said, "I don't understand either one of these guys. They quit and have nothing good to say about me, yet they want to be in the band. I'm not a psychologist, but I wouldn't want to work with people I don't like. They don't like me, but they want to work with me." He expressed regret at coining his oft-repeated L.S.D./lead singer's disease catch-phrase. "I hate that term," he said. "I regret it. I said it once years ago. . . . It actually wasn't even my term; I think it was a friend of mine who pegged it that. It's just, I guess, the nature of a lot of lead singers to think that they are it and the planet revolves around them." With reference to *Van Halen III*, he said, "It basically stiffed."

That same month, Eddie went to the dentist for a check-up and a cleaning. According to Valerie, the shape of Ed's teeth caused him to bite his tongue repeatedly over the years when he ate. She said it was often hard to watch. However, the dentist found the scar tissue on his tongue to be unusual and sent Edward to a specialist.

"We went to the specialist at UCLA Medical Center, who cut out a section of Ed's tongue and had it biopsied," Valerie said. "Cancer." To confirm, a second piece of Ed's tongue was also taken off and the test results proved the same—squamous-cell carcinoma of the tongue. The doctor called Edward and Valerie into the room to break the news to them at the same time. The doctor insisted that Ed must give up smoking immediately and permanently. From Valerie's *Losing It*:

> "I don't want either of you to misunderstand me," he said. "I want to make this very clear. Ed, you are never to smoke again. Never. I don't know if I can be any more clear. You are never to smoke again. If you do, this will return." . . . "Don't you ever

> smoke again," I said, shaking my fist at him. "Because if that doesn't kill you, like the doctor says it will, I will kill you."

Within a few months, Eddie resumed smoking. Valerie was completely floored. "I couldn't believe it when I saw him puffing away," she said. "Was he insane? He'd heard the doctor's warning: the cancer would return. Even if he didn't care about his own life, what about me and Wolfie—most of all Wolfie?" Valerie confessed to crossing the line during an argument when she said, "Why don't you have another cigarette and get some more of your tongue cut off? Keep it up. Soon you won't be able to talk." That was effectively it for Val. Her patience had officially run completely out. She flatly said, "Ed and I were terrible examples of what a husband and wife should be. . . . Wolfie deserved better."

To celebrate her 40th birthday on April 23 that year, Valerie insisted on having a girls-only weekend to get a break from Eddie. Before she left, he took her out to their favorite restaurant. Finding fault with everything he did, she was irritated that Ed had set up the dinner so that they could dine in private before the restaurant opened to ensure they would not be interrupted. In Valerie's mind, she just thought that was rude to the staff to make them all work to suit their schedule. She said that Ed was sweet, pleasant, and calm the entire evening. "Why are you being so nice?" she thought. "I need to figure out how to leave you."

In May of 2000, Eddie began undergoing weekly "preventative" treatments at M.D. Anderson Hospital in Houston. Although they tried to keep it private, the media began reporting that Eddie had cancer in May. His trips to Houston were too noticeable. Press releases followed to the contrary, but fans were on high alert, for sure.

Alternative Treatments

Like so many other things, cancer was something Edward was determined to take on in his own way. In early summer, Ed and Val flew to New York to meet with a different kind of specialist working in alternative cancer treatments. From Valerie's autobiography:

> I don't know how he found this so-called expert, whether it was through a recommendation of from the *Internet*. But the doctor definitely seemed like a quack. He arrived at our

> hotel room smoking a cigarette and carrying a bottle of wine. "That's the doctor that's going to help you?" I said after watching the two of them smoke and drink through the initial meeting. However, Ed was of the belief that his cancer had been caused not by cigarettes and alcohol but from a reaction between the metal in his artificial hip and a metal guitar pick he bit on during rehearsals and performances. There were fans online that elaborated on his theory, citing as possible causes electromagnetic waves, radiation attracted by the pick, and even the nickel-plating in his guitar strings that rubbed off his fingertips and into his mouth. There were also people who wouldn't have blinked twice if Ed claimed he could turn water into wine.

In 2006, during an infamous Howard Stern radio interview (to be covered later in depth), Ed implied that the method he used to treat his cancer with Dr. Steve McClain in New York was actually illegal in the United States, but he did not clarify the statement. He noted that a significant piece of his tongue was removed—at the time, about one-third in total. He said the healthy pieces of his tongue were used to grow his cells outside of his body, and the testing was done externally rather than internally. His tongue samples were experimented on. The resulting "secret" method was then performed on Edward.

Dave's Private Return

At this exact same time in 2000—from the dentist appointment, to UCLA, to Houston, to New York—Edward had been keeping another secret from the public. He had been working in the studio with Dave on and off for all those months. *MTV News* reported the rumor in March. That spring, the entire original Van Halen lineup convened at 5150 two times for jam sessions of their classic material. Dave later said, "It sounded amazing." Things went so well that they continued to work together and moved on to laying down new material. "I played him a few new tunes, we bullshitted a bit, had some laughs, and everything seemed cool," said Eddie. "He was even kind enough to turn me on to his uncle, Jack Roth, a cancer surgeon and research specialist at, coincidentally, M.D. Anderson, in Houston, where I had been going once a week for treatment." It would turn out that the timing of Dave's recommendation of his uncle was likely not until after April of 2001 based on a later statement made by Dave.

By July 2000, the original VH had three songs tracked and ready to go. That same month, Michael Anthony was interviewed in the short-lived publication *Yamaha All Access*. He was asked who the new singer was going to be and said, "We're saving the announcement for the right time. . . . It's going to be huge. It's a name people will know." Still in the media spotlight, in August, Edward and Valerie were spotted taking Wolfgang out to the Britney Spears concert at the Forum and again in November at the 'N Sync concert at the MGM Grand Garden Arena in Vegas.

Things for the band came to a halt around September when, for reasons easily deduced, a team of lawyers got involved to carve down into the nitty-gritty. "Everything looked pretty positive about gettin' together," he said. "But before you know it, attorneys are involved. These cats had me so beat down and confused, it made the cancer seem like a tiny zit on my ass. Everything seemed to fall apart after these guys got involved. I mean, we used to do it on a handshake."

There was no official "fuck you!" this time. It simply fizzled out. The rumor mill was in full burn and churn mode for months. When a picture of Dave from about 1980 appeared on the cover of *Spin* in August, a lot of us thought it was a done deal. To pour it on, Warner Brothers reissued remastered versions of only the first six albums, boosting the sonic quality for modern sound systems. The silence throughout 2000 was deafening, even though it had actually seen the reformation of the original lineup of the band in the studio cranking out several brand new tracks—tracks that have never seen the light of day. Sammy made a lot of news running his mouth with speculative comments that Dave was back but got kicked out again and other gossip. But Ed rode out the remainder of the year being extremely quiet.

A Generous Man

In December 2000, Edward was taking golf lessons from his instructor Ron Del Barrio when Ed confronted him with an offer of outrageous generosity. As per Ron:

> [Edward] "I know you're unhappy being Mr. Golf Teacher to the Stars. I mean, people are using you, ripping you off right

> and left. What's your passion? What's your gift? What do you really think you should be doing?"
>
> "Playing golf, working on my own game, competing," I say.
>
> "So why not just do it?" asks Eddie.
>
> I tell him how much money I need each year—$1 followed by too many zeroes—to quit teaching and try to earn a Tour card.
>
> Says Eddie, "No, you don't understand. I know you can play. I've seen you hit some golf shots. I'll give you 10 years of backing if you need it. Right now money for me is just a tool to help the people I love. I fucking love you. So let's go!"
>
> Eddie looks me in the eye, and I look back at him. We start crying right there and sob away like two big babies. A few weeks later I sign a contract with Eddie's management company. I stop working with most of my teaching clients and spend most of my time working on my own game. I sign up for the satellite tournaments on the Pepsi and Buy.com tours. In my first five starts, I get five top-five finishes.

In early 2001, a follow-up exam gave Edward cause for alarm—yet another cancer scare. "Enough with the alternative clinic crap; go to the best doctors in L.A.," said Valerie. According to Ron in May, with regard to Ed fighting cancer, he said, "[Edward] says he's winning, that his chemo treatments appear to be working." This is important to note as Edward later said during the infamous 2006 Stern interview that "I beat it without chemo or radiation."

Ed attended the January 2001 NAMM convention only by video and his message was simply that the new Peavey Wolfgang guitar wasn't ready yet and that he wanted to continue testing it until it was "bullet proof." Michael Anthony was there in person, though, and intimated that a new album and tour might be in the works toward the end of the year. That spring, a rumor erupted that Van Halen had secretly begun booking stadiums for the fall.

Things were still not going well with Valerie and Eddie. Feeling neglected and underappreciated, Val had been carrying on an online relationship with an Atlanta businessman named Mark, whom she met through her brother David. In March, Valerie threw an Oscar watching party at their home, and Mark was in attendance. She went out of her way to dote on Mark to intentionally make Edward jealous, and it worked. Ed pulled Valerie aside and peppered her with questions about this guy, and her answers apparently placated Eddie for the time being.

For spring break, Ed, Val, and Wolfie rented a Winnebago and went on a long road trip to Arizona and back. They checked out the Grand Canyon and the Arizona meteor crater and camped out at KOA campgrounds like any other family. According to Valerie, it was one of their most ideal moments as a three-piece family.

Cancer Revealed

Dave put out a message on his website that March that said, "There's a lot of really good rumors and some of 'em are even true about me goin' on out there, and I would like to tell you now, that if you wanna hear the truth, the whole truth and nothing but my version of the truth, you're only gonna hear it from me." The mill was in a complete frenzy when Dave finally issued a public statement on April 19:

> About a year ago, myself and the great Van Halen band played together once or twice and it sounded amazing. In the following several months, Edward and I — Edward Van Halen and me, David Lee Roth — created some of the most amazing, phenomenal . . . the hands fell off the clock, ladies and gentleman, and we wrote three astonishing tunes. That was last July, and since then I haven't been up to the studio, we haven't really been in touch, and we haven't made any music. But I am holding forth; I am in the shape of my life, and I got the high note — I'm ready to go.

Only a week later, the official Van Halen website—which had not been serving the purpose of keeping the fans informed—released a personal message from Edward on April 26:

> I'm sorry for having waited so long to address this issue personally. But, cancer can be a very unique and private matter to deal with. So, I think it's about time to tell you where I'm at. I was examined by three oncologists and three head & neck

> surgeons at Cedars-Sinai just before spring break and I was told that I'm healthier than ever and beating cancer. Although it's hard to say when, there's a good chance I will be cancer free in the near future. I just want to thank all of you for your concern and support.

Dave's response was immediate. "I was stunned this morning to learn Eddie Van Halen has cancer," he said. "My condolences. You can whip this, champ. See you down the road." This statement would make it obvious that Ed had kept the cancer issue completely to himself and did not even let Dave know at all what was going on. While it could've saved Dave and the fans a lot of heartache, as Ed said, cancer is a unique and private matter. It was clear that Dave was simply going to let things go for the moment. He actually returned to the road playing classic Van Halen songs yet again that summer.

On May 19, a very thin Edward stepped out into public for the first time in well over a year. He took Wolfie along with him to play in the LAPD annual charity golf tournament. He briefly answered questions, and he acknowledged that the three songs he had recorded with Dave would likely never be released. When asked directly if the band was back together, Edward responded by saying, "The band has always been together. Whether we have a singer or not is a different story. . . . Depends what we do." The comment about the three songs was devastating for fans of classic Van Halen, and his follow-up was overly ambiguous.

Valerie was offered a role in the CBS series *Touched by an Angel* in June, which would eventually require nearly eight months per year of shooting. Valerie was torn between being on location in Park City, Utah and staying home with Wolfie. Edward encouraged Valerie to take the role and offered to take on the responsibility for taking care of their son, which included back and forth to school every day, karate lessons, basketball and baseball games, homework, hot lunch deliveries, and PTA activities.

Ed's Golf Instructor Ron

Eddie picked his clubs back up and sunk himself into golf as a respite from his cancer drama. As a result, most fans were shocked when the only real interview he had given in years was for *Maximum Golf* magazine in August 2001 (the article detailed an afternoon from the previous May). Even more so, readers were shocked by his candidness while being interviewed by his golf instructor Ron who was credited with writing the story (along with Andy Meisler). One excerpt detailed his battle with cancer:

> Eddie also tells me about the initial fear and shock he felt when he was diagnosed with cancer, but says now: "I know I'm kicking its ass out. The way I look at it is like this, I've run too many red lights and gotten away with it for a long time, but it kinda caught up with me. I believe that God doesn't lay this on you unless you're supposed to learn something. And boy, I've learned more in the last year and a half than I ever thought I'd learn in a lifetime. Sometimes when things are right in front of your face, you don't see them. It seems simple, but all that really matters to me is my son and my wife. Everything and everybody else can pretty much kiss my ass. Even making music—which is pretty much my life—takes a backseat to my family and my health."

Most importantly though, Ron says that their outing occurred "just a few days after he announced via his fan-club Web Site that he's battling cancer." Again, Ron specifically said, "He says he's winning, that his chemo treatments appear to be working." This would confirm that Edward's cancer treatments first started at M.D Anderson in Houston in January 2000 for "preventative treatments." He then moved on to New York for an unspecified amount of time in the summer of 2000 for treatments with Dr. Steve McClain that he would later describe as "illegal in this country." And finally, upon Valerie's insistence, he moved to chemo treatments via Cedars-Sinai in Los Angeles in January 2001 for which he was still undergoing chemo treatments at the time of the interview in May.

While touring Ed's home for the interview, Eddie showed off a photo of him, tour pro Fuzzy Zoeler, Bob Hope himself, and former president Gerald Ford. "When people see this picture they always ask me, 'What the hell did you talk to the president and those other guys about?'" said Edward. "I tell them: What do all guys talk about when they're away from their wives? Pussy, what else?!" Ron also addressed Eddie's game. "He's . . . not great," he said. "He tends to spoil his fluid, natural swing by gripping the club too hard or swinging it too fast, which throws off his hand and body positions. But his poor technique is saved occasionally by fantastic hand-eye coordination; hours of poor shots are redeemed by 275-yard bursts of brilliance."

With regard to his struggle with the bottle, Edward light-heartedly said, "I figured I might as well go straight, because drunk, I was a complete idiot; straight, at least I have the chance of just being half an idiot." Again addressing his now public battle with cancer, Ed said, "I don't know why people want to know what only my wife and son and maybe my best friends have a right to know. I say to everyone else, 'Look, all I have to say is that I'm doing great.' But I'm not about to go into the details until the cancer is completely gone." Clearly in May, Eddie's cancer was still active. In the article, he also addressed how the attorney involvement in the recent attempted reconciliation with Dave ruined the whole thing for him particularly by, in effect, minimizing his cancer battle. He admitted, "The last time I spoke to or saw Dave was back in September of last year."

CHAPTER 35
The Dissolution

Just a month after the golf article was published, the September 11, 2001 attacks on America had a profound impact on Valerie. Amazingly, the producer of the "Right Now" video, Carolyn Ann-Meyer Beug was aboard American Flight 11, which hit the north tower of the World Trade Center—the second plane to hit. Valerie wanted to see Wolf immediately, but the director for *Touched By an Angel* insisted that work continue on as normal. She was able to get down to L.A. for the weekend, but the trip was too quick for her, so Ed made plans for him and Wolfie to come and visit her in Park City two weeks later.

Upon his arrival, Valerie noticed that Ed's behavior was odd. "He was trying too hard to appear normal," she said, "and made an effort to go to bed at the same time I did, which was always his way of showing me that he wasn't doing drugs." The following day, Valerie noticed Ed was moving his jaw around, a tell-tale sign of cocaine intoxication. Having been with him for so many years, she picked up on it immediately, and secretly went through all of his belongings. Unfortunately, when going through his wallet, she discovered a packet of coke. She was furious. Again, considering this was only two weeks after the 9/11 attacks, she thought, "How could he have brought coke with him on the plane when security was at red alert level? How could he have brought it while traveling with Wolfie? . . . Fuck him for doing this, for being so unbelievably stupid to fly with drugs on him, and with Wolfie." Her trust was now depleted. Their relationship was coming to an end.

In a calculated effort to get back at Ed, Valerie seized on an opportunity to have an affair with her friend Mark in Park City. She said, "Once I found the coke, it was like fuck you, now I get to hurt you." Although the affair had been brewing for quite a while, they spent only one evening together. The following morning, Valerie was wracked with guilt, and as Mark departed she knew she'd never see him again, and she didn't. But she knew that was the marriage killer, period, and the time had finally arrived.

Back in L.A., Valerie gathered up Alex and her longtime friend Barbara to confront Edward at their home on October 15. They met at the house on a Saturday afternoon only to find Eddie still asleep in bed. Valerie expressed amazement that he could sleep after doing so much cocaine, but Alex replied, "It must be the valium." In her autobiography, Valerie described the confrontation as follows:

> "When you came up to Park City, I found your coke," I said.
>
> "What do you mean?" he asked. "What coke?"
>
> "The coke in your wallet."
>
> "I didn't have coke."
>
> I got up from the bed and looked down at him. It was a standoff.
>
> "Ed, I'm not debating the issue. I found it. And if you don't get help and stop doing coke, I'm going to divorce you."
>
> "Fuck you, divorce me." . . .
>
> "So I'm hearing this right, then," I said. "You're ready to stop."
>
> "Fuck you."
>
> "You're going to choose this over trying to build this family back together."
>
> "Fuck you."

Shortly thereafter, Valerie took Wolfgang out of school for a week and brought him with her to Utah. "Ed protested," she said, "but I think deep down he knew he was in no condition to take care of Wolf." Valerie said that Eddie eventually built up an incredible amount of anger toward her. "Angry, in pain, and still using drugs," she said, "Ed badmouthed me non-stop. In person and on the phone." Val said that Ed was convinced the whole thing was her fault—she was of the opinion that he routinely blamed others for his own problems.

He really fought Valerie on her reasoning and her timing for the split. He noted that she had partied alongside him in their early years and that she had enabled his bad habits. Ed also questioned her why she would do this when Wolfgang was now ten years old—a horrible time for a child to go through a divorce. She said, "I new I'd love [Ed] again one day but hated [him] as we went through the emotional reality of separating."

They agreed not to tell Wolfie that they were splitting until Valerie had found a new house of her own, which would take more than half a year. They also vowed to keep it completely out of the media. In the meantime, they slept in separate rooms. To add to the general gloom and doom, Van Halen—the multi-platinum selling kings of rock and roll—was dropped by Warner Brothers in January 2002. The band officially had no record label, and Alex briefly became the default manager of the band.

That spring, beaming father Eddie played with Wolfie in his school talent show. They performed "I'm Alright" by Kenny Loggins with Ed on guitar and Wolf on drums. Valerie had been assigned to videotape the occasion, but was so moved by her son's performance, she didn't run the camera. When she told Ed, he said, "You *what*? You forgot to tape it?"

In April, Valerie finally found her own place, and it was time to break the news to Wolfgang. Their son was extremely distraught. Val said, "He took his yellow belt from karate and tied himself to the balcony outside his bedroom and said he wasn't going to leave." He eventually acquiesced and did settle into Valerie's new digs without much of an issue. She was taken aback that after only a few weeks, Ed had a girlfriend move in with him, but as she admitted, "Who was I to say anything? I'd left him."

Free of Cancer

During one of the worst periods of his life, Edward finally got some excellent news. Valerie said, "Fortunately, a test by a trio of oncologists at Cedars-Sinai Medical Center came out clean, and Ed was given a clean bill of health—as well as a stern warning about what to do to stay cancer free." Valerie noted that Edward continued to drink and smoke. Her love for him was already gone, but any bit that may have been lingering anywhere absolutely evaporated.

Eddie was finally ready to take the news to the public on May 9, 2002. On the band's official site, he posted the following message:

> I know I promised I'd get back to you and I'm sorry for the delay but I wanted to let you all know that I've just gotten a

> 100% clean bill of health—from head to toe. I wanted to share the good news with you immediately. And of course, I thank you all for all your good wishes and prayers along the way. Now it's time to really get back to the music and fun . . . so party on and you'll be hearing from us very soon. All my love, Eddie

That was it—the man had beaten cancer, totally and completely. One way or the other, Eddie Van Halen kicked cancer's ass. Throughout the ordeal, Alex said that Ed was always positive he would beat it, but Alex was not. "It was a health scare," said Alex, "and believe me, as his brother who didn't know if he was going to make it through the next week, it was a very strange experience."

Unfortunately, Ed and Val were devastated when *People* broke the news of their split in June. The article featured a quote from Valerie's mom saying she was sure they were headed for divorce. But it also had a quote from Ed in which he said they were still friends and that he still loved her. In July, the media ran with the story officially: "Estranged from Van Halen, Bertinelli buys own home / Couple separated in October after 20 years of marriage." Subsequently, Valerie's weight skyrocketed and she ended up as heavy as she'd ever been or would be in the following year.

Public demand for anything Van Halen was so high, the most unlikely pairing in rock history came together and joined forces to wave the VH banner high and proud. David Lee Roth and Sammy Hagar embarked on a summer tour together. They alternated the opening and headlining slots every other night. The tour was playfully called the 2002 Heavyweight Champs of Rock 'N Roll Tour. I caught the show on July 28 in San Antonio. Dave opened that night. His show was completely straight-on, no frills rock and roll, playing only classic Van Halen songs, period. He sang them with gusto and his band brought the music in a most respectful and faithful-to-the-original fashion. Dave never once said the word "Van Halen" or "Eddie" or "Edward" or anything of the kind. Sammy, on the other hand, claimed that he wanted to do the tour "just to piss off Van Halen."

Sammy's stage set was set up to look like a mini Cabo Wabo bar, with a section for people to actually sit on the stage with the band. By 2002, Sammy's weight had definitely caught up with him, and he was not terribly animated during the show. We were definitely blown away though when Michael Anthony appeared onstage to play with Sammy.

We had absolutely no idea that he would be there. That was actually pretty cool. But if it was indeed a "match," Dave won—by a knock out. Clearly though, Dave was upset that the fans had to settle for just the two singers and the bass player. "What the Van Halens are about is wasted time," Dave said. "If you think one second isn't valuable, then ask the little girl who just missed getting a gold medal at the Olympics by one second." He continued, "If you think one month is not valuable to somebody, then ask the lady who just had a premature baby how valuable that month is. Eddie Van Halen and his sister have wasted years." Ian Christie noted: "Crowds appeared at the 'sans Halen' shows waving anti-Eddie signs and mutilated cardboard Eddie cutouts."

CHAPTER 36
A Public Meltdown

Eddie's work with Peavey was slow and arduous and they had nothing new to bring to the market as of the January 18, 2003 NAMM convention. Yet Edward was obliged to show up. His appearance shocked, scared, and disappointed scores of fans and admirers. Unfortunately, for Eddie, the entire thing was captured on tape, and a fair level of intoxication was obvious.

What follows is a transcript of the entire ordeal. I have added comments for clarification along the way. The ellipses during Ed's dialog indicate pauses in his speaking pattern; not a single word has been removed.

[Ed walks into the room wearing odd clothing—a hat, finger-tip-less gloves, a jacket around his waist, and a bag on his shoulder. He honestly looks like a bum. He sits down and twirls around in a chair. There is brief light applause and woo-hoos that die down. Ed pulls an open mic down toward and him and begins.]

> EVH: Thanks for joining me . . . Hi!
>
> Audience: Hey, Edward!!! WOOO!!
>
> EVH: What're y'all doing here? [He says this without much humor, to some light applause.] No, what're you doing here?
>
> Audience member: Waiting for you!
>
> EVH: [A long pause. No answer. Ed then turns to chug a bottle of water.] OK, here we go. [Returns to massively chugging bottle of water to cheers, as if in a drinking contest. He pauses and looks at the plastic water bottle.] Vodka . . . [He then unwraps the microphone cable from the stand so he can move more freely and does a bit of an Elvis dance to the crowd's amusement. He then sits back down and puts his hand on his knee to prop himself up.] Anyway . . . [Long pause.] Hi . . . [The crowd

cheers.] A little louder, please . . . [The crowd cheers louder.] Hi . . . [He waves.] In ten years of doing the 5150 amp, and . . . dealing with you guys that put it together, it just hit me like a brick wall the other day that after ten years I've only blown one amp. One amp. It wasn't his fault or mine or bad loading or bad food. OK? So, the Wolfgang guitar, 5150, durable amp . . . beat the shit out of it, drag it around the block . . . I do not put my name on anything or let it out until, I would not put something out to you if it doesn't hold up. It better outlast my life. It better exist after I'm dead and gone, OK? Which isn't gonna happen any time soon, but . . . [Applause.]

So, I've been with the company for ten years and it's time for me to move and do bigger and brighter things with the same company . . . Anyway, I really have nothing here to show you because we've got some motherfucking kick ass punk ass shit that's gonna come out real soon that . . . We've been working our ass off for the last year to get this stuff done. OK? We dropped everything to do what I needed done. Didn't have enough time. OK? So, I'm not even gonna talk about it. But it's some shit that's never been done. I got a patent on one of them. And . . . it'll blow your socks off. That's why I don't wear them anymore, because, you know, it ain't no fun. Umm . . . there are a couple of things that are in the, uh . . . [He turns to consult with the Peavey rep]. I think we got a ¾ scale guitar and, uh, 5150 [inaudible] which kicks ass. Umm, there's a couple few things that were a little more difficult than we thought, just to come up with some twisted ass ideas. And . . . when they do come out . . . [This is followed by a very long, awkward pause.]

Look at your neighbors around here. Is there a company around here that does anything but follow us? I'm serious. You know? Hooked them up with some badass shit. It's great, sounds great, and we have to prove to ourselves first that it's worthy of putting out. I don't do anything . . . I'm not monetarily motivated. It's not about the money. It's about stuff I need to do what I need to do. You know? So, sometimes somebody in the company will go 'Well why would somebody want something like that?' [He says this in a overtly mocking tone.]

Well, and I tell them again, *I* want it—someone else will want it. OK? So, I'm proud to be part of Peavey, gets to be a whole new beginning. I've been through a lot of personal shit in the last couple three years, and the light at the end of the tunnel is not an oncoming train. I came out healthier than I've ever been, ummm . . . [The crowd cheers.] Thank you for anything spiritual, you name it . . . I am . . . I'm happening, and so is James, so is Matt, so is Bill. [He is referring to the Peavey reps. James is James Brown, the amp guru who worked with Edward on creating the first 5150 amp.] Hardly ever know about Bill . . . [This is followed by light laughter.] Where'd he go? Where'd his folks go? But anyway, I don't have a hell of a lot to say except we got some wicked ass shit coming up as soon as we as a team are happy with it and are comfortable that it will not break after beating the living shit out of it. It will be available to you. So I can't put any date on it, it sucks, we're busting our ass to get it out, OK? And I got some personal stuff to do right now, so, I'm not signing any autographs, no interviews, uhh, I'll take care of every one of you and your aunts and uncles and third cousins next time I see you. OK? So, that's about all I got to say. [There is some noise from the crowd.] Huh?

Audience member: Play a little guitar for us! [This is followed by a long, sustained applause.]

EVH: Somebody bring me a cello. I only play the piano and the cello. [The crowd continues to bait Ed to play something. Edward stands up and takes a very defensive posture.] What the fuck am I gonna play here that you haven't heard already? I'm not—no, wait, wait, wait—I'm not gonna play you something new. [The crowd goes completely silent as a shocked response to the snarky comment. Slowly though, members of the crowd begin baiting him again to play some classic bits.] Just listen to the fucking record. I haven't even listened to the record to remember what I did. OK, what do you want to hear?

Audience: [Members of the crowd shout several things like "Eruption," etc. During a moment of brief silence, one audience member makes a very clear, audible request.] "Mean Streets!"

EVH: You know, I like forward movement. [When the audience realizes he is not going to respond to their requests, many members groan loudly.] That too, cause it's funny. I stop at the gas station and people go "How come you ain't doin' nothin'?" I go just because we're not putting nothing out doesn't mean I ain't doin' nothin'. Wrote a movie, wrote a sitcom, wrote the music for it. [Ed's purported movie and/or sitcom has never been further discussed and most definitely has never seen the light of day.] I got enough music for five records.

Audience member: We just want one.

EVH: It's just a matter of, uh . . . . [This is followed by a very long pause.] I've just got too much shit goin' on. And I haven't had the time to put it out. But soon . . . whatever that means. [A Peavey rep hands Ed a Wolfgang, Ed looks it over and turns to the Peavey rep.] You got a caliper? [The audience laughs as Ed fishes a pick out of his pocket.] I do not travel without. [Ed straps on the guitar and starts jamming a bit. He plays a few chords, adjusts the amp, and tunes the guitar. He proceeds to play quite well, and then stops to fiddle with the amp some more.] Somebody get your punk ass up here and sing. [Ed continues to noodle, but stops in a fit of frustration.] I'm trying to think, and when I think, it don't work.

Audience member: It's workin'!

EVH: No, it ain't. You ain't seen me when it works. I've written so much stuff lately, I'm trying to think of it.

Audience member: Pick one!

EVH: Well, no, because you're recording this shit. C'mon, you heard me. [There is no response from the audience to this comment. Utter silence. Ed proceeds to play some using various odd effects from amp. He plays a lot of different bits, occasionally stopping for applause. All he is doing is start-and-stop noodling. He pauses and actually puts his hand to his foreheard in frustration.] Wait a minute. [He turns to grab his water bottle.] Everybody put your camera on pause . . . [He then proceeds to chug the water as if he was excessively dehydrated.] You like my lid? [He is referring to his hat. The audience claps a bit and Ed returns to playing. He continues to play to varying degrees—at times brilliant, and at times very sloppy. His noodling, again, is very start-and-stop—he simply goes from one disjointed idea into another. Almost nothing flows together and at times he just makes pure noise and feedback—his guitar sound is incredibly washed out in reverb and echo. Ed stops playing.] What is with that, the, the, the 'verb shit? [There is some awkward laughter.] No, what is that? [He says this pointedly to a Peavey rep off camera.] What? [One of the reps obviously adjusted the amp before Ed takes a quick practice bend at the 7th fret on the G string, and hears that the reverb is gone.] Thank you. I don't use none of that crap. [He is playing an amp that he personally designed . . . He continues to noodle, working some harmonics passages before he again comes to a very abrupt halt.] Damn it! [He is visibly frustrated that he can't execute what he's trying to do.]

Audience member: Do the elephant sound!

EVH: What? Ahh, that's old, man. [He reluctantly does the "elephant", and actually mumbles something incoherent that sounds like "I've heard the touch". Then he looks at James to his right and makes an aggressive "what's the deal" gesture to him. James gestures away, possibly indicating that he didn't have any say-so or control over the amplification settings whatsoever, and Ed turns away and gives a clearly exasperated "Aww, man." Ed looks angry but continues to play. James then stands up behind Ed and whispers to him for several seconds and pulls away. It is clear that James is doing the best he can to redirect Edward's behavior. Ed nods, and before James sits down, he actually moves back in to continue to whisper to Ed, apparently adding to his initial comments. Ed replies with an audible, "Naw, man" straight into the microphone. He continues to noodle briefly before coming to yet another stop.] God damn it, all. It's too fuckin' early. I'm nocturnal, you know. [He stands up and stands still, looking toward the ceiling as if waiting for inspiration to hit him.]

Audience member: Play the blues, Ed!

EVH: [Ed responds by playing a very short blues lick.] I'm too happy. [This statement is followed by laughter. Eddie continues to noodle, very briefly working in a tiny bit of "Runnin' with The Devil." Ed then happens upon a bluesy sounding tapping part and stops and mumbles something unintelligible about the blues and continues to play.] I was jamming with this guy the other day. Started doing this lick. [Ed executes a tapping lick]. I don't know, I don't know how to play like those fuckers—ah buh deed ah [unintelligible]. So I just thought, 'I can do that'. I never tried that before. [He sits down and plays a lick and becomes very frustrated.] Oh, fuck! [James taps Ed on the elbow as if to suggest he calm down. As he shakes his head, he pauses, looks around briefly, and then plays a very simple plain rudimentary blues riff in a mocking way toward the guy that asked him to play the blues. The audience continues to yell out various requests for classic bits.] I don't remember! And you'll all get me on film, fucked or not. [He finally plays the intro to "Mean Streets" with a great deal of variation.] Let's do it AOR style . . . [He plays "Mean Streets" at about a quarter speed for a few seconds.] Let's do it country style . . . [He plays "Mean Streets" with some country flourishes. He continues on and eventually plays the full intro to "Mean Streets" as recorded in fairly haphazard fashion until he messes up the ending and halts abruptly.] Fuck! Man! It's been, it's been four years since I played the damn thing. [Ed goes back into "Mean Streets," still not great, but better. Then he stands up and goes and stands in front of the amp for feedback. Eddie concludes this bizarre section of the act by violently banging the neck of the guitar against the top of the amp. He then turns to someone in the front row of the gathered crowd and actually steadied himself by putting his hand on their head. He then went back awkwardly to James and hit him on the top of the head with the neck of his guitar, in a joking but still rude manner. Ed then takes a seat and appears to apologize and James gives him the "don't worry about it" shake off and they proceed to have a private conversation off mic. Ed then turns around with the cables for his guitar and microphone tangled up and then sits down.]

OK, I'm bored . . . [James and Ed continue to converse privately while Ed begins to play and works his way up into a loud interlude. The entire time, he is constantly changing between parts and songs and styles—just start and stop. He utters something completely unintelligible. He continues to play until he eventually gets to the point where he abruptly stops playing yet again.] Fuck, man! I wanna play! [As he is sitting, his knees are jumping and jittering with personal disgust.] I've been playing piano and cello so much this thing is like a two-by-four to me right now. [He continues to play in varying styles and is actually playing better at this point. His improvisation is all over the map and he finally gets up to a relatively dramatic climax and stops cold; the crowd applauds.] I wrote this fuckin' boogie man, it's so fast . . . [He gets himself prepped and whips out bits of a truly amazing riff going against his agitated pledge to play nothing new. He plays the same riff for a while before venturing into a very slow a painful wail over and over and over.] The blues . . . [Ed continues to play in a bluesy fashion, and some licks are truly amazing.] That's Skynrd's classic lick. [He plays their trademark lick and continues to improvise as his strap falls down and he comes to a stop, breaking down.] Goddamn man, I hate this thing.

Audience member: We love ya, Ed!

EVH: And I love you. You know what I'm talkin'—that's right, there's nothin' new right now because I guarantee what I'm givin' you. I don't want you buying anything with my name or the Peavey name on it that's gonna break on your ass. Y'know what I mean? [Ed shrugs and sits back, and then he steps to the mic.] "And this won't."

[He does a slide up and down the neck of the guitar on the microphone stand a la Hendrix, but follows with a violent strike to the microphone stand, banging the neck of the guitar against the stand with alarmingly blunt force. He hits two chords that are still in tune, and stops abruptly after the thrashing. There is some awkward laughter from the crowd.] I don't know what else to do. [He talks briefly to the audience before again returning to playing improvised material. He stops playing again.] Now I wish I'd fucked with that dude. [He now takes a drink of what appears to be a dark-colored drink in a small, clear plastic cup.]

> Audience member: Can I leave the thing for ya?
>
> EVH: Leave the thing. [Ed then goes into a complete mock blues performance, complete with over-the-top grinding vocals.] "It's hot in here! I do believe I need some air! I said it's hot in here! I do believe I need some air!" How do you feel about that? [He then sits down and continues to noodle and concludes with a big shrug.] I swear . . . when we're done with the shit we're workin' on . . . and we're working 25 hours a day on this shit. It's a waste of time sitting here talking to you punk asses . . . [The room immediately seized up with thick tension.] What're you talkin' like—man, I'm kidding! [Edward forces a laugh to ease the tension in the room, and he stands.] I just wanna thank you for being here, just trying to show that cloning does work, 'cause Ed? He's dead. [He makes a sleeping gesture with this head, and answers some question with a remark about a fish tank.] Hey, I love you guys, thanks for being here. We will not let you down. And . . . I will take care of autographs, all that bullshit, next time. OK? [He shakes a few hands for a bit and acknowledges a few people.] Until next time. [He starts to exit but quickly returns for the black bag he's brought with him. Then he exits. The spectacle is over.]

The poster of the seven-part YouTube series of videos, nobrownmnms, included the following in his description of Ed's appearance:

> Not only did he get on stage two and one half hours late, he spent all that time drinking red wine in the Peavey NAMM booth angrily lambasting the Peavey ownership and executive staff about how fucked up EVERYONE else was, except him. I've seen some pretty ugly displays of egotistical drunken anger and animosity, both onstage and off, but this was one of the all time worst displays of a Rock Star Behaving Badly, as Edward had NO consideration for his endorsement deal at that time, but worst of all, he had NO consideration or regard for his fans. He was in such bad shape, that when I finally shook his hand after the performance, I looked at his almost dead skin, matted hair and yellow teeth and I really thought he was going to die within the year. The fact that he has made it this far proves

> that the human body is an incredibly resistant machine. It's a shame, since Edward's late father was also a life-long alcoholic. I hope, pray—and I am not a religious guy—that Edward gets his act together one day and puts out new music soon, and on a consistent basis.

"I just wanna thank you for being here, just trying to show that cloning does work, 'cause Ed? He's dead."

That last line was way, way too close to a Hendrix or Cobain quote than anyone ever wanted to hear. Ian Christie noted, "The reaction to Eddie's appearance and behavior was a mix of pity and anger."

I exchanged e-mails with James Brown, the Peavey rep who had tried to keep Edward cordial. I empathized with his circumstance, and he said, "Thanks for your compliments. It means a lot. . . . I'm just glad he's better now." When I asked James flatly what exactly was going on that day, he simply told me, "I think the video speaks for itself!"

CHAPTER 37
Sowing the Seeds of a Spectacular Failure

God only knows what forces conspired to bring Edward together with Limp Bizkit in the spring of 2003, even if it was for only one jam session. The flash-in-the-pan rap-rock band was abandoned by guitarist Wes Borland, and they were looking for a replacement and filling time. So paths crossed and Edward ended up over at their rehearsal spot for a day's worth of jamming, and who knows what else. *MTV News* reported an article including the line "After auditioning as many as 11 guitarists, including none other than Eddie Van Halen . . ."

"When Eddie jammed with the band, they reined in their typical down-tuned rap metal and played sharp hard rock in the vein of classic Van Halen," said Ian Christie. "The real-life mash-up was a tear in the fabric of the rock universe." He continued, "The story grew strange, however, when Eddie allegedly returned to the rehearsal area twenty minutes after leaving, agitated, and looking for his guitar. They insisted he had taken it with him, but he persisted in grilling them suspiciously." Some rumors were much uglier (loose reports of big bodyguards and firearms), although they are currently unsubstantiated. A half-assed version of "You Really Got Me" by the band Camp Freddy with Fred Durst on vocals appeared on YouTube in 2008.

Edward effectively went completely into hibernation in 2003. Red wine had become his drink of choice, and he began drinking straight out of the bottle, just treating the wine as if it was a big bottle of beer. This habit began to wreak havoc on his teeth. Soon they were stained, and worse, his back teeth were simply rotting. His beverage of choice was Smoking Loon—an unflattering brand name laced with vicious irony.

In April, Sammy released a live solo album. Contributing bass and vocals on one track was Michael Anthony. And as if to stick it to Edward even more, Gary Cherone was even featured on a track with Sammy and Michael all together. There's a message there. Obviously, all those guys can get along together, so what's Eddie's problem? It's all his fault, right?

The problem here with Sammy is that he has almost to a fault never given Edward any rope for being an alcoholic, a man that needed serious help and needed to be steered in the right direction by every single person that cared for him. Valerie had tried, but failed. Alex seemed numb to the whole thing. Michael Anthony was living day to day in his own world—and Sammy's world—and wouldn't have had any influence over Ed any way.

But Sammy Hagar, the son of an alcoholic himself, treated Edward's alcoholism with an outdated mindset—that the alcoholic had only themselves to blame and there would be no problem if they could just stop drinking. But alcoholics are called alcoholics because they cannot process or handle alcohol like "normal" people do. Alcoholics metabolize alcohol much faster than an average drinker—the initial spike of rush of alcohol to the brain is not like what normal drinkers experience. Alcohol is far more akin to cocaine that way. It's a bell curve for normal people. It's a series of spikes for alcoholics—and each spike requires more and more and more until you pass out or make yourself sick. No one would *purposefully* do that to themselves. No one would actually *want* to do that to themselves.

Alcoholics are genetically predisposed to metabolize alcohol differently, period. It is a disease the same way diabetes is a disease. You cannot wish it away no more than you can diabetes or even diarrhea. It has been proven that the rate of metabolism in alcohol varies by racial lines, and it is commonly understood that Asian and Native American peoples metabolize alcohol faster than other racial groups. The power of alcohol ends up being stronger than the power of your own brain to overcome it. Few things are that strong and addictive, but alcohol is one of them. And—as a recovering alcoholic myself—I do know what I'm talking about, unfortunately. As a by-product of the heavy onset of the disease, Ed let himself go. He let the house go. He let his hygiene go. He rarely bathed or changed clothes.

Michael Anthony revealed in a June interview that he hadn't spoken to Edward or Alex in over a year at that time. He also said that he knew they were clearly unhappy with him sticking with Sammy. He had reason to hold hope though . . . for one more insane go-around.

The *Rolling Stone* Insult

One of the most insulting acts in the history of Edward's career was perpetuated by *Rolling Stone* magazine in August of 2003 when they came up with their own list of the top 100 guitarists of all time. It was no surprise to anyone that Jimi was ranked #1, in fact, everyone was very cool with that. I know I was. I recall having the issue in my hands and started scanning for Eddie's name. He was not in the top 10, several of which were suspect. Then it began to get ridiculous. Not even in the top 20, not even in the top 50. Ed was listed at #70! Joni Mitchell, the absolutely amazing guitar genius (*ahem*), was at #72. I remember feeling like it was something done on purpose, as in "make sure Eddie Van Halen is nowhere near the top of the list." An outright public insult and a journalistic disgrace. Just eight years prior, in April of 1995, *Rolling Stone* had called him "the single most admired, influential, revolutionary guitar slinger of his generation."

Two Guys from Iowa

Just before Thanksgiving, a morning radio duo out of Davenport, Iowa—Dwyer and Michaels (Greg Dwyer and Bill Michaels of Q106.5 FM)—somehow got a hold of Ed's phone number and called him up at random. They were surprised that he actually answered, even though Eddie was quite agitated upon first receiving their call. However, as the conversation progressed, Ed warmed up to the pair and let his guard down. Eventually, Ed would welcome their calls with grace and good humor. The radio duo became Edward's principal speaking outlet between 2003 and 2006; he spoke to them on six different occasions.

Dwyer and Michaels speak over each other so often and sound so similar that both of their dialogs have been consolidated into simply one voice, "DJ," for the remainder of the text. All of their interviews with Ed are for the most part intact. Most edits were simply made for readability and flow. Excerpts from the spontaneous November 25, 2003 interview follow with commentary

> EVH: [Ed's phone is ringing. He answers with music blaring in the background.] Hello?!
>
> DJ: Eddie! Hey!

EVH: Who is this?

DJ: This is Dwyer and Michaels from Q106 radio.

EVH: Got the wrong number. [He comes off quite serious.]

DJ: Oh, come on.

EVH: Hey, man . . .

DJ: Come on . . .

EVH: I'm workin'.

DJ: Everybody's callin' us—

EVH: I'm *workin'*. [Agitated.]

DJ: I realize that. Can you tell us anything?

EVH: Nope. [Terse.]

DJ: Can you tell us anything more than "nope"? [Awkward laughter.]

EVH: The N, or the O?

DJ: [Laughter.] Will we be surprised and happy—

EVH: Two simple letters: N-O.

DJ: Will we be happy in—

EVH: *Nothing* to say. [Agitated.]

DJ: Come on!

EVH: I don't say *anything* until it's done.

DJ: How big is the stage setup gonna be for the, for the summer tour?

EVH: Goodbye now . . . What summer?

DJ: We're dyin' here, Ed. You understand?

EVH: Well, that ain't my problem.

DJ: Alright . . . [Sounding resigned.]

EVH: I'm cancer-free, well alive, and makin' a lot of music. Sorry I can't help ya.

DJ: That's alright. That's okay, we understand. We had to ask. We're dyin' to know.

EVH: Hey, you know, you can ask all you want, you're gonna get one or two answers. Yes, or N-O. [Laughs—his mood has lightened.]

DJ: Um, it sounded like you were playing music in the background. Is that new stuff?

EVH: Yeah.

DJ: New stuff you're workin' on?

EVH: Yeah. It's just me. I'm playin' drums, guitars—I'm doing everything.

DJ: Can you give us a riff?

EVH: Huh?

DJ: Can you give us one sample riff?

EVH: [Slight pause.] No.

DJ: [Laughter.] At least he didn't say "nope."

EVH: No riff before it's time.

DJ: There will be no riff before it's time.

EVH: That's right.

DJ: Alright, we understand, but we wanted to check.

EVH: It will be a fat, motherfuckin' cabernet.

DJ: Really? Ohh . . . We'll bring it. We'll we're looking forward to anything, my friend.

EVH: Hey, it's gonna be good.

DJ: You promise that, huh?

EVH: Come on. What do you think I've been doing for the last four years?

DJ: Well, we haven't heard a whole lot. You're healthy and everything, right?

EVH: Yeah, makin' music.

DJ: Yeah. Are you antsy to get back out on the road?

EVH: You know, I got a hip replacement, uh . . .

DJ: Hey, you were always hip to us.

EVH: Nah, I got a total titanium hip. Uh, Valerie and I are gettin' along better now that we're divorced. [Laughter.]

DJ: Now, wait a second. Did you hear the thing about now she has a crush on Mike Wallace?

EVH: Oh, yeah.

DJ: What's that all about?

EVH: Fuck if I care, she ain't my wife any more, it doesn't matter. [Laughs.]

DJ: She wants to date an 85-year-old guy and pull an Anna Nicole, that's fine by you.

EVH: Well, maybe she'll like me when I'm that old.

DJ: [Laughter.] But the hip is good, the tongue is good. You're ready to go.

EVH: No cancer. I got an amazing son.

DJ: Yeah?

EVH: This cat is more talented than anyone I've ever met.

DJ: Really? What's his, what's his chosen instrument?

EVH: Umm, drums, keyboards, guitar, bass, and sings like a mofo.

DJ: Really?

EVH: I swear to God.

DJ: So the rumors about Sammy are not—

EVH: Are you recording this? 'Cause, you know, I'm sayin' some things here that, it's like, you know—when the his balls drop . . .

DJ: [Lots of laughter.]

EVH: Hey, he's gonna be my lead singer.

DJ: [Laughter.]

EVH: This motherfucker can play anything, and can sing his ass off.

DJ: Is he all self taught?

EVH: Yep, yep. Can't read a note, just like me. I can't read music.

DJ: Even now, you still can't read music?

EVH: I need to see what my fingers are doing. I'm not Jose Feliciano or Ray Charles. I don't care what color my piano is, though. It's the only thing I've got in common with them. [Laughs.]

DJ: Well, you've obviously seen all the rumors swirling around the internet.

EVH: I, I tell ya, I don't look at, you know, at any of that.

DJ: Seriously? None of the fan web pages, you don't check out?

EVH: What's the point?

DJ: Well, I don't know, just keep tabs—

EVH: I have a life. 25 hours in a day is not enough for me to accomplish the things I need to do, let alone the things I want to do.

DJ: Yeah. It's got to be cool that you're still so important to all the Van Halen fans.

EVH: You know, I really appreciate it, but, believe it or not, I have to please myself first.

DJ: Well, that's the best way to approach it.

EVH: Well, you know, people have taken that for selfish into selfishness.

DJ: Yeah.

EVH: You have to be selfish, otherwise I can't be there for anyone.

DJ: Uh-huh.

EVH: If I don't care of myself.

DJ: But four years worth of work, and you promise it's gonna be—

EVH: I got, I got enough ten fuckin' records.

DJ: [Laughter.] Well, let's just concentrate on the next one.

EVH: It's just a matter of, hey, pick any CD. You know? There's a record.

DJ: By the way, on the next record, who's gonna be singing?! [Laughter.]

EVH: It just might be my son.

DJ: [Laughter.] Well, hey, we appreciate you talkin' to us, Eddie.

EVH: Ah, you're welcome.

DJ: Happy Thanksgiving.

EVH: Same to you.

DJ: Bye.

EVH: Bye-bye.

Setting the Stage for Sammy's Return

Edward's one and only bit of output in 2003 was on Steve Lukather's Christmas album *Santa Mental.* Steve's rocking version of "Joy to the World" is punctuated with a series of fairly nice solos by Eddie. It gave fans a reason to rejoice, not just for the season, but for the fact that Ed was indeed doing something, and that something was still playing—even if that playing took place on a hokey semi-metal Christmas album.

The almost complete and total lack of inactivity was startling in a way, and in a lot of ways simply made no economic sense. As such, Irving Azoff, who was managing Sammy at the time, stuck his nose in to get the ball rolling. Alex and Sammy had always had a generally positive relationship and had always stayed in touch with each other once or twice per year. At the urging of Azoff, Alex made a call to Sammy in late 2003. Sam told Al he and his family were soon going to be in Laguna Beach and that Al should come visit. On New Year's Eve, Alex brought along his new wife and their son and talked through some things from noon to midnight. During the visit, Edward called Alex on his cell phone. Al simply handed the phone over to Sammy and Ed immediately lit into him asking "Why'd you quit the band?" Sammy said, "It was late at night and I figured the guy was wasted."

On January 9, 2004, Dwyer and Michaels called up Eddie again at his house unannounced and proceeded to get a lot of information out of him. A transcription of nearly the entire interview with some commentary follows:

DJ: [It's] the dudes in Iowa! . . . How are ya, buddy?

EVH: Great.

DJ: Good holidays?

EVH: Yeah.

DJ: Awesome.

EVH: Every day's a holiday.

DJ: One quick question and then we'll let you go. Where are you gonna be tonight? Any place in particular?

EVH: Sleeping.

DJ: Are you sure? Before that? Like say . . .

EVH: I'm still up, I'm writin'.

DJ: And, and tonight . . .

EVH: [Ed is playing guitar.] Huh?

DJ: That sounds cool.

EVH: What do you mean? You didn't hear anything.

DJ: We did! We could hear—do it again.

EVH: Nah, I can't do that.

DJ: I'll just do it—Walnut Creek, California? Does that mean anything?

EVH: Walnut Creek?

DJ: Good, you're writing it down, because you're supposed to be there to announce a big Van Halen reunion.

EVH: Yeah, I heard about that.

DJ: Yeah, that's where Sammy's playing tonight, so you, Sam, Mike . . .

EVH: That's where he's playing tonight?

DJ: Yeah. . . . your brother. It's all gonna happen. No truth to that, huh?

EVH: So Sammy's playing, my brother's playing, and I'm not?

DJ: No, no, no, no—your brother's probably gonna pick you up around 6:30, seven . . . that's why we called to make sure you're ready.

EVH: Wow . . .

DJ: Man, you're the best secret-keeper that we've ever talked to.

EVH: Hey, you know, I just make music. That's all I do. I don't know about secrets, I don't know what the hell you're talking about.

DJ: So if your brother were to pick you up tonight, does he know where the Walnut Creek venue is?

EVH: More importantly, I'd have to listen back to our records and learn to play the shit.

DJ: Well, we're thinking . . .

EVH: 'Cause I don't sit around, I don't sit around listening to our old music—I'm always writing.

DJ: Ahhh . . . Well, that's what we were thinking maybe . . .

EVH: Do you realize it took me ten years—my son, Wolfgang—ten-years-old before I ever played him any of our records? I, I, I started crying. I called Warner Brothers and I asked them for our whole catalog in a box, a box of each of our records. I pick him up from school, and they're sittin' on the bench in the shop here by the studio . . .

DJ: Yeah . . .

EVH: And I pick him up from school and we walk in and he goes, "What are all these, Dad?" And I went, "Oh . . . god."

DJ: You gotta be kidding me.

EVH: Ten-years-old. He looks at me and goes, "This is all you?" And I went, "Oh, god," and I just turned around and cried. "I'm sorry."

DJ: Wow . . .

EVH: He went straight from Britney Spears and N'Sync to Daddy's world.

DJ: Hey, that's awesome.

EVH: And the next day, quote-unquote, verbatim, you know what he said to me?

DJ: What?

EVH: "How come nobody makes music like this anymore?"

DJ: Did you tell him "'Cause they're waitin' on you, Wofie?"

EVH: Hey . . .

DJ: "The world's waitin' on you."

EVH: You should hear this cat, man. He is scary.

DJ: That's what you were saying—who can play your old music better? You or him?

EVH: Oh, he's, he's taking it further.

DJ: Yeah?

EVH: Yeah.

DJ: Taking it up a notch. You seriously, you don't . . .

EVH: I jam, I jam with him.

DJ: If you had to rip into "Eruption" now, you couldn't play it?

EVH: Oh, yeah. That's easy.

DJ: Let—prove it.

EVH: Oh, come on. I just broke a—I just snapped a string on my guitar. I was just goin' in.

DJ: Really?

EVH: You caught me just in time.

DJ: Well, the Eddie we know could play it on four strings.

EVH: Yeah, except the string I need—I only need one string. [He is referring to the B string for the tapping section.] Except it happens to be the one string that's broken.

DJ: Well, you've heard the rumor obviously and we didn't expect you to confirm or deny anything but we felt we . . .

EVH: Well, all I can say is this, that, uh, yes, there are rumors, and I guess it's true that there are rumors. Those rumors are rumors and that's true.

DJ: And the rumors are true?

EVH: No.

DJ: No. It's just true that there are rumors. OK.

EVH: Well, as far as I know.

DJ: But it's something you would like to do, I would think, right? Play live again in front of thousands of people?

EVH: Hey, it'll happen.

DJ: It'll happen.

EVH: Well . . . [Stammering.] I will play in front of people some day again.

DJ: Some day, some day this year?

EVH: What year is it? 2004?

DJ: 2004!

EVH: Look, you know, *time is irrelevant to me*. [Pause.] As you can tell. But I haven't slept yet—it's 8 o' clock in the damn morning.

DJ: Which is why . . .

EVH: I'm just going to bed.

DJ: Which is why we get the best stuff from you right now!

EVH: Yeah, that's also why it's very difficult for anyone to have a goddamn relationship with me because I'm kind of like a, a dog or a cat or an animal. I, I eat, go to the bathroom, and sleep whenever necessity . . . you know, whenever it hits.

DJ: As long as it's whenever and not wherever, I think you're OK.

EVH: Well, that's, that's, you know, I live in the hills so it doesn't matter, you know? It's like, does the, does the pope shit in the woods?

DJ: [Laughter.]

EVH: Oh, I . . . Are you guys, are you guys radio?

DJ: Yeah! . . .

EVH: Oh, sorry about the "shit."

DJ: No, that's OK, that's OK. Hey, would you, would you like to—can we go on the air with you? Because we're not on the air right now.

EVH: Oh, come on, you're recordin' this.

DJ: I know, but it would be better to have you live on the air.

EVH: No, no, no—I can't do that.

DJ: Can't do that?

EVH: Nah.

DJ: OK. Can you tell us at least if you . . .

EVH: [At this point, Edward sounds aggravated.] I can't tell you anything. I don't know.

DJ: Well, but this, this is a personal question about your job. Can you—can you . . . are you and Sammy getting along?

EVH: We never did not get along.

DJ: OK. OK. That's cool.

EVH: You know? He just wanted to pursue a solo career and, so he quit. We never not got along.

DJ: Michael Anthony? He's still in good graces with you?

EVH: Mike? I don't know. I haven't talked to that cat in two years.

DJ: Really?

EVH: Yeah. I don't know what he's off doing. I think he's with Hagar.

DJ: But you don't have a problem with him. You still get along with him?

EVH: I don't have a problem with anything.

DJ: Not even us calling at weird hours?

EVH: I don't know. It doesn't matter to me.

DJ: We're actually, we're actually putting any and all, uh, confirmation of anything behind by chit-chatting, aren't we?

EVH: Well, I mean . . . What the hell? You know, God put your eyes in front of you and your ass in the back, you know? So, look forward. I don't look back.

DJ: God, I love your philosophy, man.

EVH: Well, I mean, you know . . . The waste comes out the back end and the fresh stuff comes in the front side. [Ed laughs.]

DJ: Are you making time to play golf still?

EVH: Actually, you know, I've been grooving, I've been writing so much damn music it's ridiculous. So something's bound to pop sooner or later.

DJ: Yeah. That's what we're all waitin' for.

EVH: Sooner than later, I guarantee you that.

DJ: "Sooner than later."

EVH: Oh, yeah.

DJ: OK. We're chomping at the bit here. Lyrics? Music? Both?

EVH: And singing.

DJ: Oh, well, of course! And that's where you want . . .

EVH: A lyric with music without singing is, you know, music with lyrics.

DJ: So when you wake up from a deep sleep . . .

EVH: Well, what would you, what would add to this: bah bah bah bum [Beethoven's *Fifth*]. You know, Beethoven. What could you possibly add to that lyrically, counter-melody-wise . . . what could add to enhance that? Sometimes, simplicity is the best.

DJ: So, it's gonna be an acoustic album with no singing?

EVH: Nope. No guitars, no amps . . . we just walk onstage and go, "Hey, how's it going, people?"

DJ: Have you ever been approached by other musicians to do projects? You know, Steve Vai? Uh, Joe Satriani? Those . . .

EVH: Now why would I want to do that?

DJ: Well, I don't know. Because you—

EVH: I make too much damn noise for anyone else to play with me.

DJ: It worked with Michael Jackson.

EVH: Yeah, well I kind of rearranged the song and . . . I, I, I actually, uh, edited the song and changed it.

DJ: Yeah. Best song he ever put out.

EVH: Huh?

DJ: That was the best song he ever put out.

EVH: Well, I don't know about that. I mean, songs to me are, CDs, records, whatever you want to call 'em—I prefer to call them records because they're still recordings, you know—they're kind of like kids. They're all a little different, you gotta love 'em all.

DJ: Well, to, just to restate what you said, the wait will be sooner rather than later for new Van Halen music.

EVH: Hey, you know? It's like . . . I've got so much stuff. If I stopped writing right now, I have enough for at least ten records. What do you think I've been doing for the last four years? Besides fighting cancer, and ending a relationship, and raising a son, and getting a hip replacement, and this, that, and the other.

DJ: Hey, how was Wolfie's—

EVH: All I do is make music. That's all I do.

DJ: How was Wolfie's—

EVH: Of course, in between *jobs* . . . No, I'm kidding. [Eddie laughs.]

DJ: What did Wolfie get for Christmas from Santa Claus?

EVH: Oh, man. I gave him my original, umm, striped guitar that was my . . . I built three of them. Umm, I gave him the backup one from the 1984 tour. The original strings from that tour are still on it. You know, I used duct tape and rolled it up to put picks on . . . the picks—you couldn't even pull 'em off.

DJ: Because they were so stuck on.

EVH: Well, they'd been twenty fucking years!

DJ: And that was the first time you had touched it since that, the end of that tour?

EVH: Yeah. I opened the case, the only thing I, I, I changed was . . . uh, I got a patent on this, uh, drop to D on the low E-string.

DJ: Yeah?

EVH: I added one of those but I left the same string.

DJ: What was his reaction when he opened it?

EVH: Ah, he cried. He, he, he just freaked.

DJ: It sounds like, man, you guys share a real cool love together, you know?

EVH: Man, I tell ya, this kid . . . we jammed, wrote a badass tune the other day. He is so creative it is ridiculous. It's just, he's just a natural, beyond anyone I've ever met. And this is not his dad talkin', I'm talkin' as a producer, as a musician, as a, uh . . . He wanted play double-kick. OK? So I set him up a week and a half ago. Then he wants a cowbell. OK? So I bring over a cowbell.

DJ: Shouldn't that be uncle Alex's job?

EVH: Well . . .

DJ: Sendin' over all the drum stuff.

EVH: No, well, Al gives me this stuff to give, you know, whatever.

DJ: OK.

EVH: He, uh . . . anyway, four or five days go by, and he goes, "Dad, let's jam." He's . . . he's like he's been playing double-kick all his damn life! And don't forget, he only started making music when he was 10! And he's only 12!

DJ: And again—no lessons, all self-taught.

EVH: He plays bass better than . . . *a lot* of people I know.

DJ: Better than anybody that plays on a Jack Daniels bass, let's just say that.

EVH: Or, no, let's just say anyone who *drinks* Jack Daniels.

DJ: [Laughter.] Let me ask you this. After he opens—

EVH: This cat is *sexy*—I'm tellin' you, he's got a, he's a, he's a—I know no one . . . I mean, I started making music when I was six playing piano. OK? I didn't start rock and roll or playing guitar until or drums until I was 12. Well, by 14, I was like him. You know? And he doesn't practice. He just started. He goes, "Daddy, I've been practicing." I go, "Yeah, right." You know? I gave him four guitar lessons and he plays in front of his whole school flawlessly. And he only practiced for an hour. He's never played guitar before. Four lessons. OK?

DJ: I think it's in the genes.

EVH: Now, drums, I tell ya—I just recorded it on one of those little, uh, Radio Shack, uh, microcassette things?

DJ: Yeah.

EVH: I played it for Alex yesterday—'cause Alex and I, we play every day, we jam, you know, and write, whatever. I played it for Alex, he's going, "My god . . . I can't believe it." He just tripped. He's going . . . he's just born with it, you know? The way I look at that, and I don't mean to get deep on ya, but, it's like—everybody is born with a gift. You know? Most people are just hapless and cheap. You know, they don't even bother to, to feel or to, to . . . I don't know. It's like, have a passion. I don't care if it's needlepoint. You know? . . . My point being that I think you are born, everyone's born with a gift. And when someone says, "Boy, that kid's talented." You know, talent is what you do with the gift. . . . To me. Some people phone it in because they have the gift and think they can, but if you work that gift, then you're talented. And my son—I don't even know if he's my son because the other day, I had to turn around, and I go, "That's not my son." He's blowing my fucking mind. I could not look at him and play.

DJ: What does it feel like to watch him play your guitar?

EVH: What'd you say? I'm talking when he's on the drums, it's like jamming with my brother. So I had to turn around, I go, "I can't look at him . . . I can't look at my son because then I can't play 'cause I'm watching him and hearing . . ." (laughs) I don't know how to explain.

DJ: You're watching him but you're hearing your brother's, uh, level.

EVH: Yes! I'm hearing a peer. He's a damn peer. I'm telling ya. I've cut tracks with him.

DJ: Wow. Well that's, that's pretty incredible stuff to hear, Ed.

EVH: I don't mean to go off on my son, but it's like, it's like, they say kids pick their parents, well, you know, I thank God he picked me. I'm blessed—one blessed person.

DJ: What did he get you for Christmas?

EVH: Himself. That's enough.

DJ: But there wasn't like something under the tree, though?

EVH: Oh, actually, um, um. Oh, this is too funny. Uh, he picked out, uh, you know, like a necklace thing. . . . And Valerie and him went shopping and they figured they'd get the family a necklace with a picture of him. And, well . . . I didn't get one. And I go, "How come that?" And this is Saturday night before last, Valerie goes, uh, "Well, it's a, it's a little too feminine looking." And, and Wolfie goes, "No, it's not!" You know? "Daddy'll wear anything."

DJ: Well, he did just see you in all your old albums.

EVH: Yeah.

DJ: Well, listen, man, we appreciate you talkin' to us and we hope you understand our . . .

[Phone is disconnected; they ring his line again.]

EVH: I think the box cut us off.

DJ: Sorry, man.

EVH: No, I think my message machine, so I got, I got the whole thing on tape, too.

DJ: OK. [Laughter.] I hope we don't sound stupid.

EVH: You or me?

DJ: [Laughter.] Us. I'm worried about us.

EVH: No, but, let me finish real quick. To what I was saying about the necklace—is Wolfie goes, "Oh, Dad"—'cause he picked it out—OK?

DJ: Yup.

EVH: And Valerie didn't wanna give it to me, she thought it was little too, uh, over-the-top, beyond gay kinda deal, you know?

DJ: [Laughter.]

EVH: And . . . I said beyond gay, not gay.

DJ: I understand.

EVH: Gay's okay, beyond gay? I don't know.

DJ: OK.

EVH: But um, so anyway I say, "Let me at least see it." So I look at it and I put it on, she goes, "I can't believe it, it actually looks good on you." [Laughter.] And Wolfie goes, "See! I told ya he'd like it!"

DJ: [Laughter.] Awesome. Are you wearing it right now?

EVH: Yeah.

DJ: Cool. Well listen, I hope you understand our curiosity and I sure appreciate your talking to us but, umm, well, you know the level of interest in this whole story.

EVH: I really don't. You know? I, I . . .

DJ: Well, that's why we called. People are going nuts, us included.

EVH: You know, it's like people . . . what the hell is a rock star? I'm a musician.

DJ: Yeah.

EVH: I make music.

DJ: Well, you know, you touched on it. Why people are so interested—nobody's making the kind of stuff that you used to make.

EVH: Well, because there're very few people that're musicians. Most of 'em are just rock stars.

DJ: Yeah.

EVH: What is that like a meteor, comet or something?

DJ: By the way, happy anniversary. Twenty years—the release of 1984. On this day.

EVH: Well, why didn't you call me and congratulate me on the release of the first album in 1978!

DJ: Well, you know what? Ed—you're not always there. Well, you're always there, but sometimes when we call, you're not. And uh, it's like a, it's like a philosophy lesson every time we call.

EVH: I saw the phone ringin', and I was—I play very loud.

DJ: Yeah.

EVH: And, so, I picked it up a couple of times and nobody was—I couldn't hear anything, so . . .

DJ: You didn't get that, you didn't get that string fixed on the guitar so you could kick into "Eruption" for us?

EVH: Nope. I was just goin' out to, uh, I was just goin' out to, uh, microphone broke on me on a kick drum yesterday, so I was gonna . . . I'm engineering, I'm doin' everything now. I just . . . It's life cleaning, so to speak, not spring cleaning.

DJ: Life cleaning meaning we're startin' over fresh.

EVH: Well, I just, just, you know—one way to, uh, I beat cancer was just moving, removing all negative BS from my life.

DJ: Yeah.

EVH: You know, I mean it's like, everything is multidimensional. You know? It's not one—they're not gonna come up with a Bayer pill that's gonna cure a damn thing.

DJ: Gotta change everything.

EVH: You know, it's like, why did God put your head on top? It controls everything below it except what's above it—your hair. [Laughter.] Cannot, cannot control your hair.

DJ: One last question, we'll get you back to, uh, your work in the studio or your gift in the studio . . .

EVH: Actually, I'm, I'm leavin' it as it is, and I'm goin' in and goin' to sleep.

DJ: Alright, then. Don't forget, tonight, Walnut Creek, alright? Sammy will be waiting for you.

EVH: You know, when I think of a walnut, I think of like a peach, and something else that looks similar to it.

DJ: [Laughter.]

EVH: And it's not the creek.

DJ: Right!

EVH: Maybe a crack but not a creek.

DJ: Well, hey, thanks so much for talkin' to us, Ed. We appreciate it, man.

EVH: What're you guys' names, anyway?

DJ: It's Dwyer and Michaels. And we're in, believe it or not, Davenport, Iowa.

EVH: That's cool.

DJ: We love you.

EVH: Hey, uh . . .

DJ: We're gonna stay in touch if that's okay. We won't be pests, we promise.

EVH: You know, I . . . I'm easy.

DJ: OK.

EVH: You know?

DJ: We're the little guys in the radio world, so . . .

EVH: Hey, I'm just a little guy standin' here makin' music.

DJ: Heh—I think people would disagree with that. We'll take your word for it.

EVH: How tall are you?

DJ: [Laughter.] Together—twelve feet tall. Thanks buddy, appreciate it.

EVH: That's if you fold it in half, right?

DJ: Yeah.

EVH: Anyway, have a great day.

DJ: You too.

"Time is irrelevant to me . . ."

A few days later, Sammy arrived back at the 5150 studio waiting for Edward to come down. What he saw shocked him.

CHAPTER 38
A Year to Forget

Sammy made several assessments upon his first encounter with Edward in ten years. "He looked like he hadn't bathed in a week," Sam said. "He certainly hadn't changed his clothes in that long. He wasn't wearing a shirt. He had a giant overcoat and army pants, tattered and ripped at the cuffs, held up by a piece of rope." He continued, "I'd never seen him so skinny in my life. He was missing a number of teeth and the ones he had left were black. His boots were so worn out he had gaffer's tape wrapped around them and his big toe stuck out."

Ed went straight up to Sam to embrace him in a hug, which was awkward. Sammy said he immediately had a flash of a thought to get the hell out of there. Sammy said straight out that he thought Ed was "crazier than a loon." When Sam noticed that Edward was drinking wine straight out of the bottle, he asked him why he didn't just drink it out of a glass. Ed held up the bottle and retorted, "It's in a glass." Sammy also noted that Edward was repeatedly disappearing into a bathroom, often claiming "I gotta take a shit" almost as a not-so-subtle code phrase. Sammy said, "I never saw what it was, but he was doing something." Clearly, Ed was still steeped in coke usage.

When Edward brought Sammy into the house for the first time in ten years, he was completely astonished:

> There were bottles and cans all over the floor. The handle was broken off the refrigerator door. It was like a bum shack. There were spider webs everywhere. He had big blankets thrown over the windows. . . . He was sleeping on the floor with a blanket and pillow. There was no food in the cupboards. I had never seen a dirtier place in my life. It was like the house out of that movie *Grey Gardens*.

Sam also claimed that the source of Ed's missing teeth was Eddie acting as his own dentist. Hagar said Eddie told him, "I pulled my own tooth—this thing was bugging me so I got a pair of pliers and yanked it." Sammy also said that at that time—in early 2004—that Eddie was "living with a pathologist" that was continuously checking Eddie's tongue for cancer, even though he had proclaimed to the world that he was cancer-free in May of 2002. Sam belittled his obvious horrific condition, calling him a "fruitcake."

The band proceeded to fumble their way through what might be called a recording process. Sammy said they sifted through any number of old tracks from all three eras/incarnations of the band. Sammy said that getting Eddie to stay focused in the studio was incredibly difficult as Ed was constantly either starting and stopping or tinkering with equipment to no end. The first song that Sammy was finally able to bang out lyrics for was titled "It's About Time," which he claimed was all about the breakup and reunion. One word: trite. Another song was called "Learning to See," which was something approaching sappy country-rock. Yet something amazing did come out of the sessions. Sammy was able to write what could possibly be the single worst lyrics in the history of rock music, outranking himself on a claim to infamy he already held.

The song was called "Up for Breakfast" and was—wait for it—written with sexual metaphors about . . . breakfast. I hesitate to reprint any of the lyrics, but feel I must for context. "She put the cream in my coffee (first thing in the morning) / Put that butter on my biscuit (honeydew my melons) / Cherries on bananas (gonna need a second helpin') / You know I'm up for breakfast so early in the morning." This chorus was preceded by a verse line that included the phrase "Pump it up, baby, make it bigger." It's not clear why Hagar didn't just call the song "Let's Have Sex" and have the lyrics be "Hold my penis until I get an erection / Then let's put it in your vagina / And I will hump you until I ejaculate." But that would probably be too subtle for Mr. Hagar. The lyrics for this material was going to go nowhere.

Once again, they brought in Glen Ballard to produce, but he had a lot of trouble sticking with Ed's schedule which was typically starting at 9pm and going for three or four days straight before collapsing and taking a few days off. Of the actual recording, once the basic tracks were down, Sammy and Michael cut all of their vocals—lead and background—in a half-day. The remainder of the recording took three additional months (which included Eddie playing bass on all three tracks—he refused to let Michael Anthony record any bass parts or give him any songwriting credit). About how long it took Ed to finish the recordings, Sammy said, "The Eddie Van Halen I first met could have done that in an hour."

Word Leaks Out

During the sessions, they finally let the word out that VH had reunited with Hagar in March. Late that month, Sammy went on Howard Stern's show for an interview by phone. Stern absolutely crucified him. He played a series of clips of Sammy badmouthing Van Halen and Eddie and Alex from the late 1990s, making Sammy look like an insincere fool. "How did it come about that you had a complete change of heart?" asked Stern. Sammy responded with, "Howard, I'm gonna kill you." Sammy danced around the issue using platitudes like "things change." Stern asked about Ed, and Sammy said, "Eddie's fine. He's great. He's playin' better than ever." Sam must have been visibly squirming.

Dwyer and Michaels came calling again on April 9. They proceeded through a short but hilarious interview with Ed:

> EVH: Hello?!
>
> DJ: Eddie?
>
> EVH: Yeah.
>
> DJ: Hey, it's Dwyer and Michaels in Iowa!
>
> EVH: *And* . . .
>
> DJ: Oooh! How ya doin'?
>
> EVH: Uhh . . . I'm on the phone with a . . . *female companion.*
>
> DJ: By the name of . . .
>
> EVH: [Pause.] Of what?
>
> DJ: We're just tryin' to see what her name was?
>
> EVH: Oh.
>
> DJ: Is that more important than talkin' to us? 'Cause if it is, we'll understand.
>
> EVH: Well, yeah it is.

DJ: [Laughs.] Okay!

EVH: Unless you give good head.

DJ & EVH: [Lots of laughter.]

DJ: Well, you're not gonna get that from us. So . . .

EVH: Well, I can play you part of a great fuckin' song, right now.

DJ: Okay.

EVH: But, she's more important, so you're shit out of luck. [Laughs.]

DJ: Okay. Hey, can we, can we call back in a little while?

EVH: Uh, I'm gonna be asleep, man. I've been workin'.

DJ: Oh, okay.

EVH: Like, I've been gettin' three hours . . . three hours of sleep a night. 'Cause . . . I'm, I'm mixing. [Pause.] We're . . . [Pause.] We're recording—finishing the third tune here at my house and we're mixing somewhere else, and, I—hold on a second. [Ed goes to other line to talk to his girlfriend for about 5 seconds.]

DJ: Okay.

EVH: [Returns.] Alright, you know what she said?

DJ: What?

EVH: She goes "Tell 'em to fuck off."

DJ: Nooo! Sounds like someone who knows us.

EVH: [Laughs.] No, it's, uh, not a chick with a dick . . . but she's definitely got balls.

DJ & EVH: [Lots of laughter.]

DJ: So, are you guys rehearsing right now, then, getting ready for the tour?

EVH: Our first fuckin' gig is June 12th.

DJ: Yeah. Well, I don't know. I'm hoping you're already ready to go.

EVH: Um, I was *born* ready. If the rest of the guys aren't, that's their problem.

DJ: Yeah, so you're, you're working on track number three for the, for the CD.

EVH: Yeah.

DJ: I heard Sammy's—

EVH: Oh, come on. Eh, you know, I'm not gonna tell you any of this shit.

DJ: No, that's *alright*.

EVH: Yeah, for *you*!

DJ: Well, right!

EVH: Shit. You know, who gives a fuck, really? I don't give a shit, you know? Put it this way. Obviously, the hat is out of the bag (sic), right?

DJ: Yeah, right.

EVH: Fuck. I gotta go. Alright?

DJ: Okay. [Laughter.] You could call us—

EVH: Call me tomorrow. Call me tomorrow.

DJ: We'll call you tomorrow.

EVH: Alright?

DJ: Yeah.

EVH: *Bye*. [Sweetly.]

DJ: Thank you.

EVH: You're welcome, bye.

The Cabo Wabo issue came up again, which was not a good sign. Ed was dead set against Sammy using the tour as a springboard of any kind at all to promote the club or the tequila (the same went for Michael Anthony's brand of hot sauce). Through management, Edward insisted that not one venue feature a single poster or advertisement for Cabo Wabo, or even serve the brand. In response, Sammy had an enormous tattoo of the Cabo Wabo logo inked on the lower part of his right upper arm. He figured that every single night, the tattoo would be front and center on the video screens every time they showed a close-up of Sammy. Just like he said about the 2002 tour with Dave—that he did it "just to piss off Van Halen"—Hagar clearly did this to get under Edward's skin more than to actually promote his brand. That tattoo alone would ultimately play a huge role in the permanent dissolution of the Hagar-based incarnation of the band.

The tour rehearsals were rocky, and led to a formal intervention attempt. According to Sammy:

> Eddie was having trouble finishing songs. . . . All he wanted to play at rehearsal was the three new songs. He wouldn't learn the old songs. Something was always wrong. I'd walk into a rehearsal and he'd be tearing apart his speakers. . . . He fired the monitor guy, fired the sound guy, fired the keyboard tech, fired at least five guitar techs, and that was just during rehearsals. . . . It was the craziest, most whacked-out stuff. I knew it was a disaster. I told Irving. . . . Irving agreed to hold an intervention with Eddie. He brought a big beefy security guard and met Al and me at 5150. Eddie walked in, carrying his wine bottle. Irving did all the talking. He told Eddie the tour was going to be difficult, that he needed to go away for a week or two, that we could postpone some dates if we needed. We all agreed Eddie needed to clean up. He smashed the bottle. "Fuck you," he said. "I will kill the first motherfucker that tries to take this bottle away from me. I left my family for this shit. You think I'm going to fucking do this for you guys?" That's how sick the cat was at that moment. It was going to be a long tour.

The Disastrous 2004 Tour

The 2004 tour kicked off on June 11 in Greensboro, as usual, and the show was very well received. The setlist for the summer shows featured a much higher volume of Roth-era material than previous Hagar-era tours. The show opened with "Jump," and featured rare nuggets like "Somebody Get Me a Doctor" (with Mike on lead vocals) and even "Unchained." The latter had only been performed by Hagar a handful of times on the 1993 tour. Ed teased his way up to the intro of the song until he exploded and launched into the classic, grinding yet beautiful chord progression. But barely a week after the tour started, a performance of "Unchained" in Worcester, just outside of Boston, was painfully off on Ed's part, littered with sloppy playing. At one point, he even picked up something to drink off of the drum riser while continuing to play with his left hand in mid-verse.

Early on in the tour, Ed began to wear his hair like a samurai—a ponytail on the top of his head. "Whenever he came out with no shirt on and his hair tied up samurai-style, he seemed fucked up," said Sammy. "That was his little signal. I don't know what it was. He would come out first with his hair down, go back to change guitars, or after Alex's drum solo, and come back with his hair up. I'd look at Mike and we'd roll our eyes—here we go again." At one spot on the tour—they addressed the hair directly. Ed was clearly drunk out of his mind—his teeth looked horrible. He looked like he could barely stand. Sammy, looking tanned and healthy, sat down next to Ed on the drum riser and they put their arms around each other and had a very friendly chit chat off microphone. They went back and forth with Ed offering kisses and Sam offering hugs in front of the cheering crowd. After a solid thirty seconds, Sammy says to the crowd, "I gotta tell ya, this is the shit I'm talkin' about! Right?!" The crowd roars, Sammy puts his shades on and Ed grabbed the mic. "Anybody that can put up with this shit," and pointed to his samurai hair. "I got no problem with this shit, OK?!" said Sammy, referring to Ed's hair. "Gimme some fuckin' scissors, here, gimme, gimme some scissors! So, let me ask Ed a question here in front of 18,000 people . . ." Ed grabbed the mic and said, "You cut my hair, I shave yours." Sammy responded with humor. "Ed, I'm already shaved buddy," he said. "I'm already shaved, I take care of my shit. Aww, yeah. My old lady likes it like that, you know what I'm sayin'?" It was a rare moment of levity.

Shortly after the two Worcester shows and just before two shows in East Rutherford, New Jersey, *The Boston Globe* reported on June 23, "Showing his softer side, Eddie Van Halen surprised guests at the Ritz-Carlton on Avery Street the other night by playing a few jazz standards on the piano. In town to perform at Worcester Centrum Centre, he played the grand piano in the hotel's lounge, paused to smoke a butt outside, then played some more."

A highlight of the Worcester shows was when Wolfgang joined his dad onstage during his guitar solo. Ed knew what was coming and he knew it was going to be emotional for him. He started to play "316," the song he had dedicated to Wolfie, but stopped. He was visibly weeping. He mouthed "thank you" to the audience and soaked in the applause. He continued to play until he came to rest completely on his back. At that point, Wolfgang—only 13-years-old at the time—came out playing "316" exactly like his dad. He walked over and sat down next to his pa, who was overcome with emotion. Ed showered him with kisses and they jammed on "316" and then a little bit of "You Really Got Me" together.

Just a few days later on June 29, *Blathermouth.net* ran with the headline "Eddie Van Halen Drinking Again?" The article ran as follows:

> Eddie Van Halen, who has set up camp in Boston while his band tours the East Coast, made a couple of bizarre appearances at the Back Bay boite [last week], leaving patrons and employees wondering if Eddie's in big trouble. First off, the big-haired axeman wandered into the Newbury Street hotspot with his own bottle of wine, which the management promptly took away. Eddie returned a few nights later, seeming rather disoriented. He went up to a table where [a young couple] were dining, stuck his fingers in their water glasses, then proceeded to bless them — papal style with the water — and stumble out. The rocker's camp, when contacted yesterday, had no comment.

Edward was inseparable from his wine. He would likely have gladly paid a hundred dollars simply to drink his own preferred brand that he kept in hand. The incident with the young couple was just a smart-ass throwback to his Catholic upbringing and not a God complex thing in any sense. Sammy described Eddie as often being a "rude wise-guy." While Ed did get the final "fuck you" in with the restaurant, the press attention and scrutiny he was getting in 2004 was fairly harsh.

In East Rutherford, Edward continued to take the second line of the second verse of "Why Can't This Be Love?" as he had back in 1998. His vocal did not hit the mark, and his guitar playing did not either. Reviewing dozens of videos of various concerts in 2004, Ed ranges from brilliant to horrific. Nearly every song features an obvious sloppy mistake, and occasionally worse. "I couldn't listen to Eddie," said Hagar. "He made some terrible mistakes and it seemed like he couldn't remember the songs. He would just hit the whammy bar and go *wheedle-wheedle-wee*. I'd listen to Mikey to find my note."

In late July, while playing the United Center in Chicago, Edward literally petered out during his guitar solo. *Los Angeles Times* writer Geoff Boucher said, "Hagar said that Eddie Van Halen was drinking heavily and, on some nights, it showed. In Chicago, Eddie stumbled throughout the set and, at one point, quit playing and sacked out, telling the crowd: 'I done run outta gas.'" It was also reported that Edward either tripped on his cables or simply fell down on the stage repeatedly.

On July 23, a venture between Eddie and Charvel Guitars was announced. They were going to co-produce custom one-off guitars under the name EVH Art Series. The Charvel press release said: "The Charvel Custom Shop will work closely with Van Halen to create no more than 100 pieces, all of which will replicate the original down to every detail, including original specifications, as well as its nicks, scratches and wear marks." It was a fairly clear sign that the Peavey relationship, soured by the 2003 NAMM appearance, was coming to an end.

In Oklahoma City, on July 29, Sammy had arranged for Toby Keith to join him onstage during his acoustic segment. Sam had set it up so that Keith would join him while singing Keith's "I Love This Bar." Just before Keith went out to join Hagar, Eddie confronted him backstage and asked why he was going on with Sammy and not with the band. Keith told Ed that Sammy had invited him and Eddie hadn't. "Why are you wearing that cowboy hat?" Ed asked Toby. "I'm a country guy," he said. Ed retorted with, "No, it's because you're bald." Keith went on anyway and, of course, being in his home state, the crowd went nuts. "Eddie went crazy the rest of the night," said Sammy. "He destroyed his dressing room after the show. His son, Wolfie, was in my dressing room, scared and crying."

Valerie said Wolfgang "had a handful of eye-opening experiences with his father." In her words:

> I don't know all the details concerning the drinking, drugs, and anger. When I asked, Wolfie would cut me off with "Mom, I handled it." Later, as I pushed for more details, he would say only that he was able to say, "Dad, I don't like it when you do this." For the first time, he got an accurate picture of what Ed was really like. After all, I'd protected him his whole life. But this was no-holds barred. Wolfie saw everything.

As soon as tickets went on sale, my friends and I jumped on them for the show in San Antonio on September 28. When Van Halen hit the stage that night in San Antonio, the crowd went absolutely nuts (although the venue was not quite sold out). I was not a critical audience member, I was simply there to have fun.

During Ed's solo, he approached the center stage microphone, which was something I had never seen him do. He said, "I'm just fuckin' around, I hope you guys don't mind." The crowd cheered. Then he followed that up with, "I normally play the same thing, but I just feel like fuckin' around tonight. Alright?" I noticed then that his speech was slurred. It occurred to me that he was probably drunk.

For the end of the show, my good friend Brando and I pulled the old sneak. Through a combination of lax security and early departures, we ended up as close as you could possibly get to Ed's corner of the stage—the left-front corner of the stage was about five feet from us. As they ended the show, we were just baffled by how close we were to Eddie. After the last song, Ed led the crowd to thunderous applause. From the stage, he yelled, "1-2-3!" several times and gestured for applause. I will never forget that we were so close that we could actually hear Ed's voice from the stage, no microphone. All in all, we had a blast.

On the drive back to Austin, someone said, "I think Eddie was wasted." The thought got passed around the car, and I pointed out that his speaking and behavior during his solo was a little odd. As we drove further down the road, someone else offered up, "Did you notice Sammy stayed on Mike's side of the stage the whole night?" I remember adding, "Did you notice that Sammy barely even moved during the whole show?" It didn't take long for the adrenaline to wear off, and we all assessed that what we saw was indeed fun, but it was far from the real Van Halen. At the time, I had so much going on personally that I didn't pay much attention to the press surrounding the tour. I had not read any online reviews so I went into the concert absolutely tabula rasa. I just wanted to let loose and have a blast. If I had known what had been going on, I might have paid more attention. But all I really wanted to see was Edward and I most certainly accomplished that. I was so psyched that I just did not notice his hair or teeth or his skin. One friend that saw the show in August in Salt Lake City had close seats. He told me that Eddie's skin looked "green." I just didn't notice.

Meeting Darrell "Dimebag" Abbott

The day after the San Antonio show, on September 29, Van Halen played in Lubbock, Texas. There to meet his idol was Damageplan/ former-Pantera guitarist Darrell "Dimebag" Abbott. "That was the first time Dime ever got to meet Eddie Van Halen," said Rita Abbott, Dime's wife. She continued:

> They hung out before and after the show. Dime even got to play on his rig at sound check. He was like a kid in a candy store . . . the way his eyes were lit up. He told me later—in the limo—which Van Halen provided—how cool is that? Anyway he leaned over and looked me right in the eyes and said, "If I died tonight, it wouldn't matter, 'cause I've done everything now, I've met Eddie Van Halen!" and he had the biggest smile on his face . . . he was so happy!

Afterward, Dime called Ed's cell phone. He left Edward an exuberant voice mail about how great it was to meet him and hang out. The voicemail was something that Ed seized on as a pick-me-up. He decided to keep the message saved; Ed liked validation from the new guard. While they were hanging out, the two of them discussed the EVH Art Series guitars that had just been announced, and Dime made a specific custom request for a replica of the *Van Halen II*-era black and yellow striped guitar. Ed promised to secure one for him.

The situation within the band worsened throughout October. Sammy told several different stories of Edward getting beyond out of control after shows. One notorious incident was more or less caused by Sammy and Michael staying after a show to simply shower and pick up some sandwiches. At the airport, an impatiently waiting Edward had been growing more and more furious by the minute. Sammy wrote:

> "Don't ever fucking make me wait," he said. "Without me, you're nothing. You'll see. At the end of this tour, you guys will have nothing. You're going to have to call me if you ever want to tour again." He was facing one direction, I was facing the other. I turned and said, "Ed, shut the fuck up, man. Come on. We just did a gig." "Fuck you," he said, and started bashing his

> bottle on the plane window. . . . The stewardess and the pilot started freaking out. They were reluctant to take off with this madman on the plane. Finally, Al got him to take it easy and we took off.

From there on, the two traveled separately. Sammy and Edward would never take a plane together again ever, actually, nor stay in the same hotel or ride in the same limo. The only times they would ever interact again would be just before show time and during performances. Sam did not do sound checks in order to save his voice for the actual show.

That old VH rumor mill was smoking again, so much so that Sammy went out of his way to post a message on his personal website on November 2. "The Last Leg of the Van Halen Tour is about over. It ends on Nov 19th to be exact in Tucson at the Anselmo Amphitheater. Last two shows. Huh! . . . You can't make it? Get real! See ya in Tucson! Everything has been great, the fans awesome, the fun meter in the red. Listen here, all these crazy rumors flying around cyberspace are that. Plain and simple, I never said I was quitting Van Halen. There has been no discussion as to when or where we're going to pick this show up on the road and do it all over again cause quite honestly, 80 shows since June 11. Wow, I'm bushed . . . HA!"

Black Friday

November 19 in Tucson would become known to some Van Halen fans as Black Friday. It was the second night of an end-of-tour, back-to-back pair of shows at a small 4,200-seat arena. The November 18 show was relatively unremarkable. The choice of songs at sound check on November 19 would give some indication as to Edward's general mood and potential "future" direction. Sound check jams caught on tape included set list staples "You Really Got Me" and "Jump." The former classic VH tune was actually sung in part by Wolfgang. During a playful version of "Jump," Mike sang lead and Ed screamed the lyrics in a fun call and response with Mike; it also featured some major jamming between Ed, Mike, and Al at the end. Another jam, though, was a song only occasionally played on the 2004 tour, "Runnin' With the Devil." Mike sang lead with enthusiasm, and Ed chimed in with some of Dave's own classic vocal fills including, "I tell ya all about it." One spontaneous jam of "Drop Dead

Legs," however, was something very different. It was a very short little jam, less than a minute, and most of that was the outro. This song had *never* been performed live—not even on the *1984* tour. The jam was cut short abruptly in a teasing manner by Ed. This 53-second jam has been viewed (or heard, rather) nearly 100,000 times on YouTube. Another major jam during the sound check was the unearthed treasure "I'm the One." Mike sang lead and Edward sang all of his lines right in unison with Mike. At the end, Eddie's shouted lines of "Show your love!" literally sounded like Kurt Cobain. The lucky few in attendance cheered along with the practically never-heard tunes.

As it neared show time, though, Edward's world boiled over. As per Hagar:

> He came up to me before the show, when I was talking to Irving [Azoff], and rolled my sleeve down over my tattoo. I didn't even acknowledge him. I just rolled it back up. He rolled it back down. I rolled it back up. "Don't be fucking with my shirt, dude," I said. "That thing ain't gonna last," he said, showing me his Van Halen tattoo. "See that? That's better. That's going to last longer."

When Sammy was signing exactly 120 bottles for all 120 members of the crew, Edward suddenly wanted a bottle. Sam went out of his way to get Ed a bottle from his fridge, from which Ed immediately took a few slugs, but Eddie wanted to know why he couldn't have one of the other bottles, not having processed that Sam was signing a specific number for the entire crew. It was clear that well before show time, Ed was already off in his own very angry world, like a bomb slowly being detonated.

Valerie came with her then-boyfriend/now-husband Tom Vitale to watch Wolfie perform one last time on the tour. Valerie's brother Pat came to proudly watch his former brother-in-law from the wings of the stage during the last show. During Hagar's now protracted acoustic segment of the show, Edward angrily approached Pat and exploded on him for no apparent reason at all. Ed then attempted to choke Pat, who was much larger than he was. Valerie wrote in *Losing It*:

> Taken by surprise, Pat defended himself by grabbing Ed's hand and saying, "You don't want to do this. You don't want to do

> this." With his free hand, Ed tried to take a swing at Pat. Pat blocked his punch, took hold of both of Ed's arms, and yelled, "You don't want to do this!" Fortunately, one of the burly backstage security guards agreed. He grabbed Ed and dragged him away. . . . By the time I got to the side of the stage, Pat was walking away and Ed was going back on stage. "What the hell happened?" Pat said upon seeing me. "I don't know," I said, "You tell me." "I can't believe that asshole," Pat muttered. "He's out of his mind. Something's wrong with him."

The show built up until the very end, and during one his most infamous onstage acts, Edward smashed his main two Peavey Wolfgang guitars. The end of the second smashing was caught on film. During the 22-second clip, Edward has his green guitar with both hands on the neck of the guitar, swinging it directly over is head and smashing the body onto the stage. The neck did not break off of the body, so Edward took the guitar with his right hand on the neck with the body near his feet. Ed then braced himself for a windup and swung the guitar at about 200 degrees, meaning that for the most part the guitar went up backward over his head and landed essentially in the center of the stage. The guitar had some serious hang time and velocity on it. Ed turned around to watch it land, raised his arms above his head and clapped. He then walked over to an open microphone and said something unintelligible and gestured toward Michael and Sammy departing on stage right. He said "Woo!" into the mic, and turned to exit stage left, saluted the audience, clapped, gave a thumbs up, and staggered off stage.

Ion Hobson of *Tucson Weekly* said:

> Seeming to have fallen off the bandwagon yet again, EVH's mood changed drastically as the final performance ended. Constantly yelling, "That's it, it's over," all night, Eddie made the crowd ponder if another breakup was on the horizon. This was later fueled after "Right Now," when EVH smashed his guitar repeatedly before swinging his ax, almost nailing Hagar. This immediately drew a "What the fuck?" reaction from his band and the crowd.

Hagar told *Billboard* that he and Eddie almost came to blows after the show. "They just pulled him one way, and me the other," he said. "We didn't even say goodbye to each other. It was a horrible way to end the whole thing." Valerie said that Ed destroyed his dressing room after the show. Later Hagar said, "They tell me he pulled some crazy shit on the plane home. . . . Some funky shit went down on that plane. My man was completely gone and out of it." He added, "I never spoke to him again after telling him to keep his hand off my shirt."

Again, Wolfgang witnessed the whole thing. Valerie was concerned about how Wolfie would take the whole incident, but he seemed to take in stride, for better or worse. For Edward, the culmination of the tour was capped off by a horrific tragedy that hit him hard given the recent contact he had with the victim, which was magnified in Edward's mind since it happened barely over a week after the Tucson incident.

Ed's guitar tech for the 2004 tour, Lonnie Totman, gave an extended interview for *Guitars101.com.* "Ed is an interesting person," he said. "He's a smart guy and . . . a person with a big heart. Believe it or not out of any player I have worked with he is the most thankful appreciative guy. He constantly thanks you for all your hard work and lets you know that you're doing a great job. That means a lot." When pressed about what took place in Tucson, Lonnie would only say, "I'm not interested in commenting on this with the exception of stating that it had nothing to do with anything gear related. He wasn't frustrated because something wasn't working properly." Ben Italiano, the webmaster of another VH fan site, snagged an interview with Lonnie just a few days later. Prior to start of the chat, Italiano posted the following message: "One thing Lonnie and I both agree is to please do not ask about what went on at the Tucson show. This is strictly prohibited."

Alex was worried. On December 1, he called up Valerie to tell her that he was planning yet another formal intervention only two weeks after Tucson. His efforts fell apart though, in part due to the tragedy that followed only a week later.

The Death of Dime

On December 8, 2004 (the same day John Lennon was shot and the same day my own brother's plane crashed), Darrell "Dimebag" Abbott, whom Edward had just met barely two months before, was tragically shot and killed on stage while performing with his and his brother Vinnie's new band Damageplan. The shooter was a deranged, disgruntled Pantera fan. He killed four people in total before being shot dead by a responding police officer. When the word hit that there would be a public memorial in Arlington near Dallas, Edward hopped a plane and took off.

The voice message from Dime that Edward had saved now took on new significance. Ed felt that his message showed the true Dime and he played it through his cell phone to the audience. "I just wanted to give you a . . . call to tell you thank you so . . . much, man, for the most awesome, uplifting, euphoric, spiritual rock and roll extravaganza ever," Dime said in the voice message.

Edward and Ozzy/Black Label Society guitar legend Zakk Wylde, who was a close friend of Dime's, were principal speakers at the memorial. They repeatedly downed shots openly during the service, and during one toast, Edward squeezed his tall, plastic shot glass so hard that it shattered into pieces—a moment captured in photograph. In an interview with *Revolver* magazine, Zakk said his grief was compounded by having to deal with Eddie's "bizarre" behavior. "I don't know what the hell happened to Ed," he said. "He hasn't just gone off the deep end—he's living in Atlantis! I couldn't get in a word without being interrupted by him. If I mentioned God, he'd say, 'There is no God or Jesus, only yes or no.' It was like he thought the whole thing was about him. He wasn't thinking about Dime, or even Vinnie and Dime's old lady, Rita, for that matter."

Ed's selfless saving grace, however, was his donation to the burial a few days later. Edward had known that Dime wanted a replica of the black and yellow *Van Halen II* guitar, but considering the totality of the circumstances, Edward brought the original guitar itself which was placed inside Dime's casket. Dime's wife Rita told *Metal Monthly*, "When Ed came in at the viewing, he had the guitar, but it wasn't the guitar we expected . . . He told Vinnie and I that 'Dime was an original and only an original deserves the original!' He popped open the case and there it was . . . His original '79 still with the rusted set of strings on it! It was so amazing!!!" She continued, "I took it in to Dime and I said, 'See, baby, you didn't get a replica! You got THE one,' and I gave him a kiss on the forehead and placed it in there with him . . . Ed was awesome and I thank him still!"

It would take *years* to recover from 2004.

CHAPTER 39
The Lost Years

If Edward had a few lost years, they were 2005 and 2006. He was essentially in seclusion. Peavey quietly announced that the guitar that was once the Wolfgang was to be renamed the Carina, only to be renamed yet again the HP Special in January 2005. That was the end of the Peavey Wolfgang. Ed would eventually end up where he wanted though—making things himself exactly like he wanted it. Those old Wolfgangs have a cult following and are amongst the most highly sought after guitars on the aftermarket. There are plenty of websites dedicated to devotees of the instrument, with places to enter your serial number and find out all kinds of information about any specific instrument. They hold up well.

Dwyer and Michaels out of Iowa was his only media outlet in 2005. He granted two interviews to the duo throughout the year, and that was all he would say publicly.

On May 11, the duo really nutted up and approached Ed with more aggressive questioning than they had in the past. The early parts of the interview were actually extremely contentious, with the radio hosts serving as fan advocates and saying some pointed things directly to the reclusive genius himself. Excerpts from interview follow with commentary:

> DJ: So are you just, are you not interested in . . . recording rock—
>
> EVH: I'm always recording! [Angry.] Where the hell do you think I am?! If I dropped dead right now, there'd be enough damn music for—pfft—at least twenty, thirty fuckin' CDs. You know?
>
> DJ: But it shouldn't take you to *drop dead* to get it released.
>
> EVH: Hey! You know, it's like, you know . . . I can't do it all myself!

DJ: You could put an album out right now without a singer and it would be huge. Van Halen fans would *love* it. Eddie Van Halen fans *need* it.

EVH: Look, we just finished a damn tour in November!

DJ: I know there was a tour, and that's great, so put the tour out on disc so people can at least capture it.

EVH: Well, hey, you know—nobody else wanted to do more than *three songs*! [Very angrily.]

DJ: What do you mean?

EVH: Nobody wanted to do it. You know? I did. I wanted to do a whole record. But, uh . . .

DJ: You mean *nobody else* in the band wanted to put out more than three new songs?

EVH: Yeah.

DJ: *Everybody* was against it?

EVH: Well, I said, "Let's do at least do half and half." You know?

DJ: And who said no? Sam said no?

EVH: *Well, who else is in the band*?! [Sarcastically.]

DJ: So, you were outvoted three to one?

EVH: Hey, there have been songs that I've written that I personally don't even like that I got outvoted.

[Later in the interview, Ed actually plays and sings a tune over the phone. He's playing an unamplified electric guitar.]

EVH: No, wait. [He then starts to play pieces of a rather nice chord progression.] Here's the fuckin' song, wait . . . [Eventually, he starts singing along with the riff.] "Death by Hollywood / A little too fabulous for his own good." [Laughs.] That's the kind of lyrics I write.

DJ: That's awesome. That's Eddie Van Halen. What is, what is the name of that?

EVH: "Death by Hollywood / A little too fabulous for his own good." Heh-heh-heh!!!

DJ: That's great. That's great. And you just wrote that tonight?

EVH: Ah, I guess. It just popped in my head.

DJ: Yeah. I wanna know what kind of wine you like.

EVH: Well, I mean, it's . . . Well, okay, now I'm gonna . . .

DJ: No . . .

EVH: Now I'm gonna piss everybody off.

DJ: No, who cares.

EVH: No, 'cause I don't want 'em to think . . . [Edward's worry was likely that he did not want to admit he had returned to drinking after such public battles in the past. He continued.] Uh . . . It's not very expensive, but it's, uh, it's very consistent. It's called Smoking Loon.

DJ: Smoking Loon?

EVH: Yeah.

DJ: We're all writin' it down! Okay, Smoking Loon. Where's it out of?

EVH: Uh, California.

DJ: 'Cause see I was gonna, I was gonna send you a bottle of wine because you talk to us all the time, but I didn't know what you like. You like a cab? Or something—

EVH: Yeah, yeah, yeah, it's a cabernet.

DJ: Okay.

EVH: Heavy cabby. Cab.

DJ: Heavy cab.

EVH: I don't, I'm not, I don't go for that fruity crap, you know?

DJ: Okay. How can we ship it to you?

EVH: Oh, damn. I don't what my P.O. box number is any more. [Laughs.]

DJ: What's the address there at the house?

EVH: Oh, come on, I can't give that out!

DJ: [Laughter.] Well, we're not gonna give it—

EVH: I got enough, I got enough stalkers already. [Laughs.]

[Later in the interview, Ed discussed the 2004 tour for the first time.]

DJ: Hey, what was it like on that opening night? You guys were in what—North Carolina?

EVH: You know what's really odd is, last tour, I would just show up at sound check, and I go, "Hmm? *Why* do extra laundry?" So, I would just wear whatever I'm wearin' and take my shirt off and play. But more importantly, this was the first time ever that I got up on stage and I was not nervous at all.

DJ: Really?

EVH: Yeah. It's like it was, we were about a month into the tour, and I'd even preface before I started my guitar solo. I'd say, "I'm just gonna F-off, you know? And somebody throw somethin' at me if you don't dig it." You know? I just totally let go, and I was actually writing on the stage. I was just coming up with stuff as I was playing. About a month, three weeks, two months into the tour, Alex, my brother, goes, "Ed, don't you think you should play *something* off the records?" [Laughter.] Because, you know, I was having so much fun just, just goin' out there and, not necessarily jerkin' off, but sometimes, I don't know . . . My philosophy is fall down the stairs and hope you land on your feet. And most of the time I did. Sometimes, you know . . .

DJ: So, the best, the best part of being on stage was when you were improvising a solo for yourself. What is the best part on stage do you think when it comes to connecting with fans out who have come to see you?

EVH: Oh, I was gonna, I was gonna say the other best part is when Sammy's doing his thing with his little electric palm tree, and, since I'm not married, I'm behind the amps havin' fun.

DJ: [Laughter.] And it's not with a bottle of Smoking Mallard or whatever the hell that is. Crazy Loon? Smoking Loon?

EVH: Oh . . . She be—she be smokin' something else.

DJ: Okay! Alright!

When Dwyer and Michaels posted the interview clips with Edward, they also posted a recent interview segment from Michael Anthony. "I hate to talk smack about anyone in the band or whatever," he said, "but, you know . . . Eddie, you know, he's, he's still doin' a bit of drinking and everything. There were nights where it was kind of like a roller coaster, up or down, and, and, myself, I would've like to have seen him totally clean up if we were gonna take this further and like, 'cause, gosh, you know, we could've gone all around the world with it."

Ed was photographed out at a WNBA game with an unknown blonde on August 13. They were taking in the game from the front row, dining on beer and popcorn. Edward was still wearing those same damned, worn-out boots wrapped in gaffer's tape. It's possible the boots were the only stable thing in his life at the time.

Opening Up to Dwyer & Michaels

Later in August, Eugenia died at 90 years old. Valerie openly expressed concern for Ed's well being after having lost his other parent. She wrote:

> They had a small, touching ceremony for her on a boat near where they'd said good-bye to Mr. Van Halen. The occasion was extremely sad. I had a lot of fond memories of her. . . . The boys had her lying in bed. I kissed her on the cheek. After my lips touched her skin, I was struck by how cold her body was.

On October 3, Edward really opened up and gave an overly extensive interview with Dwyer and Michaels. Once again, excerpts from the interview follow with commentary:

DJ: Umm, hey, we got our, our buddy Eddie Van Halen is back on the phone with us. And during that record we were chattin' about, umm, your help with Big Brothers Big Sisters down in Scottsdale, Arizona. You donated, uh, a painted guitar that, umm . . .

> EVH: *Yee-haw*!!! [Very exaggerated and hilarious.]
>
> DJ: [Lots of laughter.] You're, you're ex-brother-in-law asked you if you would be part of this—

EVH: Actually, Stacy, his wife, did. [Ed went out of his way to credit Pat's wife Stacy, and not Pat whom he had physically attacked in Tucson.]

DJ: Okay, his, his wife. So you're on speaking terms, then, with, with your former in-laws?

EVH: I'm on speaking terms with anyone that'll speak with me.

DJ: Okay.

EVH: I'm speaking with you guys, ain't I?

DJ: [Laughter.] Yeah! And we're pretty low on the list, right? There aren't a whole lot of people you're turning away!

EVH: I wouldn't say that.

DJ: [Laughter.] So, let's see—

EVH: That's not speaking too highly about yourself.

DJ: Right. So your, your guitar was in there with, uh—

EVH: I don't know who else. All I know is this. My mom passed away a month and a half ago.

DJ: Oh! I'm sorry to hear that.

EVH: Um, well, you know, how much longer do you want to live than 90 years old?

DJ: Depends on quality, I suppose.

EVH: Then I rest my case.

DJ: Okay, so . . .

EVH: And she rests in peace. But, uh . . .

DJ: Well, that kind of brings everything down to a screeching halt here.

EVH: Nah, not really. I mean, she's much better off where she is, and . . .

DJ: Had she been sick? I didn't hear anything about this.

EVH: Uh, well, you know, I usually don't have much to say except to you guys.

DJ: Yeah.

EVH: 'Cause you seem like, you know, you sent me a bottle of Poizon and I guess it's okay to talk to you.

DJ: We didn't, we didn't mention that on the air yet, but the last time we talked to you, we got into a lengthy discussion over, uh, Smoking Loon wine. Which, by the way, after we talked to you about that, all the stores here in town sold out of it. So, we were gonna send you some of that, but we couldn't get it, so—

EVH: Well, don't send me something I can get right down the street.

DJ: Well, but that's why . . . You live in California! Every wine is right down the street for you! But you did get it, right?

EVH: Yeah.

DJ: Okay, and what did you think of it?

EVH: Uhh, interesting packaging.

DJ: [Lots of laughter.] When I tried to send this wine, umm, I had no concept in my head as to—I mean, do you walk down to the end of your driveway to get your mail? Does the UPS guy stop by your place?

EVH: Actually, I just, I just got a new, uh, you know, like P.O. box kind of deal where FedEx can drop off because I used to use my studio address and people would start ripping me off and I wouldn't receive things and, so, I got a different address.

DJ: Well, tell them the story about having talked to the lady at the, the vineyard to have it shipped to him. Well, I . . . She needed a name on the address, she couldn't just send it to the studio, and you can't send it to a P.O. box, unfortunately. And I call up and I, I tell 'em who I'm sending the wine to. And she's like, "Could you tell me that name again?" And I'm like, umm, "Edward Van Halen." I'm like, "V-A-N . . ." She's like, "Oh, my god! *The* Edward Van Halen?!" I'm like, I'm like, "Yeah, we're, we don't even . . ." And I had to say, "I don't even know if this is really his address." And then she went into a long story about how they provided wine for a Metallica wedding. [Awkward silence.] Which I know, which I can tell really impresses you. [Laughs.]

EVH: No, no. I was just trippin' on "the." Should I just walk around calling myself "The?"

DJ: Well, that's what I wanted to know. If, you know, because, how was I supposed to know, a DJ in the middle of Iowa, whether or not anything you would send . . . Anything that got sent to Eddie Van Halen in care of anything would ever get to you. I thought that was a victory in and of itself.

EVH: Yeah, and I drank it.

DJ: Yeah, well, okay! I guess, and so, I guess we're all happy now! And it was good, but what? It doesn't compare to Smokin' Loon?

EVH: A little fruity for my taste, you know, but . . .

DJ: Umm, what's that other, uh, cabernet you like real well? Silver Oak. You want a bottle of Silver Oak? We're getting into the spendy stuff, Eddie.

EVH: Aahhh, Smoking Loon's just fine.

DJ: Yeah, but we're trying to broaden your horizons a little bit. And we're trying to suck up and kiss your ass an awful lot!

EVH: What you don't get is I didn't *start* with this. I honed it *down* to this.

DJ: But at seven bucks a bottle, you can't beat Smoking Loon for consistency.

EVH: Oh, I got a bottle in my hand . . .

DJ: Yeah.

EVH: It is . . . good. [Edward gargles wine into the phone. There is laughter.] Can I do the weather again?

DJ: No! In case you're just tuning in, that's Eddie Van Halen gargling wine. That's what we do every morning.

EVH: I thought I did a pretty good job on the weather last time. Whether you like it or not!

DJ: Hey, you know what? In talking about this charity thing with the, uh, the guitar and everything—

EVH: The guitar. Let me tell you the original idea I had for that thing.

DJ: Okay.

EVH: And, because for one, you know, I named my son after the pizza guy Wolfgang Puck.

DJ: Okay. [Laughter.]

EVH: Amadeus Puck. [Laughter.] You know, I don't know how many people know this, but, uh, I don't know if it's a Barney song or whatever, but everyone uses it, and it's called "Twinkle, Twinkle Little Star." Well, that melody, that song's written by Amadeus.

DJ: That I did not know. Was it really?

EVH: Wolfgang Amadeus Mozart, yes. Minuet is C or some B.S., something like that, but—

DJ: Well, the Barney people owe him some money, then, I would think, in royalties.

EVH: Well, no, it's, it's public domain, or whatever you call it.

DJ: Public domain.

EVH: Public domain, yeah. So, what I was gonna do, is just, you know, treble, treble clef and write "Da da—da da—dee dee duh," and underneath it write "Do you really have to know how to read music" and underneath the strings, to the bass clef, and go "Duh duh—duh duh—dee dee duh," and write "In order to write music?"

DJ: Okay. That's pretty cool. And then, that didn't, but that's, that's not what the final product is.

EVH: Well, my mom was dying. Okay?

DJ: Mm-hmm . . .

EVH: At home, and she was, what, two minutes away from me, or she did. So, that kind of threw a little wrench in the works. And, anyway . . . The concept was "Da da—da da—dee dee duh / Do you really have to know how to read music? / Duh duh—duh duh—dee dee duh / In order to write music?" And on the back, I'm gonna put a big fat "No!"

DJ: [Laughter.] Okay. Right!

EVH: Because I can't read music, because—*ideas* . . . You know, the only reason they even transcribed or wrote music down was because they didn't have tape machines. You think Mozart, Beethoven, any of these guys, you know, Bach, would have *bothered* . . . You know? To write, to write this stuff down?

DJ: Had they been able, had they been able to record it back then.

EVH: "Hey, here's 24-track, shit! Yeah! [Laughter.] And it's *exactly* how I want it to sound!"

DJ: What did the final outcome—

EVH: Well, you know, because my mom was, you know, preparing to move to wherever we're all going . . .

DJ: Yeah.

EVH: Umm, I waited 'til, I don't know, about three days before they were coming to pick it up even though I had the thing for a damn month and a half. And, so, I said, "Wolfie," you know, because Wolfie and I did it together. And I said, "Doesn't look like gonna have time to do the original concept." He said, "That's cool." I go, "We'll think of somethin'." I go, "I know. Let's go to Big Five, buy same paint, paint guns." You know? Paintball guns?

DJ: Okay! Paintball guns.

EVH: Well, I had no idea that this paint was water soluble.

DJ: Yeah.

EVH: So, we did this really neat, just, you know did a . . . job on it—you know? "Pop-pop-pop-pop-pop!!!!" You know, we murdered the damn thing, you know? And, and wrote some funny stuff on it. And it's like, on the headstock, I think that was still there, I put "Bumper," you know for the name of the guitar, not "Fender." Because bumper will dent your fender. [Laughter.] So a "Bumper" guitar.

DJ: And you titled it *Father and Son*, or did they title it that?

EVH: No, we just signed it.

DJ: Okay.

EVH: And, uh, it was it. It was pretty cool. But guess what? I go visit my mom, you know? Spend the night over there.

DJ: Yeah.

EVH: Come home in the morning. [Pauses.] Water soluble paint. Sprinklers went off and everything washed off. [DJs laugh.] And Wolfie and I went, "Now what?!" Concept number two, which, I didn't know where it came from. This time, I didn't leave it outside. I pull it up in the garage. Guess what? The gardeners come with their damn blowers and the paint wasn't dry yet.

DJ: Uh-oh. So, there's some grass clippings attached to it that wasn't supposed to be there?

EVH: There was all kinds of dead bugs and grass and leaves and you name it.

DJ: This has, like, turned into an episode from *The Honeymooners*!

EVH: So, I had to remove it all . . . And then, version number three. And this time, I painted it, closed the garage doors, covered it, and that's the version that ended up.

DJ: What did it sell for? Any idea?

EVH: I don't know. . . .

DJ: What day-to-day car do you drive? Take Wolfie to school, what do you drive?

EVH: Right now, a '52 Ford pickup.

DJ: '52 Ford pickup. What was the first car you bought when you started seeing some cash? Like, the first toy.

EVH: Uh, you mean the first car I ever owned?

DJ: No, no, no. When Van Halen hit big and you had some money to throw around, the first, uh—

EVH: A Porsche.

DJ: —indulgence. A Porsche. What, what kind?

EVH: Ah, it was a piece of junk, actually. It was, no, well they were like . . . No, they were both a piece of junk.

DJ: Like a nine, an old 914, or something new?

EVH: No, it was a 911e Targa.

DJ: Okay, alright. That's a pretty good place to start! And how many speeding tickets did you get in it?

EVH: How many what?

DJ: Speeding tickets.

EVH: Forget speeding tickets, man. It was how many times did I spin the damn thing?

DJ: [Laughter.] Whew. Wow, that's . . . So okay, and now do you still have that car? And I don't know why we're—

EVH: No.

DJ: You don't any more.

EVH: No.

DJ: I didn't know if you were a collector, or just a buyer and user, or . . .

EVH: I, I don't know what I am either. I just buy things, use 'em, and I barter.

DJ: On to the next one.

EVH: And then, someone goes "Hey, that's cool," and I go, "You want it? Go ahead, take it."

DJ: Can I come and visit some time? And bring a—

EVH: Any time you like because, I tell you, I can't walk in my house.

DJ: Oh, God! Alright, Eddie, can—hang on one minute, we gotta do a couple of commercials but we'll be back. Okay?

EVH: Okay, but, okay, but, shit . . .

DJ: Try not to say that though.

EVH: Oh, I'm sorry.

DJ: That's alright. Hold on, we'll be right back, Eddie Van—

EVH: I've got things to do!

DJ: We know! We know! But it, it . . .

EVH: It's four in the morning, here!

DJ: Yeah, but it's 6:30 here, it's just gettin'—

EVH: *4:30*!

DJ: It's getting good!

EVH: Come on. I'm right in the middle of, of working—

DJ: Of what?

EVH: —on my Wolfgang prototype guitar.

DJ: For who?

EVH: I've gotta send this stuff off. I'm redesigning all my equipment. And if I don't get this off to these people *today*, then, you know, nothing at NAMM show.

DJ: You're not, you're not much for deadlines, are you?

EVH: Uh, no, no, no . . .

DJ: You had the fourteen-foot guitar . . .

EVH: No, no, no . . . Here's the problem. Very few people keep up with my ass. It's like, I'm always doing something. And people think I take on too much. No, I don't. It's like, when someone tells me they can do something, I expect them to pull through some time. *I* do.

DJ: We would be, uh, we would be completely not doing our job if we didn't ask you if you would take phone calls from, I don't care, you decide how many. How many, how many Van Halen fans would you accept a phone call from if we just put you on with them right now?

EVH: Right now? Two.

DJ: Two? Okay. 355-5343 is the phone number.

EVH: I need to go to the bathroom, and I need to restring a guitar, go to the studio, and check.

DJ: Do you want to do that first? Or do you want to do the calls first? He's gotta go to the bathroom, let him go. I know but what if he doesn't come back? He will!

EVH: Well, if you guys would just get on with it we wouldn't have anything to worry about.

DJ: You sound like our boss now! "Would you guys just get on with it!" Alright, we'll take two people that can talk to Eddie Van Halen right now. 355-5343. Hey, when,

when we talk about these charity things that you've donated for, Big Brothers Big Sisters, etc., we do a thing for Toys for Tots here. And is there any way we could get, I don't know, a plate, a guitar, you know, uh, pickguard to you, have you sign it for us and ship it back to us for our Toys for Tots auction?

EVH: Sure, why not.

DJ: You're a pretty agreeable dude.

EVH: Hey, I got no problem, you know?

DJ: You just kind of roll with it, don't you?

EVH: I'm probably the simplest guy you'll ever meet. . . .

DJ: Alright, here is Peg. We'll start with a gal, okay? Uh, Peg?

Peg: Good morning.

DJ: You're on with Eddie Van Halen.

Peg: Good morning, Eddie. How are you today?

EVH: Uh, actually, I don't know yet, it's a little earlier here than—

Peg: It's pretty early, it's pretty early.

EVH: Say again?

Peg: My question is I'm very interested in what your future holds with your son. Are you going to be cutting a song with him? An album that we're gonna hear? Or?

EVH: Well, I've recorded so many songs with him already.

Peg: Any idea, when will it be?

EVH: Say again?

DJ: She wants to know if it's going to be released any time.

EVH: Oh, uh . . . I don't know.

DJ: So, is Warner Bros.—

EVH: I've got hundreds of songs *I* haven't released.

DJ: Right. But is Warner Bros. saying "Hey, why don't you and your son release some of that stuff?"

EVH: Come on, I mean, he's 14 years old.

DJ: Hey! How old were you when you broke into the business?

EVH: He's a world-class musician. I jam with him almost every day.

DJ: Who plays the drums when you two jam?

EVH: Him. And me.

DJ: You don't call Al? Call Uncle Al and have him come over, and . . . [Laughter.]

EVH: No. I don't know.

DJ: Do you two play differently, you and Wolfie, when you have tape rolling than when you're just sitting around the living room?

EVH: No. Uh-uh.

DJ: So, there you go, Peg. They have recorded stuff, it hasn't been released, though.

Peg: Okay!

DJ: Alright?

Peg: I look forward to it in the future. Thanks, guys!

EVH: One thing I did want to say is that for . . . Oh, bye!

DJ: She had to go. She had to go take a leak and restring her guitars, also. [Laughter.] What did you want to say, though? She can still hear.

EVH: Is that for, for graduation ceremony back in June . . . You know, he's in ninth grade now. He's only fourteen. And, well, I don't know, the school that he goes to, uh . . . [Pause.] Well, they gave a damn rock show. . . . The lead singer of the band told everyone, because it was coming to the end of the gig, so to speak, and the ceremony, or whatever it was.

DJ: Graduation?

EVH: Yeah, it was graduation day, I don't know if it was the ceremony or, what the hell. You know? But right before the last song before the band, the band, uh, came out, the lead singer came out and he delivered, "C'mon down front!" And everyone came up, you know, got up out of their seats, and, you know, it became a true rock show.

DJ: So, this was Wolfie's band? Like a bunch of school friends?

EVH: Yeah, yeah, yeah.

DJ: What's the name of their band?

EVH: I think this one was called The Shisa.

DJ: The Shisa?

EVH: Which means "the shit" in German. 'Cause that's what, whenever I like something I always say, "Now, that's the shit, Wolfie!" You know?

DJ: [Laughter.] Oh! No! You can't say—umm . . . Wait, you said you would talk to two listeners, let's bring Brett up and then we'll, we gotta let you go. We'll get on with what we have to do. Brett?

Brett: Good morning, Eddie!

EVH: Hey! How's it going?

Brett: I've been a fan forever, man. You're awesome!

EVH: Well, thank you.

Brett: My question to you is that Harley that you used to have, or you may still have it, I don't know. Did you ever get it sold on, uh, eBay?

EVH: No, I didn't sell it, I gave it to the guy who, uh, bought about *four* of 'em.

Brett: Did you ride it when you had it? That's a pretty dumb question.

EVH: The deal, the deal was whoever bids the highest on one of my guitars on eBay—because, because I didn't put a price on 'em. Otherwise, I would've just sold 'em in stores. But I figured, hey, I'll just let the people decide what it's worth to them.

DJ: Okay.

EVH: You know?

DJ: Man, you are unorthodox.

EVH: And whoever spends the most on one of the striped guitars that I played on tour, uh, I'll give you my Harley. So, I gave it to the guy who spent around forty grand.

DJ: So, he got a guitar and your Harley for forty grand?

EVH: Well, actually I think he bought about four guitars.

DJ: Yeah, a bunch of guitars. And Brett wanted to know did you ever ride the Harley before you got rid of it?

EVH: Yeah, yeah, yeah, until—you know, it's kind of like an Elvis bike, so to speak, you know? I mean, it was a great bike, it was just, "Wow, I wonder who's riding that?"

DJ: Yeah, okay.

EVH: You know, it's got a "VH" on the tank, "Eddie" on the seat, it's got, you know, striped up like my guitar. [Laughs.] It was, it's like, "*Duhhhh* . . . I wonder who *that* is?"

DJ: [Much laughter.] It's kind of a giveaway when they see you coming down the street is what you're saying?

EVH: Yeah.

DJ: Okay. Alright, Brett. Thanks for the question, man.

Brett: Thanks, guys.

DJ: Alright.

Brett: Take it easy, man.

DJ: Alright. Well, hey, we appreciate you talking to us. If you can, hold on one second so we can get the address, and seriously, we'll send you a, a pickguard for our little Toys for Tots.

EVH: Uhh . . . Call me back in about ten . . . I got—

DJ: Hold on, hold on. You go do, you go get your guitar, you go take—go to the bathroom, whatever, and, and we'll get the info from you, okay?

EVH: Yeah, and then call me back.

DJ: Okay.

EVH: Alright?

DJ: Alright, Eddie. Thanks again, man. Good talking to you.

EVH: You're welcome.

DJ: Take care. Bye.

EVH: Bye. Call me back.

DJ: Alright, we will—ten minutes.

The D-Word

After four long years of separation—and even what Edward already considered a practical divorce—Valerie finally officially filed for divorce on December 7, 2005. The Associated Press carried the story as "Bertinelli Divorcing Rocker Eddie Van Halen." The article included a quote from Valerie's spokeswoman confirming, "Yes, that's true. They have been separated for four years and it's amicable." The divorce petition simply cited irreconcilable differences. In reference to Edward and the band, the AP writer said, "Van Halen, 50, is one of the most celebrated lead guitarists in rock music. . . . The group [Van Halen] was known for wild excess both on and offstage in its early years, and [Edward] Van Halen, once a heavy smoker, was treated for cancer in 2000 and 2001."

In some ways, the fans and even the general public weren't in general very happy with the guy. Edward never quit smoking cigarettes, and maintained that they had nothing to do with his tongue cancer. His position in this issue caused many an eye to roll, and very few to understand. Slowly, Ed was in the process of becoming a new person, but there were still a few layers left to peel away, a few things left to get out of his system. A chance to hit rock bottom. And a public spectacle so unfortunate to the point it would be used to shame him into getting himself together.

CHAPTER 40
Strange Days

2006 started out quietly, much like some of the biggest storms one will ever encounter. Eddie had begun at least a friendship with a woman named Joey House, the owner of House of Petals, a flower shop in West Hollywood. Ed and Joey went to what seemed like a minor event—Elton John's Oscar party on March 5—but it turned out to be much more than that. The two actually walked out on the red carpet together, although Joey, an unknown, stayed mostly off to the side. The paparazzi snapped several pictures of Eddie, one of which would become infamous—one of the first photos that pops up when one Googles for an image of Eddie Van Halen.

Ed looked terrible. The unfortunate timing of the shot caught an expression that made him look like he was decades beyond his age. It also revealed just how awful his teeth had become—obviously missing many, the rest brown, and demonstrating an obvious lack of concern for his own hygiene. And he was still wearing those worn-out boots at the bottom of a sloppy black ensemble. It was as if he simply didn't care about his public persona in any way whatsoever.

Fuse carried the headline, "Holy Sh*t, It's Eddie Van Halen." In the mid-2000s, crystal meth abuse had become an alarming problem in the States, and one of the most obvious side effects of the drug is the decaying and rotting of the teeth. No one in the public had any idea at all that his teeth were in such bad shape because he had been drinking wine straight out of the bottle and pulling his own teeth with pliers, and that crystal methamphetamine had nothing to do with it whatsoever.

My reaction was immediate. I was stunned. The whole crystal meth thing had been getting so much media attention at that time, and the anti-abuse ads they ran nightly showed before and after pictures of meth addicts. You get that whole complexion worsening and teeth going to hell image burned in your head. When I saw the picture, I just cringed for him. But another part of me was angry, although I had no right to be. At that moment in my own life, my alcoholism was edging ever closer to the breaking point (which was only few years away). Nevertheless, I thought, "This bastard. Why?! Come on, man—come out of the woodwork and kick these guys like Tom Morello and John Mayer and Jack White in the *ASS*!" I sent out an e-mail to my tight-knit group of rabid Van Halen fans after digesting the photo. I still have it. It is brutal. "Look at these photos: . . . The man could afford to have a dentist office in his house. He is clueless. He has 5-10 years max to live. . . . I am worried that he isn't able to pull out of this. Where are the loyal friends? It seems that if he could be saved someone would've stepped in already. It's all very disheartening."

In Eddie time, he responded rather quickly to the negative press and gossip surrounding the photographs. Who to turn to other than Dwyer and Michaels for another random, off-the-cuff interview? Excerpts from their last ever interview with Eddie on their April 7 show follow with commentary:

> EVH: I went to Elton John's party, I went to another party to help a friend push her flower shop. Hey, because of cancer, my teeth are all fucked up 'cause I got six of 'em yanked, you know? And they gotta focus on that and say I'm doing crystal meth, give me a fucking break. Hey, my teeth are fucked up.
>
> DJ: Who's the chick you were with?
>
> EVH: Uh, her name is Joey House and she has a flower shop called House of Petals.
>
> DJ: Uh huh . . .
>
> EVH: And she's a friend of mine.
>
> DJ: Just friends?
>
> EVH: [Ed does not acknowledge the "Just friends?" question.] I was just . . . you know . . . What's funny is on the internet there's a picture of me, you know, somebody asked me some stupid question and I'm like going "What?!" [He is describing the photograph.]
>
> DJ: Right.

EVH: . . . a card of her flower shop in my hand. And the caption underneath says something like, "Eddie Van Halen used to be cool, man, now it looks like he's holding his dentures in his hand."

DJ: [Laughter.]

EVH: No, it gets funnier. Because people started e-mailing back going, "Looks more like a pack of rubbers to me!"

DJ: [Laughter.] Which hopefully you're not bringing to Elton John's party!

EVH: [Awkward pause.] Ahhhhh . . . .

DJ: Hey, I had to take it, man, you laid it up there. Hey, listen to this . . .

EVH: I really don't have the time right now. [Getting terse.]

DJ: Ohh . . . Really? Just one second, OK?

EVH: No, hey, c'mon.

DJ: We ain't gonna piss you off.

EVH: No, you're not pissing me off, I just, I just I gotta get some sleep, it's four o'clock in the fucking morning here. [More persistent.]

DJ: OK.

EVH: And I'm just making a copy of what I just played and . . .

DJ: Alright, well, we'll call you again soon.

EVH: OK. Hey, I don't mean to be rude. You know, I love you guys, you know?

DJ: No, no, no—that's cool, we understand.

EVH: You guys are cool, you know?

DJ: It's your studio, man. Maybe this summer, we'll bring you into town and you can play in our charity golf tournament?

EVH: That sounds like a plan.

DJ: We gotta get you some teeth first though because the media is gonna be all over the place.

EVH: Look, you know, if I went down to Ralph's right now and bought that shit that you can make your teeth white, that'll kill you quicker than leaving them the way they are.

DJ: [Laughter.] But a nice set of dentures with like fangs or something? That'd really trip people out.

EVH: I'll put 'em in upside down and backwards and really freak people out.

DJ: [Laughter.]

Ed said that he had six teeth yanked because of his cancer. In fact, it appeared that he pulled at least some of his own teeth himself, and his teeth were discolored from drinking Smoking Loon wine directly out of the bottle for a solid two years. The amazing thing is that that much public ridicule still wasn't enough for him to get straight. After all, that was just an unfortunate pose and his teeth are messed up from cancer—it wasn't what it appeared, according to Ed. The bottom line is that the picture told more words than Edward could have ever imagined. Nevertheless, Ed pursued an interest that would cause his fans and the public a minor panic. Edward was dabbling in pornography—financing it and providing some music. And he was having the movie filmed at his house—where his son lived with him part of the time.

In April, Sammy Hagar went out of his way to say, "[Eddie's] never going to see my ass again unless he goes and gets himself some help." At the same time, he announced that he and Michael Anthony were going on the road as The Other Half—as in the other half of Van Halen. It was a debatable distinction, to be sure. They played Van Hagar songs. Sammy said, "I just think I need to play those songs, the fans need to hear those songs and it's just unfair to let it sit and die."

Alex and Edward jammed onstage with Kenny Chesney when he came to Los Angeles. They actually performed "Jump" and "You Really Got Me" on June 17, 2006. Ed worked up an improvised solo jam before launching into "You Really Got Me," and Kenny and his band took turns singing the verse lyrics. Before the solo, Kenny yelled, "Come on, Eddie!" During his solo, Ed was mobbed by three photographers that took position on the stage as Kenny watched Eddie play. They were literally crowding him as he played; they barely gave him room to move. Combatively, the *Van Halen*

News Desk (VHND)—by then the single-most important website for all Van Halen fans—titled the news item "Another Half."

Still involved in helping Joey and her floral boutique House of Petals, Edward performed at a private function at her shop in late July. *Undercover* reported that, "Eddie Van Halen debuted some new music at the House of Petals in Los Angeles this week. Van Halen played Wednesday night jamming with Patrick Leonard (on keyboards). Leonard is best known for songwriting and production work with Madonna." They had a drummer backing them as well. Video shows that the songs were strictly experimental psychedelic jazz. Ed was wearing jeans with massive holes in the knees, and his shirt was tied around his waist. It was a pure free-flow jam session and it was rather hit or miss. It could definitely strike some as incredibly sloppy and not well thought out.

VHND broke an almost surreal news story about Edward with the line, "Imagine the shit storm this is gonna kick up." On July 26, the news was released that Edward had recorded two solo tracks for an upcoming pornographic film called *Sacred Sin* directed by an adult entertainment industry director whose work Edward greatly admired. The two songs are perfectly suitable for modern porno sex scenes. They do feature some decent playing from Edward, but they were songs for a porno movie. The songs were called "Catherine" and "Rise," the latter was released as a sample video teaser. It featured Ed in those ragged jeans with a black sport coat playing none other than the classic Frankenstein guitar itself.

Jared Rutter of *Adult Video News* wrote:

> In a major crossover move, rock superstar Eddie Van Halen has joined forces with adult director Michael Ninn to write and perform two songs for the upcoming Ninn Worx feature, *Sacred Sin*.
>
> Although several big-name rappers have contributed material to XXX movies, Van Halen is probably the first major rock star to lend his name to an adult project.
>
> Van Halen told AVN.com he's not bothered by possible criticism. "I'm working with a friend. Very simple. I like his work," he said. "Michael Ninn is like a Spielberg to me: the imagery, the way he makes things look, just . . . sensual."

Edward had closed off his free-wheeling Dwyer and Michaels interviews for the whole world to hear him speak spontaneously while being asked some rather tough questions, even if it was by a couple of guys in Iowa. But, on the other hand, Edward had been trying to track down Howard Stern for months for an interview. Getting them together was a serious challenge.

Finally, on September 8, 2006, Edward gave his most infamous open-ended, spontaneous interview of his career. As hard as some of Dwyer and Michaels' questions had been, Howard and his clan pushed Ed hard on some claims they found a bit preposterous (as well as every listener).

The 2006 Howard Stern Interview

The interview started off normally—Ed cursed and quickly asked about a seven-second delay. Howard told him that they were on satellite and didn't need one, to which Ed responded, "Well, fuck me runnin' if you can catch me!" Howard started off by asking Edward about Hendrix and then Clapton. Edward responded with his usual Hendrix story, that Jimi did some excellent things but when Ed was younger, he couldn't afford all of Jimi's pedal hookups so he focused on Clapton instead. When Howard asked Edward about Clapton now, Ed callously replied that he thought Clapton was better when he was addicted to heroin and was now a weak imitation of B.B. King.

Howard asked Edward about his cancer battle. During the interview, Ed confirmed that he was cancer-free, not in remission. *Rolling Stone* reported that Eddie said flat out: "I had squamous-cell carcinoma of the tongue. And I beat it without chemo or radiation. . . . I really can't talk about because I did it in a way that is not exactly legal in this country." He intimated that this development could put pharmaceutical companies out of business. Stern pressed Eddie for details, and, surprisingly, Ed gave them up. He said he had founded a pathology lab with Dr. Steve McClain in Long Island. He said that they removed healthy pieces of his tongue and grew healthy cells outside of his body, while at the same time complaining though that all in all he was missing one-third of his tongue.

As most people already wondered, Stern pressed Eddie about his decision to continue to smoke after being treated for cancer. Edward said directly that cigarettes did not cause his cancer. From *Rolling Stone*:

EVH: Smoking didn't cause it.

Howard: How do you know that?

EVH: Because! Uh, uh, uh, a metal charge to a metal, uh, uh, uh . . . Electric charge . . . Okay, EMF, electro magnetic field, or electro magnetic energy, which I live in about 14 to 18 hours a day in my recording studio with a metal pick hanging out of my mouth, it's basically like playing golf in a lightning storm.

Howard: Hmm . . . You're saying a metal pick gave you tongue cancer?

EVH: Yep.

Howard: Because it picked up the radiation from all the equipment you use?

EVH: That's right.

Howard: This is *crazy*.

Howard did imply that the explanation was hard to believe, but brushed it off and continued on with the interview. When told that he spoke fine even though so much of his tongue was missing, Eddie joked that he was always intoxicated before, and that was why he still sounded the same.

When the subject turned toward the band, Edward referred to Sammy as the "Little Red Worm" and Michael Anthony as "Sauce" Soboleski. The latter was a reference to Michael's hot sauce brand and a jab at him using his given name. Howard called Ed out for using Anthony's given name—a common putdown in the entertainment industry. Edward simply replied that that was his real name, period. Ed also complained loudly that Hagar and Anthony were touring as The Other Half (as in the other half of Van Halen). He said flatly that *Alex* was the other half of Van Halen.

With regard to Dave, Eddie called him "cubic ziroconia" rather than Diamond Dave. But he did admit that they tried to record with him back in 2000 but it just did not work out because Edward said Dave was a "loose cannon."

Suddenly, the interview took a very strange left. Turns out that on the phone with Edward was pornographic film director Michael Ninn. Edward claimed he entered the adult movie business by "default," which he clarified by saying, "Nine out of ten people masturbate, right? And the tenth person, person is just full of shit." He said he enjoyed Ninn's films so much that he sought him out personally and asked to help out with his next movie however he could. Ninn obviously jumped at the chance and drafted Edward not only to compose music for the "film" but also to use Edward's palatial estate for the actual filming (the estate where Ed's then 15-year-old son lived approximately half of the time).

Howard was shocked, as was everyone who heard the revelation. When Edward told him that his home was used for the filming, Howard sounded incredulous when he asked, "And you let this go on at your house?" Edward, however, continuously defended his involvement, revealing that he didn't consider it a "porno" or even pornographic. He said it was simply sex, and described the film as "*Braveheart* with a cum shot." Ninn and Edward revealed that there would be two versions of the movie: an X-rated version called *Sacred Sin* and an R-rated version called *Rise*.

Once the conversation steered away from *Sacred Sin*, Howard asked Edward if he was seeing anyone and Ed said that yes, he was, and that his new girlfriend was standing right there. Janie Liszewski and Edward met through Michael Ninn, for whom Janie was doing promotional work. Ed confirmed for Howard that Janie was indeed a smoking hot lady, and although they had only been together for two months at that time, they were already spending a great deal of time with each other.

Edward then began to talk about his recent experience jamming with Wolfgang. By the summer of 2006, Wolfgang had truly come into his own as a musician. Eddie, Alex, and Wolfgang had begun playing as a trio and Edward was blown away by Wolf's abilities, referring to him as a peer. Given Edward's less than flattering statements about Michael Anthony, Howard posed what was becoming an obvious question:

> Howard: I'm hearing Michael Anthony is out and your son is in.
>
> EVH: Uh, let's just say my son is in, and "Sauce" Soboleski can do whatever the hell he wants.

In retrospect, it is not as shocking as it was when it was first uttered. But when it was first uttered, most fans simply could not believe it. As if the interview wasn't already simply bizarre, Howard chose to one-up it by asking Edward if Wolfgang—again, only 15 at the time—was getting laid yet. Ed responded by saying that he thought so, but that he knew for sure that Wolf was "spanking it" because he was spending 45 minutes in the bathroom without taking a shower. I will never forget my brain going on pause, trying to confirm that I had just heard Edward Van Halen tell the entire world that his 15-year-old son was masturbating and having sex, all on top of Ed himself admitting he got into the adult film industry by "default" via masturbation.

About the future of the band with Wolfgang, Edward said, "The name Van Halen, the family legacy, is gonna go on way after I'm gone, 'cause this kid is just a natural." Once the interview had concluded, Howard and his co-hosts did an immediate post-interview assessment which illustrated how baffled they were by Ed's words. Finally, Howard took a call from a listener:

> Howard: Jeff, you're on the air in Portland. . . .
>
> Jeff: You know, I think Eddie is one of the most brilliant artists this country has, but when exactly did he lose *his fucking mind*? [Laughter.] Oh, my God. That interview *scared the shit* out of me! [Laughter.] I *love* Van—Van Halen is, is, is the most incredible rock band that I think has ever come around in this country, and that *scared* me. I, I, I'm dumb-—I sat here *dumbfounded* for that whole interview.

The fallout was almost immediate. To sum it all it up, *Rolling Stone* writer Andy Greene's article on the interview was titled "Eddie Van Halen Goes Bananas on Howard Stern" (however, the transcripts of the *Rolling Stone* excerpts were fairly inaccurate and paraphrased greatly, and were thus, in a sense, taken out of context). In hindsight, one has the ability to go back and listen to the interview over and over and even here, one can read some of the text of what was said and slowly digest it. But the listener that called in—Jeff from Portland—perfectly captured everyone's *immediate* reaction to the interview. It could leave one speechless.

How many things did people have to digest in that voluntary 30-minute interview? Clapton was good when he was a heroin addict. He called Dave "cubic zirconia" and a loose cannon, but that he was essentially open to working with him. He called Sammy Hagar "the Little Red Worm." He called Michael Anthony "Sauce" Soboleski and said he had been replaced in the band by Wolfgang. He said that he knew Wolfgang was masturbating and having sex at fifteen.

When he finally decided to release some solo material—that his fans had been wanting for years and years—he did two songs for a porno movie, but it wasn't really a porno. Ed said he got into the porno business "by default" because "everybody masturbates." He called the movie—filmed within his own home—"*Braveheart* with a cum shot." It was made by renowned pornographer Michael Ninn, but Ed claimed he was "not really a porno guy." And Edward helped finance the movie—a pornographic endeavor. The video for the song "Rise" featured Eddie playing his original classic Frankenstein guitar wearing jeans with holes in the knees and a black sports coat with no shirt. The song wasn't bad, but it was definitely suitable for a porno soundtrack. Even though it wasn't really a porno as per Edward.

Perplexing Claims

He beat cancer without chemo or radiation, even though his golf teacher Ron confirmed he was undergoing chemo treatments as of May of 2001. He said he founded a pathology lab, McClain Laboratories, with Dr. Steve McClain in Smithtown, Long Island and that they had twenty-nine employees. Eddie said he opened it in collaboration with McClain, but he also said that he owned it. He self-diagnosed that his cancer was caused by electromagnetic fields interacting with his titanium hip and a metal guitar pick (the only mention of using metal guitar picks came very, very early in his career and in no article or interview regarding his technique prior to his cancer diagnosis were metal guitar picks ever discussed; it was well-known that he preferred simple Fender Medium guitar picks). The leading cause of squamous-cell carcinoma in the head or neck is clinically proven to be tobacco and alcohol.

There is a complicating factor here. For Edward to attribute the cause to something out of his control may very well have been the contributing factor for his mental determination to defeat the cancer, which plays an enormous role in overcoming the disease. Any negativity in the brain can contribute to stressors being released into the body which only serve to worsen the condition. As always, any threat to Ed's control put him dark places.

As far as his contribution to McClain Laboratories, I exchanged e-mails with Dr. Steve McClain in May of 2011. I simply wrote to confirm that Edward was indeed a founder of the lab, but McClain punted and referred me to Ed's publicist. I wrote back and made clear that I wanted to know absolutely nothing about Eddie's diagnosis or treatment in anyway whatsoever, and that I was strictly interested in information regarding the founding of the McClain Laboratories. Finally, Dr. McClain provided me with a fair amount of information. He wrote me the following:

> McClain Labs is a medical lab, founded by me in 2004. We presently have 7 full-time employees. We analyze and report on tissue biopsies and excisions for cancer and other diseases. We conduct research into improving the performance of clinical assays and have published on early diagnosis of cancer and Melanoma. We do research specimens for Universities, publishing on wound healing and burn healing. Those are matters of public record. My partner is a matter of public record. Nearly all that has been written in the past is incorrect. . . . –Steve

I gave McClain a chance to clarify what exactly was written in the past that was wrong. I also gave him an opportunity to respond to Valerie's nearly libelous claims that he was a "quack" but he chose not to, which is completely respectable. It also turns out the McClain's credentials are quite respectable as well: he is board certified in anatomic and clinical pathology and dermatopathology; academic appointments in dermatology and emergency medicine at SUNY-Stony Brook Medical Center; member of the American Society of Dermatopathology and the Association for Pathology Informatics; once Director of the Division of Dermatopathology and Director of Pathology Informatics in the Department of Pathology at Montefiore Medical Center in New York.

Whatever methods they came up with gave Edward the mental confidence he needed to overcome cancer, and one cannot know the extent to which these treatments provided a placebo effect. It is not truly clear why, in addition to denying that cigarettes were a contributing factor, that he denied that he underwent chemo when in fact he did at Cedars-Sinai Hospital in Los Angeles. Again, perhaps it was because chemo was something out of his control, and he didn't like that.

Fans like me were worried that things were just getting worse and worse every year. However, the one key to Edward's eventual major turnaround seemed relatively minor at the time, but it was the beginning of his relationship with an adult entertainment industry publicist, Janie Liszewski.

That same summer, Dave participated in a bluegrass project that proved just how universal classic Van Halen music truly is. Roth sang versions of "Jump" and "Jamie's Cryin'" on a CD titled *Strummin' With the Devil: The Southern side of Van Halen.* The disc featured some of the absolute top session players in all of bluegrass and the interpretations of some songs written by Edward Van Halen and David Lee Roth were absolutely incredible (the album featured no songs past *1984*). The version of "I'll Wait" by Blue Mountain is simply excellent. The vocal delivery by Tim Stafford and Wayne Taylor sends chills down the spine. Dave was doing his best to keep the VH brand going and in good shape, and this project was a step in the right direction. Dave even performed the bluegrass version of "Jump" on *The Tonight Show.*

CHAPTER 41
The Slow Journey
Back to the Top of the Mountain

On September 30, 2006, Edward threw a monster bash at his own home—referred to as The Gathering Party—to celebrate the release of *Sacred Sin.* The party was attended by hundreds if not a thousand people. Hundreds of photographs and extensive video of the party exists. Edward was heavily intoxicated. There were pictures of Eddie with Janie as well as pictures of him with Joey House. Some close-up photos focused on those unbelievable bum boots he insisted on continuing to wear for at least three or so years by this time. At one point, someone captured 18 seconds of Ed playing the piano in the house. A small, well-dressed crowd had gathered around and Ed while he played some furious classical jazz on the piano that built up to an incredible peak before he actually semi-collapsed. He rested his forearms on the top of the piano and dropped his head down as if he was barely coherent. No one actually applauded, although lots were snapping photos during his performance.

He casually performed with a makeshift band on a stage in his backyard during the event. The band played classics like "Ain't Talkin' 'Bout Love" and "Jump." The performances were loose jams, not exactly an arena spectacle for 30,000 people. The performance of "Jump" was *extremely* loose with another player taking on the keyboard parts while Edward noodled, missing several notes along the way. His guitar solo for "Jump" was actually dead on, though. For the most part, he jumped around like he was pretty out of it, and his bent-leg jumps barely got himself off the ground and, even as low as he jumped, he had trouble landing with much grace.

Edward even treated the party crowd to a six-and-a-half minute guitar solo that started with "Eruption" and segued into "Cathedral" and then back again. However, for "Cathedral," he wasn't quite getting the sound he needed—the presence of the guitar was too low for the echo to pick up on the notes. So, he actually came to a stop and motioned in a funny way for the crowd to be quiet so he could hear. He started back into "Cathedral" starting and stopping twice. It just wasn't happening. As he continued to solo, he eventually did get to a point where he was kicking some ass. But it was not a great performance overall. The truth is, obviously, that Ed was just playing in his backyard and didn't think about or care if anyone filmed the party show with their camera or their phone. Unfortunately, in the modern age, that thing is going straight to YouTube and it is going to be viewed tens if not hundreds of thousands of times. Everyone that saw it had a reaction, and everyone that had seen him in his prime was concerned.

Just a week later, Edward returned to House of Petals for yet another jam session to promote Joey's high-end flower shop. The bash was referred to as "House of Petals presents Harlottique Hosted by Eddie Van Halen." Party attendees included several celebrities, most notably Ton Loc, who made a fortune of off sampling "Jamie's Cryin'" for his song "Wild Thing." This time though, Ed was accompanied by Janie who was becoming more and more of a constant companion. He had recently met Janie through Michael Ninn and she was involved in promotional work for *Sacred Sin.* While in some matters, Ed tended to move glacially, in this matter, he did not. By the end of 2006, Janie had quit her job as an adult industry publicist with High Profile Media. Her new job would be to serve as Edward's exclusive personal publicist in all matters related to media and promotion of any kind associated with Edward's name. He put his trust into her 100 percent—fully, completely, and totally.

Janie Enters the Picture and Wolfgang Enters Van Halen

Doing publicity for people like Michael Ninn was only one small part of Janie's career. She was actually a professional stunt woman and appeared in dozens and dozens of well-known movies and TV shows including *Spider Man 2, The Wedding Planner* (as a double for Jennifer Lopez), *CSI Miami*, and *Baywatch.* She was even a bit of a video vixen, appearing in an Enrique Iglesias music video. The timing of their meeting would turn out to be absolutely perfect. She was fifteen years Ed's junior, but was already in her mid-30s when they met. She was one of the most significant catalysts for Eddie to get his life and his career turned around.

The other major factor was Edward's son. Starting in the summer of 2006, Wolfgang and Eddie started playing together on a regular basis with Wolfgang picking up the bass and Ed playing guitar. Eddie said that the first time Wolf ever played bass with him was on "the blonde five-string bass with four strings on it!" Alex came over for a regular session with Eddie, and Wolfgang slipped into the studio quietly and started slamming away on the bass. Edward said, "Al said, 'Hey! How are you playing guitar and bass at the same time?' I got on the talkback and said, 'Say hi, Wolfie!' and [Wolfgang] went [in high voice] 'Hi, Uncle Al!' . . . Al went, 'Who's playing bass?' I told him it was Wolfie, and it blew Al's mind. . . . That's when I asked [Wolfgang] if he'd like to be the bass player in Van Halen. He said, 'Yeah, as long as I don't have to do a certain thing,' which I won't mention.'" Wolfgang clarified and said, "I just don't want to do a bass solo."

Of particular significance, however, was that Wolfgang—much like is own mother publicly professed—had an overwhelming preference for Dave rather than Sam or any of the Sammy-era material. Chris Gill of *Guitar World* asked Wolfgang, "When did you start listening to your dad's recordings with David Lee Roth? What do you like about them?" Wolfgang said, "I love it for the same reason everybody else loves it. It's awesome. It's just good music. It lasts. It was made a while ago, and it still lives today." Edward also recalled, "I'll never forget when we were coming home from Castle Park [a family entertainment center]. 'Hot for Teacher' came on the radio and Wolf was going, 'Who is that singing?' I said, 'That's Dave.'"

The three Van Halens played every Wednesday and Saturday for prolonged rehearsals and jam sessions. After about six months of playing with no one on vocals, Ed gave an interview to *Guitar World* in which he intimated that Dave had already been asked to come back and he was simply waiting on a response. "I'm telling Dave 'Dude get your ass up here and sing, bitch! Come on!'," Edward said. "As it stands right now, the ball is in Dave's court. Whether he wants to rise to the occasion is entirely up to him, but we're ready to go."

This was no minor verbiage. This was *it*. That was the green-light-go for dreams coming true. I remember reading those words and losing control of my jaw. I could not believe it. Fortunately, Dave slightly hesitated, but didn't take very long to answer the call. Ed recalled to *Guitar World*:

> EVH: We rehearsed probably six months before Dave showed up. We were almost over-rehearsed. We got to the point where we were goofing around.
>
> Wolfgang: That's when we started playing "Little Dreamer" in double time.
>
> EVH: When Dave walked in it blew his freakin' mind.
>
> Wolfgang: That night was magical. That was the fist time I heard vocals with everything.
>
> EVH: Dave couldn't believe how good you are.

Ed and Dave on the Same Team

In almost no time at all, the *Los Angeles Times* reported on January 26, 2007—Edward's 52nd birthday—"Eddie and Dave, together again." The article revealed that Dave, Eddie, and Alex would be reuniting, but that Michael Anthony had been replaced by Wolfgang Van Halen. Geoff Boucher wrote: "The band had been planning a splashy press conference in L.A. to announce the news, but word leaked out Thursday. There had been intense speculation that the reunion might happen after the announcement this month that the band would be inducted into the Hall of Fame in New York on March 12."

Just a few days later, the band officially announced it. *Rolling Stone* picked it up and reported: "Van Halen is Back: Van Halen Officially Announce Summer Tour With David Lee Roth."

> Los Angeles, CA—In what is no doubt one of the most anticipated moments in rock and roll, Van Halen officially announces their 2007 North American tour.
>
> The tour will mark the first time since 1984 that original Van Halen front man David Lee Roth will perform with Eddie and Alex Van Halen along with new bassist Wolfgang Van Halen for 40 shows this summer.
>
> Van Halen fans can look forward to legendary high intensity performances, featuring a set list of the most iconic hits ever produced by America's premiere rock band.

> Eddie Van Halen states, "I am very excited to get back to the core of what made Van Halen."

"The core of what made Van Halen" is no small string of words coming from Edward. No matter what outside influences or reasons Edward personally had for finally burying the hatchet and partnering back up with Dave, the timing was right. It had been clear Ed wanted to play on a regular basis in some capacity with his son, and at almost sixteen, Wolfie was finally able to carry the weight and the responsibility. He wasn't poured into the situation. It was a slow, careful, and deliberate process of incorporating him into the band. Their focus had been the material on the first six albums. The timing was finally right. At least it seemed for so for a few weeks.

Meanwhile, Sammy Hagar, the Buzz Aldrin of Van Halen, wasn't taking it so well. He told the *Cleveland Plains Dealer* on January 6 that the only reason Michael Anthony wasn't still in Van Halen was because the two of them were friends. He also openly scoffed at the idea of Ed working with Dave. "I don't see it in a million years," he said. "Dave's gonna want it to be all about him. Ed's gonna want it to be all about him. . . . I'll probably just be sitting over in the corner, cracking up." That same month, Sammy flapped his gums again about Wolfgang being in the band, casting some rather foul dispersions to *Billboard.* "That's a lot of pressure for Wolfie," he said. "Just 'cause he's Eddie's son doesn't mean he can go out and play in arenas and perform and entertain an audience for two hours." Sammy offered an alternative musical route for little Wolfgang. "I would love to see Eddie and Alex get behind Wolfie, with a kid of his age singing, and produce the record for him and help him launch a career," he said. "I'd rather see it go that way than come out and say 'Wolfie's the bass player in Van Halen and maybe singing, too.' Van Halen's got way too much history to have that put on him." Sammy and probably millions of other fans obviously didn't think about what impact their words would have on a fairly young Wolfgang. The charges of nepotism in the face of pure Van Halen family talent were absurd. But they were also hurtful. Additionally, Edward had openly confessed from the time Wolfgang was five that he couldn't wait to play with him some day. He reiterated that Wolfgang wasn't forced into music or to take lessons. He simply grew up surrounded by music and absorbed it, the same way Edward had with his father. Wolfgang had *it.* Yet the hardcore Michael Anthony and Sammy Hagar fans were greatly displeased.

Dave finally made a public statement to *Rolling Stone* which ran on February 15. "Eddie and I wrote the songs, every note, every syllable, as if we invented a language that only we can speak . . . When you speak a language that you both created, it's natural to go, 'I know you.' So it was very easy. There wasn't any stumble at all. I just showed up, and twenty minutes later, it was the usual, 'How's the wife, how's the kids, let's play.' When you're born to do that language, you speak it naturally. I never forgot it." Dave said the chemistry during their rehearsals was "combustible." They had taken a now classic photograph that was intended to be the front cover of the very next issue of *Rolling Stone*. It was incredible image. A tall, long-haired Wolfgang; a mischievous Dave chomping the handle of his sunglasses; a tough-looking Alex; and a long-haired Eddie with his sunglasses on his nose and beanie hat on with a huge smile. Tour dates were just about to roll out when things got sidetracked again, almost as if on schedule.

"Al made it clear he didn't want to tour unless Ed was sober," said Valerie. She also said that Wolfgang came home very upset after a photo shoot—possibly the *Rolling Stone* cover shoot. "He'd also run out of patience and said something like, 'That's it. I'm telling Dad I'm not doing the tour.'" Considering his career and his relationship with his son were potentially on the line, Ed made the best decision possible.

Just one week after Dave's brief interview, *Rolling Stone* followed up with: "The Official Word: Van Halen Tour Kaput; Van Halen's road plans have taken a rocky turn." Finally, on March 8, with Janie as Van Halen's publicist, Eddie released a public statement:

> I would like Van Halen fans to know how much I truly appreciate each and every one of you. Without you there is no Van Halen.
>
> I have always and will always feel a responsibility to give you my best. At the moment I do not feel that I can give you my best. That's why I have decided to enter a rehabilitation facility to work on myself, so that in the future I can deliver the 110 percent that I feel I owe you and want to give you.
>
> Some of the issues surrounding the 2007 Van Halen tour are within my ability to change and some are not. As far as my rehab is concerned, it is within my ability to change and

> change for the better. I want you to know that is exactly what I'm doing, so that I may continue to give you the very best I am capable of.
>
> I look forward to seeing you in the future better than ever and I thank you with all my heart.
>
> Love, Ed

The story was carried by other outlets with the headline "Eddie Van Halen to Enter Rehab." It was yet another profound admission directly from Edward himself. He made no bones about it—no dancing around the issue, period. He was going to rehab to work on himself. There was a new circle in place, and you were either within the circle or not in the circle. Those on the inside of the circle now had a policy of keeping everything inside the circle *inside* the circle. Those people were Edward, David, Janie, Alex, and Wolfgang. Virtually no word regarding Van Halen would *ever* be released to the media again without the careful orchestration and consent of some or all of the above parties.

Unfortunately, March 12 was the date of the Rock and Roll Hall of Fame induction ceremony, so there was no way Edward was going, and Alex would never have gone without his brother. Dave expressed interest in attending. In Van Halen's place would be short-lived supergroup Velvet Revolver featuring Scott Weiland of Stone Temple Pilots and members of Guns 'N Roses. Discussions over Dave performing with Velvet Revolver did not go well. They offered to play "You Really Got Me," but Dave didn't want to perform a cover song at his own induction. He insisted they learn and play "Jump," but that wasn't going to happen. So Dave bailed on the ceremony as well.

Scott Weiland gave the opening remarks, and then Slash said, "Eddie Van Halen. Guitar genius and innovator. God to fans and musicians alike. David Lee Roth, the ultimate front man." Finally, drummer Matt Sorum stated, "The Rock and Roll Hall of Fame would like to induct Sammy Hagar, David Lee Roth, Eddie Van Halen, Alex Van Halen, and Michael Anthony." Only Mike and Sam appeared to accept the award—both of whom were no longer even in the band Van Halen. "Right Now" played as they took the stage.

For all the acrimony with Michael Anthony, what he said when he first took the microphone will never lose its impact, and shows what kind of a man he truly is. Knowing how much Edward disliked him at the time, he said "First off, I'd like to, uh, say God bless you to, uh, Edward Van Halen." He continued. "I wish you were here, buddy. You couldn't be here tonight." The crowd gives applause for the selfless, caring act. Mike continued, "He's home gettin' some help, and I love you, man." Once Michael concluded his remarks, Sammy took the microphone. The first words out of his mouth were, "Well, I can't tell you how much I wish, uh, everyone could be here tonight. And it's out of our control, and it's out of some other people's control. And I think it's a good thing. I think Eddie's gonna come out on the other side a better person and maybe we can get our buddy back." Only Sammy referred to Roth even once during their remarks, simply adding an "and Dave" to one of his statements.

A Complete Transformation

Edward entered rehab in mid-March a pale, scraggly looking shell of his former self. Wolfgang turned sixteen while Eddie was checked in. By April 22, Ed's first post-rehab public appearance was at an all-American NASCAR race. He was an honorary race official and he greeted all of the drivers as they were introduced. Edward Van Halen looked like a *completely* different person. He had, between March 6 and April 22, completely transformed his appearance. The ratty matted hair was shorn. In its place was a sharp, short trim with highlights on top. In place of his pale skin was smooth and tanned skin. He was sporting a short Van Dyke. And in place of those yanked, brown, rotting teeth were sparkling white, beautiful veneers. His thin frame had some bulk back on it. He appeared so smiley and healthy and happy it was enough to stop you in your tracks. In fact, some fans put up before and after pictures and the difference between March 2006 and April 2007 is nothing short of a complete and total physical transformation. He could easily have been the winning contestant on one of those extreme makeover shows—his physical recovery was that magnificent.

On May 25, Eddie released yet another public statement acknowledging his recent rehabilitation experience:

> I want to say thank you to all the Van Halen fans for the tons of emails and all the support they provided when I was in rehab earlier this year. It was an intensely personal thing that I'm not

> really comfortable talking about right now, but I want everyone to know that their support has and always will mean the world to me. I want everyone to know that I am truly grateful.

Just one day before the race, Ed unveiled his latest amazing guitar venture. He entered into a deal with Fender's Chris Fleming, senior master builder in Fender's custom shop, to produce one hundred identical replicas of the classic Frankenstein guitar—these things would sell for $25,000 a piece. As part of Ed's NASCAR appearance, he presented the winner of the race with one of the replica guitars. Doug, a close friend and bass player for one of a few bands this author plays in to this day, was a Guitar Center employee at the time the Austin store received their one Frankenstein. At such an incredible price tag, special clearance was required to even touch the guitar, much less play it. Doug worked it out so I could not only check out and hold the guitar, I was actually able to plug it in and play it for ten to fifteen minutes. A small crowd gathered around me in awe—clearly not at me, at the guitar. However, I did Edward proud and plowed through "Hot for Teacher," "Unchained," and "Eruption" to the delight of the small crowd. I can easily say it was the most financially valuable object I have ever held in my hands, period. It was an amazing experience and absolutely electrified me. The detail of the reproduction was insane—down to the rust marks and date on the quarter nailed to the guitar! I had Doug snap a picture of me with the guitar, but it has sadly been long-lost on an old, crappy 2007-era cell phone.

Along with the Frankenstein replica guitar, Edward had also been working on a new amplifier with Fender built exactly to his specs with no questions asked. The EVH 5150 III amplifier first became available on July 1, 2007. Although made in collaboration with Fender, the guitar and amplifier manufacturer marketed all of Edward's gear under the name EVH Brand with his very close friend Matt Bruck as his business partner in the venture. This not only included the Frankenstein replicas and the 5150 III amplifiers, but also picks, cables, amp covers, straps, strings, and even low-friction volume knobs. The EVH brand, however, also extended to a deal with MXR to make custom effects pedals (painted with red, black, and white stripes)—essentially reissues for their classic phaser and flanger pedals which were critical to Edward's early sound. Taking it one step further, one could now purchase EVH Brand sneakers. Edward said he got the idea after seeing so many fans make their own custom striped shoes. About the clothing venture, he said, "I'm not trying to be a clothing designer . . . I just think that my tennis shoes are cool."

"A New Brother"

Edward was back in good, sober shape for the first time in a decade, and the newly christened foursome returned to grinding out rehearsals for four straight months. The machine was as finely tuned as humanly possible. Once they were ready, they stepped out to no holds-barred press conference fielding questions of every kind imaginable. All four appeared together on August 13 on a stage in front of the classic original *Van Halen* album cover logo. Facing the stage, from left to right was Alex, Dave, Ed, and Wolf. A transcription of the press conference follows with commentary:

> DLR: Good afternoon, everybody! How are you this afternoon? This is the press conference that you probably never thought that you would see happen. Certainly not while we are all young, skinny, and good looking. Welcome, one and all. Make yourselves at home—we did. I think, uh, you know all the names of everybody here. And, uh, I thought I was newest guy in the band, but, uh, that turns out to be even part of the colorful Van Halen, uh, history. It is a new band. Man, when you hear the sound of what we've got going now . . . We've been rehearsing this more often than not. I've done more rehearsal in the last four months than I've done in the last twenty summers. We started this, uh, approximately last October. And, uh, the whole sound has, is better than it's ever been. Wolf brings a young energy and a spirit to this that'll knock you out of your socks. The vocals—
>
> EVH: He kicks all of our ass.
>
> DLR: The vocals are better than ever. He's a task masker. It was Wolf who picked the song list. And we've got close twenty-five of your greatest hits. All of the favorites that you've been hearing tearing out of the back of a pickup truck at the Burger King drive thru over for how many summertimes. It's all very well intact. The same attitude

but with a whole new look. Stereo sound and hi-fi style. I think you know everybody here. Wolfgang, Edward, myself Diamond Dave; here, this is Alex. I'd like to start out with this.

[As Dave said "myself Diamond Dave," Ed, standing next to him, pat Dave on the back several times. Then Dave embraced Edward and Edward embraced Dave in a beautiful moment. Their hug was tight and meaningful, and Edward used both arms to really grab Dave, unlike his one-armed non-hug back in 1996. After several seconds of holding each other tight, they backed away, Dave with a huge smile. There was much applause to accompany their hug. Ed stepped up to the microphone.]

EVH: I got a new brother. [After saying that, Ed put his arm around Dave's neck and pulled him for a big kiss on the cheek. Dave's million dollar smile was in full effect. It was a beautiful moment that was a long time coming.]

DLR: Questions, please! Who's got a question? Somebody yell something out. Go ahead right there.

[A mostly unintelligible question from the press corps asked about performing "Me Wise Magic" and "Can't Get This Stuff No More."]

DLR: Are you talking about the two new songs from back when? You know, there is a, uh, catalog that is as familiar as "Duh-duh-duh-DUH!" [Beethoven's *Fifth*.] People, uh, to this day, stop me at crosswalks and act out the guitar solos in front of me in twenty-three different cities here. It's sort of a provided thing. You know, when the Three Tenors get together, you only wait for "O Solo Mio" and the rest of it you can barely pronounce. With this, you know *every single song*. You know every guitar lick, every "Wooo!," every kick, every jump, every drum lick, and we can't afford to shirk that duty.

EVH: Besides that, we haven't learned those two songs yet. [Edward shrugs to some laughter.] I gotta take responsibility, okay? [More laughter.]

Question: . . . How does it feel to be together on stage for the first time in, oh, so many years?

EVH: [Very calmly.] Incredible to me, man. I'm very excited, uh, you know, to be makin' music with my son, my brother, my new brother . . . [He throws his arms up as if he has all he could ever ask for.] It's, it's the shit. That's all I can say.

DLR: It feels completely natural. Strangely enough, after this many summers, I myself am certainly more aware of that than ever. Of how valuable this band is to me and my history. How valuable it is to the neighborhood, to the communities that this music appeals to. And that's a *lot* of communities. [Dave says a few sentences in Spanish.]

EVH: It is totally blowing—it is totally blowing our own minds, and I think it will yours, too. It's better than it's ever been.

Alex: I grew up on this stuff! [Laughter.]

DLR: I can't walk twenty meters down any sidewalk near any college campus without somebody stopping me and going, "You're that white guy!" [Lots of laughter.] . . . This is not a reunion. This is a new band. This is a revision with hits that you're so familiar with, it's as familiar as the roof of your own mouth is to you. But the ambition has, has *nothing* to do with old history. Usually when an old band like us comes back like us, it's rockers with walkers. And this is everything but. Meet us in the future, not the pasture. Next question. [Tons of applause. Ed and Dave lock hands in mutual agreement.]

Question: Has your guitar playing approach changed since your sobriety? If so, how?

EVH: Umm . . . [Ed puts his hand on his chin and pauses.] No. It doesn't change. [Shrugs and pauses.] You'll just have to come by and check it out—see what *you* think.

DLR: Again, usually when you talk about sobriety, everything kind of *slows down into mental age* [very exaggerated].

EVH: Well, I'm still playing my ass off.

DLR: Yeah, and we usually have to adopt words like tolerant and forgiveness and that is not the case here. The bar is set *unbelievably* high. We know what your expectations are. Are you prepared for it to be better than it ever fucking was? [Lots of applause.] Please, yell it out.

[An unintelligible question about Michael Anthony is asked.]

DLR: No. Michael Anthony is part of this band's history. There's a lot of great alumni who have been through this band. I'm shocked than any of us are still vertical after thirty years. Okay? And as far as why Wolf is in the band, may I speak for you Ed? Tap me on the shoulder in the limo on the way home if I'm wrong here. But while we're at the top of our game, and we really are, I understand how he wanted to play with the boy because his is *amazing* and you heard me say that. When you hear these vocals, when you hear what's going on in this rhythm section now—it is young, it is skinny, and it is *fucking* vicious. Get ready. [Edward was smiling proudly. Wolfgang continued to stand there, firmly holding his ground with a perpetual half-grin.]

Question: It was my honor to be at your studio and listen to the three of you play earlier. And there was a lot of magic there. Any apprehension working with all of these backing vocals, and these new voices being inside your head?

DLR: No, and Evan, aren't you a porn star? [Lots of laughter.] Because you occupy a very special place in my, uh . . . [Laughter.] . . . in my video setup! I don't spend any time looking at you though!

EVH: Be nice, he's a friend of mine. Be nice, he's a friend of mine. [Ed places his hand on Dave's shoulder and squeezes it, and then playfully pokes him in the arm as the press corps laughs at Dave.]

DLR: No, you have a good question here. There's a whole lot of change going on, okay? There's update. We upgraded, the same we they moved the Mustang into the future back when—the little bit, there. And that's what you expect. You don't want to see the same old band. The U2 guys with the mullets, you know, and doing etc. You want something that delights, that entertains, that astonishes. And that's by the second song. Next question, please.

[A female reporter asks Dave "How is your athleticism?" Dave's response kills the crowd.]

DLR: Well, let's have a look at you, hot stuff! [Lots of laughter. The entire band cracked up, especially Wolfgang. Ed leaned to Dave and appeared to ask Dave, "What'd she say?"] The athleticism is . . . I'm a lifetime martial artist. I started on my birthday when I was twelve years old. And, uh, it makes the music bring visual—it makes it looks like it sounds. You don't even have to understand English to know what's going on here. You don't even have to like rock and roll to have your mind *roasted* by what's going on on this stage.

Question: . . . Drum solos, guitar solos, bass solos—can we expect this? And please tell me you're playing "Unchained." [Laughter.]

Alex: Yes. Yes. Yes. [Laughter.]

DLR: We decided to do everything that you expect, but to make it *high speed, low drag.* Make it modern, make it move. Like, like, everything that got me fired from radio. Did you know I was in radio? [The crowd laughs at Dave's classic self-deprecating sense of humor. Edward laughs a lot.]

EVH: [Turning to look at Dave.] I heard something along those lines. [Edward laughs heartily.]

DLR: Yeah, you're gonna get your expectations, but it's been upgraded, updated. The same way we've gone from cassette to CD, baby. Next question, please.

Question: Wolfie? . . . What kind of stuff are you listening to now? . . .

Wolfgang: AC/DC, I guess. [Laughter.]

EVH: I turned him on to it.

Wolfgang: Yeah. Uh, it's really not that different. I listen to, uh, well AC/DC, Tool, White Stripes. Pretty much like that.

DLR: What brings Van Halen music into focus is more than anything is that there's constant difference in the collection here. I only listen to it if it's got an R&B bass. I went to an integrated junior high, high school, junior college, etc. (The) Van Halens come out of Europe. That's a whole different background. Their dad was a professional musician. [Dave points to Alex.] And I remember you, what was it—every Friday night? We had to stop rehearsal because you had to go play with your dad.

Alex: That's right. That's where I learned the trade.

EVH: Me, too. [Laughter.]

DLR: We would, we would be rehearsing and your mom would come out and go, "That's it. You gotta stop." And they'd go play a little place about half the size of this stage.

EVH: Do what you're paid to do.

DLR: Yeah, and he had to play with his dad. And they'd play at the, uh, what was it? It was the, what club was that?

Alex: This was the Continental Club on the corner of Cahuenga and Hollywood Boulevard. When I was thirteen.

DLR: Playin' standards.

Alex: Good experience.

EVH: It used to be called the Continental Club.

Alex: Then we'd play music. [Laughs.]

DLR: Yeah, and he was driving when he was thirteen, 'cause his dad wasn't driving because there was too much gear in the truck. So, there's a family tradition going on here. I remember loadin' the drums into the car with you.

Alex: Absolutely, absolutely.

DLR: God bless him. We miss him. Next question, please.

Question: When's the new album coming out.

DLR: A good question. We're already plotting and planning. Saving the world is Bono's job. We just wanna save a hundred cities. [Laughter.]

EVH: Just know this—

DLR: Then we wanna save Europe. Then we wanna save Japan and Australia, [turning to Edward], and I wanna talk to you about Hong Kong—Wolf, you don't know what you're missing. [Much laughter.] *Then* we make an album. Lots of big dreams, here. Lots of ambition. It's a good point, and we've already talked about it.

EVH: Just know this. We're a band, and we're gonna continue. [A loud burst of applause follows as Ed looks down with the smile and determination of a new man.] A whole new beginning.

DLR: Yes. In the back, there, sir.

Question: One for Wolf. How did you get asked to join the band?

Wolfgang: [Laughs.]

Alex: He wasn't asked. He forced his way in. [Laughs.]

DLR: He's the only one who had no choice. [Laughter.]

Wolfgang: We just, like, started playing one summer and I sort of, just sort of slipped in.

Alex: Yeah. Wolfie's groove is very deep. He's got a very deep rhythmic sense. And I think that comes obviously from his father. I can describe Wolfie in two words. D-N-A. Right?

DLR: That's a musician joke. [Lots of laughter.] It's actually true. No—you either have it or you don't. That's in any type of instrument, and these are organic instruments. If you will—these are actual instruments. You're not talking about synth. You're not talking about the computer. You're talking about real bass, real drums, real guitar. That takes thousands of hours of to master. And no matter if you spent it or not. If you don't got it, you don't have *that groove*. The impossibly, unbreakable groove, and he's got it.

EVH: It's *sexy.*

DLR: Yeah, it's sexy. That's how you spell that. Next question. Young lady in the back.

Question: As rock icons yourselves, do you guys have a comment with regard to it being the thirtieth anniversary of the death of Elvis Presley? What is it about his legacy? And why is it still alive?

DLR: Well, if there was a god, Elvis would still be alive and all of the imposters would be dead. [Lots of laughter.]

EVH: I think I own—I think I own a Spam.

DLR: If Elvis was alive, so would Michael Jackson, I think, today. [This comment pre-dates Michael Jackson's death in 2009. Lots of laughter, followed by light taunting.] What are you booing me for a Michael Jackson joke? This is a Van Halen audience! Come on!

EVH: *Yeeeeee-haw*! [Lots of laughter.]

Question: [Unintelligible question about Valerie Bertinelli.]

DLR: Why do think I'm separated?

Wolfgang: Let's just say she's watching me closely.

DLR: The questions are pursuant to Valerie, Wolf's mom, Valerie Bertinelli. Everybody knows, you know, who she is and stuff. And, uh, the next obvious question will be how am I getting along with Valerie Bertinelli, and I want to say, that now we're getting along fine. The first time we ran into each other up at the studio—she had the kind of look like she was down at the family gym and the Devil showed up looking to throw a ball around. [Lots of laughter.] "You want your kid to go on the road with *this* band?!"

EVH: Well, one thing I can say is that she can hold her own.

Question: Alright, one more question, and then we'd love to get you guys on stage for a picture.

Matt Linus: Hey guys, Matt Linus, *MTV News* here in the back, right here in the center.

DLR: Certainly.

Matt Linus: So, when the tour was postponed in March, um . . . Eddie entered rehab. You said you didn't feel like you were at your best. Why'd you make that decision? And do you feel at your best right now?

EVH: Because I am. [That's all Ed says.]

DLR: Yeah, there's a high standard, here. You know? We could waddle out there. We could kind of, uh, halfway do it. But like I said—a band like this coming after an absence of this amount of time can get away with a lot if you do one tour. That's not our ambition, here. This is not like The Police. The idea is that this will continue on and on and on. And that, uh, you gotta get a good start with that. We're all together with this, whether it's with Ed, or anything else that involves any one of us. We really have reformed this team like a brother team that is *never* was before. I think you hear that in my voice, here. And we think we got it right this time. You come and judge the performance *harshly*. *Please*. I beg you. Come on down and see.

EVH: None of us wanna give you less than our best. And we are at our best. [He nods.]

DLR: Thank you for joining us, God bless you all!

Following the press conference, the guys moved all their microphone stands out of the way and posed, arms around each other, for nearly a minute while a thousand flashes peppered the band. The press corps yelled out for the guys to remove their sunglasses. Eddie and Wolfgang took theirs off, but Alex and Dave did not. After multiple yells for them to remove their glasses, someone yelled, "Take off your clothes!" to much laughter. With that, "Jump" came over the speaker system, and the guys left the stage. On their way off the stage, Wolfgang patted Dave on the back.

Now to hit the road. Edward would struggle with the routine of being on tour. It would be a glorious ride, but with one rock big enough to temporarily block the entire road.

CHAPTER 42
Almost Too Good to Be True

The resurgence of the Edward and Dave era of Van Halen landed like an atomic bomb in North Carolina on September 27 in Charlotte and two days later in Greensboro (their traditional opening city). Opening night in Charlotte was a huge triumph for Edward and the latest incarnation of Van Halen. The footage is there—Edward was completely back on top of his game. This latest incarnation of the master himself was enough to make anyone reflect upon their age. Eddie was 52 years old at the time, and he was performing cut and shirtless, with just cargo pants and tennis shoes. He was rocking, jumping, soloing, and singing like the flood of a creek after a drought.

The band launched straight into their set of classic material with "You Really Got Me," almost as if to get it out of the way while simultaneously reminding the listener of just exactly what it was they were seeing. By the time they hit "Dance the Night Away" about a half-dozen or so songs into the set—it was clear that this monster had a life of its own. The middle section was lengthened with some beautiful guitar work by Ed, but then the band brought the song down very low. Dave sang out the first line: "Dance the night away . . ." The entire crowd chimed along in unison singing along spontaneously. It was an absolutely beautiful moment. A simply perfect performance. Ed's individual solo spot was dead on. His delivery was fantastic and fluid. The beauty of the conclusion of his solo was that old, familiar three-ring circus voice coming up from behind: "Ladies and gentlemen, Edward Van Halen!" They were simply firing on all cylinders. Wolfgang's performance was at a level where no one should have missed Michael Anthony at all.

Rolling Stone reacted to the first show immediately with the headline "Gods of Rock Deliver the Goods: Van Halen Kick Off Reunion Tour." The review was exceedingly glowing, even referring to *#70* Edward Van Halen as a "guitar god" and focusing on Dave's Olympic-precision performance with awe and due deserve, the reaction of a common fan best summed up the impact that their opening night performance had on the public. Weeping fan Matt Caramella said, "Did this really happen? . . . Man, that was like a fucking dream."

The dream continued on two nights later in Greensboro—as familiar turf as Van Halen has in the United States. When Edward said they didn't want to give any less than their best and reassured everyone they were at their best, all he had to do was continue to prove it. The second show of the tour would become legendary. Your classic hand-drawn cartoon came back in updated digital animation in full stereo sound. By 2007, essentially every single show of the tour would be taped one way or another and posted to YouTube. In the 21st century, your performance is essentially broadcast immediately and the microscope was on Edward and Dave.

While the first twenty-five songs of the set went perfectly without a hitch at all, "1984" came in followed by the pre-recorded synth backing track from "Jump." The moment Edward came in, it was painfully obvious that he had a guitar tuned down a half step to E flat rather than in standard 440 tuning [the majority of all Van Halen songs are tuned down about a half-step, but a keyboard song, like "Jump," is always in standard tuning]. Edward attempted to make adjustments throughout but the guitar was so painfully out of tune against the backing track—it was simply a half-step off. He had the wrong guitar. If he had the correct guitar that was properly in tune with the backing track, that would have been great. But it was the wrong guitar, and it was painfully off and left some to wonder why Ed didn't simply swap out guitars given how overtly obvious it was that the tuning was off. It was a horrible way to end a 99.5% perfect performance. Just a few nights later in Philadelphia, the set-closing performance of "Jump" was spot on and flawless. At the end of the song on October 1, Ed improvised a brilliant wah-wah solo over a spot where it had never existed before, and it was triumphant and masterful. The October 12 "Jump" performance in Toronto was also excellent and ethereal.

It turned out quite a bit of the set would require delicate interplay with prerecorded backing tracks, especially in "The Cradle Will Rock" and "I'll Wait," in addition to "Jump." During "The Cradle Will Rock," Dave completely melted the crowd with what would become his oft-repeated refrain of "Have you seen Wolfie's grades?!" At the tail end of the song on October 1, Edward masterfully drifted briefly into "Smoke on the Water" before kicking the famous "wooshing" sound of "Cradle" and slamming it for a tight ending.

One of the biggest highlights of the early shows was the interplay between Edward and Dave on stage. They came across as so genuinely happy and sincere and loving toward each another. The only thing that could equal that was the interplay between Eddie and Wolfie on stage especially during tunes like "Romeo Delight." To see Dad come over and muss his son's hair on stage was one hell of an extra treat for the crowd. Occasionally they would get down on their knees in front of each other and pick at each other's instruments just to get each other to laugh. It wasn't unusual at all for Ed to grab Wolfgang by the neck and give him a kiss on his head.

Getting Angry and Getting Lost

On November 3, Ed was officially on public bad behavior. He had a stage monitor that was either not working or not mixed correctly. Ed lost his mind with anger. He gestured off-stage with fury, pointing at and screaming about the monitor in a huff. Finally, Edward had enough. He took his guitar off and he picked up the stage monitor. He carried it toward the front edge of the stage and hurled the monitor down the steps just as the song ended. It was not pretty at all. There is some irony here. Long ago, during Dave's Jungle Studs travel days, he said that all of his hardships taught him not to sweat the small stuff. In fact, he specifically once said of such incidents, "'Hey, man, the monitor just blew up.' That's all right. I remember the beat." At least "Jump" was in tune for the most part. But all in all, he was not happy that evening.

By November, video surfaced of Ed getting lost in songs. The first such incident was during "Hot for Teacher" in Uniondale. Ed was behind Wolf and Alex, missing notes, and having gear trouble. At one point, he gestured to Dave for guidance upon which Dave belted out for the whole crowd to hear, "I think we're gettin' ready for the final outro . . ." Video was also posted showing Ed getting lost during the funk breakdown/solo/breakdown part of "Mean Streets" and giving an overall not-there guitar solo.

The show at a sold-out Madison Square Garden on November 13 is truly legendary. Edward's solo spot was amazing and flawless and he brought it 10,000%. During "Cathedral," he was so in the zone and the crowd knew it that Ed broke into a huge smile and nodded to the crowd as if to say, "Yeah, it's happenin'!" The crowd reaction during his solo was amazing and thunderously loud, again rounded out with Dave's classic carnival barking, "Ladies and gentlemen, Edward Van Halen!" "Panama" sounded brand new. During the middle breakdown, instead of going into a contrived, nonsensical diatribe about living for "right now" etc., Dave got down to business, taunting a woman in the front row, "Don't stick that tongue out at me unless you intend to use it, hot stuff!" Dave, Ed, and Wolf all stopped and went extra long on the "now" in "Ain't no stoppin' now" a Capella. Amazingly, it is actually an improvement upon the song's original arrangement.

At the Garden that night, Edward's vocals were amazingly strong on "Unchained" and complemented Wolf's and Dave's perfectly. The best part was the classic breakdown of the song when Dave teased Wolf saying, "You'll get some New York leg tonight for sure, Wolf! Tell us how you do!" Wolfgang took to the microphone, and the entire band completely stopped. "Dave . . . ?" Wolf said and paused about three seconds before following it meekly with, "Can you give me a break?" Dave gave the crowd his huge open-mouth smile and the crowd roar surged even higher. Of course, Dave came back in screaming, "One break, coming up!" They finished the song strong, with Ed just amping up his solo and taking it extra long through the outro while Dave taunted him like a chief summoning fire. Dave went to a rare symbolic stage gimmick for the band—two gigantic pieces of chain that he held high and then dropped to the stage during the very end.

Just a week after the New York City show, the band played the Staples Center in Los Angeles—the modern-day equivalent to the unfortunately outdated Forum. Amazingly, things were just getting better. The November 20 performance of "Unchained" is damn near unparalleled in Van Halen history [I invite you to look up the video]. The majority of the performance is a spot-on, album-version recreation. Edward's guitar solo is as excellent and extraordinary as you are ever going to hear in your entire life. His performance during the "Unchained" outro induces goosebumps. They were peaking. It was unbelievable. It is an amazing digital age in which anyone can now go and watch hundreds if not thousands of individual performances by Edward and Van Halen at their fingertips—but it was amazing when it was happening. When the night was done, the rush was on to upload the videos to YouTube for the whole world to watch damn near each and every performance. If only I had the digital camera I do now back in July of 1984—now that would have been something.

Van Halen had a strict every-other-day booking set-up. Rarely if ever did the band play on back to back nights. By rule, there was essentially a one day break between each and every show. This tactic seemed to work well for the band as they wrapped up the second leg of the tour with back-to-back shows at the MGM Grand in Las Vegas at year's end. Eddie and the band were firing on all cylinders throughout all of November and December—save for the accidental "Jump" butcher, Ed's monitor fit throwing trip, and getting inexplicably lost in "Hot for Teacher" and "Mean Streets."

The next few months would be beyond glorious and a bit painful. But the pain would be over soon. And there was still plenty of ass kicking left to do.

CHAPTER 43
Glory and That Rock in the Road

Before the band returned to the road in late January, the second leg of the tour, Edward and Wolfgang gave an interview to of Chris Gill of *Guitar World* for an article that was eventually published in the April 2008 edition of the magazine. The interplay between father and son in the interview was so pure and charming. It was *Leave it to Beaver* with f-bombs. Ed was like a stoner Ward Cleaver and Wolfgang was a long-haired Theodore.

Wolfgang emphasized how the approach to his joining the band was very organic and natural. "We didn't lay out a plan or anything," he said. "It just fell together. We played together a good four months without any vocals, and we looked at each other and knew it was awesome." Ed followed it up with a quote from Dave: "It's like Dave says, 'Three parts original, one part inevitable.' And it was inevitable." He joked that he joined on bass since it was the only open slot. In response to critics such as Sammy Hagar, Edward said, "Before we went on tour a lot of people were saying Wolfgang got the gig just because he's my son. But after that first gig, forget it. It's just hands down, hands up, hands sideways: he's a musician and a Van Halen." Everyone that went to the 2007-2008 shows knows at least two or three fellow fans that said, "It's just not Van Halen without Michael Anthony." That is common knowledge. Most people probably don't realize Wolfgang heard the same thing, too, over and over again. But his level of talent—especially in the eyes of his father—was easily that of an equal and he said so directly. "Every now and then when we're on stage playing, I look at him and go, God, that's my son!" he said. "He's only 16, but he's not 16. He's an equal. Age doesn't matter."

In the interview with Chris Gill, Edward summed up the situation at the time. "For me it's the fact that I get to play with my son, my brother and Dave," he said. "Every night is special." And my special night was right around the corner.

San Antonio and Dallas were the second and third shows of the third leg. It was something I had been looking forward to since I was twelve in 1984. Almost 24 years had passed—twice as many years as I was old at the time.

The San Antonio show on January 24 was absolutely fantastic. One thing that was very obvious, however, was that Edward had either a bandage or a wrap of some kind around his left hand. It did not seem to affect his playing at all, but everyone noticed and wondered what it was.

I have to admit that I was so thrilled and astounded that my reaction during the show in San Antonio was more that of numbness. I was extremely sedate during the show with a case of a blown mind. I also knew that just two days later, we would be seeing them again in Dallas at Reunion Arena. That concert would be sold out, and the band would even come back to Dallas later in 2008 for a second show at the same enormous venue.

For the Dallas show, I figured that there was at least a lingering possibility that this show could be the last I'd ever see with Dave and Edward on the same stage together—I was just fearful, even though I was eternally positive for Edward's future and the future of the band, which seemed to be going completely in the right direction after so many years of drifting. My best friend Michael, with whom I had seen Van Halen with in 1984, couldn't make it to the San Antonio show, but he did make it for the Dallas show.

It was winter in Dallas on January 26, 2008—Edward's 53rd birthday. Michael and I sat next to each other in pretty much the nosebleeds of Reunion Arena. I brought with me our original 1984 tour ticket stub and we laughed about it before the show started. The lights went down, up came the rumbling thunder of music from the stage, and into "You Really Got Me" they flew. I had that shot-out-of-a-cannon feeling again. It was fantastic. Song after song was masterful. Ed's hand was still bandaged, but none of us could figure it out—if it was a wrap or a wound cover. Again, it made absolutely no difference in his playing at all, so that made it even more perplexing, because Edward Van Halen was on fire on the evening of his 53rd birthday in Dallas, Texas.

"Romeo Delight" was the tune that Dave had something in mind to acknowledge Eddie's birthday. Nevertheless, Wolfgang jumped up to the microphone and said, "Let's sing Eddie 'Happy Birthday!'" The crowd cheered briefly and Dave turned to Wolfgang and said, "Shut your fuckin' mouth, Wolfie. Play the song, Eddie!" Edward started "Romeo Delight" and played one single time through the riff and stopped as if he wasn't sure what exactly had just transpired. He actually paused for nearly ten full seconds before Dave said, "Play the song on the guitar!" and Edward went directly back into "Romeo Delight," restarting it from the beginning. They launched into a rendition of the highest order of badass, it was straight out over the top. Ed and Wolf's background vocals were ridiculously spot on. Edward's guitar solo was absolutely off the charts, completely and totally. The breakdown was astounding with Wolfgang taking some of the tapping parts on the bass in mini-solo of his own.

As the breakdown reached its lowest ebb, Dave started into "Happy Birthday," prompting the entire crowd to sing along. "Happy birthday, dear Eddie," Dave sang, "Happy birthday to you!" Ed stood there smiling, just soaking it in. Afterward, Ed and Dave embraced, with Edward giving Dave his trademark kiss on the cheek. Wolfgang stood close by clapping. Edward got on the microphone and said, "You get to make a wish, right? I want you all to have a great motherfuckin' time tonight!" With that they launched back into "Romeo Delight." Just before the "Feel my heartbeat" refrain, Dave said, "You see, Wolf, I just couldn't sing 'Happy Birthday' in the other goddamned key!" Wolfgang walked over and laughed. No harm done. They segued into a jam of "Magic Bus." You will rarely find a single performance of "Romeo Delight" better than what happened in Dallas on January 26, 2008. It was an eight-minute exercise in rock music entertainment excellence. It was as transcendent as a rock performance could possibly be. I saw it and I documented it. It was *crazy* good. The whole train though was also less than a month from derailment.

The Amps Came Crashing Down

By the time the band hit Tampa on February 18, Ed's solo segment began to deteriorate. He spent just as much time making feedback and echo effects as he did actually playing. He wasn't able to get his timing right on "Cathedral" at all. He came to a stop and went to the microphone and said, "Who's out there? Who's out there at this point?" He continued on into some of the blazing parts of "Eruption" but was mostly improvising and to the hyper-critical observer, he was a bit all over the map. It wasn't his greatest performance, and there may have been good reason.

On February 20, in Sunrise, Florida, at the Bank Atlantic Center, the show seemed to be going well. "Everybody Wants Some" was superb. Ed and Dave's engine sound competition was classic. Dave would use his voice to imitate a car engine and Edward would use his guitar. Dave would give up, saying "I can't beat that." During the final chorus, Edward got up on Wolfgang's microphone with him as they both belted out "Everybody wants some!"

But behind the scenes, things were falling apart. Fans reported that Wolfgang would not engage with Eddie at all during the show despite a dozen or more attempts by Ed to get Wolfie to loosen up. Clearly, things were off between the two. The ending of the concert was another one of the ugliest moments in Edward's onstage history. At the end of "Jump," Edward threw his guitar to the stage and then wandered around for nearly twenty seconds before finally saying "thank you" to the crowd. For the customary band bow at the end of every show, Edward had to actively reach for Wolfgang's hand. Wolf was hesitant to give him his hand, period. But he did and they bowed. Immediately thereafter, Wolfie practically ran off the stage. He was followed by Al, but as Ed left the stage, he violently rocked Wolf's amps back and forth until a stack of cabinets collapsed to the stage. Smooth as ballet, Dave just casually stepped back as several hundred pounds of amplifier fell about six inches from his feet. Something was very wrong. There were reports of a "furious backstage bust-up with his son."

The next move was a difficult one, but absolutely critical. The tour had to be postponed. Edward was clearly tired of having to address his alcoholism publicly and acknowledged that in his statement regarding rehab back in March of 2007 when he said, "It was an intensely personal thing that I'm not really comfortable talking about right now." This time, the word rehab was banned from the discussion of Edward's status at that time. On March 3, 2008, The *Associated Press* carried the headline "Van Halen Postpones Shows, Eddie Undergoes Medical Tests." At first, only four shows were postponed, but just a week later, it was announced that in fact seventeen shows would be affected and the tour was put on hold for a month. And just one week after that—all seventeen shows were rescheduled. There was really only a brief two-week window or so that left fans to scratch their heads, but once the postponed shows were rescheduled, everyone realized that this was just temporary and that the band would indeed be back in action in short order.

During the hiatus, Valerie chose to tell *People* that Eddie was in fact still sober and not in rehab. Even though she seemed to be proactively denying what seemed to be so obvious, she refused to go one level deeper. "He's being proactive about his illness," she said. When asked to elaborate, she pulled back, saying only, "I don't think it's my place [to comment.]" However, Valerie released her well-received autobiography *Losing It* on February 25—just immediately before the tour was derailed. Other than Dave's 1996 autobiography, Val's book was the only other publication at that point in time that truly revealed what it was like to live with Edward Van Halen. Her book hit the best-seller's list and while many readers identified with her issues of weight loss and self-perception, another great many were shocked at the descriptions and depictions of Ed at his worst. However, Edward was reportedly fine with the book, just the same as he was fine with Dave's book. He didn't make any big waves to stop the publication or make counter-claims in any way whatsoever. The timing of his derailment (February 20), however, coincides neatly with the release of Val's very revealing book (February 25).

Wolfgang was also putting a spin on things when he appeared at Nickelodeon's Kid's Choice Awards on March 29. He told a *People* reporter, "Don't listen to the rumors—he's doing great—seriously!" Medical tests, ailments, illness (*People* even called it a "mystery illness")—it seemed like an obvious spin and twist using semantics. Ed had been so public and so open about his struggles before, even though he had said he wasn't really comfortable talking about it. By this time, it is simply likely that enough was enough. Everyone knows he is a struggling alcoholic. The tour got derailed for a month. The picture was already painted before anyone could even open their mouth.

Dave gave a brief interview on March 27 to Rocco G, a fashion reporter who caught up with Dave at the Mercedes Benz LA Fashion Week Fall 08. Rocco asked, "So how's everything going with the music? What've you been up to?" Dave's response was funny, nonchalant, and positive. "Oh, it's going superbly," he said. "We have an unexpected break in the action here but that's kind of what you pay Van Halen for. It's like NASCAR: are you here to see the winner or the crash? Don't answer—we have both! And we'll be starting up our engines again in a couple of weeks."

At this exact same time, Edward and Alex finally sold their mother's home. The house was co-owned by the brothers, the same home they had purchased for her after her pelvic injury back in 1987 after Jan had passed away. It had been three years since Eugenia passed, but the brothers still had not sold the house. One could argue that the last link to their parents and their past and their upbringing was finally gone with the sale. Ed had said the house was only two minutes away from him and that he often slept there overnight. It was finally time for Edward to permanently move into the future and forget about the pasture—as Dave would put it. Just like his guitars and amps and effects, Edward had to ultimately rebuild himself his own way. In the end, it doesn't matter how many times it takes someone to see the light, just so long as they finally see it. It is no small postulate that this was *it.*

A Supreme Rock and Roll Machine

Before the tour resumed in Reno on April 17, Edward and Janie were caught by paparazzi at the airport on their way from L.A. to Nevada. Most of the pictures were simply, "Hey, here's me and my girlfriend going to the airport just like everyone else." But one picture highlighted the ridiculousness of the TSA during the post-9/11 era. There is a photo of Edward with his shirt pulled completely up revealing his stomach and chest, his hands up, and the blue-gloved TSA agent literally unbuttoning Ed's jeans! It was one of those caption-contest type photos. But it is possible Ed is on everyone's list because of the "gun thing."

When the band hit the stage in Reno, a song title from their debut album perfectly described the caliber of the band at that moment, and that would be "On Fire." Reviewing all of the footage from the Reno show truly revealed that Edward and the entire band came back even stronger, as if that was actually possible. The Van Halen of April and May of 2008 was ridiculously super-charged and delivering a supreme product. I personally reviewed hundreds of videos over those two months [there are thousands on YouTube from just April and May 2008 alone]. I did not find a single performance that was subpar in any way shape, form, or fashion. Anyone who saw Van Halen during April or May of 2008 witnessed the peak of the band's performance power.

The day after the Reno show, the press reviews were glowing. Writer Jason Kellner for the *Reno Gazette-Journal* said, "The band was in top musical form, with Eddie ever the astonishing guitarist . . . Even Roth didn't hold back, save for a few of the banshee screams that went missing. The band played every song in its original key, evidence that Roth can still hit the highest highs . . ." Kellner also commented on Ed and Dave's camaraderie as well as Wolfie's musical prowess: "Despite past animosity between David Lee Roth and Eddie Van Halen and a couple false starts in the reunion department in the past 10 years, there was no bad blood to be seen on stage. Eddie and Dave both wore genuine grins . . ." About Wolfgang, he said outright, "The young dude is a fine bass player, great backing vocalist . . ." The band followed with back-to-back shows in Vegas that were spectacular.

One of the shows was officially a fundraising concert for the Tiger Woods Foundation (this was a good two years before Tiger's well-publicized indiscretions). Tiger himself was a self-proclaimed longtime Van Halen fan and personally picked the band to kick off Tiger Jam XI. Woods himself personally introduced the band and there are numerous pictures of the famous golfer with the various band members. Noteworthy was the fact that Edward, Dave, Alex, and Wolfgang each gave $100,000 personally to the Tiger Woods Foundation. In an official statement, the band said, "Playing Tiger Jam XI has certainly been one of the highlights of the tour so far. It was an honor to be involved and a pleasure to rock for a cause."

After Vegas, the band played Cincinnati. For some reason, it would be the last show that Edward would perform shirtless for the tour. For all fifty-seven shows so far, he played without a shirt, often garnishing praise for his admirable physique at age 53. But as of their return date to Dallas on April 24, Ed began wearing comfortable shirts for the remaining nineteen shows of the tour. With a shirt, without a shirt—Edward was beyond the top of his game. What's more, he was consistently on top of his game for the entire two-month stretch of April and May. His playing was fluid, lucent, and inspired. Near the end of this third leg of the tour, Jed Gottlieb of the *Boston Herald* wrote on June 3: "There's nothing wrong with Eddie Van Halen. Nothing. After undergoing a thorough two-hour examination by thousands of people at a nearly sold-out Manchester Verizon Wireless Arena on Wednesday night, Van Halen has been given a clean bill of awesomeness."

In early June, Edward gave a brief interview with Brian Hiatt of *Rolling Stone*. Hiatt asked if the band [read: Dave and Ed] was getting along well on a personal basis. "Oh, yeah," said Eddie. "We always really have. To me it seems like the press made more of a stink out of shit than we actually did. 'Cause everybody kind of parts ways and tries to find their own niche, you know, or whatever, but no hurt feelings about anything." After so many years of acrimony, those words rang out like beautiful bells. They were obviously genuine as well.

The tour officially wrapped with an excellent show in Grand Rapids. Respectfully, Van Andel Arena in Grand Rapids was renamed Van Halen Arena for June 2, 2008. The *Grand Rapids Press* wrote: "The temporary name change involved obtaining special permission from the band, the Van Andel Family and the city. 'The Van Andel family agreed to the renaming of the arena for the day,' [Grand Rapids Mayor George] Heartwell said. 'It's fitting to celebrate a Dutch name in a Dutch city.'"

Just three days after the Grand Rapids show came a surprise announcement that Van Halen would kick off the Quebec City Summer Festival on July 3. *Blabbermouth.net* reported that the band played in front of 90,000 people, a record crowd for the festival. Even after an unplanned month's break, the band's prowess was still at its peak. The ending of "Hot for Teacher" was mind-blowing. The crowd was going nuts and Ed, Wolf, and Al were just hammering away building up to the end. Dave walked over and gestured as if to pull even more out of the three. Dave enticed the audience with his facial expressions, and finally gave a cue to Alex and executed an amazing round-house kick for a 54-year-old man with the band ending the song precisely upon his landing. The Quebec show was a beautiful ending to the greatest ever family vacation across North America, during which the car broke down temporarily, but the family finished out the wild trip in glorious style. The world was better for it.

It was the most successful tour in Van Halen history. *AllAccess.com* reported that the band had made $93 million over the seventy-four shows of the tour; Van Halen's biggest ever. In comparison, the 2004 tour with Sammy grossed barely over $50 million on eighty shows.

Most fans expected a CD or DVD of the best performances of the tour but that did not come to fruition. It's possible that with the thousands of fan-captured videos on YouTube, as of 2008 the guys likely had a firm grasp of modern technology and its implications. As of mid-2011, Eddie's "Eruption" solo performance on December 3, 2007, in Seattle on had been viewed in excess of 2.7 *million* times (it is spectacular). With all of the YouTube videos online, a DVD of the tour may have ended up being more trouble than it was worth. As far as a live CD went, Edward's experience in the past dictated that it was something he likely refused to go through again. He knows how many fan-made videos there are online.

It was practically a foregone conclusion that the recording of a new album would begin in earnest. Unfortunately for the impatient, Edward would move on Van Halen time—which he had previously said was irrelevant to him. About a new album, Edward said that he did indeed plan to record a new album, but qualified that by saying "We'll cross that bridge when the tour is over." There were several things to deal with before even beginning to think about the actual process of recording an entire album of new material.

CHAPTER 44
A New Husband, a New Man

After the conclusion of the wildly successful tour, Eddie confessed to being a couch potato for about five months. Late that summer, while vacationing in Hawaii, on August 4, Janie accepted Edward's proposal of marriage. *People* reported, "The rock guitarist dropped to one knee and popped the question in a private room at Tiffany's, [according to] a source close to the couple." The wedding date was set for June 2009. The source added: "They are happy, healthy, very much in love and looking forward to living life together forever. . . . They are devoted to each other and to experiencing life in a whole new, positive and passionate way." A picture of Edward shirtless on the beach in Maui even ended up on the celebrity gossip show and website *TMZ*. Notorious for crucifying celebrities at their worst, *TMZ* gave Ed the tag "Eddie Van Healthy."

Just days before, Edward was given serious validation by *Roadie Crew* magazine. It is not exactly your every day coffee table periodical, but the journal did bring together three hundred of the most well-known and influential musicians—to begin listing them here would be absurd—to vote on the top fifty guitarists in rock music history. Jimi Hendrix? Number one, of course. Where did Edward place? Was it #70 as per the snobs of *Rolling Stone*? No, it was number two—right behind Jimi Hendrix. And that is exactly as it should be, because that is exactly accurate, right, and justified.

The EVH Brand

In January 2009, the culmination of all of Edward's work improving and perfecting the electric guitar arrived in the form of the EVH Wolfgang. *Business Wire* reported, "The EVH Wolfgang guitar represents Eddie's 35 years of experimenting with guitars, over two years of intense research and development, and a full year of brutal road testing during the top-grossing

Van Halen 2007-2008 tour." Edward highlighted the fact that every single last aspect of the guitar was of the highest quality and specificity using only the best woods and metals. "Everything that I've built, destroyed, stumbled onto, learned and experienced is in this guitar." Ed's partner in the EVH Brand deal with Fender, longtime technical assistant and best friend Matt Bruck, said of the creation of the guitar, "We went through about eighty sets up pickups." Ed said the guitar was on par with NASA standards.

It was the highlight of the EVH Brand line of products, although because production was kept to a relatively low number, a new Wolfgang would be high quality but hard to come by. On the other hand, the EVH 5150 III amplifiers were readily available in North America and highly sought after. Particularly, Scott Ian of Anthrax is a rabid supporter of the EVH 5150 III.

Sobriety

The same month that Ed launched the new Wolfgang, I launched the new me. By January 2009, I was remarried with a new young child and my drinking was close to killing me. I ended up in the hospital on New Year's Day 2009, my family intervened for a second time, and I checked into a rehab facility three days later. As I went through rehabilitation for alcoholism, I could not help but think of Edward and look to him for inspiration, and also to help understand just how difficult it could be. If as Ed said, you just get one big bottle and once you drink it, it's all gone—that's how it was with me. Once I'd had my last drink, I had my last drink. It was the single-most difficult and important thing I have ever done in my entire life. Had I not stopped drinking that day, I simply may not have survived much longer. I put myself into many situations where intoxication could have very easily caused an accidental death.

My life is a lot different than Edward's is for sure, so the nature and habits of our drinking are not very comparable. I had to work my drinking into a strict schedule around having a day job and getting the kids to school. Edward's schedule was fairly wide-open. But the alcoholism is the same. We both have that gene, the X-factor, the genetic predisposition. My uncle died from alcoholism (cirrhosis is a horrific way to go). And it's not fair, because, man, I loved to drink. And I'm not a big guy but I could seriously put away some beer, more than I should ever have been able to—up to eighteen in one day at my worst. And just like Ed, I started drinking at exactly the age of twelve. I put in a good twenty-four years worth, with the last three to four being off the charts. Alcohol just simply is not part of my life anymore. It is most certainly perfectly fine for people who can handle it—"normal" people. For me and other alcoholics, it's simply the worst thing imaginable. It is a demon. It is hard to accept that the drug is actually stronger than the chemicals in your own brain, but once you do, you're on your way.

In the spring of 2009, Ed told *Hustler*:

> EVH: I don't really wanna get into the whole sobriety trip. But I'm just workin' on a lot of things to get better at being here in the moment and stay clear, ya know? I have been drinking, smoking, and playing guitar since I was 12 years old. I still smoke, and I'm definitely playing guitar better than ever. I guess one of the three had to go. Along with some other shit. But alcohol was the wonder drug for me. It's a trip to look back and go, "Fuck, I've been doing this for over 40 years." I'm lucky to be alive. I'm healthier and happier than I've ever been. . . . . I have the most insanely gifted, talented, wonderful son (a direct gift from God), whom I love more than he'll ever know. My brother Alex, who I just love so fucking much, it makes me wanna cry out of joy that I'm so blessed to have him since the day I was born. My best friend Matt, who I've known for over 20 years and works with me on just about everything I do. My friend Ryan and a few other people. A great career. And of course my own company, EVH Brand of guitars, amps and accessories. What the fuck more could I ask for? I feel like my life is just beginning.

The interviewer also directly asked about a new album. "First, Wolfgang graduates, and then Janie and I are getting married," Edward said. "Then we'll sit down, give Dave a call and ask him if he feels like whooping and hollering a little bit."

A Thankful Man

In early June, *Rolling Stone* reported the following significant update on the musical front. "We're a true band now," said Edward. "It wasn't just a reunion one-off thing. I've already gone to Dave's house four or five times over the last month. I've got so much music. It's just trying to figure out what Dave's into because we haven't written together in a long time. But it's great. It feels like we've always felt in the beginning. But I'm sober, so it's different. He's sober, so it's different. It's a wonderful feeling." About working with Wolfgang, Edward said to *Spinner.com*, "I thank God on my knees that I'm alive and obviously to be sober and to be working with my son. I'm so damn blessed it's beyond words."

Shortly before the wedding, Eddie was a major feature on the Spike TV Guy's Choice Awards on June 22, 2009. Robert Downey, Jr. introduced him by saying, "The man we honor tonight as our first ever Guitar God is a musical genius. He is a virtuoso. . . . I give you your Guitar God . . . EDDIE VAN HALEN!" As Eddie emerged from the wings, he looked fantastic and healthy wearing a comfortable black shirt and faded jeans. He embraced Robert before taking the podium. As he stepped up to the podium, before he could even get a word out, the audience burst into massive applause. The applause struck a nerve inside Edward.

> EVH: You're taking me down a little. [He gets visibly choked up.] I didn't have an idea of what to say on the way over here. [His voice cracked and he was on the verge of tears.] Excuse me, I'm getting a little choked up, here. [He turns away to regain his composure.] When my mom, dad, brother, and I first came to America when I was seven years old, we came here with fifty bucks and a piano. I'm living proof—anything is achievable. [Much applause.] I started drinking when I was 12 years old, when I started playing guitar. I quit a year ago—42 years later. That also shows you anything is achievable. I want to thank my best friend and my son, Wolfgang; my brother, Alex; my friend, Matthew Bruck; Ryan Noto; most of all, my wife-to-be, Janie. They have given me a reason to stop bullshitting *myself*, and that keeps me sober. I don't do what I do for *this* [the award], but,

> man . . . it feels good. From the bottom of my heart, thank you.

When Eddie revealed in late June that he finally quit drinking "a year ago"—that is essentially an admission that he had resumed drinking during the 2007-2008 tour, although review of video and the timing of the postponement of the tour made that a foregone conclusion.

Getting Remarried and Getting Surgery

Edward and Janie married in a beautiful ceremony on the grounds of Ed's estate for a small, private gathering of no more than one hundred guests on June 27, 2009. It was a beautiful and casual affair, with Ed and his best man Wolf decked out in tan suits and flip flops. Ordained minister Alex Van Halen presided over the ceremony, or as his brother calls him, "Reverend Al." Janie's mother and her fifteen-year-old Pomerian walked Janie down the aisle. The wedding served only non-alcoholic beverages—no alcohol of any kind to be found at the wedding. Mr. Roth was also not to be found at the wedding, however, Valerie and Tom were there, and Janie and Ed would eventually return the favor. Edward and Janie honeymooned in New York, Germany, and the Netherlands.

It turns out the bandage that we saw on Ed's hand during the third leg of the tour in Texas must have indeed been a brace to provide some stability for Ed's left hand. "During the last leg of our tour, I started developing pain in my thumb and my pinky," he told *Rolling Stone*. "I didn't think much of it at the time. It got progressively worse to the point that about three months ago I wasn't able to play at all. My pinky and my thumb were totally locked up and felt like there was something broken." Edward sought out the most highly regarded hand surgeons in the world and ended up in Düsseldorf, Germany. One of the doctors there immediately noticed arthritis, but eventually found a bone spur, a cyst in his thumb, and a twisted tendon. "They said the only way to fix it was surgery, which of course scared the shit out of me, but I was told it was the only way to fix it." By July 23, Ed deemed the operation a success, but that it would sideline him for a good four to six months to heal. At the time of the article, Eddie still hadn't had his stitches removed. "I am totally jazzed that they found the problem, fixed it and in about four months my hand will feel like I am 18 again. Thank God."

The *Boston Music Examiner* reported in late July: "As far as the band's future plans, they definitely include both Eddie's son Wolfgang, or Wolfie, and former singer David Lee Roth. Roth joined his old band mates for a very successful 2007 tour, and Eddie Van Halen says he's written lots of new songs which they'll be recording sometime soon, with Roth as the singer and Wolfgang as bassist." Things were just on cruise control to ensure the successful recovery of Edward's hand surgery, whose rehabilitation from which may very well have been the single most important factor in the continuance of the Van Halen entity beyond 2010. Without Ed's healthy hands, there is essentially nothing.

On TV and Still Perplexing Fans

Edward made an unusual appearance on the sitcom *Two and a Half Men* on September 21, 2009 well prior to Charlie Sheen's incredibly public meltdown ("*Winning!*"). Executive producer Chuck Lorre actually asked Ed, who was reportedly a fan of the show, to appear while Ed was on his honeymoon. "He was gracious enough to do a cameo, which is really cool," Lorre said. Eddie's appearance was fairly silly for the most part, simply offering advice to Sheen's character on how to break the cycle of constipation. Ed also later appeared on the short-lived *Lopez Tonight*'s comedic one-hundredth episode celebration and was the highlight celebrity guest of the evening appearing via prerecorded video. He gave one of his signed Wolfgang guitars to Lopez who hilariously closed out his show by pretending to play "Panama" on the guitar.

Other than a few odd television appearances, most fans had not heard anything for months and months. It was not until March of 2010 that Edward was featured in a co-interview with Tony Iommi of Black Sabbath in *Guitar World.* Post-surgery in 2009, everyone was giving Ed plenty of time to heal. By spring 2010, fans were getting downright antsy. And Edward wasn't happy about it, nor did he appear to care.

> EVH: People think they know what I should do. A lot of fans are complaining that Van Halen should put out a new record now. Everybody is going, "Eddie should do this. Eddie should do that." I've got all kinds of music that I could put out if I wanted to, but they don't take into consideration the other members of the band. Maybe the singer doesn't want to do that.

> I play classical piano. I play a little bit of cello. I write all kinds of different music that certain singers or certain musicians don't want anything to do with. So what do I do? When people see Van Halen or Black Sabbath, it conjures up a certain image in their minds. If there's just one albino pubic hair outside of that image, they won't accept it. And if we do put something out, the first thing people are going to say is that it isn't as good as the classics. Okay. Put it in your closet for 20 years and then it will be classic.
>
> People forget that we put three new songs—"It's About Time," "Learning to See" and "Up for Breakfast"—on *Best of Both Worlds* in 2004. The reviews didn't even mention those songs. When we played the new songs live, people would just stand there. Nobody said anything about them. Why go to all the trouble, spend all of that time in the studio and spend tons of your own money—there aren't even any record labels anymore to put our shit out—to record a new album when people are only going to complain about it or ignore it or somebody is going to download it from the *Internet* for free? We might not record something new. There's an element of satisfaction and joy to creating something new, but not when it comes solely at your own expense and when people are just going to shoot it down, no matter what you do.

These were some complex statements by Edward. The most distressing of which was "We might not record something new." Ed also seemed to still be hung up on his classical piano and cello trip, and suggested, "Maybe the singer doesn't want to do that." This was distressing to fans and supporters. From my perspective, Edward had the opportunity for years and years and years—and still does—to put out a solo record of classical piano and cello music. In fact, most fans would absolutely die to possess such a product. That product should be released as "Edward Van Halen," not "Van Halen." David Lee Roth should not have to worry about adding vocals to a classical piano piece (nor should anyone really [see "How Many Say I"]). Like Dave said, his specialty is ass-kicking. Edward is perfectly welcome and able to write hours of material on piano, cello, saxophone, clarinet, or triangle. What he did not seem to understand or was simply frustrated by was that fans want classic Van Halen album number seven. One would think that the validation of 15,000-30,000 people per night over nearly eighty shows in 2007 and 2008 would dictate that fans most definitely strongly desired a new VH studio album. All of those fans attended those shows without even a single note of new material. A lot of fans, like myself, considered it a mutual understanding, as if, "We'll take this tour, for sure, guys. But next time, we need something new—although we'd still go if you didn't write another note because we are loyal to a fault."

There is simply a disconnect in some of Ed's words. To put *all* new material into the same bucket, meaning the new Hagar songs from 2004 versus any new music with Dave, is a real mistake. Ed's own comments about Dave's poor radio ratings when he briefly took over for Howard Stern in New York City apply perfectly in this scenario. People just stood there when the band played those three songs in 2004 because they were not that good. In fact, at least 100% lyrically, they were awful. There may have been something musically redeeming in those songs, but as had happened over and over again in the past, Ed's new music was consistently ruined by Sammy's horrific lyrics.

To think that people would just stand there when the band actually does perform new material with Dave does not fit the analogy he made about the 2004 Hagar material. He also seemed overly concerned about people downloading it without paying for it, even though Alex stated back in 2004 that he didn't care at all if people downloaded new material. The price of a VH concert ticket in the twenty-first century is the equivalent of purchasing ten albums as it is. Edward also came off positive that no matter what they did, that it would not get good reviews. This is tough to explain because Ed is well known for statements like "fuck the critics." He was worried people would say the new material would not be as good as the classics, that people would complain about it, that people would ignore it, that people would not accept it, and that people would shoot it down. The obvious conclusion could be that the epic failure of *Van Halen III* and the 2004 tour had a profound effect upon Edward. He was perfectly successful just where he was with a successful tour behind him, working with his son, a new wife, the EVH Brand. Why risk it all by putting out new material?

He said that everyone was saying what he should do, which was essentially put out a new album with Dave. It seemed like a logical, no-brainer decision. But again, Ed would move on Ed time. That meant the world would have to wait at least another entire year for the dream to come true. In fact, Ed would distract himself with work on the EVH Brand and Dave would have to simply wait him out, find some healthy distractions of his own, and cooperate fully with Eddie if *anything* was to ever come about again.

CHAPTER 45
Waiting Patiently

By mid-July 2010, various outlets started carrying stories that Van Halen had completed a new album and that a new single would be released soon. With Janie as the spokesperson, her simple response to *Rolling Stone* was "What is going around is exactly that, rumors. I don't have any updates at this time." In August, Steve Greenlee of the *Boston Examiner* ran with the headline: "Van Halen to Record, Tour with David Lee Roth" and said that "*Billboard* is reporting that something is imminent." Later that September, Irving Azoff let slip the notion that Van Halen would be touring in 2010. All that writer David Kreps at *Rolling Stone* could conjure up for a response was, "So far no plans for a tour have been announced."

For Christmas 2010, Edward became a video game. *Guitar Hero Van Halen* was released in December and featured nearly every classic Van Halen song on the game, as well as other modern rock tracks picked by Wolfgang. For that holiday season, Eddie personally released the message, "I would like to thank all of you for your continued support. Have a safe and happy holiday and a rockin' new year! See you soon! Eddie." Ed also amped up his EVH Brand output that Christmas offering up such non-guitar products as "premium" flip flops, ties, bandanas, beanie hats, and a wide variety of t-shirts all featuring, in one way or another, Ed's classic, patented striped design.

By the end of the year, VHND reported that the band was in fact eager to tour but insisted on doing so behind new material. During Ed's quiet time in 2010, he was constantly writing, and did in fact confirm that he had already worked with Dave. The wheels were in motion, they were just churning very slowly, or perhaps more accurately, deliberately. It should have been obvious to anyone that the band was not working slowly because they were adding 32 tracks of vocals and 54 tracks of guitars. Not in the slightest. Almost definitely, the time it took was the result of two things. First, Dave and Ed could probably only take being in each other's presence for a short time, especially under the high scrutiny of the studio environment. Secondly, the filter for suitable material was likely so incredibly specific that the band was stockpiling songs and would end up pick only the very best ones. It's not the classic Van Halen approach to do fifty takes of a song. Chances are that there are far more leftover songs than the ones that would be selected, and chances are that the ones that were selected were likely recorded in just a few basic takes like any other classic Van Halen song. The band was not becoming Pink Floyd or Radiohead.

On the Cover of *People* in 2011

To start off 2011, Valerie and Tom were married on January 1. Edward and Janie both attended their small, private ceremony (save for the exclusive *People* magazine spread). One rather bizarre aspect of this event, however, was the fact that Eddie wound up on the cover of *People* magazine to start off the new year (he was featured in a small inset photo of himself, Valerie, Tom, and Janie). Many people read about the fact that Edward and Valerie had each attended the other's second wedding ceremonies, something that most people would consider as healthy as eating salad every single day. A picture of a heartily laughing Edward with his arm around Tom was featured in the exclusive spread. Just a few days later, on January 4, Wolfgang and Edward attended the Alterbridge concert in L.A. with Edward watching stage-side as Wolfgang sat in on drums. Wolf would forge a strong bond with the band Alterbridge (which features former-Creed guitarist Eric Friedman).

At the NAMM convention in January, Edward unveiled his new EVH Stealth and Wolfgang guitars, as well as a 50-watt version of his increasingly popular 5150 III amplifier. Ed appeared a bit heavier than normal, but in his case, heavier simply meant healthier. "He [Eddie] is actually using this guitar [Wolfgang Stealth] in the studio right now . . . getting ready for the new album," said Chris Cannella, an EVH Brand employee. Chris also told *Vintagerock.com*: "You're gonna see a lot more of Ed this year . . . hopefully by the summer." Ed's appearance at the NAMM show was nothing but gracious and kind, and he stopped and posed for pictures and gave autographs.

Back in the Studio and into the Smithsonian

On January 21, super-producer John Shanks updated his Twitter account with the simple message: "here we go kids . . . vh." He also posted a picture of the EVH Brand logo from one of Edward's amplifiers. Shanks production credits covered the entire spectrum of the music industry with artists as diverse as Bon Jovi, Backstreet Boys, Kelly Clarkson, Jane's Addiction, Fleetwood Mac, Keith Urban, and Hanson, amongst many others. This was not an insignificant "tweet"—this was the unofficial/official word go. Just five days later, Edward turned 56 years old.

As if January 2011 were not a busy enough month for Ed already, it was capped off by an incredible honor. A replica of the original Frankenstein guitar, referred to as Frank 2 (the replica that Edward played on the 2007-2008 tour) was acquired by the Smithsonian National Museum of American History. Museum director Brent Glass said, "The museum collects objects that are multidimensional, and this guitar reflects innovation, talent and influence. The guitar moves the museum's instrument collections into more contemporary history." Edward told *Smithsonian Magazine* that the original Frankenstein had been retired. "It took so much abuse from endless touring and recording," he said. "I wanted to pay some respect to it and let it survive and not let it get destroyed completely. At the same time it became something so well known beyond my wildest dreams that its value made it a target for theft and I wanted to protect it. I still play it every now and then. It's priceless to me."

In March, Sammy Hagar released his autobiography *Red* which has been cited many times in this text. Sammy and Michael Anthony had moved on with a new group called Chickenfoot including guitarist Joe Satriani and Red Hot Chili Peppers drummer Chad Smith. The group was well-received, but sounded simply like substitute VH music. Sammy's book sold well and was in part spurred on by his revealing comments about Edward. Given some of those comments, writer Andy Greene of *Rolling Stone* suggested to Sammy that he had completely burned his bridge as far as ever working with Eddie again. "I don't consider [it] burning bridges at all," Sammy said. "When I first joined the band, dirt was going back and forth between us and the former lead singer. I didn't burn any bridges. They eventually put the bridge back. Time washes everything clean. To be honest, Valerie [Bertinelli] said almost all the same stuff in her book about Ed. The only thing I did was talk about my personal relationship with him."

TMZ caught Edward, Janie, and Alex leaving a restaurant on St. Patrick's Day. A paparazzi videographer asked Ed if he had a lucky charm of any kind. He was holding Janie's hand and raised it up and said, "Right here!" Edward was in the zone, but he had taken a long, hard road to get there.

Tiger Parenting

Many social trends were highlighted in the early twenty-first century including bullying and gay intolerance. One trend that was covered was called "tiger parenting" that specifically referred to some Asian mothers as "tiger moms." Lac Su, a psychologist and author of I Love Yous are for White People, wrote an article about tiger parents for CNN in early 2011. While it is clear that Edward loved his mother, he did make several statements at various times that questioned her harsh parenting skills. Ed recalled that she told him he would be a "nothing nut, just like your father." Edward said flat-out that that was damaging to his self-esteem. Eugenia was also the one to bash Alex's hands with a wooden spoon, lock Eddie guitar in a closet, and never even really accepted Ed and Al's success as musicians—the exact thing she did not want them to be. Su wrote that "abusive parenting is motivated by [the mother's] unhappiness." Tiger moms are so consumed with the achievement goals they set for their children that they often belittle them in the process. Lac Su wrote something that mirrored Edward's experiences in a way: "Now in my mid-thirties, I'm sure I appear successful and happy on the surface. I'm a published author, a successful executive, and I have a Ph.D. in psychology. In spite of this, my parents' approach failed. I'm torn to pieces on the inside. I've been through countless hours of psychotherapy, and my lack of self-worth beckons me to rely on alcohol to numb the pain."

Onward and Upward

By mid-2011, Edward had not touched alcohol for three years—his longest stretch since he was twelve years old. Wolfgang was now a ripe twenty years old, no longer a child. In May, Slash told U.K.'s Rock Radio, "I'm a *huge* Van Halen fan. They're finishing [up their new album right now], actually. I don't wanna speak on their behalf, but one of the guys that works for us works for Van Halen in the studio and he told me that they're in the mixing stages." In June, Alterbridge guitarist Mark Tremonti said, "Recently, I was in Los Angeles and Wolfgang invited me to his Dad's house and I got to go to 5150 studios and watch Eddie and Alex and Wolfgang play their new record from front to back. So I was one of the only people who have heard the new Van Halen. It was incredible."

On July 11, 2011, David Lee Roth changed his website to read only the following two words: "Get ready." The world was ready and waited patiently for the return of the world's greatest rock band led by the world's greatest living rock guitarist, Edward Van Halen.

AFTERWORD

The life and times of Edward Van Halen are an incredibly important part of American cultural history. His personality and character traits are complex. He can at times be stubborn and rude, but for the most part—as many have described—he has a huge heart and is a very loving, kind, brilliant, creative, and also quite a funny human being. There were times when I was reading or listening to an interview that Edward made me laugh out loud when I was completely alone. Any time he says "*Yee-haw!*" is absolutely hysterical.

My hope was to capture the essence of the man's entire life, from his childhood up through the current day. As a voracious consumer of rock biographies, I incorporated elements of what I think makes for the best possible rock biography. One of those elements was to include a great deal of verbiage that came directly from Edward's mouth. I spent countless hours transcribing interviews in order to bring the reader his exact words. We are fortunate to live in an era when access to media of all types is virtually at your fingertips. By including important, extended interviews and/or diatribes, there leaves no doubt what the man was saying, or trying to say, or what he was saying without saying it. As such, I included commentary throughout many of the extended quotations to clarify and guide the reader through the story. Unfortunately, I was not granted permission to reprint a few of the better interviews. In those instances, I was forced to paraphrase.

This work is the result of a full year's worth of research aided greatly by 21st century technology. I was not able to interview Edward Van Halen: that should be clear. I did come into contact with a handful of people that provided critical information. I estimate that I pulled from easily a thousand sources. The invaluable advent of YouTube accounted for a great deal of those. Yet I also have stacks of *Hit Parader* and *Circus* magazines from the 80s. The trick was to weave it all together into one cohesive tale.

A good deal of Edward's story is sad and unfortunate, and even at times flat out disturbing. A friend of mine is apt to say, "Geniuses don't play well with others." I agree completely. Charles Cross referred to "the role of madness in artistry" when breaking down Kurt Cobain. This notion is applicable to innumerable artists throughout history: Mozart, Van Gogh, Dali, Elvis Presley, and perhaps, to an arguably lesser extent, Edward Van Halen. "Madness" itself, however, is a vague term. It is ultimately up to an individual to assess its impact on any subject. If "madness" led to the creation of a completely new type of guitar and the introduction to "Mean Streets," I wish madness for us all. If it led to *Van Halen III* and the 2004 tour, that is another story.

However, the balance inevitably falls on the side of the fabulous and wonderful things Eddie Van Halen has brought to the lives of his family, friends, fans, admirers, and the history of music on this planet. His life has come full circle. My sincerest hope is that Edward will live a long, long life and continue to make music into his old age with Dave, his brother Alex, and his son Wolfgang. And of course, we all look to Wolfgang to keep the Van Halen legacy going for at least another eighty years or so.

My own VH necklace from the *1984* concert in Houston. Photograph © Kevin Dodds

ABOUT THE AUTHOR

I worshipped Eddie Van Halen. Worshipped him. And I still admire the hell out of him. When people that know me well think of me, the words "Van Halen" will shortly follow somewhere in there. I can honestly say that I have probably listened to each of the songs on the first six albums thousands and thousands of times. Occasionally, someone will ask me why I never get tired of it. I can't answer that query in less than at least four hours. I have *Van Halen II* in my car as I type. I had my first copy of that album at age 11, and I'm still listening to it today, and I will listen to it when I'm 90.

I grew up where Edward grew up—in the suburbs of the United States of America. It was within those suburbs that rock music truly lived and breathed in the 1970s and 1980s. My father was a guitar player, but stuck to mostly fundamental chords and very simple riffs. But with his help, he launched me onto a path that would sometimes cause him consternation.

By the age of eleven, after having watched Edward's performance at the 1983 US Festival repeatedly, I knew what I wanted to do. I wanted to be a rock guitarist, period. After the *1984* concert, my best friend and I embarked on a band project that continues to this day. Our early performances and success in high school only strengthened my resolve to be a professional musician. But my father would not have it and insisted I take the safe route and go to college. I figured I would just do both—go to college and try to make it music, which I did indeed attempt to do.

Unfortunately, the timing of our band's ultimate rise coincided closely with my college graduation, and instead of diving headlong into the band life and travelling further to play, I was told in no uncertain terms that I was to get a job using the college degree that had just been paid for. So, I did, and the band was forced to remain relatively confined to Austin and the surrounding Texas area, although we did indeed get opportunities to play all over the United States, including Los Angeles—where we had a hilarious chance encounter with none other than Eric Clapton in a Venice driveway. Having always taken care of every single thing ourselves, our only two forays into "professional" management were for the most part eye-opening, disturbing, and expensive. At the same time, my best friend Michael had two children back-to-back. Shortly thereafter, Mike's wife was diagnosed with an illness that made it absolutely impossible for her to care for the children while we played out of town, or even in-town, for that matter. After well over a decade of full-on dedication, we went into semi-retirement in 2002. However, we still play together a few times per year to this day.

Because of my communications degree, I ended up in publishing. I have been a layout designer, desktop publisher, writer, editorial production manager, managing editor, and ultimately a publishing project manager. It is because of this experience that I had little reservation about my ability to write a complete book. The honest truth is that this happened only because I was simply looking for a definitive biography on Eddie Van Halen and was shocked that one did not exist. The encouragement I was given by author Charles R. Cross (*Heavier than Heaven* [Kurt Cobain] and *Room Full of Mirrors* [Jimi Hendrix]) might seem relatively minor to him, but was of incredible value to me. World renowned rock guitar journalist Jas Obrecht—who conducted the very first interviews with Edward himself—cannot be thanked enough. His correspondence and approval of portions of the text, as well as his open allowance of me to repurpose his material was invaluable. Also, the encouragement of my friends and cohorts to dive in and do it myself was priceless. My appreciation of their encouragement cannot be understated.

These days, I am a project manager at a large publishing firm in Austin, Texas and a freelance writer. I still play in a few different bands. I am free from the chains of alcoholism. I am a happily married man with two young sons, aged eight and three. My eight-year-old has already performed publicly several times and it is clear that he has the guitar-playing genes. He even knows the main riffs of "Runnin' with the Devil" and "Unchained." My three-year-old appears poised to follow in his brother's footsteps and is always plinking on a guitar or bashing away on a kid-sized drum kit. My three-year-old even tells me, "Get your guitar, Daddy" as he picks up the drum sticks. They're going to have to go to college, too, though.

If you the reader find any mistakes of any kind, please e-mail them to me and corrections will be made prior to the second edition of the text. Send e-mail to Kevin Dodds at kbd372@hotmail.com.

APPENDICES

1. My Toto Story
2. My *1984* Concert Story
3. My Guitar Teacher Story
4. My 1986 Performance Stories
5. My Unabridged 1986 Texxas Jam Story
6. My Unabridged Monsters of Rock Tour Story
7. My Unabridged 2004 Tour Story
8. My Unabridged 2008 Tour Story
9. A Little Bit About My Brother

1. My Toto Story

In 1979, I theoretically came within one degree of separation from Edward when I was only six (just a few weeks before I turned seven). My father's best friend and business associate at the time was a childhood friend of Bobby Kimball, the lead singer of the band Toto. When Toto came to Houston in March of 1979, their hit "Hold the Line" was absolutely peaking. My mom, dad, brother, and I all got to go backstage after the concert.

It turned out the show was actually on Bobby's birthday. We got backstage just in time to see their organization present a birthday cake to him. I had a beater camera that my mom had given me and actually took pictures of both Bobby and a picture simply of his birthday cake. I was wide-eyed and in complete awe.

Also backstage was obviously guitarist Steve Lukather, who would become one of Edward's very closest friends. While I don't recall meeting Steve, I do recall that we were introduced to the whole band (which included Jeff and Steve Porcaro). Everything backstage was extremely kid-friendly. It was the first experience I ever had that pointed me down a musical path. After that concert, I remember asking my parents if it was okay if when I grew up, I played in a band that played all Toto songs.

I still haven't founded that Toto tribute band, but I still have that backstage pass and the picture of Bobby's birthday cake to this day.

2. My *1984* Concert Story

I was twelve years old and Van Halen ruled my world. I let the sports craze of my youth fade away as my love for guitar grew rapidly, especially in 1984. Down came the Roger Staubach posters and up went all of the classic original Van Halen posters of the early 80s, including the classic poster of Ed in his red, white, and black striped overalls wielding the Frankenstein. I was already two years into playing guitar, something I picked up from my father. And the moment at which our interests came together was when my brother Brandon brought home the 45 for "(Oh) Pretty Woman" and both of my parents stood in Brandon's room while we listened to it. My dad liked it and said, "Hell, that's my music!" It was immediately after that that my father taught me my first guitar riff on his guitar. The next day, my parents bought both my brother and I our first guitars in the spring of 1982. A few years later, in the summer of 1984, my then 16-year-old brother took his guitar apart and made it into an almost exact Frankenstein replica.

When the word came down that tickets for the *1984* show were going on sale in Houston, Brandon, who was fifteen at the time, me, and a few of his friends went and camped out all night for tickets (this was the *olden days*). The shows sold out immediately. We ended up getting our tickets in two batches of four each; four were very close to the left side of the stage and the other four were in the upper promenade of the Summit. My best friend Mike and I were relegated to sit with my older sister and her husband way up in the upper prom, with my brother and his friends commanding the close seats. I was none too pleased with that arrangement.

Before school let out that year, my brother and one of his ticket-holding friends had a go at it in the school hallway over one thing or another. Things were so tense that on the day of the concert, my brother sacrificed his two personal tickets and traded them to me and Mike so that he didn't have to deal with sitting next to a guy he had just had a fight with. Mike and I were ecstatic—actually, it was more than that, we were in disbelief. For about four months, we had prepared ourselves to watch from a mile away and now we would be as close to the stage as almost anyone else in the arena.

My sister ushered us to our seats and told us not to move under any circumstances and that she would come down and check on us periodically. Before we went to our seats though, we bought concert shirts and VH necklaces (I still have both the shirt and the necklace to this day).

When Mike and I sat down in our seats—a mere 40-50 feet from stage right (Michael Anthony's side)—we were simply in shock. We knew where we were. We knew what was about to happen. We knew that all of these people were here for the same thing. We lucked out and witnessed the opening night in Houston of a three-night stand (the tour closed out with another three-night stand in Dallas). The wait for the band to come on was excruciating and seemed to take forever and ever.

Then the lights went down. Our eyes were as wide as our lids allowed. There they were on stage right in front of us. Even though it was nearly thirty years ago and I was only 12 years old, I still remember the evening as if it were yesterday. The most important thing that will never, ever leave me was the audience response. After the opening "Unchained" was over, the crowd gave a literally unending ovation. They did not start the second song—they just stood there and let the crowd yell. Then Dave summoned the other three to the front of the stage and they simply bowed in unison. This was after the first song! Again, the crowd roar never abated—it did not decay in any way. It was constant; a perpetual noise. We were certainly the two loudest 12-year-olds in the arena!

3. My Guitar Teacher Story

I heard the news about Sammy from my new guitar teacher, Andy—a high school senior surfer dude with long shaggy blond hair and the most incredible white vintage Fender Stratocaster one could possibly imagine. I had taken "straight" lessons—a la the Mel Bay style—for two solid years from a well-meaning but otherwise boring instructor, Bruce. It got to where instead of mastering "When the Saints Go Marching In," I wanted to know how to play specific rock songs, including a lot of Van Halen (I was ambitious). Bruce consistently refused to take that route with me, and one of the last events was the introduction of a basics of classical guitar book; I clearly could have benefitted, but I was thirteen and had acquired a cheap but playable Eddie copycat guitar—and it was 1985. So I switched to Andy.

By this time, I had learned some of the basic chord progressions for some of the simpler songs like "Runnin' with the Devil," "Ain't Talkin' 'Bout Love," "Dance the Night Away," and "Panama." But "Unchained" eluded me. During my first lesson with Andy, he said, "So what would you like to learn, Kevin?" I said, "I want to learn to play 'Unchained' like on the album." He hesitated, as an instructor, and said, "Don't you think it's more important to learn the theory, the scales, and all that, before just learning a song without understanding what exactly it is you're playing?" I explained rather clearly and somewhat aggressively that I had been taking basic lessons for two years straight, and what I wanted to know from him was simple: "Why doesn't it sound right when I play 'Unchained?' What am I doing wrong? I want *you* to tell *me* what the problem is. That's what I want to learn here, right now."

Andy was taken a little aback, but acquiesced and began writing out the chords on a sheet of lesson paper. He also mentioned, "Eddie tunes down to D for this song, and a lot of songs on *Fair Warning*." I said, "What the hell is 'tune down to D'?" Andy laughed and explained that the low E string is tuned down to D, a full step lower, which gives it a much heavier sound. I tuned down to D and played it and said, "It still doesn't sound right." Then Andy said, "Oh, well, he tunes a half-step down to begin with, so it's actually in C#." He told me to tune my guitar with the song, so I did and had an epiphany. One of the many reasons that you can't just pick up a guitar and sound like Ed is because of his tunings—they vary in pitch from song to song—from a quarter-step down from E to straight E flat and even a quarter-step below E flat, and then occasionally tuning the low E down a full step to D on top of all of that. That was why it was so damned hard to sound and play like him. But I felt like it was really the first time I had figured out one of his tricks. I would dedicate countless hours—hours upon hours and years upon years—trying to figure out his tricks.

One day I came into the guitar shop for a lesson during the early fall of 1985—a full year after the *1984* concert had changed my life—Andy said, "Man, did you hear that Sammy Hagar's in Van Halen now?" I couldn't believe it at first, but after just a few seconds, completely under the Van Halen spell, I said, "Wow! That's a trip! That's cool!" I was focused on Edward at the time, not Dave. I wasn't taking guitar lessons to be like Dave. Andy retorted, "Aw, man, I can't stand Sammy Hagar." I honestly recall recoiling in slight horror at the suggestion that Edward would possibly make a bad decision by getting Sammy into the band. I guess I wasn't too surprised by the ugly press that followed. In fact, I ate it up, and at the time, I took Eddie's side. He was my idol.

On top of that, my older brother Brandon was a huge Sammy Hagar fan in addition to our mutual idolization of Edward. Brandon lived the Sammy dream, driving a Camaro with T-tops down to Galveston beach with *Van Halen II* or *VOA* in the tape deck every weekend—and sometimes during the school week depending on what side of the bed he woke up on.

4. My 1986 Performance Stories

By the end of my 8th grade year in the spring of 1986, my friend Mike and I had formed a full band with a bass player and a drummer, with Mike dropping guitar duties and taking on lead vocals, something not many 8th graders had the balls to do. My playing had improved greatly, but I was still a few months from turning the corner. Nevertheless, our band played in the cafeteria on the last day of school. Primitive versions of "Runnin' with the Devil," "Ain't Talkin' 'Bout Love," and "You Really Got Me" absolutely floored our fellow students.

I was bringing the Van Halen love to the people at the intermediate school level. By fall of 1986, we had entered high school and we were the only freshmen at all in the school talent show. My playing improved by leaps over the summer and we debated long and hard about which song we were going to play. We almost played "Best of Both Worlds" but went with "Good Enough." It was videotaped—we were not absolutely terrible for 14-year-olds.

5. My Unabridged 1986 Texxas Jam Story

The tour continued through the summer and this author had one hell of a life experience the weekend of July 19, 1986. Me, two of my best friends, Dave and Chris, my brother Brandon, and his friend Gary all went to Dallas for the annual Texxas Jam. These festival shows at the Cotton Bowl were absolutely legendary. Van Halen had played several, including one on their first tour, and Sammy had the distinction of being the artist to play the festival the most times. The bill was Keel, BTO, Krokus, Loverboy, Dio, and Van Halen.

At 14-years-old, looking back, we were probably too young to be at a festival like that. My brother and his buddy were full-blown 17-year-olds ready to do some damage, but me, Dave, and Chris were bug-eyed at what we saw and experienced. One of the first was seeing someone take their binoculars and magically unscrew one of the eye-pieces and chug whiskey out of it. That was my official introduction to binocular flasks. We saw fistfights. We were sardined in the hallways just trying to get a Coke or get to the bathroom. I'll never forget Gary's yellow "banana joints"—all supposedly rolled using banana rolling papers.

But that was nothing compared the *Up in Smoke*-sized joint the group in front of us was passing around. Literally the diameter of a tennis ball, although no more than two inches long, that thing made its way around the entire section. One single puff and you'd hit a cherry the size of thirty joints at once, and coughing fits ensued. No offense to Krokus or Loverboy, but I was literally so high that I partially fell asleep during their sets. Eventually, of course, we all came back around to a happy summer haze by the time Dio came on and we ditched our seats and jumped down to the "floor"—the football field at the Cotton Bowl. We were only about thirty yards from the stage when Dio ended, so we figured we were in great shape for Van Halen's set.

We weren't. During the wait for VH to take the stage, the crowd surge was beyond what three 14-year-olds between eighth and ninth grade could handle, so we bailed back to the side sections near the stage, leaving Brandon and Gary, plenty capable of taking care of themselves. Dave, Chris, and I all ended up with great seats right at the bottom of the nearest seated section on Ed's side of the stage. We had an incredible view when the band took the stage.

The band was honestly on fire and had the crowd of well over 70,000 in the palms of their hands. It was easy to tell that it wasn't just an ordinary night for the band. Ten, fifteen, twenty-thousand people adoring you—that's amazing. But tens and tens of thousands of lighters going at the same time is a whole other thing. The electricity was incredible. I was transfixed by Ed's solo. I will never forget that he played Beethoven's "Fur Elise" with both hands on the fret board. By the end of the show, my 14-year-old body was convinced I'd seen something that rivaled the *1984* show. But each show had such a different feel, it was apples and oranges.

6. My Unabridged Monsters of Rock Tour Story

The show came to Houston on July 2, 1988, and, of course, my brother and all of our friends were there. It was a scorching hot Texas afternoon, and Rice Stadium was filled to the upper decks. To appease Texans, the show was co-billed as an unofficial Texxas Jam (the very last Texxas Jam was held the following year—after that, it was gone forever). We got there fairly early and the entire stadium was general admission so we moved around all day.

When Metallica took the stage, the air changed. Smiles turned to slacked-jaws the minute they started. James Hetfield, Kirk Hammet, and Lars Ulrich had the audience at their command, and newcomer Jason Newsted spent half of the set flipping off the crowd (likely in response to hecklers on behalf of deceased bassist Cliff Burton). We moved to the floor for a great deal of their set and were absolutely floored and excited. Metallica's popularity subsequently went through the roof.

Dokken had the grave misfortune of following Metallica, and worse yet, they were plagued by P.A. problems, and they didn't handle it well at all. Dokken had gotten their show started when the entire P.A. completely cut out and you could actually hear the drums acoustically from the stage. The sound continued to go in and out. Singer Don Dokken threw his microphone stand to the stage in disgust, with guitarist George Lynch following suit by hurling his guitar angrily across the stage. We were joking that Metallica had blown the sound system out with their set. Upon Dokken leaving the stage, I decided then and there that it was the single worst performance of any live band I had ever seen in my life (it remains true to this day).

While anything following Dokken would have gone over well, The Scorpions really brought a great show. The sun had set and the air had cooled. The Scorps played hit after hit and their Spinal Tap-like choreography was just flat out fun—almost Broadway or Vegas-style but without a hint of pretention. I suppose I felt a certain excitement during their set because of the 2,000 times I had watched The US Festival video from 1983 when The Scorpions immediately opened for Van Halen.

After The Scorpions, and now being a sixteen-year-old, my testosterone-fueled buddies and I were tall enough and strong enough to brave the stadium floor and nothing was going to stop me from getting as close I possibly could to the stage on Ed's side. We pushed, shoved, and cursed our way to within twenty to thirty yards of the stage directly in front of Eddie. Any further and we'd have been crushed.

The band came out slamming and played a great set—no P.A. problems. However, I will never, ever forget the look on Eddie's face when one of his sequencers nearly failed. It was a first for Van Halen to play to recorded tracks—Edward had partly abandoned playing keyboards onstage live and nearly all of the keyboard and synthesizer lines were sequenced in. During one song, the sequencer cut out for at least five full seconds. Because of the fact that I watched Edward the whole time, I saw his face the moment it cut—he went from a smile to sheer horror in microseconds. Since Al was wearing headphones to play along with the track, Ed turned to him to give him that "What the hell do we do?!" look, and right about the same moment, the sequencer kicked back in in perfect time, as in it was only briefly muted and didn't skip or start over. The band continued on and Ed looked back toward the audience after shaking his head in disbelief and giving the "Whew!" expression. Technology has its drawbacks.

7. My Unabridged 2004 Tour Story

As soon as tickets went on sale, my friends and I jumped on them for the show in San Antonio on September 28. While 2004 was ultimately not a good year for Edward, it was surely not a good year for me either. That spring, after thirteen years together (nine married), my marriage ended just after our son had turned one. To her credit, I changed after my brother died. I became a different person—some things for the better, some things probably for the worse. Honestly, I was not the person she married. It was painful because our young son was in the middle. As a result, my already questionable level of drinking increased significantly.

The drive down to the show from Austin was drenched with beer drinking. Most of us, especially me, were already fairly lit by the time we arrived. We then proceeded to buy as many $8 beers as we had cash for. Nevertheless, I remember the evening and the concert very clearly—probably solely attributable to adrenaline. When they hit the stage, the crowd went absolutely nuts (although the venue was not quite sold out). I was not a critical audience member, I was simply there to have fun. I called a friend who had moved out to San Francisco from my cell phone so he could hear some of the show. I also called my answering machine at home and tried to capture Eddie's solo (it sounded like fax noise when I checked it later).

It was during Ed's solo that I did notice something. He approached the center stage microphone, which was something I had never seen him do. He said, "I'm just fuckin' around, I hope you guys don't mind." The crowd cheered. Then he followed that up with, "I normally play the same thing, but I just feel like fuckin' around tonight. Alright?" I noticed then that his speech was slurred. It occurred to me that he was probably drunk, but what the hell did I care? I was just as drunk as he was.

For the end of the show, my good friend Brando and I pulled the old move and walked around the venue hall until we came to the lower stage section on Eddie's side. Through a combination of lax security and early departures, we ended up as close as you could possibly get to Ed's corner of the stage—the left-front corner of the stage was about five feet from us. As they ended the show, Brando and I were just baffled by how close we were to Eddie and how easy it was for us to pull the sneak. After the last song, Ed led the crowd to thunderous applause. From the stage, he yelled, "1-2-3!" several times and gestured for applause. I will never forget that we were so close that we could actually hear Ed's voice from the stage, no microphone. All in all, we had a blast.

On the drive back to Austin, someone said, "I think Eddie was wasted." The thought got passed around the car, and I pointed out that his speaking and behavior during his solo was a little odd. As we drove further down the road, someone else offered up, "Did you notice Sammy stayed on Mike's side of the stage the whole night?" I remember adding, "Did you notice that Sammy barely even moved during the whole show?" It didn't take long for the adrenaline to wear off, and we all assessed that what we saw was indeed fun, but it was far from the real Van Halen.

At the time, I had so much going on personally that I didn't pay much attention to the press surrounding the tour. I had not read any online reviews so I went into the concert absolutely tabula rasa. I just wanted to let loose and have a blast. If I had known what had been going on, I might have paid more attention. But all I really wanted to see was Edward and I most certainly accomplished that. I was so psyched that I just did not notice his hair or teeth or his skin. One friend that saw the show in August in Salt Lake City had close seats. He told me that Eddie's skin looked "green." I just didn't notice. The next day, he met Darrell "Dimebag" Abbot for the first time.

8. My Unabridged 2008 Tour Story

San Antonio and Dallas were the second and third shows of the third leg of the 2007-2008 tour. It was something I had been looking forward to since I was twelve in 1984. Almost 24 years had passed—twice as many years as I was old at the time. Because of the fact that there was no talk of recording an album, I was slightly wary that this might very well be the only time I would ever get to see this again in my life. I wanted to bring my decent quality but bulky digital camcorder to document it just for me personally, but I figured that security would be over-the-top, so I brought just crappy, older digital camera on which I was able to capture about ten minutes of lousy video. But it wasn't about the video or the quality of the video as much as it was simply documenting what was happening. I deemed it an historic event. It needed to be documented. The security in San Antonio was so lax I could have walked in there with a film camera on a tripod. I cursed myself for not bringing my digital camcorder, which at the time could have captured an hour on one tape.

The little that I did document in San Antonio on January 24 was absolutely fantastic. One thing that was very obvious, however, was that Edward had either a bandage or a wrap of some kind around his left hand. It did not seem to affect his playing at all, but everyone noticed and wondered what it was.

I have to admit that I was so thrilled and astounded that my reaction during the show in San Antonio was more that of numbness than "Woo! Yeah!" I was simply thinking, "Holy shit, is this real?" I let the whole event just kind of run through me, just soaking it in. I was extremely sedate during the show with a case of a blown mind. I also knew that just two days later, we would be seeing them again in Dallas at Reunion Arena. That concert would be sold out, and the band would even come back to Dallas later in 2008 for a second show at the same enormous venue.

For the Dallas show, I figured that there was at least a lingering possibility that this show could be the last I'd ever see with Dave and Edward on the same stage together—I was just fearful, even though I was eternally positive for Edward's future and the future of the band, which seemed to be going completely in the right direction after so many years of drifting. I figured that if the security was lax in San Antonio, then it would be lax in Dallas, so I decided to bring my digital camcorder with me to capture some songs in the best quality I possibly could for posterity. My best friend Michael, with whom I had seen Van Halen with in 1984, couldn't make it to the San Antonio show, but he did make it for the Dallas show. Again, we had been waiting 24 years to see this. In fact, we really went out of our way to mark the occasion.

A club in Austin called Beerland was hosting a Van Halen hoot night and we jumped at the chance. Our lineup was a little bit from all of the different bands that we have played with and included me, Michael, bass player Doug, and drummer Brando. We billed ourselves as The Brown M&Ms and played "Mean Streets," "Little Guitars," "Somebody Get Me a Doctor," and "So this is Love." We did our absolute best to be as faithful to the originals as possible. Video exists. It's not exactly terrible.

It was winter in Dallas on January 26, 2008—Edward's 53rd birthday. It was another reason I knew I had to capture some video. I was sure they were going to do something special for Ed's birthday and there was no way I was going to miss it. The walk from the parking lot to the venue was fairly short, and I was bringing up the rear. Brando was up in front of me and turned back to me and said nervously, "Hey man, they got metal detectors, dude." So, there I was, camcorder in hand. I thought about it and decided that it meant so much to me that I was going to attempt to bluff my way past security. The other guys went ahead of me and stared back like deer caught in headlights. I had put the camera in the back of my pants under my jacket. I set off the alarm. The security lady wanded me and my belt buckle beeped. She said, "You've got something right there." I pulled my pockets inside out, which were empty, and she said, "Okay, go on through." I just had my ticket scanned and walked on into the venue. I'll never forget Michael's immediate reaction was, "I loved your whole 'What?' thing about it. That was classic."

Michael and I sat next to each other in pretty much the nosebleeds of Reunion Arena. I brought with me our original 1984 tour ticket stub and we laughed about it before the show started. The lights went down, up came the rumbling thunder of music from the stage, and into "You Really Got Me" they flew. I had that shot-out-of-a-cannon feeling again. It was fantastic. Song after song was masterful. Ed's hand was still bandaged, but none of us could figure it out—if it was a wrap or a wound cover. Again, it made absolutely no difference in his playing at all, so that made it even more perplexing, because Edward Van Halen was on fire on the evening of his 53rd birthday in Dallas, Texas.

"Romeo Delight" was one I knew I had to capture in my one-hour limit of tape because it had been so great in San Antonio and always one of my favorites. I had my camera rolling before the song started. This was the tune that Dave had something in mind to acknowledge Eddie's birthday. Nevertheless, Wolfgang jumped up to the microphone and said, "Let's sing Eddie 'Happy Birthday!'" The crowd cheered briefly and Dave turned to Wolfgang and said, "Shut your fuckin' mouth, Wolfie. Play the song, Eddie!" Edward started "Romeo Delight" and played one single time through the riff and stopped as if he wasn't sure what exactly had just transpired. He actually paused for nearly ten full seconds before Dave said, "Play the song on the guitar!" and Edward went directly back into "Romeo Delight," restarting it from the beginning. They launched into a rendition of the highest order of badass, it was straight out over the top. Ed and Wolf's background vocals were ridiculously spot on. Edward's guitar solo was absolutely off the charts, completely and totally.

The breakdown was astounding with Wolfgang taking some of the tapping parts on the bass in mini-solo of his own.

As the breakdown reached its lowest ebb, Dave started into "Happy Birthday," prompting the entire crowd to sing along. "Happy birthday, dear Eddie," Dave sang, "Happy birthday to you!" Ed stood there smiling, just soaking it in. Afterward, Ed and Dave embraced, with Edward giving Dave his trademark kiss on the cheek. Wolfgang stood close by clapping. Edward got on the microphone and said, "You get to make a wish, right? I want you all to have a great motherfuckin' time tonight!" With that they launched back into "Romeo Delight." Just before the "Feel my heartbeat" refrain, Dave said, "You see, Wolf, I just couldn't sing 'Happy Birthday' in the other goddamned key!" Wolfgang walked over and laughed. No harm done.

They segued into a jam of "Magic Bus." You will rarely find a single performance of "Romeo Delight" better than what happened in Dallas on January 26, 2008. It was an eight-minute exercise in rock music entertainment excellence. It was as transcendent as a rock performance could possibly be. I saw it and I documented it. It was *crazy* good. The whole train though was also less than a month from derailment.

9. A Little Bit About My Brother

My brother was three years older than me. He was the classic, stereotypical older brother in every sense of the word. He was the extreme protector and the extreme torturer. There were two things that complicated our relationship growing up.

Brandon was not a great student in grade school. He seemed to always struggle with his grades, but it was always obvious he was not a dumb kid at all. On the other hand, good grades came natural to me. I don't recall having to put in a huge amount of effort or that I was somehow superior. I just got good grades and did all the way through high school and college. This was always a point of contention between my brother and I, and he would often use his larger physique to settle whatever score there was to settle whatever day he chose to settle it.

We had a family van. It was loosely passed down to my brother, but I was also learning how to drive by backing it up and down the driveway. One day, I hit the garage and dented the van. Brandon came out and flipped out on me, cursing me for being, specifically, "stupid." My retort was cruel and referred specifically to our grades and Brandon physically attacked me on the driveway, grabbing me by the neck. But then he stood up and walked inside and didn't say anything.

Later that night, my dad called me into his room and told me that Brandon told him what had transpired. Dad then taught me the lesson that there are some things you just don't say to another person when you're mad or at all, and that that was one of them. I felt terrible.

The other point of contention between my brother and I was playing guitar. We both got our first guitars on the exact same day from the exact same pawn shop. Brandon was thirteen, so he got a cheap electric and an amp and I got a $20 acoustic guitar because I was ten. Right away, I knew I had a natural proclivity, and after several years, it was obvious that Brandon did not. Bless his heart, he just didn't have the natural talent required to be a decent guitar player. By the time I got to playing Van Halen songs note-for-note, it was driving him nuts. He refused at first to acknowledge my band's accomplishments, but by the end of high school, he did come to our talent shows. As our band in Austin in the 90s was doing well, he was able to be around a few times to catch a few of those shows, and he always told me how proud he was of me.

One point of contention my brother and I did *not* have was Van Halen, and, specifically, Edward Van Halen. While my brother continued to love all eras of VH, I steadfastly remained loyal to the Dave era and it certainly caused its share of arguments between us.

When we first ever discovered Van Halen, it was really my brother that was bringing it into the house and essentially broadcasting it from his room. I will never forget those days when I was only nine or ten and I was rocking out with my brother to *Diver Down*. I cannot even begin to recall how many hours we spent listening to records and looking at pictures and just talking about how cool Eddie was. It was our thing.

As we got older and were in our twenties, my brother and I completely settled our differences. I made a rule that he could no longer refer to me as his "little brother" but simply as his "brother," period. I was so proud of him for overcoming his scholastic career and kicking ass in flight school and becoming a commercial pilot. He was proud of me and my band and the fact that I had graduated college. We spoke often even when we were over a thousand miles apart.

My brother and his wife Susan had been living in Los Angeles for several years, and Brandon worked at the Van Nuys Airport. He used to call me weekly with his latest "celebrity" report—the Van Nuys Airport is a celebrity ant trail. Brandon actually ended up befriending Phil Hartman (the voice of Waldo in the "Hot for Teacher" video). Brandon even got to fly Phil's plane to Catalina with Phil in the passenger seat. Brandon also went to his home and met his wife and his children. They were friends. When Phil was murdered by his wife in the summer of 1998, I was the first person that broke the news to my brother, and he broke down and wept on the phone.

By 1998, Susan had taken a job in Miami, so they hit the road again. Brandon struggled to find a job at first but got a call back from an airline that exclusively flies executives to the Bahamas from Fort Lauderdale. As part of his hiring process, Brandon was required to make three runs before he could be given the job. The first two runs were simply from Fort Lauderdale to the Bahamas and back. The airline does not fly at night and Brandon was slated to come back the next day to do his third run. But someone at the airline insisted that Brandon do his third run that evening, just a quick touch-and-go landing off of a small airstrip near Lake Okeechobee, and he could start work the next day. My brother was in the pilot seat with a supervisor in the passenger seat and the head of safety for the airline in the back of the plane when he took off for his third run on December 8.

The plane never returned. Susan called my mother and father to tell them he was missing and my father then called me at work. What followed was a bizarre haze of eight long, twisted days and nights in Florida looking for him and the plane. Eventually, the plane was found in Lake Okeechobee; after sunset, the lake sky becomes pure black with only a few lights on the horizon. The plane was essentially undamaged, indicating that they had hit the water at a level heading. When the plane was removed from the water, the altimeter read 1,500 feet. The plane hit the water so smoothly that the only cause of death for my brother was drowning—he had only hit the side of his head.

Van Halen lost one of its most hardcore fans of all time that day. My life was never the same. I could not even bring myself to play a show with my band until they convinced me it was the best medicine. I rejoined the band for a high-profile New Year's Eve show at the biggest club in Austin. It was tough for me. Brandon was the one that really brought Van Halen into our household, into our lives, and into our brains. We were better for it. He only lived thirty years—but he packed them full of adventure, including having put his arm around Eddie Van Halen.

REFERENCES

References include books (retrospectives, visual histories, autobiographies, biographies, collections of interviews, and general rock history); web resources; magazines (online and print); broadcast (TV and radio; material used only as permitted); press releases; and transcriptions of broadcast interviews (recorded in whole or in part and/or broadcast on TV, radio, or internet; this material used only as permitted).

Note: All of the Eddie Van Halen-Jas Obrecht quotes are from the *Jas Obrecht Music Archive* at www.jasobrecht.com. Used by permission. All *Dwyer & Michaels* interviews transcribed by Kevin Dodds and approved by Greg Dwyer. Used by permission.

Alphabetical by Author

Agostino, John D. "Pop Music Review : Van Halen's Altered State In San Diego." *Los Angeles Times*. May 4, 1992.

Aledort, Andy. "Get Up.'" *Guitar for the Practicing Musician*. September 1988, p. 67.

Aledort, Andy. "Transcription to 'Eruption.'" *Guitar for the Practicing Musician*. December 1987, p. 23.

Aledort, Andy. "Transcription to 'Ice Cream Man.'" *Guitar for the Practicing Musician*. November 1986, p. 67.

Andeman, Joan. "Van Halen returns to the party." *Boston Globe*. October 31, 2007.

Andrews, Rob. "Van Halen: The Rock Brigade." *Hit Parader*. September 1984, p. 16.

Arnold, Thomas K. "Hagar Lets Van Halen Floor Pedal to the Metal." *Los Angeles Times*. November 16, 1988.

Arthur, George. "Van Halen: No more disappointments with '1984.'" *Circus*. February 1984.

Atkinson, Terry. "Rough Sailin' For Van Halen." *Los Angeles Times*. April 6, 1986.

Baltin, Steve. "Eddie Van Halen Thanks God for Sobriety and Guitar Riffs." *Spinner.com*. June 11, 2009.

Bertinelli, Valerie. *Finding It*. New York, NY. Free Press, 2009.

Bertinelli, Valerie. *Losing It*. New York, NY. Free Press, 2008.

Boehm, Mike. "Van Halen All Smiles at Pacific." *Los Angeles Times*. September 12, 1991.

Bomb, Adam. "High School Musical '77." August 30, 2007. http://www.myspace.com/adambomb2012/blog/304696074.

Boss, Joseph. "Edward Van Halen: Player of the Decade.'" *Guitar World*. February 1990, p. 46.

Boucher, Geoff. "David and Eddie, together again." *Los Angeles Times*. January 26, 2007.

Boucher, Geoff. "Van Halen's road plans have taken a rocky turn." *Los Angeles Times*. February 23, 2007.

Boucher, Geoff. "Van Halen's back on tour — with the Hagar lineup." *Los Angeles Times*. June 07, 2004.

Brown, Glenn. "Van Halen: Biggest U.S. Band?" *Circus*. March 1983, p. 35.

Brown, James: e-mail to author. June 26, 2011.

Bully, Debbie. "Valerie Bertinelli." 1987. *Homonculus.com*. http://www.homunculus.com/articles/bertinellivalerie/bertinelliinterview87.html.

Burk, Greg. "A classic Van Halen eruption." *Los Angeles Times*. November 22, 2007.

Bustillo, Miguel. "Con Artist Uses Charm and Lies to Steal Car, Police Say: Crime: Man who claims to be an assistant to a rock star also disappoints a group of quadriplegic." *Los Angeles Times*. March 4, 1994.

Cherone, Gary. "Letter to Eddie Vedder by Gary Cherone." *Vox-nova.com*. http://vox-nova.com/2007/06/20/letter-to-eddie-vedder-by-gary-cherone/.

Chilvers, C.J. *The Van Halen Encyclopedia*. Oak Lawn, IL. Malpractice Publishing, 1999.

Christie, Ian. *Everybody Wants Some: The Van Halen Saga*. Hoboken, NJ: John Wiley & Sons, 2007.

Cioffi, Billy. "Edward Van Halen: King Tapper." *Guitar School*. April 1989, p. 18.

Clehane, Diane. "Valerie Bertinelli: Eddie Is Not in Rehab." *People*. March 12, 2008.

Cohen, Jonathan. "Van Halen Putting Tour On Hold For A Month." *Billboard.com*. March 10, 2008.

Cohen, Scott. "It's Only Roth and Roll." *SPIN*. April 1986.

Connelly, Chris. 1996 MTV Interview with Edward and Alex van Halen. *YouTube*. Poster: modernVintagefilms. http://www.youtube.com/watch?v=azJ4dOC5TwM&feature=related.

Corgan, Billy. "Best of Both Worlds." *Guitar World*. April 1996.

Crisafulli, Chuck. "Ain't Talkin 'Bout Love." *Los Angeles Times*. October 20, 1996.

Cromilen, Richard. "Van Halen Rocked by Social Conscience: Pop Music: Band noted for party image turns to defense of fans rights." *Los Angeles Times*. April 25, 1992.

Cross, Charles R. *Heavier Than Heaven*. New York, NY. Hyperion, 2001.

Crowe, Jerry. "Sammy Hagar Marches On With Life After Van Halen." *Los Angeles Times*. May 17, 1997.

Crowe. Jerry. "Van Halen Jumps Into Era III." *Los Angeles Times*. March 15, 1998.

Dansby, Andrew. "Eddie Van Halen Has Cancer: Guitarist vows to beat disease." *Rolling Stone*. April 30, 2001.

Dansby, Andrew. "Van Halen Says He's Cancer Free." **Rolling Stone.** May 9, 2002. dbeck03. "Eddie Van Halen gets sober." *HubPages*. http://hubpages.com/hub/Eddie-Van-Halen-gets-sober.

Del Barrio, Ron with Meisler, Andy. "18 With . . . Eddie Van Halen." *Maximum Golf*. August 2001. di Perna, Alan. "Crazy Eddie?" *Keyboard World*. July 1988, p. 26.

DiMartino, Dave. "David Lee Roth: Foul-Mouthed Reagan Shocks The World." *Creem*. June 1986.

Djansezian, Kevork. "Van Halen Postpones Shows, Eddie Undergoes Medical Tests." *Associated Press*. March 3, 2008.

Dodds, Kevin. Transcription. Van Halen press conference, August 13, 2011. Public domain.

Dodds, Kevin: Transcription. Dwyer and Michaels radio interview with Edward Van Halen, November 25, 2003. *Dwyer & Michaels.* Used by permission.

Dodds, Kevin: Transcription. Dwyer and Michaels radio interview with Edward Van Halen, January 9, 2004. *Dwyer & Michaels.* Used by permission.

Dodds, Kevin: Transcription. Dwyer and Michaels radio interview with Edward Van Halen, April 9, 2004. *Dwyer & Michaels.* Used by permission.

Dodds, Kevin: Transcription. Dwyer and Michaels radio interview with Edward Van Halen, May 11, 2005. *Dwyer & Michaels.* Used by permission.

Dodds, Kevin: Transcription. Dwyer and Michaels radio interview with Edward Van Halen, October 3, 2005. *Dwyer & Michaels.* Used by permission.

Dodds, Kevin: Transcription. Dwyer and Michaels radio interview with Edward Van Halen, April 7, 2006. *Dwyer & Michaels.* Used by permission.

Dr. Shoop, Stephen A., and John Morgan. "Eddie Van Halen gets hip—literally." *USA Today Health. December 1, 1999.*

Dwyer, Greg, e-mail messages to author: July 12, 2011; July 13, 2011; July 18, 2011; July 19, 2011.

Evans, Paul. "Balance." *Rolling Stone.* March 23, 1995.

Foyt, Caitlin M. "Van Andel Arena is named Van Halen Arena just for a day." *The Grand Rapids Press.* June 3, 2008.

Fricke David. "Van Halen Hot And Happy Without David Lee Roth." *Rolling Stone.* July 03, 1986.

Fricke, David. "After Sour Grapes of Roth, Van Halen Finally Finds Happiness." *Rolling Stone.* July 3, 1986.

Fricke, David. "Head for the bomb shelters! It's Van Halen." *Circus.* May 1980 (reprinted October 1982), p. 32.

Fricke, David. "Women and Children First." *Rolling Stone.* June 26, 1980.

Garbarini, Vic. "The Well Tempered Guitarist." *Guitar World.* October 1999.

Garbarini, Vic. "Three of a Perfect Pair." *Guitar World.* March 1998.

Gill, Chris. "Eddie Van Halen Interview: Of Wolf and Man." *Guitar World.* February 2009.

Gill, Chris. "Tony Iommi and Eddie Van Halen: Cast a Giant Shadow." *Guitar World.* March 3, 2010.

Gordon, Matthews. *Van Halen.* New York, NY. Ballantine Books, 1984.

Graff, Gary. "Q & A With Edward Van Halen." *SFGate.com.* March 22, 1998.

Greene, Andy. "A Mostly Reunited Van Halen Hit Madison Square Garden." *Rolling Stone.* November 14, 2007.

Greene, Andy. "Eddie Van Halen Goes Bananas on Howard Stern: The Full Highlights." *Rolling Stone.* September 14, 1996. http://www.rollingstone.com/music/blogs/staff-blog/eddie-van-halen-goes-bananas-on-howard-stern-the-full-highlights-20060914

Greenlee, Steve. "Report: Van Halen to record, tour with David Lee Roth." *Boston Globe.* August 9, 2010.

Guy, Paul. Untitled. *Fuzz Magazine.* 1998.

Hagar, Sammy. *Red: My Uncensored Life in Rock.* New York, NY. Harper Collins Publishers, 2011.

Hedges, Dan. *Eddie Van Halen.* New York, NY. Vintage/Musician: Vintage Books, a division of Random House, 1986.

Heller, Greg and Vaziri, Aidin; edit by Selvin, Joel. "Hagar's Life After Van Halen." *SFGate.com.* October 27, 1996

Henk Schulte Nordholt. "Indonesia and the Netherlands: Sharing histories?" February 4, 2009. This lecture is organised in collaboration with the Ethnographic Society Delft. www.verreculturendelft.nl

Henke, James. "Album takes Roth from crooner to Beach Boy." *Rolling Stone.* March 1, 1985.

Hiatt, Brian. "Secrets of the Guitar Heroes: Eddie Van Halen." *Rolling Stone.* June 12, 2008.

Hiatt, Brian. "The Official Word: Van Halen Tour Kaput." *Rolling Stone.* February 21, 2007.

Hiatt, Brian. "Van Halen to Rock On With Roth." *Rolling Stone.* July 23, 2009.

Hilburn, Robert. "Pop Music Reviews: Monsters of Rock Opens Monster Tour: Van Halen Headlines 9 1/2-Hour Concert Marathon in Washington." *Los Angeles Times.* June 13, 1988.

Hobson, Ion. "Van Halen: Anselmo Valencia Amphitheater, Thursday, Nov. 18, and Friday, Nov. 19." *Tuscon Weekly.* November 25, 2004.

Hochman Steve. "Someday They'll Be Together, or Will They?" *Los Angeles Times.* February 6, 2000.

Hochman, Steve. "Pop Music Review: Van Halen: The Eternal Dudes Rock On and On : 17 Years Later, Juvenile Love 'n' Lust Fantasies Still Become Treasure." *Los Angeles Times*. April 6, 1995.

Hochman, Steve. "Stunned Hagar Says Growing Tension Led to His Firing." *Los Angeles Times*. June 28, 1996.

Hochman, Steve. "You May Be A Winner." *Los Angeles Times*. October 13, 1996.

Hogan, Richard. "Van Halen sings the Memphis Blues." *Circus*. May 1984, p. 41.

Holmes, Tim. "Van Halen Proves Its Mettle." *Rolling Stone*. May 22, 1986.

Houweling, Peter. "Lost Boys Calling." http://utopia.ision.nl/users/ptr/pfloyd/news/vvv.html. October 30, 1999.

Huff, David. "Ain't Talkin 'Bout Love." *Guitar World*. April 1997.

Hunt, Dennis. "Pop Album Chart : Van Halen Begins at the Top." *Los Angeles Times*. February 4, 1995.

Hunt, Dennis. "Pop Album Chart : Van Halen Still Tops for Third Week." *Los Angeles Times*. July 12, 1991.

Hunt, Dennis. "POP LP CHART : Van Halen Reigns; Pop Vets Debut Strongly." *Los Angeles Times*. July 1, 1988.

Hunt, Dennis. "Van Halen Zooms to Top in Two Weeks." *Los Angeles Times*. June 17, 1988.

Hunt, Dennis. "Van Halen's Balance Slips Just a Tad." *Los Angeles Times*. February 11, 1995.

Stewart, Jon. *Jon Stewart Show*. Interview with Van Halen. February 1995. Personal archives.

Jurek, Thom. "Van Halen: Clarkston Michigan, Pine Knob Music Theater, June 26, 1993." *Rolling Stone*. August 19, 1993.

Keeps, David A. "This is What 50 Looks Like." *Good Housekeeping*. April 2010, p. 156.

Kellner, Jason. "Van Halen pulls off 1984 time warp." http://www.rgj.com. April 18, 2008.

Kemp, Mark. "Gods of Rock Deliver the Goods: Van Halen Kick Off Reunion Tour." *Rolling Stone*. Septemper 28, 2007.

Kreps, Daniel. "New Van Halen Album Just 'Rumors' Band Says." *Rolling Stone*. July 6, 2010.

Larsen, Dave. "Van Halen 'Gun Thing' Behind Him." *SFGate.com*. April 24, 1995.

Letterman, David. *Late Night with David Letterman* (NBC). June 27, 1985. Guests: Valerie Bertinelli, Eddie Van Halen. *YouTube*. Poster: hariseldon59. http://www.youtube.com/watch?v=hoNUOrGH-bI

Leonard, Elizabeth. "Valerie Bertinelli's Surprise Wedding!" *People*. January 17, 2011.

Lewis, Randy and Kaufman, Amy. "Van Halen sets reunion tour." *Los Angeles Times*. August 14, 2007.

Loder, Kurt. "Van Halen to Headline Monsters or Rock Tour." *Rolling Stone*. March 24, 1988.

Lou Chen, Viven. "Rocker Van Halen to Face Weapons Charge : Burbank: Guitarist says he forgot to leave loaded gun out of carry-on luggage at airport, authorities say." *Los Angeles Times*. April 11, 1995.

Lou Chen, Viven. "Van Halen Enters Plea On Handgun." *Los Angeles Times*. April 14, 1995.

Marshall, Wolf. "Transcription to 'Runnin' with the Devil.'" *Guitar for the Practicing Musician*. March 1982, p. 34.

Marshall, Wolf. "Van Halen.'" *Guitar for the Practicing Musician*. September 1988, p.118.

McClaine, Steve, e-mails with the author. May 2, 2011; May 3, 2011.

McDonald, Jeff. "Smeartactics: Punk Rock Guitar Legend Pat Smear Talks . . . Finally." *University of California, Santa Barbara*. http://www.uweb.ucsb.edu/~feiny34/nirvana/article08.html.

Meyer, Josh. "Trading Licks at the School of Rock : Musicians Institute is noisy and counts Prof. Van Halen among its visiting lecturers. School's mission is to help students make careers in music." *Los Angeles Times*. June 7, 1990.

Milward, John. "For Unlawful Carnal Knowledge Review." *Rolling Stone*. August 22, 1991. http://www.rollingstone.com/music/albumreviews/for-unlawful-carnal-knowledge-19910822.

Morse, Steve. "A close shave for Van Halen." *The Boston Globe*. August 8, 1995.

Mueller, Don. "Van Halen: Caught in the Act." *Hit Parader*. November 1984, p. 66.

Multiple authors: *Guitar World Presents Guitar Legends: Eddie The Complete Van Halen*. New York, NY. A Harris Publication, Vol. 1 No. 1, 1992.

Multiple authors: *Guitar World Presents Van Halen: Eddie Van Halen In His Own Words*. Milwaukee, WI. Backbeat Books, 2010.

Nedges, Ed. "Van Halen: Animal Magnetism." *Circus.* November 1983, p. 31.

Neilstein, Vince. "Eddie Van Halen Buried His '79 Black & Yellow Guitar With Dimebag Darrell." *Metalsucks.net.* December 4, 2007

Newman, Judith. "Hot in Hollywood." *Ladies Home Journal.* July 2011, p. 72.

Newquist, HP. "Edward Van Halen Interview: EVH at Play." *National Guitar Museum.* March 1995.

Obrectht, Jas, e-mail messages to author, July 13, 2011; July 15, 2011.

Obrecht, Jas. "Heavy-Metal Guitarist from California Hits the Charts at Age 21." *Guitar Player.* November 1978.

Obrecht, Jas. "Van Halen's Michael Anthony." *Guitar Player.* October 1981.

Obrecht, Jas. "Young Wizard of Power Rock." *Guitar Player.* April 1980.

Obrecth, Jas. *The Jas Obrecth Archive.* Permission granted explicitly by Jas Obrecht to repurpose material as seen fit by the author.

Perpetua, Matthew. "Van Halen Working On New Album With David Lee Roth." *Rolling Stone.* January 24, 2011.

Perry, Tom. "Van Hagar." *Rolling Stone.* April 1, 1993.

Pond, Steve. "It's Steve, Not Yngwie, For David Lee." *Los Angeles Times.* December 8, 1985.

Pond, Steve. "Van Halen Feels the Burn." *Rolling Stone.* July 14, 1988.

Rhythm, George A. "Van Halen Brothers Ain't Talkin 'Bout Love." *Rhythm & News Magazine.* November 21, 1996.

R.M. "6: Van Halen Right Now." *Rolling Stone.* October 14, 1993.

Robins, Wayne. "David Lee Roth and The Pursuit Of Happiness." *Newsday.* February 16, 1986.

Rosen, Steven. "Eruptions." *Guitar World.* December 1996.

Rosen, Steven. "Eddie Van Halen drops the bomb on Heavy Metal." *Guitar World.* January 1984.

Rosenbluth, Jean. "New Van Halen Spells It Out for You : *** VAN HALEN "For Unlawful Carnal Knowledge" Warner Bros." *Los Angeles Times.* June 23, 1991.

Rosenbluth, Jean. "Van Halen, "Balance"; Warner Bros. (** 1/2)." *Los Angeles Times.* January 22, 1995.

Roth, David Lee. *Crazy From the Heat.* New York, NY. Hyperion, 1997.

Rutter, Jared. "Rocker Eddie Van Halen Collaborates with Michael Ninn in Sacred Sin." *Adult Video News.* August1, 2006.

Ryon, Ruth. "Estranged from Van Halen, Bertinelli buys own home / Couple separated in October after 20 years of marriage." *Los Angeles Times*. July 14, 2002.

Scoppa, Bud and Cioffi, Billy. "Ed, Eddie, Edward." *Guitar World*. July 1988, p. 52.

Secher, Andy. "Readers Vote Van Halen Most Popular Rock Act in America." *Hit Parader*. January 1984, p. 16.

Secher, Andy. "Van Halen: The High Life." *Hit Parader*. April 1984, p. 16.

Secher, Andy. "Van Halen: Wine, Women, and Song." *Hit Parader*. May 1984, p. 4.

Selvin, Joel. "Hagar ain't talkin 'bout love for Van Halen, but reunion makes it easy to steal the show." *SFGate.com*. August 12, 2004.

Selvin, Joel. "Hagar Says Van Halen Fired Him / Greatest-hits dispute led to Roth's return." *SFGate.com*. July 1, 1996.

Selvin, Joel. "New Producer, Same Result, for Van Halen." *SFGate.com*. February 05, 1995. http://articles.sfgate.com/1995-02-05/entertainment/17794842_1_unlawful-carnal-knowledge-jacky-terrasson-ugonna-okegwo.

Selvin, Joel. "Van Halen Back in Sound Health / Veteran hard rockers sharp in sold-out Oakland show." *SFGate.com*. May 15, 1995.

Shapiro, Marc. "Van Halen: A New Lineup Sparks Recording Magic—Sammy Hagar has joined the group . . . David Lee Roth has left." *Los Angeles Times Syndicate*. April 6, 1986.

Shapiro, Mark. "Eddie Van Halen: One Step Ahead." *Hit Parader*. Winter 1984, p. 31.

Sheff-Cahan, Vicki. "Eddie Van Halen Is Engaged." *People*. October 6, 2008.

Simmons, Sylvie. "Van Halen: Rough and Ready." *Hit Parader*. October 1984, p. 50.

Stix, John. "Edward Van Halen: New Priorities." *Guitar for the Practicing Musician*. August 1991, p. 81.

Stix, John. "Transcription to 'You Really Got Me.'" *Guitar for the Practicing Musician*. September 1986, p. 57.

Stix, John. "Van Halen." *Guitar for the Practicing Musician*. November 1988, p. 58.

Stix, John. "Van Halen: Life at the Top." *Guitar for the Practicing Musician*. September 1986, p. 42.

Su, Lac. "'Tiger Mothers' leave lifelong scars." *CNN*. January 20, 2011.

Tolinksi, Brad. "Ball's Deluxe.'" *Guitar World.* June 1991, p. 23.

Tolinksi, Brad. "Van Halen On Top of the World." *Guitar World.* March 1992, p. 46.

Tolinksi, Brad. "Lord of the Strings." *Guitar World.* March 1992, p. 72.

SiejeC Transcription. WRCX 103.5 Radio Interview. "On the eve of the Jason Becker ALS Benefit in Chicago, WRCX DJ Lou Brutus interviewed Edward Van Halen, Billy Sheehan, Steve Lukather and Pat Torpey to talk about the upcoming event. Many thanks to SiejeC who typed the interview and posted it to the Van Halen List." November 16, 1996.

Turman, Katherine. "For Unlawful Concert Knowledge : VAN HALEN "Right Here Right Now" Warner Bros. ***" *Los Angeles Times.* February 21, 1993.

Turman, Katherine. "Pop Music Review: Van Halen: Only Surprise is the Locale." *Los Angeles Times.* March 05, 1993.

Uhelszki, Jaan. "Gary Cherone Out of Van Halen." *Rolling Stone.* November 5, 1999.

Van Horn, Teri. "Roth Says He Hasn't Heard From Van Halen Since Session In July. Singer says he and Eddie Van Halen wrote three astonishing new songs together." *MTV News.com.* http://www.mtv.com/news/articles/1442982/roth-hasnt-heard-from-van-halen-since-session-july.jhtml.

Van Matre, Lynn. "Chatting With David Lee Roth Rock 'n' roller just wanted to have fun with his solo album." *Chicago Tribune.* March 5, 1985.

Vaziri, Aidin; Graff, Gary; Sullivan, James; Winegarner Beth, Farinella, David John; von Tersch, Gary. "New Van Halen All About Guitar." *Los Angeles Times.* March 15, 1998.

Waddell, Ray. "Reunited Van Halen Eyeing Fall Arena Run." *Billboard.com.* July 3, 2007.

Waddell, Ray. "Van Halen Tour Resumes March 11th." *Billboard.com.* March 3, 2008.

Washburn, Jim. "Pop Music Reviews : Van Halen Show One Big Party." *Los Angeles Times.* August 30, 1993.

Weingarten, Marc. "Classic Van Halen With a Fresh Twist." *Los Angeles Times.* July 06, 1998.

White, Timothy. "Van Halen II." *Rolling Stone.* June 12, 1979.

Whitehall, David. "Trading Licks Spotlight: Jimi Hendrix's 'Changes' and Van Halen's 'Ice Cream Man.'" *Guitar World*. June 1991, p. 51.

Wild, David. "Balancing Act: Eddie Van Halen, The Rolling Stone Interview by David Wild." *Rolling Stone*. April 6, 1994.

Wild, David. "Eddie Van Halen on Rocking Sober, Avoiding Beef and the Future of Van Halen." *Rolling Stone*. June 1, 2009.

Wild, David. "Van Halen: Here Now." *Rolling Stone*. February 18, 1993.

Willman, Chris. "Formula Van Halen : Check List **** Great Balls of Fire *** Good Vibrations ** Maybe Baby * Running on Empty." *Los Angeles Times*. May 22, 1988.

Wolf, Buck and Chandross, Nancy. "Music Notes: Van Halen Reunion." *ABC News.com*. http://abcnews.go.com/Entertainment/story?id=106452&page=1.

Young, Charles M. "The Oddest Couple? Can it Last?" *Musician*. June 1984, p. 46.

Zahlaway, John. "Gary Cherone Resurfaces With Tribe of Judah." *LiveDaily.com*. July 18, 2001.

Zahlaway, Jon. "Sammy Hagar talks to Howard Stern about Van Halen reunion." *SoundSpike*. March 26, 2004.

Zahlaway, Jon. "Sammy Hagar, Alex Van Halen discuss reunion tour, best-of set." *SoundSpike*. May 27, 2004.

Zahlaway, Jon. "Van Halen announces tour dates, officially christens Hagar." *SoundSpike*. March 26, 2004.

Zahlaway, Jon. "Van Halen begins rolling out fall dates for reunion tour." *SoundSpike*. April 30, 2004.

Zahlaway, Jon. "Van Halen comes out of six-year hibernation for summer tour." *SoundSpike*. March 22, 2004.

Zahlaway, Jon. "Van Halen posts strong ticket sales, adds additional dates." *SoundSpike*. April 5, 2004.

Zahlaway, Jon. "Van Halen reveals details of forthcoming best-of set." *SoundSpike*. May 20, 2004.

Zappa, Dweezil." Van Halen Star Guitar." *Dweezil Zappa World*. June 29, 2010.

Zlozower, Neil. *Van Halen: A Visual History: 1978-1984*. San Francisco, CA. Chronicle Books, 2008.

Alphabetical by Title or Description

"1982 Valerie Bertinelli & Eddie Van Halen (PM Magazine)." *YouTube.* Poster: music3874. http://www.youtube.com/watch?v=Vd0KfcYhXac.

"1984 album review." *Rolling Stone.* November 16, 1989.

"1986 MTV Year In Rock Segment! Van Halen, David Lee Roth, Tom Petty, MTV." *YouTube.* Poster: SARATT69. http://www.youtube.com/watch?v=0PTsI-CtYCM.

"1986 Van Halen 5150 Tour News." *YouTube.* Poster: music3874. http://www.youtube.com/watch?v=hLDqfgBspCs.

"5150." *Rolling Stone.* December 18, 1986.

"According to the Boston Globe, legendary guitarist Eddie Van Halen . . ." *Boston Music Examiner.* June 23, 2004.

"And One More Thing . . ." *Los Angeles Times.* January 26, 1992.

Avascular necrosis information. http://www.mamashealth.com/bodyparts/avascular.asp

"Axemen Unite for Les." *Rolling Stone.* October 6, 1988.

Beat It" facts. *Wikipedia.* http://en.wikipedia.org/wiki/Beat_It.

"Bertinelli Divorcing Rocker Eddie Van Halen." *Associated Press.* December 7, 2005.

"Burbank : Rock Guitarist Pleads No Contest in Weapon Case." *Los Angeles County News.* April 21, 1995.

"Carina Guitars Renamed 'HP Special.'" *Peavey.com.* January 10, 2005.

"Celeb Real Estate Wrap: Lost's Harold Perrineau, Socialite Alex Hitz, Jared Wright, and More." *LA.Curbed.com.* http://www.bergproperties.com/blog/rocker-eddie-van-halen-and-his-drummer-brother-alex-van-halen-sell-2917-square-foot-house-in-the-gated-summit-neighborhood-above-beverly-hills-ca-for-an-undisclosed-price-likely-in-the-2m-25m/. March 24, 2008.

"Crazy Eddie." *Rolling Stone.* February 26, 1986.

"Cream Rock and Roll Hall of Fame Induction." *Rolling Stone.* March 4, 1993.

"Dave Raves On." *Rolling Stone.* March 13, 1989.

"Dave Wings It." *Rolling Stone.* September 26, 1985.

"David Lee Roth—Interview—French TV—1985." *YouTube.* Poster: vhlinksDOTcom. http://www.youtube.com/watch?v=nMTHOW6TMcQ&feature=related.

"David Lee Roth 1986." *YouTube.* Poster: vanfknhalen. http://www.youtube.com/watch?v=nzVSnBNUkrw.

"David Lee Roth and Van Halen." *Rolling Stone.* December 18, 1986.

"David Lee Roth Good Morning America Interview 1985." *Good Morning America*; *YouTube.* Poster: 20BRX7. http://www.youtube.com/watch?v=ffxkY3fd5BY.

"David Lee Roth hosts Friday Night Videos 1986." *YouTube.* Poster: KB3M. http://www.youtube.com/watch?v=3oKMT72f75U.

"David Lee Roth Interview 1986 pt 1 of 3." *YouTube.* Poster: wksufreshair/ http://www.youtube.com/watch?v=21Nq2BKJ7ZE.

"David Lee Roth interview 1986." *YouTube.* Poster: 1984rockcity. http://www.youtube.com/watch?v=qjQm3JoxP-k.

"David Lee Roth on David Letterman" (January 1, 1985.) *YouTube.* Poster: RothArmyVideos. Part 1: http://www.youtube.com/watch?v=mgcOi5-K9bE; Part 2: http://www.youtube.com/watch?v=b_T_bxcS9YY

"David Lee Roth on Joan Rivers." *YouTube.* Poster: cowsill2x2. http://www.youtube.com/watch?v=UkGNuqn_xuI.

"David Lee Roth Self Interview (Eat Em and Smile) Pt. 1." *YouTube.* Poster: cowsill2x2. http://www.youtube.com/watch?v=46fXf5dT2nc.

"David Lee Roth." *Rolling Stone.* December 19, 1985.

"Dimebag Darrel memorial funeral" (This features Edward speaking). youtube. Poster: CameToRock http://www.youtube.com/watch?v=DzD4F1raKwk

"DLR Interview: I'll Eat You and Smile, man!" *YouTube.* Poster: cowsill2x2. http://www.youtube.com/watch?v=67d9XYhPLEE&feature=related.

"Ed Leffler; Manager of Rock Group Van Halen." *Los Angeles Times.* October 18, 1993.

"Ed Pays Respects To Dimebag Darrell." *VH1.* December 15, 2004.

"eddie messing up hot for teacher" (November 9, 2007). *YouTube.* Poster: RayMac53 http://www.youtube.com/watch?v=GPZSKXU5nVg.

"Eddie performs at House of Petals, new reunion rumor surfaces." *Undercover.* July 21, 2006.

"Eddie returns to House of Petals." *Van Halen News Desk.* October 10, 2006. http://www.vhnd.com/2006/10/10/eddie-returns-to-house-of-petals.

"Eddie throws *Sacred Sin* release bash." *Van Halen News Desk.* http://vhnd.com/old/articles/061003-01.shtml. October 4, 2006.

"Eddie Van Halen—Still Rockin' the Cradle." *Guitar.com*. January 2000. http://www.guitar.com/articles/eddie-van-halen-still-rockin-cradle

"Eddie Van Halen #2 guitarist of all time, as voted by rock guitarists." *Roadie Crew Magazine*. August 2, 2008.

"Eddie Van Halen & Tak Matsumoto 1998 interview Part One" Japanese TV interview; only parts in English. *YouTube*. Poster: Ed5150army. http://www.youtube.com/watch?v=1mLPfg5cwp4&feature=related.

"Eddie Van Halen "Very serious about staying sober." *Van Halen News Desk*. August 6, 2008.

"Eddie Van Halen 1974 jamming at home." *YouTube*. Poster: VanHalenStoreDOTcom. http://www.youtube.com/watch?v=McxV2IZHe2E.

"Eddie Van Halen and Steven Stevens Namm 1984-1986 Kramer Booth." *YouTube*. Poster: DeTucciBill. http://www.youtube.com/watch?v=RKjjIT1V5vo.

"Eddie Van Halen and Valerie Bertinelli . . . ." *Rolling Stone*. February 7, 1991.

"Eddie Van Halen Back In Rehab?" *Blabbermounth.net*. http://www.roadrunnerrecords.com/Blabbermouth.net/news.aspx?mode=Article&newsitemID=92336. March 6, 2008.

"Eddie Van Halen Drinking Again?" *BostonHerald.com*. June 29, 2004.

"Eddie Van Halen Gets Pissed Off At Sound Man 11-3-07 part1." *YouTube*. Poster: thedboss. http://www.youtube.com/watch?v=qfXHFlT37C8&feature=related.

"Eddie Van Halen throws speaker at sound man 11-3-07 part2." *YouTube*. Poster: thedboss. http://www.youtube.com/watch?v=i3Slhb8T2DQ.

"eddie van halen in his backyard" ("Ain't Talkin' 'Bout Love" at The Gathering Party.) *YouTube*. Poster: smdmf. http://www.youtube.com/watch?v=wLxk0A18VuM&feature=related.

"Eddie Van Halen Interview 1984." *YouTube*. Poster: 1980Invasiontour. Interview by Lisa Robinson. http://www.youtube.com/watch?v=SrtOQPmlTvc.

"eddie van halen interview" (Talking about the recreated Frankenstein guitar in 2007). *YouTube*. Poster: **5150EVH5150**. http://www.youtube.com/watch?v=Dvvo7SxZYx4&feature=related. July 24, 2007.

"Eddie Van Halen Jan Hammer Tony Levin Bill Bruford, Les Paul Tribute Show, Aug 18th 1988." *YouTube.* Poster: Heatmi5er. http://www.youtube.com/watch?v=atSdjLb0T14.

"Eddie Van Halen Launches the All-New EVH® Wolfgang® Guitar: Available Jan. 2009." *Business Wire.*

"Eddie Van Halen marries Janie Liszewski on Jun 27, 2009!" *People.* June, 2009.

"eddie van halen playing jump at his house" ("Jump" at The Gathering Party.) *YouTube.* Poster: smdmf. http://www.youtube.com/watch?v=pEvGe2ljPbw&feature=related.

"Eddie Van Halen Recovering After Hand Surgery." *Rolling Stone.* June 23, 2009.

"Eddie Van Halen talks about Van Halen recording again with David Lee Roth." *Boston Music Examiner.* July 26, 2009.

"Eddie Van Halen to Enter Rehab." *Guitar World.* March 8, 2007.

"Eddie Van Halen, Hard Rock Cafe, 1985, Guitar Donation." *YouTube.* Poster: http://www.youtube.com/watch?v=VRXn_O3Ygyw.

"Eddie Van Halen: Interviews of Recording Artists." http://www.mcapozzolijr.com/edwardvanhalen.html.

"Eddie Van Halen: New Photos Posted Online." *Blabbermouth.net.* January 6, 2007. http://www.roadrunnerrecords.com/blabbermouth.net/news.aspx?mode=Article&newsitemID=64844.

"Eddie Van Halen's Son Says Guitarist Is 'Doing Great.'" *Blabbermounth.net.* March 31, 2008.

"Eddie Van Healthy." TMZ. August 6, 2008.

"Eddie's Back! The Dramatic Return of the World's Greatest Guitar Hero." *Guitar World.* January 2007.

"Edward van halen—Autographing (1986)." *YouTube.* Poster: Ed5150army. http://www.youtube.com/watch?v=qvNtpr3ThKI.

"Edward Van Halen Guitar Smashing Incident 2004." *YouTube.* Poster: fiddy1fiddy. http://www.youtube.com/watch?v=sW1g0HZk2no.

"Edward Van Halen Interview Japanese TV program" (2008) *YouTube.* Poster: Planefairy/ http://www.youtube.com/watch?v=BH0Ysm3wB-4.

Edward Van Halen, NAMM Convention appearance. Transcribed by Kevin Dodds. Public domain. January 8, 2003.

"Edward Van Halen Twist Of A Knife." *YouTube.* Poster: **Ed5150army**. http://www.youtube.com/watch?v=h0JZmbmhGWA&feature=related.

"edward van halen valerie_Bertinelli_et 1982" (*Entertainment Tonight* 1982).youtube. Poster: luciendidier59. http://www.youtube.com/watch?v=FoLjLUVdRyc.

"Election 92." *Rolling Stone*. December 10, 1992.

"EVH Art Guitars and Custom Shop Replicas." *www.charvel.com* and *www.evh-guitars.com*. July 23, 2004.

"Exclusive Van Halen News: The Reunion Is Official." *Rolling Stone*. February 02, 2007.

"Exclusive: Diamond Dave Spills His Guts About Van Halen Reunion." *Rolling Stone*. February 15, 2007.

"Fire—1996-11-17 Chicago (ALS Benefit For Jason Becker) [VHFrance Videos]." *YouTube*. Poster: VHFrance. http://www.youtube.com/watch?v=DUQWK_9VnzE

"Fret Rats." *Rolling Stone*. March 26, 1987.

"From Eddie." Press release. March 8, 2007.

Full one-hour conversation between Jas Obrecht and Eddie Van Halen. Transcribed by Kevin Dodds. July 30, 1982. Used by permission of the Jas Obrecht Archives.

"Graham Nash, Van Halen and Young." *Rolling Stone*. December 23, 1993.

"Guitars101's Christopher Middleton aka SuckaInA3Piece Interviews Eddie's Guitar Tech." *Guitars101.com. http://www.guitars101.com/vb/showthread.php?t=25404*. November 29, 2004.

The Howard Stern Show (guest Edward Van Halen). Transcribed by Kevin Dodds (excerpts only). September 8, 2006.

"Interview With David Lee Roth." *Rolling Stone*. April 11, 1985.

"Jump @ Van Halen in Concert, Fort Lauderdale, 2/20/08 (Bank Atlantic Center)." *YouTube*. Poster: ericsharesvideo. http://www.youtube.com/watch?v=_0f2N5ae3wU.

Late Night w/David Letterman (NBC). Guests: Johnny Carson, Lee Marvin, Eddie Van Halen. Personal archives. May 16, 1985.

"Limp Bizkit: All Up in Their Business." MTV News feature about Eddie Van Halen jamming with Limp Bizkit. *MTV News*. http://www.mtv.com/bands/l/limp_bizkit/launch_feature_030919/index2.jhtml. 2007.

"mean street break awfull" (November 10, 2007): *YouTube*. Poster: RayMac53. http://www.youtube.com/watch?v=A_3tk8EB6ZY&feature=related.

"Michael Anthony breaks his silence." *Melodicrock.com*. March17, 2006.
MTV: The Week in Rock. Transcribed by Kevin Dodds (excerpts only). July 4, 1996.
"Names In The News : Glimpses." *Los Angeles Times*. **April 24, 1990**. Times Wire Services.
"New statement from Eddie! Plus new photo and interview." Press release (www.van-halen.com). May 25, 2007.
North Sea Flood of 1503. *Wikipedia*. http://en.wikipedia.org/wiki/North_Sea_flood_of_1953.
"October 1982: Largo, Maryland: Unchained." *YouTube*. Poster: VHfan66. http://www.youtube.com/watch?v=LDDKzbwBaSE&feature=related.
"Old Guard Shine at MTV Awards." *Associated Press*. September 5, 1996.
Oral cancer foundation entry on Edward Van Halen. *Oral Cancer Foundation* http://www.oralcancerfoundation.org/people/eddie_van_halen.htm.
"Online Chat with Lonnie Totman Tonight." *VHStrungout.com*. December 2, 2004.
"OU812 . . ." *Rolling Stone*. December 15, 1988.
"Random Notes." *Rolling Stone*. April 6, 1989.
"Random Notes." *Rolling Stone*. November 16, 1989.
"Random Notes." *Rolling Stone*. November 30, 1989.
"Random Notes." *Rolling Stone*. January 23, 1992.
"Random Notes." *Rolling Stone*. April 15, 1993.
"Random Notes." *Rolling Stone*. February 4, 1993.
"Random Notes: Jimmy Page Rock Walk Induction." *Rolling Stone*. February 16, 1994.
"Rocco G interviews David Lee Roth @ LA Fashion Week Fall 08." *YouTube*. Poster: **FashionNewsLive**. http://www.youtube.com/watch?v=OJhHfdZufH8&feature=fvw. March 29, 2008.
"Rock Legend Eddie Van Halen to Serve as Honorary Race Official For SUBWAY Fresh Fit 500™." Press release. April 22, 2007.
"Rock Star Van Halen Faces Charge of Carrying Gun Into Airport." *Los Angeles County News*. April 11, 1995.
"Roth is suing Van Halen mates." *Associated Press*. December 14, 2002.
"Sammy denies breakup, Alex says new album on deck." Van Halen News Desk. http://www.vhnd.com/2004/11/09/sammy-denies-breakup-alex-says-new-album-on-deck/. November 9, 2004.
"Sammy Hagar Interview". *HITS Magazine*. July 8, 1996.

"Sammy on 04 tour: 'There were some real problems in the band.'" *Billboard.com*. April 24, 2006.

"Simon and Garfunkel and Eddie Van Halen?" *Rolling Stone*. December 23, 1993.

"Smithsonian's Q & A with Eddie Van Halen." *Smithsonian Magazine*. May 24, 2011.

Spike TV Guy's Choice Award Ceremony. *Spike.com*. http://www.spike.com/video-clips/oh4818/guys-choice-eddie-van-halen-is-a-guitar-god. June 22, 2009.

"'Tiger Jam' about fathers and sons, opulence and spectacle." http://www.lvrj.com/ April 21, 2008. *Las Vegas Review Journal*.

Tibute to Jeff Porcaro December 1992 information: http://www.toto99.com/blog/ency.php?/archives/454-TRIBUTE-TO-JEFF-PORCARO-Concert.html.

"Toazted Interview—Eddie Van Halen" (Edward interview in Dutch in the Netherlands). *YouTube*. Poster: Toazted. http://www.youtube.com/watch?v=KF7s1WxUVRo&NR=1&feature=fvwp.

"Unreleased Van Halen—Gentlemen of Leisure." *YouTube*. Poster: azdavidza. http://www.youtube.com/watch?v=kaQlqK_QJBg.

"Van Halen—Dreams (LIVE at the Whisky A Go Go 1986)." *YouTube*. Poster: DeTucciBill. http://www.youtube.com/watch?v=-AlULXGgsM4.

"Van Halen—Drop Dead Legs Jam 2004" *YouTube*. Poster: fiddy1fiddy. http://www.youtube.com/watch?v=b2S7pJDQSyE.

"Van Halen—I'm The One 11-19-2004 Tucson, AZ." *YouTube*. Poster: Gary2112. http://www.youtube.com/watch?v=guzqu4qKO-w.

"Van Halen—Interview (1987) Entertainment Tonight with Leeza Gibbons." *YouTube*. http://www.youtube.com/watch?v=nWad15SdfEc.

"Van Halen—Jump 11-19-2004 Tucson, AZ." *YouTube*. Poster: Gary2112. http://www.youtube.com/watch?v=OsZ4T5Z5vAA.

"Van Halen—Runnin With The Devil (Tucson AZ 2004)." *YouTube*. Poster: Gary2112. http://www.youtube.com/watch?v=oPgwBRi1j-0.

"Van Halen—Toronto—2007—Jump" (October 7, 2007). *YouTube*. Poster: rootzboy. http://www.youtube.com/watch?v=QcA_J5s7zME.

"Van Halen—Twist and Shout 1974." *YouTube*. Poster: zackvanhalen. http://www.youtube.com/watch?v=gtlkLaqJsW4.

"Van Halen—You Really Got Me (Tucson AZ 2004) [w/ Wolfgang Van Halen]." *YouTube.* Poster: fiddy1fiddy. http://www.youtube.com/watch?v=kLiZdZOTYQk.

"Van Halen "Act Like It Hurts" Unreleased". *YouTube.* Poster: bornbrit777. http://www.youtube.com/watch?v=qJVDdr-6EPM&feature=related.

"Van Halen "Last Night" Unreleased." *YouTube.* Poster: bornbrit777. http://www.youtube.com/watch?v=IkQrdXaIEk8&feature=related.

"Van Halen (010 Redo)—1) I'm The One / Atomic Punk / Aint Talkin' Bout Love—Fresno 78." *YouTube.* Poster: xxNatasha007xx. http://www.youtube.com/watch?v=ZI0ekgh4mRM&feature=player_embedded.

"Van Halen (010 Redo)—1) Light Up The Sky / Runnin' With The Devil—Fresno 79." *YouTube.* Poster: xxNatasha007xx. http://www.youtube.com/watch?v=-AYjRnUqeQM&feature=player_embedded.

"Van Halen 1975 Brown Sugar Unreleased." *YouTube.* Poster: Ed5150army. http://www.youtube.com/watch?v=ThhXpq-DfjM&feature=related.

"Van Halen 1975 Good Time Unreleased live." *YouTube.* Poster: Ed5150army. http://www.youtube.com/watch?v=plr5hxVEV6M.

"Van Halen 2007 Opening Night Tour, Charlotte, NC (Dance the Night Away)" September 27, 2007. *YouTube.* Poster: tuco111112. http://www.youtube.com/watch?v=93pRh7vgOso.

"Van Halen 2007–2008 North American Tour." *Wikipedia.org.* http://en.wikipedia.org/wiki/Van_Halen_2007%E2%80%932008_North_American_Tour.

"Van Halen and Orioles in a flap." *Associated Press.* August 21, 2004.

"Van Halen and the Go-Go's." *Rolling Stone.* December 19, 1985.

"Van Halen Announces Rescheduled Tour Dates." Press release. March 18, 2008.

"Van Halen at the Cabo Wabo." *YouTube.* Poster: Ed5150army. http://www.youtube.com/watch?v=418e_vSzcaE

"Van Halen Canadian Interview 1986 w/ Sammy Hagar (October 23, 1986)." *YouTube.* http://www.youtube.com/watch?v=Bvb7vHnl8Rc

"Van Halen Caught With Gun". *Associated Press.* April 12, 1995.

"Van Halen Charlotte 2007 EVH solo" (September 27, 2007). *YouTube.* Poster: lwall. http://www.youtube.com/watch?v=VFdhGnBMZvY.

"Van Halen DLR interview clip." *YouTube.* Poster: BigRockRadio. http://www.youtube.com/watch?v=HtzMD0UWkm4.

"Van Halen feud with David Lee Roth." Interview with Edward Van Halen by Tommy Nast. *YouTube.* Poster: NedSneadbley. http://www.youtube.com/watch?v=aQ6ncBgNhGk.

"Van Halen has cooled off the snide remarks about David Lee Roth . . ." *Rolling Stone.* Mary 19, 1988.

"Van Halen Heroes and Icons Part Four." *YouTube.* Poster: Ed5150army. http://www.youtube.com/watch?v=ZMT-JxfLTfA&NR=1.

"Van Halen Heroes and Icons Part Three." *YouTube.* Poster: Ed5150army. http://www.youtube.com/watch?v=tkleR52BerU&feature=related.

"Van Halen Live—Pre-Show Warmup 1986." *YouTube.* Poster: Bacardicus. http://www.youtube.com/watch?v=hIY86LO-z8g.

"Van Halen Officially Announce Summer 07 Roth Tour." Press release. February 02, 2007.

"Van Halen On E-News 2004." *YouTube.* Poster Gary2112. http://www.youtube.com/watch?v=BxzCRxSNEX4.

"Van Halen Performs In Front Of 90,000 People In Québec City." *Blathermouth.net.* July 4, 2008. http://www.roadrunnerrecords.com/blabbermouth.net/news.aspx?mode=Article&newsitemID=100276.

"Van Halen Plays Backing Band to Hank Williams, Jr." *Rolling Stone.* January 15, 1987.

"Van Halen Sued by Ex-Manager." *Rolling Stone.* May 8, 1986.

"Van Halen: What's in a Name?" *Rolling Stone.* Mary 5, 1988.

"Van Halen really screws up "Jump"" (October 23, 2007).youtube. Poster: Valarauko. http://www.youtube.com/watch?v=yXPM6d9IdiY&feature=related.

"Van Halen Rehearsals 5150 Time." *YouTube.* Poster: Ed5150army. http://www.youtube.com/watch?v=w24q2rNyJTY&feature=related.

"Van Halen special MTV Rockmentary 1990." *YouTube.* Poster: BigRockRadio. Part 1: http://www.youtube.com/watch?v=gPOzNaqFSnU; Part 2: http://www.youtube.com/watch?v=VYAFuLuMllI&feature=related; Part 3: http://www.youtube.com/watch?v=dH_l2MUPt8U&feature=related

"Van Halen—The Man on the Silver Mountain 1975" *YouTube.* Poster: zackvanhalen. http://www.youtube.com/watch?v=6vczVqXLv-E&feature=related

"Van Halen—Waiting For The Bus 1975." *YouTube.* Poster: zackvanhalen. http://www.youtube.com/watch?v=4qJ5ljA8cQE&NR=1

"Van Halen, Call It A Comeback." *LAist.com.* http://laist.com/2007/01/24/van_halen_call_it_a_comeback.php. January 24, 2007.

"Van Halen/Vince Neil." *Rolling Stone.* June 24, 1993.

"Van Halen: I'm the One." *Guitar School.* April 1989, p. 66.

"Van Halen: New Publicist, Summer Tour Plans." *Blabbermouth.net.* January 8, 2007.

"Van Halen's Drunk Performance at Restaurant." *Contactmusic.com.* June 30, 2004.

"Van Halen's Guitar Given to Smithsonian Museum." *Associated Press.* February 8, 2011.

"Van Halen-Walk Away (James Gang cover)." *YouTube.* Poster: vhfanjack. http://www.youtube.com/watch?v=bh2L4xJ8VxA.

"VH1: Behind The Music—Pantera (5/5)". *VH1; YouTube.* Poster: Zuberzuber. http://www.youtube.com/watch?v=gfAMkQlSbDs&feature=related.

"Writin' and Rockin': The Jas Obrecht Experience." Online video (used by permission of the Jas Obrecht Archives). Transcribed by Kevin Dodds. October 10, 2009.

"Zakk Wylde: 'Eddie Van Halen Hasn't Just Gone Off The Deep End—He's Living In Atlantis.'" *Blabbermouth.net.* Feb. 17, 2005. http://www.roadrunnerrecords.com/blabbermouth.net/news.aspx?mode=Article&newsitemID=33046.